WESTERN ISLES LIBRARIES

LINICLATE

Readers are requested to take great care of the item while in their possession, and to point out any defects that they may notice in them to the Librarian.
This item should be returned on or before the latest date stamped below, but an extension of the period of loan may be granted when desired.

UIST MOBILE

DATE OF RETURN	DATE OF RETURN	DATE OF RETURN
15 JUL 2011	um 09/17	
3 1 AUG 2011	1 8 JAN 2018	
2 5 NOV 2011	1 6 AUG 2018	
	1 0 JAN 2019	
1 1 JAN 2012	- 7 JAN 2020	
1 JAN 2012	1 8 FEB 2020	
1 JAN 2012	1 8 FEB 2020	
1 0 JAN 2012	2 2 JUN 2021	
2 0 FEB 2012	2 5 NOV 2021	
	- 7 APR 2023	

D1420575

Robert and Brenda Vale

TIME TO EAT THE DOG?

the real guide to
sustainable living

Thames & Hudson

This book is dedicated to Laura and to all grandchildren, everywhere.

ACKNOWLEDGMENTS

We would like to thank the international community of people
and organizations who have made their research and information
available, both in books and on the internet; without the material
that they have so unstintingly provided, we could not have written
this book. We would also like to thank Victoria University of
Wellington for giving us the time to write.

First published in the United Kingdom in 2009 by
Thames & Hudson Ltd, 181A High Holborn, London WC1V 7QX

thamesandhudson.com

British Library Cataloguing-in-Publication Data
A catalogue record for this book is available from the
British Library

ISBN 978-0-500-28790-3

Printed and bound in China by SNP Leefung Printers Ltd

SNP Leefung Printers Ltd are committed to printing in
an environmentally responsible manner and have full
international forestry stewardship certification. The paper,
115 gsm Munken Premium Cream, is produced by the Swedish
mill Munkedals, which has a long tradition of environmental
responsibility and of implementing standards that ensure
its industrial processes have the lowest possible impact on
the environment.

CONTENTS

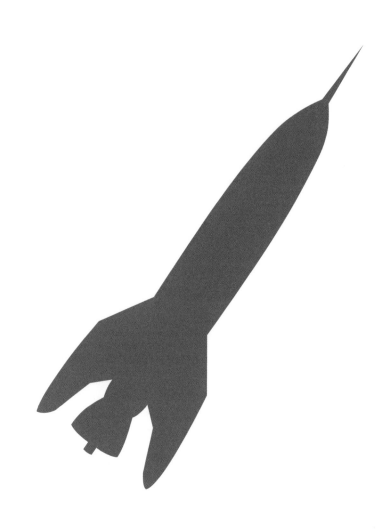

INTRODUCTION

As a boy growing up in England in the 1950s, one of the authors of this book was an avid follower of the cartoon adventures of Dan Dare, Pilot of the Future, in the comic *Eagle*. In this beautifully drawn future England of skyscrapers, spaceships, flying jeeps, gyroscopic cars and London Transport monorails, where Earth played test match cricket against Mars, Dan Dare and his colleagues in the Interplanet Spacefleet were on hand to protect society at the turn of the 21st century from a range of unexpected extraterrestrial threats and troubles. Now that we have arrived at Dan Dare's future, somehow things have not materialized quite as we were led to expect. In fact, the future has turned out to be much more like the 1950s. We do have lots of skyscrapers, but space travel is still uncommon, cars still have four wheels, London Transport still have red double-decker buses, jeeps don't fly, and Earth still doesn't have a decent cricket team.

One thing the earth does have now, unexpected by many, is a whole series of *intraterrestrial* threats and troubles. The adventures of Dan Dare presented an optimistic view of the future and of the idea of progress, but since those heady days we have begun to see that many of the things we take for granted may be doing us more overall harm than good, and that many of our activities may not be sustainable in the long term because they are based on resources that are finite. There has been a lot of talk in recent years about 'sustainability', and this book is an attempt to discover what sustainability really means. As far as we are concerned here, the only possible definition of sustainability is the ability to be sustained or to continue into the indefinite future (leaving aside the cooling of the sun in some very far distant age).

The planet earth, after all, is unavoidably finite. Admittedly, it receives energy from the sun – roughly 7,000 times the amount of energy we consume each year[1] – but it receives very little in the way of materials and resources. Dr Peter Brown of the University of Western Ontario says that every day the earth is bombarded by 80–100 metric tonnes of space dust in the form of 5–10 gram particles.[2] This sounds like a lot, but even 100 tonnes per day is very little when shared among a population approaching seven billion (we are using the US billion here, called a 'milliard' in Europe and meaning one thousand million[3]). So, in material terms, the earth as it exists is all we have. However, in spite of its obvious finiteness, we tend to treat the earth as if it were inexhaustible. Our globalized society is based on growth: growth of population, growth of income, growth of energy consumption, growth of wealth. Any interruption, or even faltering, of this process is greeted as a tragedy, as was seen in the slowing of the United States' economy in 2008, which led to stock market falls all over the world. All the resources and materials that we use for physical growth come from the earth, whether it be the rock that we dig up to make the concrete to build our expanding cities, or the coal and uranium we dig out of the ground to burn in our power stations to meet the demand for more electricity. The food and water that sustain a rising global population also come from the earth.

'PLEASE, SIR, CAN I HAVE SOME MORE?'

All this emphasis on growth raises two simple questions. The first is: 'How can we continue to grow on a finite planet?' We rely on a fixed stock of resources that were put in place when the earth was formed, and these are clearly limited. One day there will be no more oil to find, and no more limestone to turn into cement. Oil is known to be a finite resource, yet the world economy demands more every year to fuel its growth. We act as though there were no limit to the resources we can take from the earth.

The second question is: 'When will we have enough?' In the 1950s the American advertising industry predicted recession for the United States' economy: they thought businesses faced the real problem of not being able to sell any more goods since everyone in America clearly had enough of everything they could possibly want.[4] Now we have a lot more stuff, and yet it still seems that we want more. Is it possible for us all to continue to have more on a finite planet?

It is not just a question of more material possessions. The issue of increasing population also needs to be considered as part of the whole question of 'enough'. Perhaps it should come as no surprise that the species with which we share this planet are becoming extinct ever more quickly, estimated by the International Union for Conservation of Nature (IUCN) to be between 100 and 1,000 times the expected rate of natural extinction. They call this trend 'the sixth extinction crisis', the other five having taken place in prehistoric times.[5] If the earth is finite, it follows that there is a limited quantity of the elements from which living creatures are made. It seems unsurprising, therefore, that if there are more people there will be fewer animals, since there is only a certain amount of stuff to make them. However, the question that nobody except the Chinese[6] seems to want to ask is: 'When will we have enough people?' Will there be enough when we have shot the last elephant and fished the last tuna? Will there be enough when it is standing room only? Unfortunately, as the CIA's paper on global demographic trends shows,[7] population size is closely tied to economics, so a fall in the overall population or an increase in its average age may cause problems for an economy. Fewer people overall means fewer consumers and a slowdown in economic growth, and fewer people of working age means that each worker will have to support more older people. So either we have to deal with the problems caused by trying to grow in a finite world, or we must confront the problems caused by trying to live within our means. It seems to us that living according to the earth's ability to support us all is likely to be the wiser choice.

WHY SHOULD WE CARE?

It is in our own interest to sustain our environment, not least because it sustains us. Again according to IUCN, the monetary value of the goods and services provided by natural ecosystems is estimated to be roughly 33 trillion US dollars per year (a trillion here is a million million), which they say is nearly twice the value of the production that results from the human economy. (According to the World Bank, the global GDP – the total amount produced by all the world's domestic economies – for 2006 was US$48 trillion.[8]) Notwithstanding this apparent discrepancy, the environment still provides us with a lot of services. The oceans, for example, provide around

1,000 million tonnes of wild seafood a year, or 140 kg a year for every man, woman and child on the earth.[9] Economic thinking would suggest that, in order to continue making a profit, it would be good to protect the environment and what it produces, such as fish. But because no one owns the natural eco-systems, no one oversees them or prevents their over-exploitation. If a property developer in Northern Queensland buys a piece of rainforest, he can leave it alone, and the community as a whole will benefit from what it provides as a creator of oxygen, a controller of flooding or a preserver of biodiversity. Alternatively, the developer can make a big personal profit if he (or she – women can be just as ruthless in the pursuit of wealth) cuts down the rainforest and builds apartments. Developers nearly always prefer to make personal profit rather than to do good for the community. To be fair to developers they can argue that development benefits the community financially through actions like creating local jobs. The problem is that everyone thinks this way – it is the basis of modern society – but thinking this way may also cause the downfall of modern society.

ENVIRONMENT FIRST

In this book we are unashamedly considering only environmental sustainability, not economic sustainability or social sustainability. This is not an arbitrary decision, or just because we are lazy and want to leave out the economic and social bits. There are generally thought to be two models for portraying what sustainability means, called the 'weak model' and the 'strong model'. An example of how these models work, and how they differ, is given by the office of the New Zealand Parliamentary Commissioner for the Environment.[10]

In the weak model, the environment, the economy and human society are represented by three intersecting circles of equal size. They are portrayed as competing interests, and the model assumes that degradation of one can be compensated for by improvements in another. It assumes that environmental and social problems can always be solved if the economy is sound, and that a decline in the ecosystem is compensated for by an equivalent rise in human well-being.

In the strong sustainability model, the three circles are portrayed as concentric, one sphere lying within another rather than intersecting it. The economy is set within society, and society is set within the environment. This is the model we are following for this book, for the reason that if we destroy the environment, which sustains us and provides our air, water and food, then we will destroy human society; if we destroy human society, we will certainly destroy the economy. Here, the environment is the most important of the three, because without it we have nothing. We would be unwise to assume that in the long term the environment can be traded off against human well-being. Rather, we have made the assumption that pro-tection of the environment is the best way of sustaining both ourselves and everything else that lives on the earth. What this means is that one thing we do not do in this book is take much notice of conventional economics – a very different attitude from the current world-view, in which economic criteria are generally treated as the only valid basis for decision-making.

ECONOMICS: SCIENCE OR RELIGION?

Economics as it is currently practised could be described as the most danger-ous set of fundamentalist beliefs in the world. It is often called a science, but in many ways it is a religion, based on a series of shared precepts that often appear to be matters of faith rather than fact. Some of these matters of eco-nomic faith are in direct conflict with the idea of sustainability. It could be said that economists are actively trying to destroy the earth, although they probably do not see it that way. Three of the principal points of contention between economics and sustainability can be set out as follows:

- the idea that businesses and economies must grow
- the idea that things we don't pay for have no cost or value
- the idea that there should be an economic payback for actions taken

We mentioned the problem of growth earlier. We live in a finite world but behave as if it were infinite. All economic activity is based on growth. For example, Statistics New Zealand, a government department, says: 'Economic growth is generally regarded as a necessary component of any development strategies aimed at meeting ... aspirations ... for an improved quality of life.'[11] (Of course, economic growth is also driven by population growth.) We can see this focus on growth very clearly by looking at the world's oil consumption. Although oil is known to be a finite resource, we appear to have based our entire global civilization on the assumption of a steady growth in oil consumption each year. The US Energy Information Administration shows that between 1980 and 2005, world oil production increased by 125%, and it predicts a further increase of 74% in the next twenty-five years.[12] The conventional economic wisdom is that when oil becomes scarce it will become more expensive, which will drive people to find alternative fuels. However, in the past the alternative fuels were always better than what they replaced. For example, wood was replaced by coal, which provided double the energy for a given weight. Oil then replaced coal: it was both high in energy and a liquid, which made it much more practical for use in transport. (Coal, on the other hand, had been very difficult to supply to the engine, so that until late in their evolution coal-fired steam locomotives needed both a driver and a fireman to shovel fuel into the firebox.[13]) There is as yet no sign that the market has come up with a fuel that could replace oil. We are not going to consider hydrogen here, since as a fuel it is not a naturally occurring but needs to be made out of other things, using energy in the process.

Another problem in assuming that oil will be replaced by another type of fuel is the significant 'lead time' required to introduce a new energy source. For instance, if we date the invention of the motor car to 1886, when Karl Benz took out his first patent,[14] it was another twenty-two years before the first mass-market car – the Ford Model T – was launched,[15] and it was not until around 1950 that oil consumption in the United States overtook that of coal.[16] If we wait for the market to come up with a replacement for oil – assuming such a technology exists – will there be enough time to introduce it?

This then brings us to the second point on which economics and sustainability part company. The practice of economics appears to ignore things that do not have a value in financial terms. We see this in issues such as climate change and pollution. There is no financial penalty for acting in a way that causes climate change, so the global economic system carries on doing so. The worry here – to return to the issue of oil consumption – is that when oil becomes expensive, the 'solution' offered by economics will be to obtain it from unconventional sources: the tar sands of Canada and Venezuela, for instance, where the extraction of oil requires a lot of energy and results in the emission of between two and six times as much carbon dioxide as conventional production.[17] In addition, of course, we need to add the carbon dioxide emitted into the atmosphere from burning this fuel. Provided unconventional sources of oil make economic sense, they will be used, even if the damage to the world's climate amounts to ecological suicide.

Finally, to bring the whole issue of economics down to the decisions over which each of us might have some control, the whole question of 'payback' needs consideration. Economic payback is how long it takes for the money you save by taking a course of action (money saved on heating by insulating the walls of your house, for instance) to equal the money you initially spent (e.g. on insulating the walls), including the interest you would have earned had the money been placed in a bank or building society rather than used to buy insulation. Economic payback is used to justify all sorts of actions – or to justify not doing them, since it is frequently employed to excuse users from doing things that would be good for the environment. The question is, why do we demand payback on a solar water-heater but not on a new kitchen? New Zealand's Energy Efficiency and Conservation Authority (EECA) quoted a case study in which it cost NZ$5,200 in 2004 to install a solar hot-water system that saved 3,000 kWh of electricity each year.[18] We can assume this would have cost roughly NZ$6,000 in 2008. By comparison, in 2008 the website of a kitchen installer in New Zealand quoted the following prices for three grades of installed kitchen:

Deluxe	NZ$12,277
Premium	NZ$21,050
Designer	NZ$31,580

and suggested that you should plan to spend between 5% and 8% of the value of your house on the kitchen, although it gives no figures for the increase in the value of your house in relation to the money you have invested.[19] The solar water-heater's payback is said to be 9.2 years, but no payback at all is suggested for the kitchen: people want kitchens but they do not want solar water-heaters, or at least not enough to spend money on them that they could be spending on a kitchen. Interestingly, the difference in cost between a Deluxe and a Premium kitchen would pay for a solar water-heater and leave some money over.

The same sort of calculation also applies to bigger purchases. We have found that the cost of a solar photovoltaic system that will supply enough electricity to run a modest house is comparable to the cost of a moderately luxurious car. A new car, however, will lose roughly half its value over 3 years,[20] making the purchase of a solar power system for NZ$80,000 (approximately £30,000), which is guaranteed by the manufacturer for 20 years, appear a more rational way of spending the money. This system will make free electricity for you every day of its life, so it will be earning you money. A car only ever costs you money, because on top of the initial price you have to pay for fuel, servicing and tyres. If you put a solar power system on the roof of your home, the first question many people ask is 'What is the payback?', whereas if you buy a Mercedes Benz rather than a Toyota Corolla nobody ever questions the wisdom of your decision. In the current climate of 'economic rationalism', it is not considered irrational to buy a NZ$80,000 car when a NZ$30,000 model would serve you just as well for transport. If you buy a new Corolla for that price, you lose around NZ$15,000 over the first 3 years; but a new Mercedes Benz C-Class, bought for NZ$81,900, will depreciate by over NZ$40,000 during the same period.[21] So when it comes to cars, we don't care at all about payback. It may be that one of the most important tasks in the struggle to improve sustainability will be to find a way of making solar water-heaters into status symbols.

People who worry too much about payback end up not buying solar water-heaters, with the result that energy demand continues to rise. The same sort of economic thinking can be seen even at national government level. The Australian government under prime minister Kevin Rudd commissioned a report on the reduction of Australia's greenhouse gas emissions, which was then criticized by the Treasurer of New South Wales (the rather appropriately named Mr Costa) because a very significant 80% cut in emissions 'would wipe 4 per cent off the size of the Australian economy over the next 20 years'.[22] Leaving aside the emotional language, is a cut of 4% really such a big deal in the overall scheme of things? If the economic system that is supposedly working for our well-being is so rigid that it cannot contemplate any action that would avoid damaging the entire climate of our planet, for whom is it really working?

HOW CAN WE MEASURE SUSTAINABILITY?

There is no doubt that the human race could exist sustainably on the planet's resources if we all lived in the same way as at least some of our great-great-grandparents over a hundred years ago. Many people in this world still do live like this, but their lives are generally described as 'less developed' – something to be avoided, and something we are assured they would avoid if they could. Books such as the *Lark Rise to Candleford* trilogy, written in 1940s England by Flora Thompson[23] but set at the end of the 19th century, show how even comparatively recently local communities in 'developed' countries grew their own food, helped each other, made their own entertainment, travelled little, and generally lived within the resources of their immediate environment. Such a way of life could be said to be sustainable.

MEASURING LAND

When sustainability is discussed nowadays, it frequently refers to the attempt to make a Westernized way of living sustainable, with its plethora of consumer goods, increasingly large houses, labour-saving appliances, personal motorized transport and foreign holidays. But to what extent can the world's resources support a Westernized lifestyle on a sustainable basis? One way of looking at this question is to use the concept of the 'ecological footprint', first developed in Canada in the 1990s by Mathis Wackernagel and William Rees.[24] This technique allows us to compare all the goods and services that we use and all the activities that we undertake in our daily lives by considering them in terms of the amount of land required to provide each of them in a sustainable way. This method assumes that all energy is grown, and that all resources for buildings, infrastructure and so on are also grown, meaning that everything can be reduced to an area of productive land. This is a very effective and easy-to-comprehend tool for comparing a wide range of items that at first glance seem completely unrelated – because calculating sustainability is often not just a case of comparing apples with pears, as the saying goes, but of trying to compare apples with hovercraft.

The great advantage of the ecological footprint method, apart from its clarity, is that it employs as a unit of measurement the resource that is most limited on our finite planet: land. Apart from occasional examples of land reclamation – in the Netherlands, by developers in Dubai, or by the people in Hong Kong who keep filling in bits of the harbour – land is pretty much a fixed resource. The planet earth is not getting any bigger. The work of Wackernagel and Rees has already shown that we would need at least three planets like ours if everyone in the world enjoyed the average lifestyle of the modern American, and if this lifestyle were to be provided for in a sustainable way. Other research suggests that this has now risen to five planets.[25] As Wackernagel and Rees remind us, 'Good planets are hard to find.'

Unfortunately, to enjoy the American way of life is the goal of many nations, both 'developed' and 'developing'. Those who already have it, or something like it, want to keep it, and those who do not have it want to achieve it. The problem lies in the fact that the earth does not seem to have enough resources to allow everyone to live in this way. Since it currently seems that there are no more planets like the earth available for our use, we are presented with a rather depressing picture of possible conflicts over the increasingly limited resources of the one planet we do have. All that can be said of going to war over resources is that it is self-defeating. Even conventional warfare is a great destroyer of resources, a way of converting useful material to rubble and dust. Nuclear warfare is even more effective at liquidating resources. The decision to go to war also diverts resources from ordinary lives back at home, not to mention the human toll and the disruption it causes to normal economic systems.

If we want to avoid any such conflict over resources, an alternative approach would be to try to work out what sort of society could be achieved within the means that we have, whether this is assessed at a national, local or individual level. We therefore need to understand the environmental impact of the way we live now, so as to gain an indication of what the best choices for sustainability might be. This approach can also show which parts of the current Western way of life may never be sustainable. We might thus be able to arrive at a lifestyle that could be supported on the basis of what

Wackernagel and Rees call a 'fair earthshare': the amount of land available for each person on the earth, currently considered to stand at around 1.8 hectares of usable land and sea per person.[26] The one incontestable fact, however, is that the earth's population is rising, meaning that this fair earthshare is steadily diminishing. Since matters generally make more sense when put in context rather than in the abstract, the ecological footprint and the relationship between fair earthshare and population are discussed in greater detail in the following chapter, which looks at the subject of food.

MEASURING ENERGY

Apart from land area, the other measure that we make use of in this book to compare the relative impact of activities is energy. Because energy can be 'grown' in the form of trees and fuel crops, it is possible to convert one measure into the other: energy can be expressed in terms of an area of land. Energy is fundamental to everything we do in the modern world. There are lots of units used to measure it (calories, horsepower hours, British thermal units, joules), but there are two basic systems of measurement, commonly known as the imperial and the metric. In the imperial system, which dates back to the long-lost British Empire on which the sun was never going to set, energy is measured in British thermal units (Btus), but almost the only people who use it are the Americans. Everyone else, including the British and the countries of the British Commonwealth, now use the metric system (correctly called the 'Système Internationale d'Unités', or 'SI'), in which the basic unit for measuring energy is the joule. The joule is named after the English physicist James Prescott Joule (1818–89), who established that the basic forms of energy – mechanical, thermal and electrical – are fundamentally the same, meaning that one can be converted into another.[27] A joule is the work done by the force of 1 Newton acting through a distance of 1 metre. In electrical terms, the joule equals 1 watt-second: the energy released in 1 second by a current of 1 ampere through a resistance of 1 ohm.[28]

These descriptions of a joule do not give much of an idea what it actually means, but since we are nearly all used to buying electricity and to the services it provides, the electrical definition is probably easier to grasp. A joule would light a 1 watt light bulb (which would be very small, given that the average light bulb is 100 watts) for one second. It is really just a little

Table 1: SI prefixes and what they mean

kilo-	× 1,000	× 10^3
mega-	× 1,000,000	× 10^6
giga-	× 1,000,000,000	× 10^9
tera-	× 1,000,000,000,000	× 10^{12}
peta-	× 1,000,000,000,000,000	× 10^{15}

flicker. Because the joule is such a small unit, we actually use much larger units to measure energy, based on the SI's convention of adding prefixes to describe larger units. Just as we recognize metres and kilometres (a kilometre being a thousand metres), we also have joules and kilojoules, in which a kilojoule is a thousand joules. We are becoming increasingly familiar with some of the bigger prefixes because our digital cameras are rated in megapixels and our computer memories come in gigabytes. The prefixes we are going to use in relation to energy are outlined in Table 1, with each prefix multiplying the preceding unit by 1,000.

Thus a kilometre is a thousand metres, and a gigajoule is a billion joules. There are further prefixes for even bigger numbers, but they do not feature here. There is also another set of prefixes for units that are smaller than the basic unit – the 'milli-' in millimetres denoting one thousandth of a metre, for instance – but they are not needed in the discussion of energy, since the basic joule is already too small for most practical purposes.

Table 2: Energy units compared

unit	symbol	equivalent in electricity	what it can operate
1 joule	J	extremely small	almost nothing
1 kilojoule	kJ	pretty small	not much
1 megajoule	MJ	0.278 kWh	a laptop for 12 hours
1 gigajoule	GJ	278 kWh	a fridge for a year
1 terajoule	TJ	278,000 kWh	25 houses for a year
1 petajoule	PJ	278,000,000 kWh	a small town for a year

The beauty of the SI prefixes is that they enable us to employ one basic unit for calculating a huge range of energies. A joule will make a very small light flicker for a second, but a petajoule will power a town for a year, as shown in Table 2.

We will generally use megajoules and gigajoules to discuss personal energy use, and the larger units, particularly petajoules, to discuss whole countries or even the whole world.

LIFE-CYCLE ANALYSIS

Another method employed here to assess environmental impact is to consider a product over its whole life, normally referred to as life-cycle analysis (LCA). We know, because our grandmothers will have mentioned it, that buying cheap can be a false economy. Cheap goods often have to be thrown away because they cannot be repaired or are thought not to be worth repairing. On the other hand, buying that very expensive pair of shoes that you really love and will continue to wear for years, and that can be resoled and reheeled as often as necessary, could prove to be a good – and cheaper – long-term investment. This is the basis of life-cycle analysis. If overall cost is being considered, the aim is to add to the initial price the cost of maintenance over the years, and also to factor in what we could have done with the money – putting it in a bank to earn interest, for example – if we had not used it for the first expensive purchase. In this way we can see whether grandmother's advice was worth listening to. An item like a house will also have an operating cost in terms of the energy needed to run it. We could spend more money on the house initially by putting in more insulation, but this might work out cheaper, over the house's lifetime, than paying the heating bills of a house that is less well insulated.

The same method can also be used to examine which of several options has the lowest impact over its whole life. One item might require less energy but consume more resources, so these have to be balanced. The analysis can be extended to consider disposal of the product at the end of its life and its subsequent impact; this is often called a 'cradle-to-grave' analysis.

Life-cycle analysis is very useful for making comparisons, since the same assumptions can be made for all the cases under consideration, but it is less helpful when it comes to predicting exactly what the future cost or impact might be. Assumptions that have to be made include the lifespan of the object and the future costs of products for repair and of energy; in many situations these will be guesses. In this book we have attempted to use life-cycle analysis to compare different ways of doing things while making the same assumptions in each case.

DOOM AND GLOOM?

This may not at first sight appear to be a very optimistic book, but from some perspectives the future is not very optimistic either. However, rather than dwelling on the problems and the difficulties of the current situation, this is an attempt to tease out what it means, in terms of sustainability, to do the everyday things that we all do: living in a home, preparing meals, buying food and clothing, commuting to work, taking part in sports, and so on. It then presents a range of alternatives and their relative impacts, so that we can see if there are any easy answers in terms of the choices we might make, or only difficult ones. Only with some knowledge is it possible to start assembling a picture of what a future sustainable world might be like for each country and for each different part of the world. In the past, vernacular culture offered a way of life derived from the resources available to it and upon which it depended. This gave rise to the very many different cultural traditions and ways of living that have

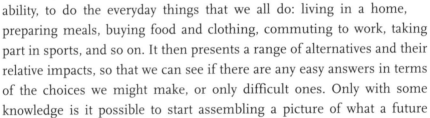

informed world history. The English, Chinese and Japanese are all keen tea drinkers, but in each country the way tea is drunk has evolved differently, because of the different systems and resources that were available. Although the fair earthshare model is a useful starting point for trying to work out

what kind of lifestyle can be sustained, it does not mean that the same resources can be grown in the same area of land all over the world. Rather, individual climates, soils and environments will dictate very different solutions to the same human needs for food, water, shelter and companionship. Because of its dependence on creating a way of life that can be continued, the sustainability of the human race may begin with a global consciousness that we share one planet with roughly 7 billion other human beings, but the solutions we arrive at will be very many and very different according to each specific place. This accords with the adage 'think globally, act locally': dating from the 1970s, it perhaps represents the first emergence of a global concern for the future of the environment.

WE STOLE THE FUTURE

In the 1950s, while one of us was enjoying the space adventures of Dan Dare, the first steps were being taken to measure the impact human beings have on the environment. One of the most significant landmarks was the establishment of an observatory on the Mauna Loa volcano in Hawaii, as a part of the International Geophysical Year of 1957–58. Among other tasks, it was designed to measure trace gases in the atmosphere, The measurements taken at Mauna Loa show that carbon dioxide in the atmosphere rose from 315 parts per million in 1957 to 370 parts per million in 2002.[29] The findings from Mauna Loa and elsewhere led to the 1972 United Nations Conference on the Human Environment, held in Stockholm. This conference produced a set of 26 principles by which humanity could live adequately without destroying the planet. Reading through these principles over thirty years later serves to highlight the years we have wasted since then. In 1972, the discovery of undersea oil, such as that in the North Sea, offered a source of fossil fuels that could have been used to build the physical infrastructure of a world envisioned by the Stockholm Conference – a world that would have supported equitable development, a stable population, and the conservation of non-renewable resources in a protected environment. Instead, these same oil resources were used to fuel economic growth, resulting in a widening gap between rich and poor,[30] a near doubling of the human population,[31] the exhaustion of non-renewable resources as the peak in oil production looms,[32] and further damage to the environment.[33]

Table 3: Income growth per capita in some rich and poor countries*

country		US$	%
UNITED STATES			
1972	disposable personal income	13,692	
2002	disposable personal income	24,479	
	increase over 30 years		79
INDIA			
1972	per capita income	1,100	
2002	per capita income	2,700	
	increase over 30 years		145
1972	income gap with United States	12,592	
2002	income gap with United States	21,779	
CHINA			
1972	per capita income	500	
2002	per capita income	4,000	
	increase over 30 years		700
1972	income gap with United States	13,192	
2002	income gap with United States	20,479	

* All figures have been converted to 1996 US dollars to take account of inflation and allow for easy comparison.

Just to show that we are not making this up, Table 3 gives some figures for the growth of per capita income in the United States, India and China. The data come from the United States Census[34] and the Organisation for Economic Co-operation and Development (OECD).[35]

The table shows that although incomes in India and China have grown much faster than those in the United States, they still fall far behind. Incomes in the latter two countries are not even close to what they were in the United States in 1972, and the gap has roughly doubled over that time. Globalization is making the poor both absolutely richer and relatively poorer.

In many ways the principles of the Stockholm Conference read as a blueprint for sustainability. For instance, by stating that the earth's natural resources should be looked after for future generations as well as for the present,[36] the second principle foreshadows the often quoted Brundtland Report of 1987.[37] This document was the result of an investigation into sustainable development on a global scale, and it defined sustainability as meeting the needs of today without preventing future generations from being able to meet their needs. Sadly, it did not define what it meant by 'needs' in this context. Principle 5 of the Stockholm Conference predicted the depletion of non-renewable resources like fossil fuels as follows:

> The non-renewable resources of the earth must be employed in such a way as to guard against the danger of their future exhaustion and to ensure the benefits from such employment are shared by all mankind.[38]

However, it now seems that the non-renewable resources of the world – what is left of them – will go to those who can pay for them in the current global market. Leaving the market to come up with answers to global environmental problems, as happens at present, runs exactly counter to Principle 14 of the Stockholm Conference: this recognized that rational planning, and not market forces, should be responsible for world development while still protecting the environment. In many ways, market forces have produced development for those who already have, often at the expense of those who have not. The final Stockholm principle described the elimination of nuclear weapons and all other weapons of mass destruction as essential if humanity is to live peacefully and equitably within the means provided by the earth's natural resources. Now it seems it is exactly those countries with such weapons that may go to war to get their hands on the remaining resources.

The Stockholm principles show that the understanding that might have allowed the world to become a very different place from what it is was already in place in the 1970s. If changes had been put into motion then, there would probably have been enough time to make a sustainable world, but nothing was done. Nearly 40 years later the situation is arguably worse, and the time left in which we can act certainly very much less. It appears that in the intervening years we have preferred to ignore sustainability and, at least in the Western democracies, have given our support to leaders who offered to make us richer. It could be said that we have voted to steal the future from our children.

DON'T MENTION THE WAR

Human beings seem to be good at responding to crises. The experience of World War II shows us that when resources are in short supply, there is greater equity and inventiveness, and the ability to adjust living habits to fit whatever is available. Unfortunately, adjustments are made only when the crisis arrives, not before. Wartime rationing in the UK meant that everyone had access to sufficient food, supplemented by what could be grown at home. Yes, there was a black market in which those who had money and influence could obtain extra supplies, but the majority of the population received an adequate diet, and the health of the nation actually improved because of this greater equity.[39] The government's mass education programme, which encouraged people to eat vegetables and outlined why they were important to health, was also part of the adjustment to living with fewer resources. Another section of the propaganda machine dealt with fuel and other resources, showing that savings in one area could lead to more resources for the war effort. As one Ministry of Fuel and Power advert stated,

> *5 lbs of coal saved in one day by 1,500,000 homes will provide enough fuel to build a destroyer. Note: 5 lbs of coal are used in 2 hours by a gas fire or electric oven.*[40]

All this gave the average person a sense of what was important and why it was necessary to preserve resources, as well as a feeling that everyone was equal (even the royal family had ration books). Since fuel had to be imported to the UK and most was destined for the military, petrol was rationed and people were discouraged from travelling by campaigns that asked 'Is your journey really necessary?'.[41] Also noteworthy about the shortages in World War II was the shared sense of 'helping each other out' because everyone was in the same situation. Deprivation is acceptable when everyone is experiencing it. This feeling was coupled with a clear picture of what everybody was trying to achieve: the defeat of Hitler and of Nazism. Of course, it must not be forgotten that the crisis was not an abstract concept like climate change, but the very real situation of having German bombers over your house every night.

THE TRAGEDY OF THE COMMONS

Although the principles of the Stockholm Conference are just as relevant today, if not more so, a cynic might comment that they were rejected by Western leaders such as Ronald Reagan and Margaret Thatcher, and therefore by voters, because they did not show how you could make a profit from an environmentally friendly future. We still face 'the tragedy of the commons' – the economic conundrum put forward by Garrett Hardin in 1968.[42] This states that when we graze our sheep on the common, each of us will benefit individually if we introduce another sheep. But a point will come when there are too many animals, all the grass is gone, and the common we all use cannot support even one sheep. If there is a finite resource we hold in common, like a piece of grazing land, each individual gets more individual profit if he or she over-exploits it, but the result of the over-exploitation is that in the end the resource itself is destroyed.

Another possible reason that the Stockholm principles were not acted upon in the 1970s is the fact that they failed to deliver a vision of what a society in equitable balance with its environment might be like. In order that such a balance might be achieved, someone has to work out what a fair share consists of, and then what life would be like on the resources allowed. This is what the UK government and its advisors did in World War II; and it is what every government, both national and regional, should be doing today while there is still some leeway. Yet there is little evidence that anything is happening, even if some grass roots initiatives are beginning to appear, such as the Transition Towns movement.[43] Most attempts to outline progress towards sustainability rely on the idea that the future will be very much like the present, only with a little more wind and solar energy, a little more recycling and less waste, a little more walking or cycling, and maybe the growing of fuels for personal, public and commercial transport. This vision could be described as 'business as usual' but with a green tinge. However, given a fair earthshare of 1.8 ha per person and current Western lifestyles that demand an earthshare of 5 ha or more, it is hard to see how giving 'business as usual' a green tinge can be sufficient. Ultimately, as resources like copper, oil and phosphorus all reach their peak production in the very near future, and as world population continues to rise, something much more dramatic will happen. What we will have is what we can grow – food, fibre for clothes and materials, and wood for structural purposes and fuel – together with what we can reclaim. Most of the 'world of the future' exists already because we do not have the resources or the time to build a new sustainable world. We will have to make the best of what we have got. The question, then, is what we can grow and what sort of lifestyle it will allow us. The other side of the same question is: what is the environmental impact in terms of energy and land of what we do now, given that this represents for many an acceptable lifestyle? These are the questions to which this book will attempt to find answers.

WE'VE DONE IT OUR WAY

To start answering some of these questions, we have adopted a comparative approach. This will allow us to discover which common activities have large environmental impacts, measured in terms of the land required (or some-times the energy needed) to support them. Often the answers have had to be based on best guesses, and it is accepted that assessments would be more accurate if more comprehensive data were available. For this reason the numbers we have used are rounded up or down. However, what the numbers do reveal are certain relative values, which in some instances are surprising. Our hope is that other people will build on this first attempt, and create a much more accurate picture and hence a vision for the future that we can all work towards. The examples we have chosen could not have been explored without extensive use of the internet. This shared source of infor-mation is one hope in a not very optimistic future. We give grateful thanks to the owners of every site that has freely shared information.

Trying to make connections between often specialized areas of knowl-edge has been the goal of this investigation. As Barry Commoner said over thirty years ago, 'everything is connected to everything else'.[44] Failure to see this is a fundamental problem of current lifestyles. No one wants to rec-ognize that taking your child to school in an SUV with an engine capacity of

4.7 litres causes ten times more environmental impact than making the same journey on foot (see 'Transport'). Given recent discussions of chaos theory and the butterfly effect, which emphasizes the fact that everything is related and that small changes can often have big consequences in complex systems,[45] this wilful inability to make the connection seems strange. We want to believe that we can carry on living as we do now and make little changes for the sake of the environment, but will it be enough to take a cloth bag to the supermarket if we go there by car? This is what we are trying to find out in this book.

Of course it will not be possible to make all the necessary connections; and the things investigated here are, to some extent, those it has been possible to investigate. However, we have attempted to cover all the normal things that are considered necessary to modern life and modern comfort. The shelter provided by buildings is considered, as is clothing. Food is a vital component of our everyday lives, and transport, too, is examined in depth. Leisure activities like sports and hobbies are also examined, alongside workplaces and the impact of working in the current economic system.

POLITICS

This is not a political book – at least not in the party political sense. We will not be advising you to vote for the Republicans rather than the Democrats, or for Labour rather than the Conservatives. However, there is no doubt that the issues discussed here have political implications. At the start of the 21st century there seems to be general agreement among most nations that the only possible model for human development is a combination of capitalism and democracy. A website called 'Conservative Resources' (and thus unlikely to be suffering from any Marxist bias) says that 'capitalism is simply what occurs when we are all left to our own economic devices; as a system, capitalism is characterized by the absence of formal systems'.[46] This informal system has undeniably produced wealth for many and a rising standard of living. However, we have also seen that the freedom to pursue the economic goals of capitalism can appear at odds with the goal of environmental sustainability. It is possible that democracy too is at odds with this aim. Democracy is defined by Merriam-Webster's Online Dictionary as 'a government in which the supreme power is vested in the people and exercised by them directly or indirectly through a system of representation usually involving periodically held free elections'.[47] In lots of ways sustainability means doing more with less. It means cycling to work rather than driving, it means eating more vegetables and less red meat, and it means making things last longer. If a political party in a democracy stands up and says 'Vote for us, we offer you a sustainable future for your grandchildren', another party is sure to stand up and say 'Vote for us, we offer you a tax cut'. People are probably going to vote for the tax cut because it is easy to understand, whereas sustainability is complicated. Sustainability is also about taking a long-term view of the future, but politicians, and also voters, in a democracy tend to think only about the short period between elections. Politicians cannot afford to take long-term decisions if they want to stay in power, and voters have too much else to think about in their lives.

In the end, it is up to us whether the world goes down a sustainable or a non-sustainable path. We cannot look to the economists or to the politicians to act for us. Both the economy and the political system operate because we let them operate. We buy the oil, the food, the cars and the newspapers and vote for the politicians that keep the whole system going. Nobody forces us to do this, although they certainly try hard to persuade us; but in the end we choose to do it. To bring about a more sustainable future we will need to change how we behave, and the purpose of this book is to explore the impact of some of our behavioural choices.

1
FOOD

One issue that has continued to develop as the world embraces globalization – with little attention to its impact on the environment – is the assumption that if demand can be met, it should be met. It is assumed that if a product is available and in demand, it should be provided. We are offered green beans air-freighted from Africa to England, deep-sea fish harvested far away by energy-hungry trawlers, and out-of-season tomatoes grown in heated glasshouses – and we buy them. If we did not buy them the shops would not sell them. This way of seeing the world, as a market and nothing else, is based purely on the financial. We all know the monetary cost of food when we go shopping, but what does it cost from a non-financial viewpoint?

THE ENERGY OF FOOD

Petrol is fuel for cars, and coal is fuel for power stations. Food is fuel for people and animals, and so, like petrol and coal, it can be measured in terms of energy. We are all familiar with the idea of calories in food – indeed, many of us worry that we are eating too many of them – but few of us probably remember that they are a unit for measuring energy. Scientists measure how much energy is in food by burning it in a device called a 'bomb calorimeter'. A sample of food is first dried and ground into a powder. Then it is placed in a strong steel container (the bomb calorimeter) that is surrounded by a bath of water. The calorimeter is pumped full of pure oxygen at a pressure of 30 atmospheres and the powder is ignited. It goes off like a bomb in the pure oxygen environment (hence the name), but the steel container keeps everything inside. The rise in temperature of the water surrounding the device can be used to measure the amount of energy released by burning the food.[1]

One calorie is the heat flow needed to raise the temperature of 1 gram of water by 1 °C, but the calorie used by nutritionists is in fact the kilocalorie (kcal): the amount of heat needed to raise the temperature of 1 kg of water (=1 litre) by the same amount. According to the United Nations Food and Agriculture Organization (FAO), an average adult male should consume food with an energy content of 3,200 kcals or 13.4 MJ per day, while an average female should eat 2,300 kcal or 9.63 MJ.[2] These calorific values may seem high when compared to recommendations for a sedentary society like the UK, for example, where average calorie intakes are estimated to be 2,550 for adult men and 1,940 for adult women.[3] However, they are world values and they take account of different peoples and more active ways of living. We have used the world values here on the assumption that a sustainable future may well be a less sedentary one.

These daily figures represent quite a lot of energy: the value for an adult male would bring about 40 l of water to the boil (or, for a woman, about 30 l). Over a whole year they add up to 4.9 GJ and 3.5 GJ for a man and a woman respectively – an average of about 4.2 GJ per adult per year, or 11.5 MJ per day. For comparison, an average New Zealand household uses around 14.4 GJ per year for heating water,[4] so the annual food consumption of a four-person household would be roughly equivalent to the energy they use for hot water.

Food represents a lot of energy not only on a domestic level, but also for the whole country. In the late 1990s the total annual delivered energy consumption (i.e. the energy delivered to customers in the form of electricity, petrol, etc.) for the New Zealand economy was 430 PJ. The New Zealand population at that time was about 3.6 million. The total food energy consumption of that population should have been around 15 PJ, but because of overeating the actual food consumption was, and no doubt still is, 39% in excess of the FAO recommendations.[5] This means that the energy value of the food actually consumed was nearly 21 PJ – a considerable amount, and in fact equivalent to about 5% of the national delivered energy consumption (430 PJ). This calculation makes no allowance for the fact that some of the population are children, who eat less than adults, but neither does it allow for the fact that teenagers should eat more than adults, so it is probably a reasonable assessment.

THE TOTAL ENERGY OF FOOD

The average figure for food energy consumption – 4.2 GJ per adult per year (or about 1,170 kWh per year, the energy contained in roughly 120 l of petrol) – represents the energy provided by food as a fuel for those who eat it. However, it also takes energy to manufacture and operate the tractors that prepare the land before the crop is sown; to make the seed drills and the sprayers; to make, package and deliver the fertilizers and pesticides; to harvest, transport, process and package the food; to transport the food to the shops; and, finally, to sell it. This energy that is used to make something is known as 'embodied energy'. Some foods need more energy to reach your plate than others. It will probably take more energy to put a loaf of bread on sale than a potato, because the bread goes through a lot more stages in its production. Research in the UK in the 1970s showed that the average amount of embodied energy needed to make food available to the population was five times the energy contained in the food.[6]

More recent figures calculated by Treloar and Fay in Australia suggest that the factor for the energy embodied in food is now closer to 10 to 1.[7] They show the total annual embodied energy of food and drink in Australia to be 42 GJ per person, which can be compared to the recommended average dietary energy requirement of 4.2 GJ per year. The figure of 42 GJ was arrived at by taking the total energy used in supplying all food and drink, including any overeating, and dividing it by the number of Australians. Assuming that Australians overeat at the same rate as New Zealanders (i.e. 39% in excess of FAO recommendations), the total food-related energy of 42 GJ/person/year is therefore 139% of what is actually needed, making a final figure of 30.2 GJ/person/year. This means that, after the basic adjustment to reflect actual consumption, the basic 4.2 GJ dietary energy requirement has been multiplied by 7.2 (30.2 ÷ 4.2 = 7.2).

On the basis of these Australian figures, the total energy embodied in the current New Zealand diet represents at least 150 PJ (i.e. an actual consumption of 21 PJ multiplied by an embodied energy factor of 7.2). The national primary (rather than delivered) energy consumption for New Zealand in 1996 was 665 PJ.[8] Primary energy accounts for the energy embodied in providing that energy. For example, burning coal in a power station to make electricity means that it takes roughly three primary energy units of coal to make one delivered energy unit of electricity. Primary energy also represents the entire energy consumed by a country. Thus it can be calculated that the energy needed to provide New Zealand's food is 23% of the country's total primary energy consumption. (This is only the food consumed by the population of New Zealand and does not include any food grown for export.) In many respects, New Zealand's embodied energy of food is likely to be lower than that of other countries since the temperate climate means that livestock live outside all year and eat grass, rather than being fed on concentrated foods in barns and sheds. Similar figures to New Zealand's would certainly apply to other industrialized countries. If at least a quarter of the energy used by a country each year goes into feeding itself, how far have we progressed from the hunter-gatherer stage?

As well as the energy it takes to feed us, we should also remember that 39% of the total 150 PJ of food consumed in New Zealand is the result of overeating. This 60 PJ we don't need represents nearly 10% of the nation's total energy use, and contributes to poor health, obesity, waste and all the other environmental ills of overconsumption.

FEEDING A WHOLE PLANET

We have looked at food on an individual and on a national scale (albeit in New Zealand, which in population terms is smaller than many cities). We can also look at the matter on a global scale, just to get an idea of what we are talking about. Is food a big issue from a planetary perspective? According to the US Energy Information Administration (EIA), world energy consumption in 2004 was 447 quadrillion British thermal units (generally called quads). It is projected to reach 511 quads in 2010, and to go on rising.[9] This represents a rise of 10.7 quads per year. We are generally using SI units in this book, so if we convert according to EIA guidelines,[10] whereby 1 quadrillion Btu works out very roughly at 1,000 PJ (it is actually 1,055 PJ), in 2007 the world used around 500,000 PJ. The US Census Bureau gives a world population for 2007 of 6,602,236,753.[11] This means that the world's annual energy consumption averaged over the total global population is roughly 76 GJ. The food energy needed by a person is 4.2 GJ (assuming no overconsumption), or 5.5% of their total energy consumption, and the embodied energy of this food, if it were grown and marketed by typical modern methods, would be about 30 GJ. If the world's population all had enough food, and if it was a conventional Western diet produced using current methods, about 40% of the world's current total energy consumption would be needed to feed us. This seems like a fairly difficult situation, not least because most of the world's primary energy comes from finite sources, as illustrated in Table 1.

Table 1: World total primary energy consumption by fuel type[12]

fuel	1973	2005	change
oil	46.2%	35.0%	
coal	24.4%	25.3%	
natural gas	16.0%	20.7%	
combustible renewables and waste	10.6%	10.0%	
nuclear	0.9%	6.3%	
hydro	1.8%	2.2%	
other	0.1%	0.5%	
total	260 quads (260,000 PJ)	480 quads (480,000 PJ)	87% increase
population	3,937 million	6,449 million	64% increase
energy per person	66 GJ	76 GJ	15% increase
% from non-renewables	87.5%	87.3%	little change

This table shows that, in 32 years of progress, the average person in the world gained access to just 10 more gigajoules of energy per year. Most of the 87% growth in world energy demand over the same period is clearly the result of the growing world population, which has risen by 64%. These figures should also remind us that because food supplies are so closely connected to energy, they are based on the use of resources that are limited.

BP, a major oil company, is the source of the figures shown in Table 2 (overleaf) for the 'reserves to production rates' for our fossil fuels. This rate is the length of time that known reserves will last at the current rate of consumption, so it is a rather ill-defined figure. On the one hand, demand for all these fuels is rising, driven by global population growth and development, which will shorten the life of the reserves. On the other hand, more reserves may be found, or the rising price of the fuels may make it economic to exploit reserves that were previously thought too expensive to extract, as happened with North Sea oil in the 1970s.

Table 2: Life of current known reserves of fossil fuels at current rates of consumption[13]

oil	40.5 years
natural gas	63.3 years
coal	147 years

There seems to be not much oil or gas, but plenty of coal; however, since coal at present supplies only around 25% of the world's energy, it will not last as long as the table suggests if it has to be used instead of the other two fuels.

According to the International Atomic Energy Agency, the amount of uranium that can be mined for less than US$130 per kg is about 4.7 million tonnes. Based on the amount of nuclear electricity generation in 2004, this would be sufficient for 85 years. The commercial development and implementation of fast reactor technology would make the uranium last for over 2,500 years.[14] Nuclear power now supplies only 6.3% of the world's energy, but if it were to replace oil and natural gas (the two fuels likely to become scarce first), this figure would rise to 62% and the uranium would thus be used up more quickly. (In reality, it is likely that more expensive reserves would then become attractive.) In addition, nuclear electricity might be less easy to use as a transport fuel than oil. You can't run an airliner on electricity.

It seems that the first fuel to become scarce will be oil. The International Energy Agency says that 'World oil resources are judged to be sufficient to meet the projected growth in demand to 2030', but then adds: 'Although new oil-production capacity additions from greenfield projects are expected to increase over the next five years, it is very uncertain whether they will be sufficient to compensate for the decline in output at existing fields and keep pace with the projected increase in demand. A supply-side crunch in the period to 2015, involving an abrupt escalation in oil prices, cannot be ruled out.'[15]

The problem with so many of these statements from official bureaucracies like the International Energy Agency is that they tend to take a somewhat short-term view. Having said that there will be enough oil until 2030, they assume that the problem ends there. They fail to consider what might happen in 2040, 2060 or 2100, when ever-increasing demand meets a finite supply. It is almost as though the officials who make these statements do not care what happens after they are dead; they seem unwilling, or unable, to express anything their employers might not wish to hear. If continuous growth in the use of finite resources and in population cannot be assured in the future, the whole global adventure of capitalism may be in for quite a challenging time. At the very least, the figures from BP suggest that oil and gas, which together supplied 55.7% of the world's energy in 2005, will cease to be available as fuels within the lifetime of someone who is just starting work or university today. This will be a big change for the world to deal with.

Just in case anyone is wondering why all this discussion of energy resources appears in a chapter about food, remember that because food is so closely tied up with energy, shortage of energy could also mean a shortage of food.

LAND FOR FOOD

As well as needing energy, the production of food also requires land. Land uses are often in conflict. If you are growing potatoes on a given piece of land, the same land cannot simultaneously produce maize for ethanol to run your car. If you concrete over the land to build a supermarket, it cannot produce food to be sold in the supermarket or ethanol to allow you to drive your car to get there.

The area of land needed to provide a particular diet for a population can be estimated using the ecological footprint method developed by Wackernagel and Rees in Canada. The ecological footprint is the amount of land required to provide a given product or service in a sustainable way. Because the ecological footprint figure for food production allows for the growing of the food on a sustainable basis, it is the most appropriate figure to use for our calculations.

The earth does not have much productive land and sea, as explained by a study made for the city of Cardiff, which has a population of just over 300,000.

> *A footprint is expressed in global hectares (gha) of 'earthshare'. If we divide the bio-productive land and sea on the planet by the number of people who need to use it, we currently get an earthshare of only 1.89 gha per person ... An average United States citizen has a huge footprint of 9.5 gha which is 5 times their fair earthshare. An Indian citizen only has a footprint of 0.8 gha, well within their fair earthshare.*[16]

As was noted in the Introduction, if everyone were to live the American dream we would need five earths, because the footprint of the average American is so large. The slightly more modest footprint of a Cardiff resident breaks down as follows:

Table 3: Ecological footprint for a person in Cardiff, Wales

category	footprint (gha)	% of total footprint
food and drink	1.33	24
energy use	0.99	18
passenger travel	0.99	18
government, services, holidays, etc.	0.77	14
infrastructure/buildings	0.74	13
consumables and durables	0.64	11
housing	0.16	3
total	5.59	
waste (if taken as a separate share of total footprint)	0.84	15*
fair earthshare	1.89	

* Waste is counted into the footprint for each heading. Waste is 15% of the total if it is taken out and considered as a separate category.

In fact, to supply its current needs, or rather its current wants (which are not necessarily the same thing), the city of Cardiff requires the products and services of an area nearly as large as the whole country of Wales.[17]

NOT 'BACK TO THE FUTURE', BUT 'BACK TO THE PAST'

As the world's population rises, each person's individual earthshare falls because more people are trying to meet their needs and desires from a fixed amount of land and sea. In 1964, when the population was half what it is now, our individual earthshare would have been 3.78 ha, which would have made everything a lot easier. Back then each of us would have had twice as much land to supply everything that we use in our daily lives; and we also each had fewer material possessions and used fewer resources, so our demand was lower. Every year the standard of living that the earth could support sustainably falls as the population increases and each person's earthshare therefore decreases. In the 1950s the world could probably have supported its whole population living the lifestyle of 1950s Europe, with leisure time, a modest use of cars, a varied diet, television and radio, and some international travel. Now, however, it is more likely that we have moved to a situation where the lifestyle that could be supported globally is a 19th-century one (no private transport other than bikes, less leisure time, a restricted diet, and limited international travel). Each year, as the population rises and as our demands increase, our individual share of the earth reduces in size and so we move further back in time. Eventually we will have a world that can support us all only with the simplest possible lifestyle.

As the standard of living that the world can support deteriorates, the likelihood of conflict over our standard of living increases. We will increasingly start to understand what we might be losing through any sort of 'levelling' process, and the countries that at the moment enjoy 'better' lifestyles will defend them to the death against others who might want to improve their own quality of life. Indeed, President George H. W. Bush declared at the 1992 Earth Summit in Rio that 'the American way of life is not negotiable'.[18] In the end, our striving to have more means that we will all have less. However, our current political system worldwide is based on the assumption that we will all have more every year. This seems contrary to the likely outcome, but because democracy is based on regular elections at inter-vals of three or four years no politicians can afford to take the long-term view, or they will be booted out of office at the next election by a party telling the electorate that they *can* have more.

Another way of looking at this issue is to see which countries currently live within the fair earthshare. This is what the environmental organization WWF has done.[19] In general, greater well-being is associated with a higher ecological footprint, but it does not have to be like that. Some countries – those that are more efficient – can achieve high levels of well-being at the same time as having lower footprints. Well-being can be measured by the Human Development Index (HDI), developed by the United Nations Development Programme, which gives a relative score between 0 and 1 according to how conducive conditions are in a given nation for people to enjoy long, healthy and creative lives (see Table 4).[20] The WWF report chose an index of 0.8 as the lowest acceptable level of well-being and an earthshare of 1.8 global hectares (gha) per person (in 2001) as the highest sustainable footprint. The only country that meets these criteria in the WWF report, and

Table 4: Ecological footprint of a number of countries compared with their Human Development Index[21]

country	Human Development Index	footprint (gha/person)
United States of America	0.94	9.5
Sweden	0.94	7.0
Belgium/Luxembourg	0.94	4.9
Netherlands	0.94	4.7
Japan	0.93	4.3
Italy	0.92	3.8
Poland	0.84	3.6
Hungary	0.84	3.5
Croatia	0.82	2.9
Cuba	0.81	1.4
India	0.59	0.8

that therefore can be called sustainable, is Cuba, which has an HDI score of 0.81 and an ecological footprint of 1.4 gha per person. The highest HDI score of any country in the report is 0.94, which was given to four countries.

It will not have escaped the eagle-eyed reader that the most sustainable country in Table 4 does not operate under the system of capitalist democracy. Some countries that do, like the United States, have large footprints; although the US appears to do well in terms of the Human Development Index, its ecological footprint is a disaster. This sends a clear message that capitalism and democracy are not necessarily a viable route towards achieving sustainability. However, it is clear from the table that the Dutch, who are also both capitalists and democrats, live just as well as the Americans but with half the impact on the environment. India, which is the largest democracy in the world, is managing to achieve a very low ecological footprint, although its HDI is currently lower than would be considered adequate. It is also clear from capitalist democratic Japan and Italy that it is possible to reduce a country's footprint even lower than that of the Netherlands with little impact on the HDI. But if only Cuba can be described as sustainable, it is obvious that those of us in the 'developed world' have some serious thinking to do about how we live our lives; at the same time, those of us in the 'developing world' need to find ways to raise the HDI without appreciably increasing the ecological footprint.

AND SO BACK TO FOOD

We can use the ecological footprint as a way of thinking about diet. Estimates of the ecological footprint of a typical Western diet vary a certain amount. It comes out at 1.3 gha per person according to the Task Force on Planning Healthy and Sustainable Communities at the University of British Columbia,[22] a result that is similar to the Cardiff figure of 1.33 gha. Another detailed calculation of food consumption found a footprint of 1.63 gha for an average resident of south-west England.[23]

For the purposes of this chapter we will make use of the data from the Cardiff study. Table 5 (overleaf) shows the breakdown of food for a resident of Cardiff, outlining the weight of each major category and subcategory of food eaten in a year, the percentage of the diet and of the footprint represented by

Table 5: Breakdown of a year's food for an average resident of Cardiff, Wales

type of food	total weight (kg)	% of diet	footprint (gha)	% of footprint	footprint (m²/kg)
MILK AND DAIRY	**142.10**	**21.0**	**0.3754**	**28.2**	**26.4 ave.**
whole milk	37.3		0.0670		18.0
skimmed milk	66.5		0.1219		18.3
yoghurt etc.*	9.1		0.0210		23.1
other dairy	9.3		0.0213		22.9
cream	1.2		0.0095		79.2
cheese	6.0		0.0893		148.8
eggs	7.6		0.0118		15.5
ice cream etc.	5.9		0.0336		56.9
OILS, FATS AND SPREADS	**5.3**	**0.8**	**0.0485**	**3.6**	**91.5 ave.**
butter	1.0		0.0160		160.0
margarine	0.7		0.0060		85.7
low-fat spreads etc.	2.2		0.0198		90.0
vegetable oils	1.1		0.0058		52.7
other animal fats	0.3		0.0009		30.0
MEAT AND FISH	**72.5**	**10.7**	**0.4402**	**33.1**	**60.7 ave.**
beef and veal	6.6		0.1380		209.1
mutton and lamb	3.4		0.0342		100.6
pork/ham/bacon	8.2		0.0208		25.4
poultry (uncooked)	9.9		0.0206		20.8
poultry (cooked)	1.8		0.0078		43.3
all other meats	33.8		0.1006		29.8
total fish	8.8		0.1182		134.3
SUGAR AND PRESERVES	**15.2**	**2.2**	**0.0143**	**1.1**	**9.4 ave.**
sugar	12.8		0.0114		8.9
preserves etc.†	2.4		0.0029		12.1

* includes fromage frais   † includes honey, syrup and treacle

FRUIT/VEGETABLES	196.5	29.1	0.1371	10.3	7.0 ave.
fresh potatoes	22.3		0.0096		4.3
fresh green veg.	18.1		0.0077		4.3
other fresh veg.	36.6		0.0188		5.1
processed veg.	49.8		0.0356		7.1
fresh fruit	41.8		0.0285		6.8
other fruit (tinned)	5.8		0.0039		6.7
fruit juices	21.1		0.0330		14.9
CEREAL PRODUCTS	79.7	11.8	0.0951	7.2	11.9 ave.
bread	35.7		0.0215		6.0
flour	2.8		0.0026		9.3
cakes	10.9		0.0237		21.7
biscuits	11.7		0.0223		19.1
all other cereals	18.6		0.0250		13.4
BEVERAGES	75.0	11.1	0.0451	3.4	6.0 ave.
tea	2.5		0.0119		47.6
coffee	1.1		0.0065		59.1
cocoa/drinking choc.	0.6		0.0043		71.7
Horlicks etc. ‡	0.3		0.0007		23.3
soups	4.2		0.0065		15.5
mineral water	10.4		0.0018		1.7
soft drinks (conc.) ∫	6.0		0.0015		2.5
soft drinks	30.3		0.0068		2.2
low cal. soft (conc.) ∫	1.8		0.0004		2.2
low cal. soft	17.8		0.0047		2.6
ALCOHOLIC BEVERAGES	73.3	10.8	0.1284	9.7	17.5 ave.
beer and lager	46.7		0.0285		6.1
wine	17.5		0.0508		29.0
spirits	9.1		0.0491		54.0

continued overleaf

‡ includes 'all branded food drinks'   ∫ 'conc.' = concentrated

Table 5 *continued*

type of food	total weight (kg)	% of diet	footprint (gha)	% of footprint	footprint (m²/kg)
CONFECTIONERY	9.1	1.3	0.0391	2.9	43.0 ave.
chocolate	5.7		0.0348		61.1
other	3.4		0.0043		12.6
MISCELLANEOUS	5.5	0.8	0.0078	0.6	14.2
total	675.5		1.33		19.7

each category, and the footprint in m² of land per kg of food for each subcategory, as well as its average footprint.

Taking the food by weight, 90.1% was eaten at home, and 9.9% outside the home.[24] However, when we look at the footprint of the food, as set out in Table 6, it breaks down very differently. All percentages are the percentage of the total food footprint represented by each item. The third column is the total food footprint including transport.

Although food eaten outside the home represented only 10% of the total diet, it was responsible for nearly a third of the footprint – probably because when we go out we often eat things that are in some way more exotic or high-footprint foods like meat.

The transport of food is often raised as a significant issue, and people have started to worry about so-called 'food miles'.[25] The Cardiff study found that 32% of the food consumed was imported,[26] which sounds as if it should

Table 6: Ecological footprint of food consumed by Cardiff residents (*gha*/person)[27]

	food footprint	transport footprint	total footprint
eaten at home	0.886	0.015	0.900 (67.6%)
eaten out	0.429	0.007	0.431 (32.4%)
total	1.309* (98.3%)	0.022 (1.7%)	1.331 (100%)

* As given in original source. The correct total of 1.315 would make the effect of transport even smaller.

be a worry. However, 99.58% of all the imported food came by ship, with only 0.42% arriving by plane.[28] Sea freight is far more efficient than shipping by road, since a container ship uses 0.12 MJ/tonne-km,[29] whereas road freight in Europe in 1999 used 0.067 kg of oil equivalent per tonne-km.[30] Since 1 kg of oil equivalent is 41.868 MJ,[31] road freight uses 2.8 MJ/tonne-km, over twenty times as much as international shipping. Air freight is even worse, at 9.7 MJ/tonne-km. These values are set out in Table 7.

Table 7: Energy use of various forms of freight transport

type of transport	energy use (kWh/tonne-km)	energy use (MJ/tonne-km)
container shipping	–	0.12
coastal shipping[32]	100	0.36
rail freight[32]	200	0.72
lorry, Europe	–	2.80
lorry, New Zealand[32]	810	2.92
air freight[33]	–	9.70

Because so much of the Cardiff food comes by ship, the transport footprint of the imported food is calculated to be very low. As Table 6 shows, the transport of food represented only 1.7% of the total food footprint for Cardiff. However, it is also clear from Table 7 that it is worth trying to avoid the transport of food by lorry, so the idea of locally produced food makes good sense. There is little environmental point in making pies in New York and taking them by lorry to San Francisco, or in baking biscuits in Scotland and carting them down the road to London, even though this currently may make economic sense.

Thus an average person in Cardiff eats roughly 675 kg of food a year: that's getting on for 2 kg a day, which needs 1.33 gha to provide it. Meat and fish at 72.5 kg a year make up only a tenth of the diet by weight, but a third of the footprint. It could be a lot worse, since the average American in 1998 chewed his or her way through 123 kg of meat;[34] by comparison the Welsh are comparatively frugal carnivores.

These footprint studies make very clear that the global economy seems to be going in the wrong direction. While we should be finding ways to feed ourselves with reduced ecological footprints, the market system, which appears to have become the only permitted way to view the world, is encouraging greater consumption of meat and fish, which have high footprints, across the globe. According to the Worldwatch Institute in 1998, world meat production grew from 44 million tons in 1950 to 211 million tons in 1997, and the world's harvest of fish from 21 million tons to 120 million tons over the same period.[35] These figures represent increases of 380% for meat and 470% for fish. Of course, more people would mean more meat and fish being eaten, but in fact population growth for this period was 131%.[36] Meat and fish consumption has been growing much faster than population size. There is obviously a need to provide adequate food for those of the global community who are malnourished, but it is not at all clear that they are the ones eating this extra meat and fish. Indeed, the Worldwatch Institute puts the increase down to 'rising affluence'.

ARE WE EATING SENSIBLY?

There are lots of ways in which we can consider these diet footprint figures. We are often exhorted to eat a sensible diet for the sake of our health, but what about a sensible diet for the sake of our planet? One question we could ask is whether we are eating 'sensibly' in terms of our food's footprint. We can use the figures from Table 5 in an attempt to find out (see Fig. 1 overleaf).

What Fig. 1 shows us is that in terms of ecological footprint (we are not going to discuss whether the Cardiff diet is a healthy one) the people of Cardiff do indeed seem to eat quite sensibly. The foods they consume a lot of by weight are generally fairly low down the footprint scale, and they eat little of the high-footprint foods. The only change that would make any significant improvement would be if they ate less fish, beef, veal and cheese, since these are high-footprint foods occupying the middle of the table by weight.

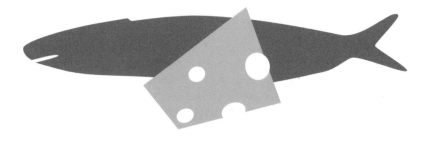

TOWARDS A LOWER-FOOTPRINT DIET?

Is the obvious conclusion from these considerations of footprint and diet that we need to eat more vegetables and less meat and fish? Would this reduce our footprint? Perhaps the first question to ask is what the size of our food footprint should be. (If we have a target, then maybe we can devise a way to achieve it.) If food accounts for roughly a quarter of the total current footprint of a Cardiff resident, we can assume that the food part of a fair earthshare would also be around a quarter of the total. At present this would work out at about 0.43 gha (based on the earthshare of 1.8 gha used in the WWF study cited above) but, since the world's population is rising, this figure is getting smaller every day. If we were to eat the same quantity of food that we do at the moment, to achieve a footprint of 0.43 gha we would need foods with an average footprint of no more than 6.4 m²/kg. Going back to Table 5, we can see that the only food items that even come close are potatoes, vegetables, bread and beer (mineral water and soft drinks are lower, but these are hardly sources of nourishment). So should we return to potatoes, vegetables, bread and beer, which sounds like the sort of diet a European peasant might have eaten in the past?

If we are considering a change of diet, we first need to think about how much we eat. How much food we need depends very much on what we do during the course of the day. We saw at the beginning of this chapter that an average adult male should consume food with an energy content of 3,200 kilocalories or 13.4 MJ per day, while an average female should eat 2,300 kcal or 9.63 MJ. These are modern global values; if we were to work as hard as peasants, we too would need more fuel.

A person's daily need for fuel (measured in calories) is the result of three main functions:

- basal metabolic rate (BMR)   60% of fuel
- activity (how hard they are working)   30% of fuel
- digestion and absorption   10% of fuel

The basal metabolic rate is the amount of energy needed to maintain the body's basic processes, such as pumping the blood, breathing, making hormones, and so on. These are things over which we have no voluntary

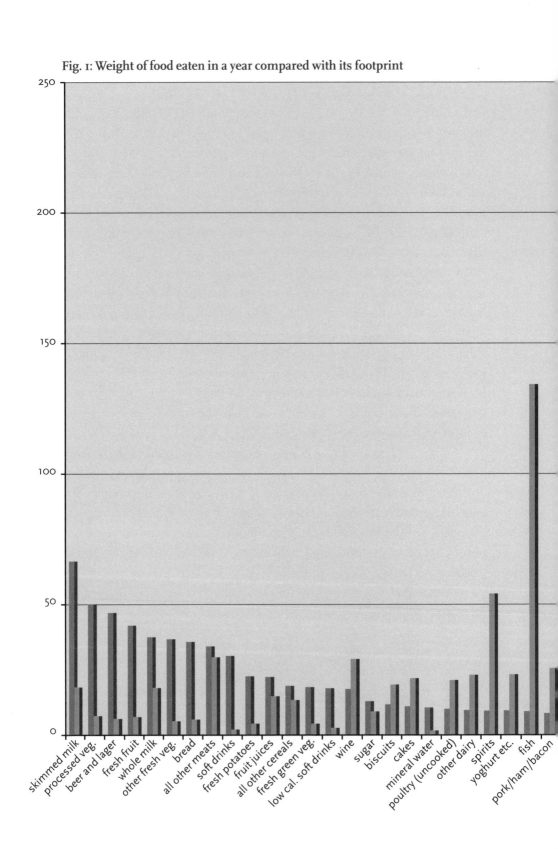

Fig. 1: Weight of food eaten in a year compared with its footprint

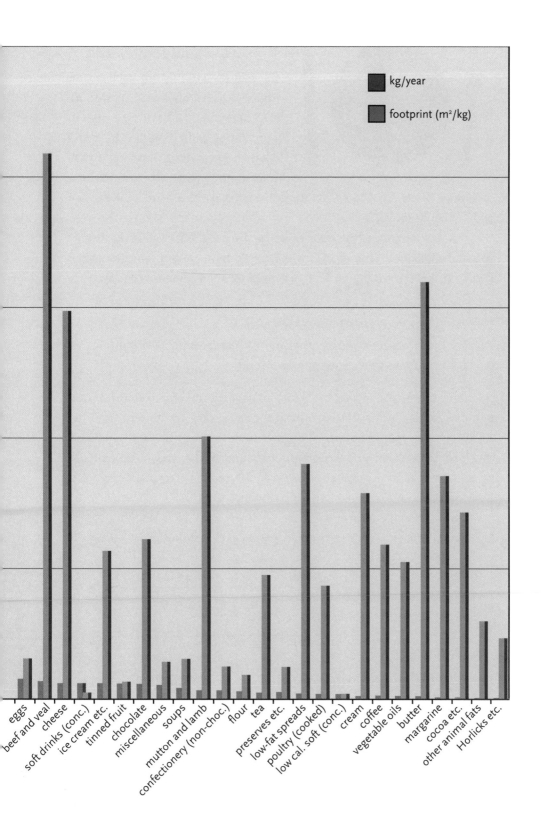

kg/year

footprint (m²/kg)

eggs
beef and veal
cheese
soft drinks (conc.)
ice cream etc.
tinned fruit
chocolate
miscellaneous
soups
mutton and lamb
confectionery (non-choc.)
flour
tea
preserves etc.
low-fat spreads
poultry (cooked)
low cal. soft (conc.)
cream
coffee
vegetable oils
butter
margarine
cocoa etc.
other animal fats
Horlicks etc.

control, and they use about 60% of the calories we consume each day. In imperial units, about 10 calories are used to maintain a BMR for every 1 lb (0.45 kg) of body weight. (The calculations here are in imperial units because this particular information originated from the United States, but they make the point well enough without being converted.)

A further 30% of the calories we eat are used to fuel all of our body's voluntary activities – things over which we do have control. The amount of fuel we need depends on our level of activity over the course of the day:

- sedentary (sitting down for most of the day)   20% of BMR
- light activity (walking, cooking meals)   30% of BMR
- moderate activity (heavy housework, gardening)   40% of BMR
- very active (prolonged physical work)   50% of BMR

A further 10% of a person's fuel intake is needed for powering digestion and for absorbing nutrients from the food. This is different from the BMR, because the energy used for digestion depends on what and how much you have eaten, and the latter depends on how active you are. Finally, we should bear in mind that we need less fuel as we get older. For each decade past the age of twenty we need 2% fewer calories.[37]

So if we take an average man of thirty years old, weighing 170 lb (77 kg) and stuck in a sedentary office job, we get the following:

BMR	170 lb = 10 kcal/lb	= 1,700 kcal
physical activity	20% of 1,700 kcal	= 340 kcal (sedentary)
digestion	10% of (1,700 kcal BMR +	
	340 kcal physical)	= 204 kcal
total		**= 2,244 kcal**
total with adjustment for age		**= 2,200 kcal**

(subtract 2% of the total)

But if our man is working hard, we get a higher figure, as follows:

BMR	170 lb = 10 kcal/lb	= 1,700 kcal
physical activity	50% of 1,700 kcal	= 850 kcal (very active)
digestion	10% of (1,700 kcal BMR + 850 kcal physical)	= 255 kcal
total		= 2,805 kcal
total with adjustment for age (subtract 2% of the total)		= 2,750 kcal

Note: Values have been rounded.

These calculations show that an active person needs 25% more food to support their active life. This becomes important when we think about ways we could reduce the footprint of our diet. In olden times we used to eat quite a lot more than we do now, because we worked harder. According to notes taken from the Food, Culture and History course at Eastern Kentucky University, a male medieval peasant weighing 120 lbs needed 4,800 calories a day – more than the requirement of a (heavier) modern office worker. In 14th-century England, the diet of even a prosperous peasant would be fairly monotonous. Meat was expensive and was generally eaten on special occasions; cheese, eggs and butter were used as substitutes. Vegetables such as onions, leeks, cabbage, garlic, turnips, parsnips, peas and beans were staples, and some of these could be stored or dried for the winter. (In the Middle Ages the potato had not yet arrived in Europe from the New World.) Fruits were available in season. The typical daily diet comprised something like 2–3 lbs of bread (made of rye, oats or barley), 8 oz of meat, fish or cheese, and 2–3 pints of ale.[38]

Thus the medieval diet adds up to a total of 2.5–3 kg of food a day, or between 900 and 1,100 kg a year – a lot more than the modern Cardiff resident whose diet we examined in Table 5, who eats only 675 kg a year. Most of the calories and protein in the peasant diet generally came from the grains (oats, wheat or rye). In Table 8 we have used the Cardiff values to calculate very roughly what the footprint of a peasant diet would have been.

At first sight, the peasant's diet would appear to be a simple one and at the lower end of the footprint values. However, we can see that a return to this way of eating is not the answer for the 21st century: expressed in modern terms, the footprint of the medieval diet (1.1 gha) is not much lower than

Table 8: Rough breakdown of a year's food for a prosperous English peasant

type of food	amount per day	annual total (kg)	footprint (gha/person)	footprint (m²/kg)
meat/fish/cheese	8 oz	83	0.5038	60.7 ave. for meat/fish
bread	2.5 lb	414	0.2484	6.0
beer	3 pints	497	0.3032	6.1
cabbage	2 cups	83	0.0357	4.3
total		1,077	1.0911	

that of the far more varied modern diet (1.33 gha). This is largely because a peasant diet involves the consumption of much more food – about 300 kg more per year. But there is another very good reason why a peasant diet will not work for us now, which was first explained by the German physiologist Max Rubner at the start of the 20th century. Rubner showed that whereas a hard-working 20th-century (male) peasant's daily diet of just over 3 kg of potatoes provided the 3,800 kcal and 54 g of protein he needed perfectly adequately, when he moved to the city and to a less strenuous job, he reduced his fuel intake to only 2.4 kg of potatoes a day, which in turn reduced his protein intake to a level that was insufficient to maintain good bodily health. He could buy meat to provide the neccessary protein in a more concentrated form, but because meat was expensive he would not then have enough money to live on.[39] The peasant diet works for hard-working peasants because the large throughput of food will allow for the absorption of enough nutrients from otherwise simple and unconcentrated foodstuffs.

CHANGING HOW WE PRODUCE FOOD

This suggests that the way to reduce the food footprint is not so much to change our diet – although it would help if we limited our consumption of high-footprint foods – but to reduce the footprints of the foods we eat. The Cardiff study found that, if all food eaten in Cardiff were organic, the

Table 9: The effect on footprint of consuming food from 100% organic sources

	100% conventional	100% organic
ecological footprint of food (gha/person)	1.315	0.799
ecological footprint of transporting food (gha/person)	0.022	0.022
total ecological footprint	1.337	0.817

footprint would be reduced significantly.[40] Table 9 shows their findings, which reveal a 39% reduction in footprint.

The Cardiff researchers found that on average the organic production of raw food required 67% less energy than conventional methods of agriculture. The argument that organic farming could not produce enough food is often brought up by the manufacturers who, unsurprisingly, want the world to stick to chemical agriculture and to use genetically engineered crops – especially those engineered to have a longer shelf life and to look attractive on the supermarket shelves. But a paper from the College of Natural Resources at the University of California at Berkeley cites the results of many trials in various countries demonstrating that, in practice, organic farming yields are comparable with those from conventional chemical agriculture,[41] so it seems likely that organic farming could provide enough food. When they assumed that the processing of organic food was as energy-intensive as that of conventional food, the Cardiff researchers discovered that the overall energy needed for organic produce was calculated to be only 17% lower than for conventional food.[42] This suggests that we may need to find ways to get our food that do not involve a lot of energy-intensive processing and packaging or other modern 'conveniences'.

THE IMPACT OF WASTE

Another part of the Cardiff report contains some data on the ecological footprint of waste, which might allow us to see whether the elimination of packaging would help reduce the food footprint. Table 10 shows the wastes that could be considered as related to food and drink. It is hard to be precise

Table 10: Annual waste production related to food and drink[43]

waste material	footprint (m²/kg)	footprint (gha/person)
PAPER AND CARD		
paper and card packaging	82	0.07
cardboard	85	0.03
non-recyclable paper	88	0.03
total		**0.13**
GLASS		
clear glass	6	0.003
green glass	6	0.003
brown glass	6	0.001
non-recyclable glass	1	0.001
total		**0.008**
FERROUS METAL		
steel drinks cans	18	0.005
steel food cans	18	0.004
total		**0.009**
NON-FERROUS METAL		
aluminium cans	118	0.010
aluminium foil	123	0.003
total		**0.013**
PLASTIC FLM		
plastic film (sacks/carriers)	85	0.02
plastic film (other)	85	0.01
multi-layer packaging	57	0.01
drink boxes (liquid cartons)	93	0.01
total		**0.05**

DENSE PLASTIC		
PET coloured	36	0.002
PET clear	36	0.003
HDPE coloured	40	0.005
HDPE clear	40	0.003
PVC	31	0.0002
LDPE	43	0.0001
PS	86	0.010
unidentified dense plastic	24	0.004
total		**0.0273**
PUTRESCIBLES		
home-compostable kitchen waste	55	0.130
other kitchen waste (meat, bones, etc)	55	0.050
total		**0.180**
overall total		**0.4173**

about the allocation of some categories, but the table provides a reasonable attempt to assess the amount of waste associated with what we eat.

The average Cardiff resident has a total waste footprint of 0.81 gha, so the waste that can be attributable to food is roughly half of the total. Of the total waste produced in the average household, the largest single individual category is newspapers and pamphlets (not shown in this table), at 0.14 gha, followed by home compostable kitchen waste. Paper, card and putrescibles are by far the largest categories of food-related waste, together making up 0.31 gha of the total food waste footprint of around 0.42 gha – that is, nearly three-quarters. It is interesting to see that plastic carrier bags, about which so much fuss is made, account for less than 5% of the food-related waste footprint, and aluminium cans make up only 3% of the total.

So if we could get rid of all waste through 'reduce, reuse, recycle' methods such as avoiding packaging, using our own shopping bags, home composting and the like, it appears that we could reduce the food footprint by roughly 0.4 gha. There would also need to be a change in shopping habits, away from supermarkets (see Chapter 3) and towards local producers' markets, since some of this waste is the packaging used in transporting bulk food from the processor to the supermarket. Alternatively, the retail sector would have to commit to both reduce and recycle all its packaging. As we saw above, the use of 100% organic food production would reduce the footprint from 1.34 gha to 0.82 gha, so if we also eliminated waste, we should be able to get the overall footprint for food and drink down to 0.41 gha – slightly lower than the value of 0.43 gha per person that represents the food footprint component of the fair earthshare.

In addition to avoiding packaging, we could reduce the footprint for food by not wasting so much of it. We waste food in various ways. As we saw above, the New Zealand Ministry for the Environment found in the 1990s that, because of overeating, the actual food consumption of New Zealanders was 39% in excess of FAO recommendations.[44] People were eating far more food than they needed. In Cardiff, they found that 100 kg of food per person per year is thrown away, representing 16.4% of the total.[45] If there were no wasted food, the total footprint would be only 1.11 gha/person.[46]

As with transport, what we need to do to reduce the impact of our diet is pretty much go back to the habits, and to some extent the diet, of 1950s Europe. When you went shopping in those days, you did not drive to the supermarket out of town: you walked to the local shops for everyday items and took the bus or the tram to town centres for things like clothes or furniture. Every day you went separately to the greengrocer (for fruit and vegetables), the grocer (for flour, sugar, butter, cheese, etc.), the butcher (for meat) and the baker (for bread, cakes, buns, etc.). You can still shop like this in the centre of Paris, but not in many other cities. In the past, you took a shopping bag to the greengrocer, and when you bought your fruit and vegetables, they were tipped into your bag without any wrapping or packaging. Now it seems we want to buy our fruit and vegetables in polystyrene trays, covered in clear plastic. Admittedly, the butcher in the 1950s would wrap any meat you bought in a piece of paper, but the meat was not pre-cut and packaged as it is in the supermarket. This custom has now mostly disappeared in many places – perhaps in the name of 'convenience', but more likely because profit is a bigger concern for those who own the supermarkets.

FEEDING A CITY

We have looked at the individual environmental impact of each person's diet, but how much land is needed to feed a whole city? Based on the values we used above, and assuming an average food footprint of 1.3 ha per person, it is possible to calculate the approximate area of land needed to support a city's population. The results are shown in Table 11.

Table 11: **Land area required to feed cities of various sizes**

city population	area of land required to supply food	
	(ha)	(km²)
100,000	130,000	1,300
1,000,000	1,300,000	13,000
10,000,000	13,000,000	130,000

Thus in order to obtain its food, a city of 10 million inhabitants needs to be at the centre of a circle of productive land about 400 km in diameter. A city of 1 million needs an area of land with a diameter of 125 km, and even a city with a population of just 100,000 people needs to be surrounded by a circle of land 40 km across.

One way of thinking about what this means for a real city would be to look at Wellington, New Zealand. Wellington is a tiny city by world standards, but it is the capital of New Zealand, and Wellington City Council plans to make it one of the first carbon-neutral cities in the world.[47] How does food fit into this? As of 30 June 2007, the population of Wellington was estimated at 190,500 people and the area covered by the city (not the whole region) at 28,990 hectares.[48] Using the footprint values from Table 11, Wellington city would need 247,650 hectares (2,477 km²) to provide its food in a sustainable manner, assuming its people eat a diet similar to that of Cardiff. This would form a circular area of land 56 km in diameter. Thus the land required to feed the city is nearly ten times the area of the city itself. Wellington is a very low-density city, with about 6.6 people per hectare. Hong Kong, on the other hand, is the ultimate high-density city – very much a built example of what the Modernist architect and planner Le Corbusier was writing about in the

1920s. Most of the population of Hong Kong lives in high-rise apartment buildings, which are frequently built on top of multi-storey shopping and entertainment centres that incorporate bus and railway stations. Hong Kong supports a highly efficient railway network, with trains every two or three minutes, as well as buses, trams and ferries. With a population of 7 million, it currently occupies an area of 1,076 km², of which 75% is open space, so the built area of the city covers about 270 km².[49] Using the same ecological footprint value as for Wellington, we can calculate that the area needed to provide Hong Kong's food is 91,000 km², over 300 times the built area of the city, or 85 times its total area. Thus the area of land needed to feed a city is likely to be between 10 and 100 times the area of the city itself, depending both on its density and on the diet of its residents.

A sustainable city also needs a sustainable source of energy. Hong Kong's energy consumption in 1999 was 17,866 thousand tonnes of oil equivalent, which is around 750 PJ.[50] A 1 MW wind turbine will produce

Fig 2: Areas of land in km² required to supply Wellington with local food and energy production

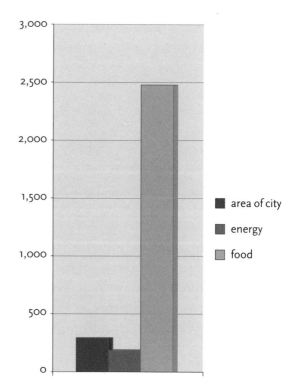

3.9 GWh per year, which is 0.014 PJ,[51] so to power Hong Kong from renewable energy would require 54,000 wind turbines each of 1 MW (or 18,000 3MW turbines), assuming the wind regime was suitable. It may not be possible to power a city or a country completely by wind power, because there are times when there is too little wind and because machines must be turned off when winds are too high. Another problem is that wind energy makes electricity, which may not be a suitable substitute for all the fuels we currently use. However, for this simple exercise it is assumed that all energy comes from the wind. The New York State Energy Research and Development Authority estimates that the total land use for a wind farm is between 17.8 and 39 acres (7.2–15.8 ha) per MW.[52] At 15 ha/MW, the turbines to power Hong Kong will occupy only 810,000 ha (8,100 km²). The Wellington region used about 43 PJ of energy in the year ending March 2002.[53] With a population of around 450,000 people,[54] the energy used by the region was about 96 GJ/person, so the energy used by Wellington city could be assumed to be about 18 PJ. The land area needed to provide this energy entirely from wind would be just over 19,000 ha, or 190 km². These figures for Wellington are summarized in Fig. 2. It is clear that, even for a low-density city like Wellington, the big issue is the land needed to grow food for its citizens.

THE QUESTION OF FERTILITY

Another issue related to food production is land fertility. To grow crops successfully over many years, the fertility of the soil must be maintained. As far back as 1909, the American agronomist F. H. King toured Japan, Korea and China studying their traditional methods of farming. His book *Farmers of Forty Centuries, or Permanent Agriculture in China, Korea, and Japan* was published posthumously in 1911.[55] King was a pioneer of what would now be called sustainable farming, although he lived at a time before the use of artificial fertilizers and machinery in agriculture was widespread. The title of King's book is a reminder that it is possible to maintain soil fertility sustainably for a very long time – forty centuries in the case of the Eastern civilizations that he studied.

In the past, the citizens' sewage was used to fertilize the food that was grown to feed them. However, a point was reached when the city's physical size made it difficult to get sewage out to the fields, particularly in the days when transport was by horse and cart. This was the case in London in the first half of the 19th century, during which the population grew from 1 million to 2.5 million.[56] In *London Labour and the London Poor* (1851), Henry Mayhew states that, before the size of the city made the collection of night soil from its cesspits difficult, this waste was mixed with other organic waste, such as hops from brewing, to make a more balanced manure, 75% of which was shipped in barges down the Thames to distant farms. The remaining 25% was carried by cart up to 5 or 6 miles (roughly 8 to 10 km) outside the city to fertilize local food production.[57] This was an attempt to make sure that natural cycles were closed rather than open-ended, so that essential nutrients would not be lost. The ability of closed cycles to retain nutrients was graphically explained in a programme broadcast by Radio New Zealand early in 2008, following the death of the mountaineer and explorer Sir Edmund Hillary. The speaker was talking about Hillary's long-term work with Himalayan village communities and how the provision of iodine in the diet had led to the elimination of the common disease called goitre, which causes a swelling of the neck. The speaker noted that, since the village houses had composting toilets, the iodine had to be provided only once: when it was in the system it went on being absorbed into each successive crop. The villagers consumed the iodine and excreted it in the composting toilets, which then turned the excrement into fertilizer to be used on subsequent crops. The iodine would be consumed once more, and so it went on.

In the 19th century the industrialized cities grew beyond the simple balance of using sewage as fertilizer, transported via the renewable methods of the barge and the horse and cart, and evolved into modern high-density conurbations that throw all this fertility away and instead rely on agricultural systems based on artificial fertilizers. However, finding ways in the post-oil world to maintain the soil fertility needed to grow food for an expanding world population may become a problem. There are three key ingredients of fertilizers: nitrogen (N), phosphorus (P) and potassium (K). Nitrogen fertilizer is generally now made from natural gas, although the nitrogen was initially obtained from the air by passing an air current through an electric arc, which used hydro-electric power.[58] It would be possible to move towards making nitrogen fertilizer from renewable electricity, but the other key components of all fertilizers, phosphorus and potassium, are derived from naturally occurring minerals, supplies of which will inevitably become depleted. The Fertilizer Institute, an industry group based in Washington, D.C., states the following:

> *The source of phosphorus in fertilizer is fossilized remains of ancient marine life found in rock deposits in North America and North Africa, and volcanic activity in China ... Fertilizer producers mine potassium, or potash, from naturally occurring ore deposits that were formed when seas and oceans evaporated, many of which are covered with several thousands of feet of earth.*[59]

A study from 2002 suggests that phosphorus ore reserves in North America will last for 25 years, or for 100 years if higher-cost ores are used, meaning that phosphorus too will become more expensive in the future, increasing the cost of fertilizer and hence of food.[60] On the other hand, they claim that there is sufficient potassium for centuries. These assumptions are based on current rates of consumption, which are likely to increase as population and living standards rise. What this means is that present agricultural methods relying on artificial fertilizers cannot be considered sustainable; eventually we will have to make sure that nutrients are recycled as much as possible, just as the Himalayan villagers recycle the iodine that was added to their diet.

Assuming that sewage works could be designed so that the nutrients in the sewage could be retained and collected, no extra energy would be needed to distribute the fertilizer to the land surrounding a city since the lorries bringing in food could return to the fields with fertilizer. A much bigger problem is that current systems usually result in the contamination of sewage with oil and industrial wastes, making it less than ideal for putting on crops that are to be eaten. To give one example, a study of sewage sludge from three locations in Colorado found traces of arsenic, cadmium, chromium, copper, mercury, lead, molybdenum, nickel, selenium and zinc.[61] Some of these are needed as trace elements in the diet, but not chemicals like arsenic, cadmium, chromium and lead. These pollutants enter the sewers not because we have eaten them, but because the sewers carry run-off from roads and from metal roofing, and all sorts of toxic wastes from industry. In the future we are going to need to clean up our sewage if we want to use it to grow our food.

DENSE OR DISPERSED?

There are two possible ways of approaching the problem of supplying a city with food. The first is to concentrate the physical development of a city as much as possible, so that there will still be highly productive land available for growing food. However, if the analysis of the writer and urban activist Jane Jacobs is to be taken seriously,[62] it is likely that this solution would actually increase the non-renewable energy content of foods. This is because market forces act to drive down the cost of food, encouraging agriculture to be more 'efficient' through the use of more mechanical processes. The replacement of human labour with non-renewable energy is a major feature of modern agricultural production.

The second way of looking at the problem is to recognize that, for a vast proportion of the world's population, the urban fabric is still an important source of food. Urban living in New Zealand (where cities are admittedly developed at a low density) was formerly highly productive. According to figures from the New Zealand Census for 1956, 20% of households in the largest city, Auckland, were growing more than 25% of their vegetable consumption and 12% of their potatoes. In Christchurch, the figures were 43% for vegetables and 35% for potatoes.[63]

Housing choices in Australasia suggest that the suburban home is the preferred model for most of the population. The suburbs could do a great deal to contribute to more sustainable solutions. Given that the population density of mainland Auckland in 2001 was 23 people per hectare,[64] most Auckland houses ought to have access to the three main ingredients of food production: land, nutrients and water. The suburban house has enough land surrounding it; sufficient rain falls on a large enough roof area to supply more than enough water for food production; and the household produces enough waste to make compost that would supply the bulk of nutrients and minerals. More detailed considerations of water supply and nutrient provision for food production at home are set out below.

WATER FOR FOOD PRODUCTION

According to MetroWater, the company that supplies water to Auckland, the average household of water-users in the city consists of 3.7 people who consume 220 m³ of water per year (220,000 l, or about 160 l/person/day).[65] It does not know how much is used for watering gardens, although it says that a hosepipe or sprinkler uses 1,800 l per hour. Data from 1982 indicate that watering the garden constitutes the following percentages of total annual domestic demand: 25–50% in the United States; 33–55% in South Australia; and 35% in Melbourne.[66] These values average at 39.6%, but if we adopt the Melbourne value for Auckland the annual water consumption for gardening would be 77,000 l per household. This water does not need to be purified to drinking standard: when it rains the garden receives raw rainwater, which nobody thinks is a problem for vegetable-growing. Thus it would seem reasonable to collect rainwater for watering the garden when it does not rain. An average New Zealand house has a floor area of 150m²,[67] and can therefore be assumed to have a roof area at least as big, since the majority of houses are single-storey. Auckland has a rainfall of around 1,250 mm per year[68] so the annual collection of water from one roof, allowing for losses of 20% through evaporation, would be 150,000 l. This is more than enough to provide all the water that garden needs. Given that the water used for gardens currently represents about 20% of Auckland's total consumption (domestic supply is 58% of the total; garden water is assumed to be 35% of domestic supply), the use of roof water for gardening would offer an immediate water-saving strategy for the city. In fact, the annual supply of water collected from roofs would be adequate both for the garden and for flushing lavatories, which typically account for another third of total domestic supply. Flushing is another type of water use that does not require water of potable quality (unless you want to drink from the bowl). The use of water from roofs for watering gardens and flushing lavatories would cut Auckland's total annual water demand by nearly 40%. The same would be possible in other countries as well, even those with lower rainfall: for example, the Autonomous House we built in 1993 in the town of Southwell in Nottinghamshire, England, obtains its entire water supply from roof-collected rainfall, although annual rainfall is only 576 mm.[69] These figures suggest that in typical suburban layouts there should easily be enough water available on site for growing food at home.

NUTRIENTS FOR FOOD PRODUCTION

A number of surveys have noted that a high proportion – at least 50% by mass – of the domestic waste that currently finds its way to landfill is organic and compostable.[70] The best way to deal with this is at source, rather than trying to separate compostable from the other types of waste after collection by the local council. The householder can use this waste to make compost for the garden, closing the loop by returning the nutrients in the waste to the soil. The result would be that 50% of household waste would no longer be 'waste' as such, but would become something of value. In addition, wastes from non-gardening households, restaurants and parks could be collected and composted in local centres before being returned to gardeners. On Waiheke Island, which comes under Auckland City Council, 90% of a permanent population of around 8,000 people compost their garden and food waste, but a waste audit carried out in 2006 still found that 28% of the rubbish put out for collection each week contained waste that could be composted.[71]

A study has shown that the embodied energy for vegetables attributable to fertilizers may vary from 11% for fresh peas to 52% for potatoes and 57% for brussels sprouts.[72] By using domestic organic waste to produce compost instead of relying on artificial fertilizers, home gardeners could eliminate their need to buy these unsustainable additives. In addition, growing vegetables at home would almost eliminate their embodied energy.

FOOD WASTE DISPOSAL

We can look at the issue of food waste in a little more detail. Would it make more sense to handle food waste in a centralized manner rather than in billions of home compost heaps? Where food waste is concerned, the action with least environmental impact is to eat everything put in front of you, and to ensure that people are served only the amount they can eat each time they sit down at the table. This immediately goes counter to some cultural traditions, such as those of the Chinese, where you are thought to be a good host only if you provide enough food for some to be left over. In the past, polite society in the West solved this problem by having servants below stairs who would consume food left over from the dining above stairs. For most households, however, this is thankfully no longer an option. So what is the best way to get rid of unwanted food and waste from food preparation?

In general, the more food that is grown at home, the easier it will be to get rid of kitchen waste, and a vegetarian diet makes this easier still. For meat-eaters who grow food at home, a pig will happily consume most table leftovers and recycle them into bacon, given additional food as necessary. However, any leftovers that have been in contact with meat or other animal products (the exception being milk) should be heated before being given to the pigs, to destroy bacteria and viruses. In the past, the bucket of pigswill was boiled; and today the New Zealand Food Safety Authority states that centrally collected leftovers from restaurants must be boiled at 100 °C for an hour before being fed to pigs.[73] This is a good illustration of the fact that the closer to source that waste is recycled, the less chance there is of serious contamination. Family pigs have been fed on family leftovers for centuries in many parts of the world,[74] and the human race has survived. In a similar manner, washed eggshells can be fed back to hens to provide some of the grit they require. However, not everyone wants or has the space to keep animals at home for meat and eggs (see Chapter 5), and the normal place for the disposal of food waste is the garden compost heap.

Anything that has lived can be composted, and this includes all leftover food. The problem is that putrescible wastes, including meat and other animal products, can smell as they break down. They are defined by the Alaska Department of Fish and Game as follows:

> Putrescible waste ... [is] organic waste that can bacterially decompose and create odors that may attract bears. These include, but are not limited to, discarded processed human and animal foods or food residues, discarded animal or plant parts, sewage solids or residue, and domestic sanitary waste.[75]

Even in places without bears, wastes that contain animal products may attract other unwanted visitors to the compost heap, such as rats. Since the most convenient place for a compost bin is fairly close to the house, putting all food waste in the compost bin is not recommended practice for a conventional compost system unless the household is totally vegetarian. However, a worm bin for composting can take meat, fish and dairy leftovers, although it is recommended that they should be well covered to avoid unpleasant smells.[76] Worm bins cannot be used for garden waste or for some foods like citrus peel, which makes the environment too acidic, so the best solution for the non-vegetarian household with a garden is to use a dual system of normal aerobic compost bins, where the oxygen in the air is necessary for creating good compost, and a worm farm. Both ensure that organic nutrients can be returned to the soil. As will be seen from Table 14, which compares a range of waste management strategies, this is a low-impact way of disposing of food waste.

For households without a garden or with only a very small garden, a worm farm is still a practical way of disposing of all organic refuse, providing there is a balcony or other place to put it where it can drain without causing a nuisance.[77] The compost removed periodically from a worm farm can be used (without the worms) to top-dress pot plants and for potting, or it could be given to a friend with a garden. Since there is no garden refuse to dispose of in an apartment, the worm farm should be able to cope provided it is treated reasonably. For households who do not wish to have even this small level of involvement with the environment, three other options remain:

- conventional disposal in landfill sites
- special collection of bio material for composting
- using an in-sink waste disposal unit

The question is, which of these four methods – the three listed above and home composting – has the least impact on the environment?

A study in the UK compared the global warming potential (GWP) of different ways of dealing with food waste: it discovered that the GWP of landfill was +743 kg CO_2e/tonne (carbon dioxide equivalent per tonne), while that for separate collection and treatment by composting was –14 kg CO_2e/tonne. The GWP of an in-sink waste disposal unit as part of a system in which the sludge goes to a sewage works to be treated anaerobically (i.e. decomposing in the absence of the oxygen), thereby making both biogas that is used to offset fossil fuel use and solids that are used on the land, has a much greater negative value of –168 kg CO_2e/tonne.[78] This would suggest that sending kitchen waste to landfill should be replaced by the compulsory use of waste disposal units, though it should be noted that the study appears on the web page of a manufacturer of such units, and in reality few sewage works yet have the facilities to make biogas and use the solids for fertilizer.

Another way of approaching this issue is to consider the energy needed to set up and operate each of these systems, and to couple these findings with an energy equivalent for the greenhouse gases produced by each type of decomposition. In an ordinary aerobic compost heap, CO_2 is the only type of gas emission and is considered to form part of the natural carbon cycle, being absorbed by plants as they grow. It is the methane gen-erated by anaerobic disposal of kitchen waste that is the problem. Table 14 summarizes the energy needed for various disposal systems over a 10-year timespan.

CONVENTIONAL DISPOSAL IN LANDFILL SITES

A Welsh study looked at the putrescible kitchen waste generated in terraced houses, council houses and semi-detached houses, comparing the results with other studies.[79] It showed that the average waste produced in the first two categories was consistently around 3.5 kg/household/week, rising to 5.5 kg/household/week for semi-detached houses, representative of more affluent households. A study for a firm making waste disposal units stated that average kitchen waste production in the United States was 2.4 kg/week.[80] An Australian study for the same firm found that households in multi-unit dwellings generated 3.5 kg/household/week.[81] For the purposes of this comparison 3.5 kg/household/week will be used.

The life-cycle environmental cost of waste collection and disposal in a landfill site needs to take account of the effect on the natural environment of all aspects related to that disposal for a specified time period. Some types of impact are the result of one-off activities, such as the extraction and carting of materials required to make a road to the landfill site. Others occur reason-ably often – the use of energy to make replacement tyres for the rubbish trucks, for instance – and some parts of the process will have an impact on the environment every time a journey is made, such as when the diesel-powered trucks emit greenhouse gas as they travel from your home to the landfill site. In this instance, the life-cycle environmental cost would include the energy used in the making and running of machinery and in the global warming potential of the methane generated at the landfill site, which can be converted to an equivalent energy unit. The US study quoted above gives life-cycle figures for the CO_2 and methane (CH_4) produced by the collection of waste and its disposal in municipal landfill as follows:

Table 12: Life-cycle equivalent CO_2 emissions from 100 kg of kitchen waste over 10 years[82]

waste (kg)	life-cycle CO_2 (lbs)	life-cycle CO_2 (kg)	life-cycle CH_4 (lbs)	life-cycle CH_4 (kg)	life-cycle CH_4 as CO_2 equivalent (kg)	total life-cycle emission (kg)
100	81	36.7	5	2.3	52.9	89.6

The household generating 3.5 kg of kitchen waste per week will dispose of 1,820 kg over a ten-year period, so the equivalent CO_2 emissions associated with its landfill disposal will be 18.2 × 89.6 = 1,631 kg.

An alternative method of considering the problem is to use the values for life-cycle energy and materials for the disposal of 100 kg of kitchen waste in landfill from the same study:

Table 13: Life-cycle materials and energy for the disposal of 100 kg of kitchen waste over 10 years[83]

waste (kg)	life-cycle energy (Btu)	life-cycle energy (MJ)	life-cycle materials (lbs)	life-cycle materials (kg)
100	80,112	84.5	338.2	153.4

To dispose of 1,820 kg of waste would require 84.5 × 18.2 = 1,538 MJ of energy over ten years, or 154 MJ/year. Assuming that all the materials associated with the disposal are steel (for the machinery, ducts, etc.), an embodied energy value for virgin steel of 32 MJ/kg[84] would give an embodied energy value of 153.4 × 18.2 × 32 = 89,340 MJ. If all the steel were recycled, its embodied energy value decreases to 10.1 MJ/kg[85] to give a value for the disposal of the kitchen waste of 153.4 × 18.2 × 10.1 = 28,198 MJ. The average of these two values for materials is 58,769 MJ. This would give a total value for the energy and materials of 1,538 + 58,769 = 60,307 MJ. This figure is used in Table 14 (below) for the purposes of comparison.

CENTRAL COMPOSTING

In this system, the wastes are separated at source and taken by road to a central composting site. Using the same US study as above, the life-cycle emissions associated with 100 kg of kitchen waste are 100 lbs (45.4 kg) of CO_2 and 0.00028 lbs of methane – an amount so small it can be ignored. In addition, some of the CO_2 is from the composting process, which means that it could also be ignored, being carbon neutral. This study gives the life-cycle energy for disposing of 100 kg of kitchen waste using this process as 143,299 Btu (151.2 MJ) and for the materials required as 89.6 lbs (40.6 kg).[86] Over the ten-year period, the life-cycle energy for the disposal of 1,820 kg of kitchen waste will be 151.2 × 18.2 = 2,752 MJ, or 275.2 MJ/year. Assuming that the energy embodied in the materials lasts the full ten years and that the related machinery is all steel, this gives a figure of 40.6 × 18.2 × 31.3 = 23,128 MJ, using the value for virgin steel quoted above. If the value for recycled steel is used, the figure would be less: 7,463 MJ. For the purpose of this analysis the average of the two embodied energy values, 15,296 MJ, is used.

IN-SINK WASTE DISPOSAL

A method of disposing of organic waste through the drains was first installed in Quarry Hill Flats in Leeds in the 1930s.[87] In this system the wastes are ground up by a macerator in the sink while the tap is running, and the resulting slurry flows directly into the sewage system. This gets rid of all putrescible waste since even bones can be ground up. The manufacturers of one particular product claim that it uses 0.5 kWha/month of power and 2.8 l/day of water for a three-person household.[88] The unit has a shipping weight of 11.6 kg, consisting of a stainless steel drum and a stainless finish. Its 1 hp motor should be able to deal with almost all food waste and certainly thin bones like chicken bones. Another manufacturer states that its 0.55 hp unit uses 5 l/day of water and 0.55 kWh/month of electricity per household.[89] Its 1 hp model is listed as suitable for households or restaurants. It is clear that this equipment does not use a lot of electricity, and for this comparison with composting and other systems a consumption of 0.5 kWh/month or 6 kWh/year (21.6 MJ/year) has been used.

Assuming that the under-sink unit is made of 50% stainless steel and 50% virgin steel, and using an embodied energy for stainless steel of 74.8 MJ/kg,[90] we come up with an embodied energy of 615 MJ for a machine that should have a ten-year life. However, to assess the total impact of using a waste disposal unit, the embodied energy of the system and its operating energy in the house need to be considered alongside the processing of slurry downstream at the sewage works.

The US study gives the total operating energy of the in-sink waste disposal system for 100 kg of kitchen waste as 45,744 Btu (48.3 MJ) and life-cycle materials of 287.4 lbs (130.4 kg). These figures will include the energy used in making the unit and in operating it in the home, and the energy used to make and operate the share of the municipal sewage system that disposes of the slurry. The methane emissions can again be ignored since they are given as only 0.00028 lbs (13 g) for each 100 kg of kitchen waste.[91] Using the same approach as for the calculation of energy associated with collection and composting over ten years, the operating energy will be 48.3 × 18.2 = 879 MJ, or 88 MJ/year. Assuming that an average embodied energy value for steel is used, the materials will be 130.4 × 18.2 × 21 = 49,839 MJ.

HOME COMPOSTING

A circular compost bin of recycled polythene with 0.28 m³ capacity weighs 9 kg and has a ten-year warranty.[92] The embodied energy for this product would be 459 MJ, using a figure of 51 MJ/kg that takes no account of any plastics recycling.[93] Since the worm farm we have at home is half the size of the compost bin and is also made of polythene, its embodied energy is assumed to be half that of the bin, or 230 MJ. A life of at least ten years is also assumed. Compost bins made at home out of wood are normally larger than purchased plastic ones, though the latter are good for small households and small gardens. A 1 m × 1 m × 1 m timber bin of 25 mm softwood boards with 75 mm × 75 mm corner posts would have an embodied energy of 147 MJ if made of air-dried rough-sawn timber.[94] To this should be added an additional 10 MJ for 1 kg of steel nails, to give 157 MJ.[95] This is a much bigger bin for a little over a quarter of the embodied energy of the plastic composter, though it would take a little time to build unlike the ready-made version. A wooden worm bin can be made from a sheet of plywood with some softwood framing.[96] If constructed in this way, the latter would have an embodied energy value of 375 MJ, which is more than the estimate for the plastic bin because of the high embodied energy of plywood, of 5,200 MJ/m³.[97] However, unlike the plastic products, timber compost and worm bins could be made from scrap materials with zero embodied energy that would otherwise be wasted. The values calculated and used in the table below assume a use of new materials.

WHICH IS BEST?

Table 14 sets out the energy required to dispose of kitchen waste using the different methods discussed above.

From this comparison, home composting looks like a good option, to be encouraged. The caveat is that composting cannot be controlled at home. Some will be managed very well and its aeration guaranteed, but as soon as anaerobic decomposition sets in methane will be generated, with its

Table 14: Energy needs of various methods of disposing of food waste over 10 years

disposal method	embodied energy (MJ)	operational energy (MJ/year)	total for 10 years (MJ)
wastes taken to landfill, anaerobic decomposition	58,769	154	60,307
kitchen waste collection for central composting	15,296	275	18,046
in-sink waste unit, total system	49,839	88	50,719
plastic compost bin and plastic worm farm	689	0	689
wooden compost bin and plywood worm farm*	532 (0)	0	532 (0)

* Embodied energy will be zero if recycled wood is used.

increased global warming potential. The worm farm has better built-in controls because, if it is not looked after, the bin will become smelly and, at worst, the worms will die, so the system offers more warnings if things are not done properly. However, since most people learn how to drive a car – a very complex activity – they should be able to operate a compost heap correctly; and the reward is lovely, rich-smelling compost at the end of the process, which can be used to grow next year's vegetables.

All the centralized systems use considerably more energy for the disposal of the same kitchen waste, with conventional landfill being marginally the worst. Energy is not the only environmental impact of these systems, but it is seen as critical since without energy it would not be possible to collect waste from each household and move it to a centralized treatment plant some distance away – unless, that is, we return to traditional waste collection using handcarts. Some systems, like the anaerobic digestion of sewage, could be scaled down into smaller local biogas plants, and composting could be done at a local level. However, to maintain systems as they are currently set up energy is critical, which is why it has been used as a measure here.

Other studies have come to broadly similar conclusions. One Australian study found that home composting of kitchen waste had the lowest environmental impact. It ranked the in-sink waste disposal unit next lowest in terms of energy consumption, global warming potential and acidification, but noted that it used more water. Centralized composting was ranked lower because of the energy required to move the waste materials.[98]

Obviously, all figures change from study to study depending upon the travel distances that have been factored in. The US study that was fed into the table above found that centralized composting was the best of all centralized systems; the latter all came out roughly the same, however, having a much greater impact than the home-based systems.

What Table 14 suggests is that anything that can be done to reduce our reliance on large infrastructure and highly centralized systems could show energy, and hence environmental, savings. Where things can be done at home, they probably should be.

HEALTHY, WEALTHY AND WISE?

The conclusion is that we could indeed return to some of our more sustainable ways. Twenty minutes a day spent growing fruit and vegetables, collecting rainwater and making fertilizer by recycling 'waste' would make for a more sustainable society. By providing both exercise and fresh organic food, these activities might help us to stay healthy (see Chapter 5); by saving money that would have been spent buying food, they might help us to become wealthier; in terms of sustainability, they might very well be wise.

WHAT SHOULD WE DO?

Where our diet is concerned, we can take the following steps:

- Always buy organic food, since it has a lower footprint than conventional chemically grown food. Transport does not seem to be a very significant part of the footprint of food, but it is a good idea to avoid produce that has travelled by air.

- Avoid processed and packaged foods.

- Compost all putrescible wastes, possibly using a worm bin in conjunction with a conventional compost heap or bin so that you can deal with cooked food and meat scraps.

- Reduce your intake of red meat, cheese and fish, unless you raise meat at home (see Chapter 5) or catch the fish yourself from the beach, the pier or a rowing or sailing boat.

- Start growing fruit and vegetables at home: this is an easy way of ensuring that your food is organic, it will use up your compost, and it eliminates transport.

- Don't waste food, and don't overeat.

2
TRANSPORT

For many people – certainly for most of the population of the 'developed' world – daily life is no longer confined by how far an individual can walk, but instead has been extended to encompass the whole planet, whether through holidays taken in distant locations or through images of exotic landscapes in the media.

Travel has become an expected part of life, but it consumes two things: time and energy. Whereas time spent standing in a rush-hour train or sitting in a car in a traffic jam is only a waste for the individual, the energy used, and wasted, in moving people around the globe in various forms of transport affects everyone. The oil used to fly you to your exotic overseas holiday destination is energy that is not available to support much-needed development in the Third World. The pollutants and emissions associated with burning that fuel will affect the whole planet. The following discussion attempts to show the environmental impact of different aspects of travel as they relate to an average Western lifestyle and to demonstrate how to travel in a way that has the least impact on the environment. What we do and how we travel is up to each of us. What is important is to understand the impact each of has on the world around us.

THE CAR

> *The poetry of motion! The real way to travel! The only way to travel!*
> *Here to-day – in next week to-morrow! Villages skipped, towns and cities*
> *jumped – always somebody else's horizon! O bliss! O poop-poop!*[1]

Mr Toad's first encounter with a motor car in *The Wind in the Willows*, written in 1908, sums up our continuing love affair with the car. Cars have risen from being a means of transport to being objects of desire. They are ubiquitous, and they have changed the way we live and make our built environment since their introduction just over one hundred years ago. How likely is it that the ideal of 'a car in every garage' will be realized in a sustainable future?

WHAT CAR SHOULD WE DRIVE?

In the United States, there is a Christian environmental campaign called 'What would Jesus drive?' that looks at the moral aspects of owning and using the private car.[2] If we are considering which cars we might use, a good starting point would be the energy embodied in making the car. Embodied energy is all the energy used to make something – to refine the iron ore into steel, to ship the steel to the car factory, to run the machinery and the assembly line, and so on. The embodied energy of a vehicle is therefore an important factor when it comes to calculating its overall sustainability, but it does depend to a large extent on how long the car lasts. The same amount of embodied energy will be far more significant for a car that lasts two years than spread over the course of twenty years.

For how long does a car continue to work? The life of a vehicle is hard to determine. For cars in the United States,

Consumer Reports ... says the average life expectancy of a new vehicle these days is around 8 years or 150,000 miles. Of course, some well-built vehicles can go 15 years and 300,000, if properly maintained.[3]

This figure of 150,000 miles is the equivalent of 240,000 km, so a car could last as long as 500,000 km. This longevity does not affect the overall embodied energy, but it makes a big difference when embodied energy is expressed in terms of energy used per kilometre travelled. If you spread the same amount of embodied energy over twice the distance, you will halve the embodied energy per kilometre of travel. The Australians have calculated that it takes 100 MJ to manufacture 1 kg of metals, plastics and other materials for vehicles, be they cars or bicycles.[4] A Volkswagen Golf 1.6 litre weighs 1,220 kg,[5] so its embodied energy will be 122,000 MJ. If the car lasts 240,000 km, this embodied energy will work out at about 0.50 MJ/km, whereas if it lasts the full 480,000 km, as suggested by Consumer Reports, then the embodied energy will be only 0.25 MJ/km. What all this talk of embodied energy shows beyond a doubt is that it makes good sense to take care of things, and not only cars, so that they last as long as possible. At this point anyone who has only a Morris Minor to drive around in should perhaps give themselves a pat on the back. In turn, Morris Motor Company should be congratulated for making an economical car that can be kept on the road for as long as sixty years; indeed, the company has long disappeared, but the cars are still going.[6] (Perhaps we should admit that at one time we were proud Morris Minor owners ourselves.)

Given that the embodied energy of cars covers a wide range, does it matter what kind of car we choose? If we go by the Australian data, the heavier the car, the greater its embodied energy, which would make sense since more metal and plastic would mean more embodied energy. But does it make that much difference? To find out we can compare a small car (the Smart Fortwo Coupé), a medium-sized car (the Volkswagen Golf), a large car (the Holden Commodore) and an SUV, or 'sport utility vehicle' (the Toyota Landcruiser). These definitions of size are fairly arbitrary, because the 'largeness' of a car is very much culturally determined. In Europe, a 2 litre engine is thought to be quite large, whereas in Australasia a 4 litre engine is considered quite normal. However, as Table 1 shows, the engine capacity of our 'normal' cars roughly doubles as we move up to the next example, so there is some logic to the choice. The final column shows fuel consumption: 'combined' means that it results from both urban and long-distance driving.

Table 1: Weight and fuel consumption for four cars available in Australia in 2007

make and model	weight (kg)	no. of seats	engine size (cc)	fuel consumption (l/100 km)
Smart Fortwo Coupé[7]	730	2	698	combined 4.7
Volkswagen Golf[8]	1,220	5	1,595	combined 7.5
Holden Commodore[9]	1,690	5	3,564	combined 10.9
Toyota Landcruiser[10]	2,325	8	4,664	combined 16.1

Table 2: Embodied energy of four cars calculated according to lifespan

make and model	total embodied energy (MJ)	ave. life (MJ/km)	long life (MJ/km)
Smart Fortwo Coupé	73,000	0.30	0.15
Volkswagen Golf	122,000	0.51	0.25
Holden Commodore	169,000	0.70	0.35
Toyota Landcruiser	232,500	0.97	0.48

From the weight of our cars we can work out their embodied energy (EE) for kilometres travelled over an average life of 240,000 km, and over a long life of 480,000 km, as discussed above (Table 2).

Not surprisingly, we can see that the embodied energy of a big car is considerably more than that of a small car, and that if we double the life of our car by taking care of it, we can halve its embodied energy in terms of MJ per kilometre travelled.

From Table 2 it looks as if the only possible choice for the sustainably minded motorist is the Smart car, but is this actually true? Using the fuel consumption data from Table 1, we can now look at the fuel use of each car and convert it to MJ/km. The conversion rate is 34.2 MJ per litre of petrol,[11] and the results are shown in Table 3.

Once the fuel consumption of all the cars has also been expressed in MJ/km, a direct comparison with the embodied energy figures in Table 2

Table 3: Fuel consumption of the four cars

make and model	fuel consumption (l/100 km)	(MJ/km)
Smart Fortwo Coupé	4.7	1.61
Volkswagen Golf	7.5	2.57
Holden Commodore	10.9	3.73
Toyota Landcruiser	16.1	5.51

Fig. 1: Fuel consumption
compared with embodied energy
(EE) for average (240,000 km)
and long (480,000 km) lifespans
(*MJ/km*)

fuel consumption (MJ/km) ■

EE average life ■

EE long life ■

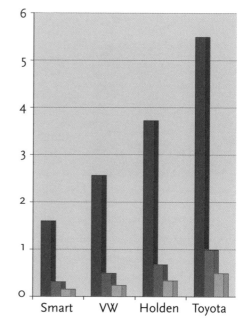

reveals that the fuel consumption is much greater, even if we assume an average lifespan so that the embodied energy is spread over a shorter total distance. Even the embodied energy of the big, heavy SUV is less than the fuel consumption of the tiny two-seater Smart. These calculations do not include the embodied energy of the fuel – the energy required to extract the oil, refine it, deliver it and sell it to you at the petrol pump – largely to make things clearer. If it were included, the difference between the cars' fuel consumption and embodied energy would be even greater. In Fig. 1 the embodied energy figures for an average life and for a long life are compared with the fuel consumption of each of the four cars, all measured in MJ/km.

It is not really surprising to see that there is a clear connection between the weight of a car, expressed in Fig. 1 as its embodied energy, and its fuel consumption. The heavier the vehicle, the more fuel it uses to push it along. Over the course of the car's life the embodied energy does make some difference to its total lifetime energy consumption, and making the car last longer reduces its lifetime energy consumption, but not by much, as shown in Table 4.

So for all four of our cars, from the smallest to the largest, it is the fuel consumption that really matters. Over an average lifetime it is more than

Table 4: Lifetime total energy consumption (fuel plus embodied) for average life and long life (*MJ/km*)

make and model	fuel consumption	total energy consumption average life	long life
Smart Fortwo Coupé	1.61	1.91	1.76
Volkswagen Golf	2.57	3.08	2.82
Holden Commodore	3.73	4.43	4.08
Toyota Landcruiser	5.51	6.48	5.99

five times the embodied energy (and more if you were to include the embodied energy of the fuel). We cannot do anything about our car's embodied energy, since it is determined by when the car was designed and manufactured. All we can do is to try to make the car last as long as possible. Fuel consumption is also determined by the design of the car. There is no doubt that, in general, the bigger the engine, the greater the fuel consumption. This is clear from Fig. 2, which shows the urban cycle fuel

Fig. 2: Urban cycle fuel consumption of private cars compared with engine size, 2001–2[12]

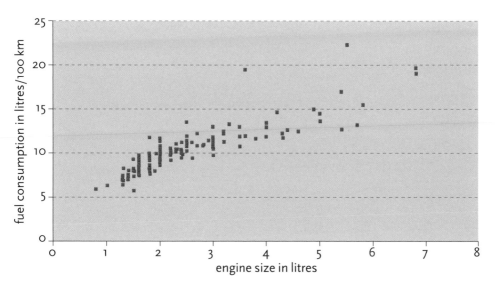

consumption (that is, the fuel used in typical city driving) of all the cars on sale in Australia in 2001–2 plotted against engine size. So yes, as with so many things, size matters.

IT'S NOT WHAT YOU DO, IT'S HOW YOU DO IT

We cannot do much about embodied energy, except to choose a small car and make it last a long time. We can, however, do quite a lot about fuel consumption whatever sort of car we drive. According to Nottinghamshire County Council, 'It's been calculated that just by changing the way we drive, motorists can use 25 per cent less fuel.'[13]

The County Council's view is supported by some data from the United States. The US car-testing organization Edmunds.com carried out a series of trials to examine the effects of driving behaviour on fuel consumption, and found that fuel savings of 37% were possible, the average being 31%.[14] Careful driving means anticipating the road conditions so that all driving reactions are smooth and do not involve revving the engine unnecessarily. It also means driving the car at its most economical setting, which will not necessarily mean driving as fast as the speed limit allows.

So we could certainly say that the fuel consumption figures for the cars listed above could be reduced by 25% if we were to drive them more carefully. The effect of this is shown in Table 5. The relative differences are shown in Fig. 3 below.

How we behave makes a big difference. The savings we can make by changing our driving style are greater than the average embodied energy of all four cars.

Table 5: Fuel consumption of four cars showing the effect of more careful driving

make and model	average fuel consumption l/100 km	MJ/km	careful fuel consumption l/100 km	MJ/km
Smart Fortwo Coupé	4.7	1.61	3.5	1.21
Volkswagen Golf	7.5	2.57	5.6	1.93
Holden Commodore	10.9	3.73	8.2	2.80
Toyota Landcruiser	16.1	5.51	12.1	4.13

Fig. 3: Fuel consumption of four cars for average and careful driving, and embodied energy (EE) for average life and long life (*MJ/km*)

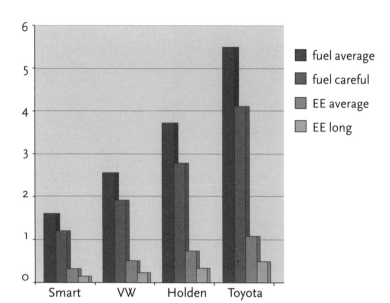

The importance of behaviour becomes even clearer when we consider the occupancy of the car. If you watch any road, you can see that most cars seem to travel most of the time with only one occupant, although they have seats for several. In the UK, according to the Department for Transport, cars being used for 'business travel' and 'commuting' have an average of only 1.2 occupants, while the highest occupancy rates of 2.1 are recorded when the car is used for the purpose of 'holidays/day trips' or 'education'.[15]

Table 1 above gave the number of seats in each of the four cars. What is the effect of filling those seats (Table 6, overleaf)?

Full occupancy of all the available seats makes the ranking of the four cars quite different; even the big SUV comes out quite well. The most efficient car when full is now the Volkswagen Golf, which has five seats but a relatively modest 1.6 litre engine.

In Table 7 (overleaf) we can now see the range of values that can be achieved by motorists in our four cars. The table shows the lifetime energy use in MJ/km/person for five different situations, which are explained in the notes below the table.

Table 6: Lifetime energy consumption of four cars (assuming average life and average fuel consumption) if fully occupied all the time (*MJ/person-km*)

make and model	energy consumption
Smart Fortwo Coupé	0.61
Volkswagen Golf	0.81
Holden Commodore	0.89
Toyota Landcruiser	0.96

Table 7: Lifetime energy consumption of four cars according to five different ways of using them (*MJ/person-km*)

make and model	(a)	(b)	(c)	(d)	(e)
Smart Fortwo Coupé	1.91	1.76	1.51	1.36	0.96
Volkswagen Golf	3.08	2.82	2.44	2.18	0.61
Holden Commodore	4.43	4.08	3.50	3.15	0.89
Toyota Landcruiser	6.48	5.99	5.10	4.61	0.81

(a) = one person, average life, average driving
(b) = one person, long life, average driving
(c) = one person, average life, careful driving
(d) = one person, long life, careful driving
(e) = all seats full, average life, average driving

It is interesting to see how much of a real difference we can make by changing the way we use our cars. We can make a small difference by making our cars last longer, and a bigger difference by driving them more carefully. However, introducing other changes, such as filling all the seats, tends to make them perform more or less the same. It has been suggested that one key to reducing the number of journeys travelled by car is reducing car ownership to one car per household.[16] If each household had only one car, then occupancy rates might also rise. Cars are generally designed to carry four or five people; if they do, the environmental impact of each passenger-km is reduced to a level similar to a journey undertaken on some forms of public transport. This suggests that cars in themselves are not bad, providing there is a renewable energy system or biofuel replacement to power them, but the habit of having only one person in a car designed for five is very unsustainable. The upshot is that choosing to be a one-car household is probably the best environmental choice. If someone else buys your second car, which you give up in the attempt to become more sustainable, that can also be considered as saving a whole lot of energy, water and materials that would otherwise be consumed in making a new car. This is not good for car manufacturers, but it is better for the environment.

Rather than changing our cars, we could use far less fuel for travelling by changing our habits: how you drive makes quite a difference, as we have seen, but the number of people you take with you makes an even bigger one. We should use the car only if we are taking the whole family or carrying a lot of friends, and choose to walk, cycle or get the bus if we are travelling on our own. Offer your neighbours a lift if you are going out. If you have to take the car to work, it would be good to organize a car pool and to take other commuters with you. This is what happened in the 1950s in England: often the father of a family took the train or bus to work; the children walked to school; the mother, who might also stay at home to look after the children, took the bus or walked to the shops; and the car, if there was one, was used for family outings at the weekend.

If you are buying a car, first look for a 'second car' that someone feels they no longer need. If you must buy new, look for the car that has the most seats and the smallest engine. If you have to drive alone, choose the smallest possible car in terms of weight and engine size.

So, in answer to the question 'What car should we drive?', if we are taking some friends along, we could drive an SUV, but if we are going on our own to work or to the shops, we would do better to choose a Smart car. Whatever we are driving, however, we need to drive carefully to save fuel.

DOES SIZE MATTER FOR SAFETY?

The findings outlined above suggest quite clearly that it is generally better for the environment to buy a small car than a large one. Small cars seem to offer all sorts of straightforward financial benefits as well: they cost less to buy; they cost less to run because they use less fuel; the tyres are cheaper; and so on. So why would you want a big car? One reason could be that you want a big car to show off. Small cars have occasionally been status symbols – look at the first Mini, for example, which became very chic – but in general larger cars are seen as more prestigious. Another reason could be that larger cars are generally considered to be safer. A detailed paper written in the early 1990s by researchers at Monash University in Australia, where the culture favours large cars, concluded: 'There is little doubt that larger vehicles are inherently more safe than smaller ones.' However, it also stated that 'the precise relationship between mass, size and safety is not clear'.[17]

So is safety a high priority for people when they choose a car, and is this why they want larger models? *Road and Travel* magazine published the results of a monthly survey of 7,000 car buyers in the United States under-taken by the market research firm BIGresearch of Columbus, Ohio. They looked at the various motivations for buying a new car. Of those surveyed, 35.2% bought a new model because their existing car had a high mileage – in other words, it was getting old. Perhaps more significantly, 22% were moti-vated by the fact they were tired of the old car and felt like a new one, this being the second most popular reason. An ecological, or money-conscious, 19.2% wanted a car with better fuel economy, and 17.6% bought a new car because their existing one had finally expired. Rather like those who were tired of their existing car, 15% liked the look of a new model. Only 14.6% bought because of better safety features. Other reasons included a need to buy a second car (14%), the need for a larger vehicle (9%), and the lure of a vehicle with more gadgets (6.2%).[18]

Safety was 8th out of the 14 reasons given for buying a new car. Only 5 of the total 14 reasons were related to the car and its design (see Table 8), and when only these design-related factors are listed, fuel economy comes out top. Styling is shown to be slightly more important than safety.

It seems from this survey that most car buyers are not particularly interested in safety. However, if you are, and if you want to buy a small car

Table 8: Design-related reasons for buying a new car, in order of popularity[19]

reason number, out of 14	motivation for buying new car	%
4	wanted a car with better fuel economy	19.2
7	attracted by the styling of newer models	15.0
8	wanted a car with improved safety features	14.6
12	wanted a car with more room	9.0
13	wanted a car with gadgets such as a nagivation system, DVD player, etc.	6.2

because it will be better for the environment, safety need not be a problem. The European Union's New Car Assessment Programme, which tests cars for their safety, lists plenty of small cars in the 'super mini' category that can offer their adult occupants a safety rating of five stars (the highest). Some also offer four stars for child occupant safety (there are no cars that have five stars for child passengers).[20]

THE BEST OF CARS, THE WORST OF CARS

We have chosen four cars to represent the range of vehicles on the market for our calculations of fuel economy and embodied energy, but we have not looked at the best and worst cars that are currently available. How much difference is there in fuel consumption between the most efficient car you could buy and the least efficient? Just to make this exercise easier, here we will confine ourselves to cars; SUVs will not be considered. Some of the most and least efficient cars on sale in the UK, according to the UK's Vehicle Certification Agency (VCA), are shown in Table 9 (overleaf).

It is clear from Table 9 that the cars with the lowest fuel consumption are small diesels. It is worth noting that the CO_2 emissions of the most efficient petrol cars (the hybrid Prius and the normal Peugeot 107) are proportionally lower than those of the diesel cars because of the fuels' different properties. The most efficient petrol car on the market is the hybrid petrol/electric Toyota Prius, but the table shows that lower fuel consumption and lower CO_2 emissions can be obtained from a diesel engine without the

Table 9: Fuel consumption of some of the most and least efficient cars on sale in the UK in April 2008

make and model	engine size (l)	CO$_2$ g/km	l/100 km[21]
Volkswagen Polo TDi Blue Motion (non a/c)	1.4	99	3.8 (diesel)
Mini Cooper D hatchback	1.6	104	3.9 (diesel)
Peugeot 206 HDi	1.4	112	4.3 (diesel)
Toyota Prius	1.5	104	4.3 (petrol/electric)
Peugeot 107	1.0	109	4.6 (petrol)
Lamborghini Murcielago 2007	6.5	495	21.3 (petrol)

complexity of the hybrid system. This really undermines the rationale of the London congestion charge, from which a range of hybrid SUVs and dual-fuel vehicles are exempt even though they use much more fuel than efficient small diesel cars.[22] We do not propose to get into the question of particulate emissions from diesels here, except to mention that the latest small diesel cars generally make use of particle filters (the particulate emissions of the Volkswagen Polo Blue Motion, for example, are given by the VCA as nil). The car with the highest fuel consumption is a two-seater sports car, and it uses more fuel than the SUV that we looked at in the earlier part of this chapter.

The tables of results produced by the VCA list only two models of vehicle in the 21–25 l/100 km category, but five pages of vehicles in the 1–5 l/100 km category, of which the worst has a fuel consumption of 5.9 l/100 km. This looks good, since there are lots of fairly efficient cars to choose from, until you see that there are also four pages of vehicles in the rather less efficient 16–20 l/100 km category. So there are lots of gas-guzzlers for you to choose from in the free market. The least efficient car in Table 9 and in the VCA lists is a petrol car. If you drove one of these, every kilometre you would be using more than five times the fuel of the most economical vehicle. It is fairly unlikely, however, that you would be doing your daily commute, taking the children to school or going to the supermarket in a Lamborghini Murcielago.

Even if you choose something a little more ordinary, what is the overall effect of your choice of car? Sticking with UK statistics (since the cars in Table 9 are all on sale in the UK market), the annual distance driven by the average car in the UK is calculated to be about 13,000 km.[23] If we were to drive this distance in the Volkswagen Polo Blue Motion, we would use less than 500 l of fuel a year. If, on the other hand, we did the same annual mileage in something reasonably ordinary like a Ford Mondeo 2.3 litre, we would use over 1,200 l of fuel.

We used to be able to buy cars with better fuel consumption than any of these, but not any more. The Volkswagen Audi Group once made the so-called '3 litre' cars: versions of the Volkswagen Lupo and the Audi A2 with very efficient diesel engines that achieved a measured fuel consumption performance of 3 l/100 km.[24] Indeed, Volkswagen drove a Lupo around the world (33,333 km) and averaged 2.38 l/100 km at a mean speed of 85 km/h.[25] Just to show that it is not only the Germans who can concentrate on fuel economy, in Japan Honda produced the Insight, a petrol/electric hybrid with similarly low fuel consumption.[26] However, production of all these cars had ceased by 2006. A '3 litre' car is by no means the limit. Some years ago Volkswagen also made and drove a '1 litre' concept car – a two-seater diesel/electric hybrid that consumed only 1 litre of fuel per 100 km.[27]

BUT THE OIL'S RUNNING OUT...

It may not help much to change our cars. In the United States in 2005 there were 136,568,083 registered automobiles.[28] Data from the US Department of Transportation show that in 2005 the average US passenger car travelled 12,400 miles (20,000 km) and consumed fuel at the rate of 22.9 miles per US gallon (10.3 l/100 km), giving an annual fuel consumption for passenger cars of 73,870 million US gallons. However, the total fuel consumption for all land transport in the same year was 179,100 million US gallons.[29] In 2008 the Indian company Tata Motors launched a new four-seater 'people's car', the Tata Nano,[30] with fuel consumption of 5 l/100 km.[31] Even if all of America's cars were replaced by the new Tata Nano, the annual figure for transport fuel consumption in the United States would be cut by only 20%.

Table 10: The gaits of a horse and their related speeds[32]

	mph	km/h
walk	5	8
trot	8–10	13–16
canter	15	24
gallop	21	34

What about riding a horse to work? A horse has four speeds (just like a car, really), called gaits, outlined in Table 10 above.

Horses are quite fast, but how far can they go? In the cross-country section of a modern Three-Day Event, horses usually cover about 20 miles (32 km) in two hours, including jumps.[33] On the other hand, gently riding along the bridleways of England you would expect to cover 20 miles (32 km) a day.[34]

Just like us, a working horse uses energy according to how hard it works. The values in Table 11 are given in megacalories and converted to the more familiar megajoules.

An average horse travelling 30 km per day could be assumed to be working moderately hard. For the sake of this discussion a horse is taken to be single-seater, and so will use around 3.3 MJ/passenger-km. We have to assume that the whole of the horse's food consumption each day is used up in working. If a horse can go 30 km a day, over a year it could provide nearly 11,000 km of transport. A horse is said to need around 5,000 m² of pasture,[35] but the Organic Research Centre, based at Elm Farm in England,

Table 11: Daily energy consumption of an 1,100 lb (500 kg) working horse[36]

	Mcals/day	MJ/day
light work	20.5	85.8
moderate work	24.6	103.0
intense work	32.8	137.0

says that you would need 15% of an 8 ha farm, or 1.2 ha, to support a working horse that eats cereals as well as grass.[37] These two figures probably represent the two extremes, since a farm horse might work harder and longer than a riding horse. If we take an average, it looks as if a horse might need 0.85 ha a year for its fuel. The land area needed to support a horse for personal transport is compared below with the land needed to run a car on various forms of replacement fuels that will be needed once the oil is gone or has become too expensive.

If we continue to use cars rather than other forms of transport, we will need to find alternative fuels for them, because oil is not going to be widely available in the future, and in order to have time to introduce alternatives we need to be thinking about them now. These alternative fuels fall into two categories:

- alternative fuels for normal cars
- alternative fuels for alternative cars

A sustainable society will not use non-renewable resources, since by their nature they will run out. This means we cannot use oil, gas, coal or uranium to fuel our vehicles, and it is no good in the long term trying to use renewable resources to eke out the supplies of non-renewable fuels, since in the end the non-renewable fuels will still run out. If we start from the premise that we have to move away completely from non-renewable resources for our future transport fuels, we can avoid ambiguity and clarify the discussion.

Finding alternative fuels for normal cars would mean that we do not have to throw away all the cars in the world and make new ones. According to Worldwatch, 'in 2002 the world's passenger car fleet hit 531 million'.[38] This probably works out at about 600 million cars in 2007, or roughly one per ten people (if all the cars were full, roughly half the world's population could be on the road at any one time). That is a lot of cars to throw away if we could no longer run them owing to the lack of oil.

Since it is hard to consider the whole world in one go, let us narrow the discussion down to one country. New Zealand has 2.5 million cars and 4 million people (and a lot of sheep).[39] If each of these cars has the same embodied energy as, say, a Volkswagen Golf (discussed at the beginning of this section), each of the cars represents 122,000 MJ. In total, those 2.5 million cars represent an embodied energy of 305 PJ. Just to give an idea of how much this is, in 2006 New Zealand used a total of 741 PJ of energy.[40] So the energy embodied in all these cars represents about 40% of the total annual energy consumption of the whole country. This suggests that, rather than producing both new fuels and new cars, it would be a good idea to find ways of running the existing cars – or at least to have a combination of approaches so that the old cars can be used until they fall apart (and hopefully get recycled).

WHAT ARE THE ALTERNATIVES?

The two likely alternative fuels for ordinary cars at present are ethanol (the alcohol you find in a glass of wine or whisky), which would replace petrol, and vegetable oil, which would replace diesel. Both can be used in an ordinary car, but the car first needs to be converted. For example, to burn ethanol instead of petrol would require, among other modifications, changing the size of the carburettor jets; likewise, using vegetable oil would need some kind of warming device, since it is thicker than oil-based diesel. However, assuming that you can convert the car, what are the implications of using these fuels? Could we grow enough?

According to Journey to Forever, an organization promoting sustainability, there is a wide range of oil-producing crops, each giving a very different yield, that could be grown in New Zealand, as Table 12 shows.

Table 12: Oil yields from a range of crops (l/ha)[41]

oil-bearing plant	oil yield
avocados	2,638
olives	1,212
rapeseed	1,190
sunflowers	952
linseed (flax)	478
maize	172

Table 13: Land area that would be required for meeting the current demand for diesel in New Zealand from plant oils (*ha*)

oil-bearing plant	land area
avocados	106,000
olives	231,000
rapeseed	235,000
sunflowers	294,000
linseed (flax)	586,000
maize	1,628,000

The range of yields is huge. If all of New Zealand's diesel fuel were produced from avocados, a lot less land would be needed than if it came from maize. New Zealand currently uses around 280 million litres of diesel per year, and 2,000 million litres of petrol.[42] To produce this quantity of diesel fuel (which runs trains, buses and lorries as well as some private cars) from the crops listed above would require the amount of land set out in Table 13.

New Zealand has just under 2.4 million hectares of land that is of high or medium suitability for growing arable crops,[43] so depending on how the oil were produced, more than half the suitable land could be taken up with fuel production. Remember that these figures only consider diesel fuel, which constitutes only 12% of the total liquid fuel consumption; and of course land is also needed to grow food.

To replace the 2,000 million litres of petrol with ethanol would also require land. Table 14 (overleaf) shows ethanol yields from a range of crops, and it can be seen that ethanol yields generally tend to be higher than vegetable oil yields. The yields quoted here are from optimal growing regions, and the location from which each yield was derived is shown in brackets. Note also that the energy content of ethanol is about 67% that of petrol.

Making ethanol is just like making whisky: first you ferment your crop with yeast, then you distil it to drive off the water and leave the alcohol. Data from the US Department of Agriculture that shows the energy use

Table 14: Ethanol yield from crops that could be grown in New Zealand (*l/ha*)[44]

crop for ethanol production	yield
sugar beet (France)	6,679
maize (US)	3,311
wheat (France)	2,592

intensity of ethanol conversion (that is, distillation) give a range of 48,772 to 54,239 Btu per US gallon, which in metric units is roughly 3.8–4.2 kWh/l, or 13.6–15.1 MJ/l.[45] We saw earlier that the energy content of a litre of petrol is 34.2 MJ, so if ethanol has 67% of the energy content of petrol, it equates to around 22.9 MJ/l. However, if an average of 14.4 MJ is needed to distil each litre of ethanol, we need to multiply the area of land required by 22.9 ÷ 14.4 = 1.59 to allow for the distillation energy. Admittedly, the energy used in distillation might not come from ethanol, but some sort of biologically derived fuel would be needed, and this calculation provides a reasonable allowance for this.

If sugar beet were used to produce ethanol to replace all of New Zealand's current petrol consumption, around 475,000 ha of land would be needed; this figure would increase to around 950,000 ha if maize were used as the source crop instead. We are assuming that the lower energy content of ethanol would be compensated for by slower driving, so the consumption of ethanol is taken to be the same as the current consumption of petrol. This is probably a little optimistic, but what we are doing is trying to gauge the scale of things, not provide absolute figures.

Table 15: Land area required to produce vehicle fuels to replace current New Zealand consumption (*ha*)

fuel	land area
vegetable oil	300,000
ethanol	750,000
total	**1,050,000**

If we assume that, in both cases, a mixture of crops is used to produce ethanol and vegetable oil, we can see the likely impact in terms of land requirement of trying to run all of New Zealand's vehicle fleet on renewable fuels (Table 15).

The ethanol uses more land, in spite of its higher yield per hectare, because far more petrol is used than diesel. The total land required approaches half of the area currently available for arable crops. The conclusion is that in a post-oil future we could expect to be able to grow some biofuels – probably enough to run buses, trains and some lorries, and perhaps enough for some occasional private car use – but we cannot continue as we are at present and not run out of food on a global scale.

DIFFERENT CARS?

Maybe we need to 'bite the bullet' and look at changing our vehicles? One solution could be the electric car – or could it? This enthusiastic description points out the possibilities:

> Now it is possible for a vehicle to complete 100 miles [160 kilometres] or more ... upon a single battery charge ... The advantages of the electric vehicle are so pronounced as to impress everyone. It offers smoother running; vibration is absent; control is easier ... it is cheaper to maintain ... it is cleaner to handle, and when standing still, it does not eat up fuel, the current being switched off during such periods of inactivity. It possesses all of the mobility of the petrol-driven car with none of its shortcomings.[46]

This quote comes from a book written in 1916. Thus over ninety years ago you could buy an electric car with a range of 160 km, which is hardly the case today – showing how in some respects things have not improved. The New Zealand Labour government's *New Zealand Energy Strategy*, published in 2007, thought that electric cars would be an important option in the future:

> Our scenario assumes electric vehicle sales reach five per cent of market share in 2020, followed by a period of rapid growth that reaches a plateau of 60 per cent by 2040.[47]

The Mechanical Engineering Research Group in the Department of Engineering at the University of Waikato, New Zealand, has been working on electric car design, and in 2007 it produced a prototype called the 'Ultracommuter'. The group has estimated that New Zealand would need five hundred 3 MW wind turbines to power a national fleet of 2 million battery-powered electric cars (400,000 single-seaters, 600,000 two-seaters and 1,000,000 five-seaters).[48] Note how the Waikato researchers have selected cars that are suitable for a range of tasks rather than assuming that all cars need to be five-seaters.

To give an idea of the number of wind turbines that would be needed to run all these electric cars (a total requirement of 1,500 MW), in early November 2007 New Zealand had 321.8 MW of operating wind turbines plus a further 46 MW under construction, making a total of 368 MW. So to run a fleet of electric cars, the country would need considerably more wind turbines than it currently possesses. However, in November 2007 consent was granted for the construction of a further 609 MW of turbines, and 1,137 MW were still going through the consenting process.[49] If all these projects were completed, there would be a total of 2,114 MW. This puts the 1,500 MW of turbines that would be needed to run the electric cars into perspective. It is still a lot of turbines, but 1500 MW of additional wind energy capacity to power a fleet of electric cars would represent less than a doubling of the scale of wind energy developments currently proposed in New Zealand. And this is in a country described by the New Zealand Wind Energy Association as being 'some way behind the installed [wind energy] capacity for other developed countries', with less than 0.5% of its total power derived from wind.[50] So a country could have a national fleet of renewably powered electric cars without going very far beyond current levels of renewable energy installation.

To come down to a local level, in 2006 the Wellington Region had about 210,000 cars.[51] Using the figure arrived at by the University of Waikato (each 3 MW turbine could provide power for 4,000 cars), we can calculate that the whole region would need around 53 turbines. A wind farm of 53 turbines is comparable in scale to the West Wind wind farm at Makara near Wellington, which started construction in November 2007 and is stated to provide enough power for '110,000 average homes'.[52] The Wellington

Region currently contains 155,838 households,[53] so this new wind farm will be able to supply power to 70% of the households. To have electric cars and wind-powered homes, Wellington is going to need at least one more local wind farm on this scale.

We can now compare some of the options in terms of the land area required to provide sustainable car transport. Figures given in the Waikato study allow us to calculate the average annual distance travelled by their three types of electric cars as 11,500 km. If we assume that an average biofuel car will achieve the fuel consumption of a carefully driven Holden Commodore (8.2 l per 100 km; see Table 5 above), each of the liquid-fuelled cars will need 943 l of fuel per year to cover this distance. The figures for biofuel production show that to grow source crops for a litre of oil requires 10.7 m² of land, while to grow crops for a litre of ethanol needs 3.75 m² of land, including the land needed to produce the fuel used in distillation. On this basis, the diesel cars will each need 1 hectare of land per year, and the ethanol cars will each need 0.35 hectare per year, to grow their fuel.

What if the cars were not 'average' cars, but the best available? Recent small diesel cars in Europe such as the Audi A2 TDi and the Volkswagen Lupo 1.2 TDi achieved a fuel consumption of 3 l/100 km, while the petrol-driven Toyota Prius hybrid has a fuel consumption of 4.3 l/100 km on the European combined cycle.[54] If all our cars were this good, we would need 345 l of vegetable oil per year for the diesels and 495 l of ethanol for the petrol cars.

We can also calculate the amount of renewable electricity generation needed to power battery electric cars. The University of Waikato study shows that the 2 million electric cars would need 4,878 GWh in total, which is roughly 2,440 kWh per car per year. A photovoltaic (PV) array in New Zealand will, depending on location, produce between 1,000 and 1,200 kWh per kW, and a kilowatt of PV is about 10 m² in area. So, in a worst-case scenario, you would need about 25 m² of PV panels on the roof of your garage or carport to allow a year's motoring.[55]

In addition, we can work out the area needed to generate all this electricity from wind turbines. The base of a wind turbine is relatively small, and the surrounding land can be used for agriculture. The New York State Energy Research and Development Authority estimate that the total land use for access roads, substations, and so forth on a wind farm represents 5% of the total project area, which it estimates to be 17.8 to 39 acres (7.2 to 15.8 ha) per MW.[56] So the land taken up by a MW of wind turbines is 5% of 7.2 to 15.8 ha, or between 0.36 and 0.79 ha. This means that, even in the worst case, each wind-powered electric car would need only 6 m^2 of land area for generating its annual fuel, providing this land area forms part of a wind farm.

FUEL CELLS AND FREEDOM

If we are discussing alternative vehicles, should we consider fuel cells? The US government thinks they are a good thing and has set up a programme called Freedom CAR to develop them.

> *The corner gas station will become the corner hydrogen station, and America's motorists will motor cheaply and environmentally clean if the Department of Energy's 'Freedom CAR' program succeeds.*[57]

But the key to making a fuel-cell car is not only making a fuel cell that works, but also making the hydrogen to power it. According to an invited paper written by Dr Ulf Bossel for the European Fuel Cell Forum conference,

> *it takes about 1 kg of hydrogen to replace 1 U.S. gal of gasoline. About 200 MJ (55 kWh) of dc [direct current] electricity are needed to liberate 1 kg of hydrogen from 9 kg of water by electrolysis.*[58]

This means that to make the hydrogen equivalent of a litre of petrol will need 52.8 MJ, or 14.7 kWh. If we had to replace the 2,000 million litres of petrol currently used by New Zealand's cars with hydrogen, we would need to generate 105.6 PJ of electricity. This sounds like a lot, considering that in 2006 New Zealand used 741 PJ of all forms of energy for everything, not just motoring. In 2005 the country's total electricity generation was 149.7 PJ,[59] so to change to a fleet of hydrogen cars would mean nearly doubling the size of the national electricity industry. The study of electric cars by the University of Waikato quoted earlier showed that five hundred 3 MW wind turbines would be needed to power a national fleet of 2 million electric cars, and each turbine would produce 10.51 GWh (roughly 0.04 PJ) per year. Using wind power to make enough hydrogen to replace the 2,000 million litres of petrol New Zealand currently consumes would need about 2,800 turbines – a lot more than the 500 needed for battery electric cars.

Ah, but surely new fuel-cell cars would be far more efficient than current petrol cars? Well, if they were twice as efficient, the country would still need 1,400 new wind turbines, compared with the 500 needed for electric cars that use batteries. The reason for this is that the process of operating a fuel cell on hydrogen has more steps than the process of charging a battery. The result is that for every 100 kWh of renewable energy generated, 69 kWh ends up as useful transport energy for a battery electric car, but only 19–23 kWh is available for driving a hydrogen fuel-cell car.[60] So the fuel cell needs at least three times as much energy input, which means that there would need to be three times as many wind turbines as for battery cars.

Presumably the main reason that hydrogen is being promoted over battery electric cars – in spite of being three times more energy-intensive – is because it is used like petrol. It requires filling stations, tankers, pipes and all the infrastructure with which the oil industry is familiar. If we have electric cars, however, we will just plug them in at home at night: there will be no filling stations, pipes or anything else. With electric cars, the transport fuel system would be transferred to the electricity industry, whereas with hydrogen it would remain in the hands of the oil industry. This is a likely enough reason for efficiency to be ignored, especially in America, where the oil industry seems very influential.

We can now construct Table 16 (overleaf), which shows the area of land needed for a year's sustainable motoring in a variety of vehicles and with a variety of fuels.

Wind power clearly offers a good solution. What is also intriguing is the level of discussion and effort made to introduce biodiesel while no one mentions old-fashioned horsepower, which occupies second place in the table. The advantage of using wind power is that the land on which the wind farm is sited can still be used for agricultural or forestry purposes because it is not actually growing the fuel. Growing biofuels and making solar electricity involve harvesting in the horizontal plane only, taking up land space, but a wind turbine harvests the wind vertically and leaves surrounding land free

Table 16: Land area needed for a year's motoring using a range of sustainable fuels (*m²*)

liquid fuels	land area required per vehicle
current diesel cars burning vegetable oil	10,000
horse running on grass and cereals	8,500
efficient diesel cars burning vegetable oil	3,700
current petrol cars burning ethanol	3,500
efficient petrol cars burning ethanol	1,900
electric cars	
hydrogen cars using solar power	75–90
hydrogen cars using wind power	18–22
electric cars using solar power	25
electric cars using wind power	6

for other uses. The problem with wind power, as with many renewables, is that it is intermittent. This is normally less of a problem where a bigger area is covered by grid-connected wind power, since it is likely to be windy at one end of the country even if it is not at the other. In New Zealand, the problem is solved through the large hydro-electric component of the grid. The hydro lakes are in effect a form of electricity storage: the water behind the dams can be run through turbines to make electricity whenever it is required.

So what conclusions should we draw for personal and local transport? Once again, it is likely that we will move to a situation more like that of the 1940s or 1950s. As the existing fleet of vehicles wears out, it will be gradually replaced both by more efficient conventional vehicles and by alternatives like electric vehicles. In the future we will generally go to work or school on foot, by bike, or on the bus, trolleybus, tram or train. Freight will go by rail or coastal shipping where possible, with only local transport of goods by road. Some people will use battery electric cars – maybe charged by solar panels on the garage roof or by a windmill in the garden – for local trips of up to 100 km or so.

GETTING ABOUT IN A SUSTAINABLE FUTURE

The scenario above suggests what transport options might be available in a sustainable future. But since they still need planning, it might be useful to know which existing transport methods have the lowest environmental impact. In a world working towards sustainability, the lowest-impact methods should be encouraged now.

COMMUTING TO WORK AND TO SCHOOL

Industrialization had a double impact on the use of energy. First, the use of the coal-fired steam engine meant that more work could be done, and more goods produced, for less labour. Second, the larger factories and places of production that resulted from the introduction of the steam engine increased the separation of home from work. To begin with, houses were clustered around factories at high densities, since walking was the only means for people to get to work. Today, commuting between home and work may take hours and is very likely to involve the use of oil for the train, bus or car. How are we going to get to work when the oil runs out?

With 'unpowered' modes of transport, like walking and cycling, there are apparently no issues relating to fuel (although we will come back to this point), but there are certainly issues relating to resources. The first is the energy that it takes to make and maintain a pair of shoes or a bicycle. And then we should consider the energy and resources needed to construct the pathway used for walking or riding. Since it could be argued that the same construction is suitable for both walking and riding, and that very often all that separates the two is a painted white line, for the purposes of a simple comparison between walking and cycling the footpath can be ignored.

SHANKS'S PONY

Walking would naturally appear to be the lowest-impact form of travelling because it seems to involve no resources, but this turns out not to be the case. To start with, walking a particular distance burns roughly twice the number of calories as cycling.[61] This is good news if you want to lose weight, but it may not be good news in a future world that is short of food.

An American website shows that a (somewhat overweight?) man of 190 lb walking at a 'moderate pace' of 3 mph uses 302 cals/hour (1.26 MJ, or around 350 watts of power – the same energy it takes to power a large plasma television). Thus to walk a distance of 1 mile, he will use about 100 cals and take 20 minutes. Converted into metric terms, this same man of 86 kg and walking at 4.8 km/h will use 63 calories (0.26 MJ) to travel 1 km in 12.5 minutes.[62]

The same man on a bicycle using 'light effort' to travel at 17.5 km/h uses 518 cals/hour. This is 2.17 MJ and represents 600 W in power, or about the same energy needed to run a blender. The cyclist uses about 30 cals (0.13 MJ) to cover a kilometre in about 3.5 minutes. If you cycle faster, you will use more energy, so a cyclist using 'vigorous effort' and travelling at 24 km/h will use 863 cals/hour (3.6 MJ, or a power of about 1 KW, more or less the energy consumed by a toaster), but this is still only 36 cal (0.15 MJ) over 1 km.

Now we can construct Table 17. This reveals that, although our cyclist is always using less energy overall to travel a given distance than if he were walking (the same applies to a woman, but the example being used is that fairly large man), he is always using more power, because, whether he rides gently or flat out, his rate of working is higher than if he were walking. If he were to cycle at walking pace, he would use less power than walking, because cycling is basically more efficient than walking, but going so slow he might wobble and fall over. This is why the cyclist in our model feels that he needs a

Table 17: The energy used to travel to work, using a car as a comparison

activity	energy used (MJ/km)	power required (W)	time taken to go 5 km
cycling gently	0.13	600	17.1 mins
cycling hard	0.15	1,000	12.5 mins
walking	0.26	350	62.5 mins
1.6 litre car	2.55*	21,250	10.0 mins

* Average urban fuel consumption of all 1.6 litre cars available in Australia in 2003 was 7.445 l/100 km. Conversion is 34.2 MJ/l for petrol.[63] It is assumed, perhaps optimistically, that the car will average 30 kph on a commuting journey.

shower when he gets to work, whereas the walker does not. The cyclist has worked up more of a sweat because he works harder, but the cyclist gets there much quicker than the pedestrian, so he has time for a shower. But nothing in sustainability calculations ever turns out to be straightforward. What, for example, if the cyclist lives in Australia and has a shower heated by electricity generated by burning high-carbon brown coal? We will come on to this later.

Table 17 shows that cycling is a much more efficient way to travel than walking, since the journey is quicker and less energy from food is required to travel the same distance. In terms of the energy required, walking is ten times more efficient than driving a smallish car, and cycling is twenty times more efficient.

However, the energy we need to power our travel is only part of the story. The walker might say that it is all very well showing that cycling uses less energy than walking, but what about all the energy needed to manufacture a bicycle? Does the energy saved in cycling ever make up for all that manufacturing energy?

The first thing we need to know is how much energy it takes to make a bike compared with a pair of shoes, or even a car. Fortunately, the Australian Greenhouse Office, a federal government department, has done some of this analysis. The life-cycle energy for manufacturing a normal metal bicycle weighing 15 kg is given by them as 0.075 MJ/passenger-km (rounded up to 0.08), assuming that the bicycle has a life of 20,000 km.[64] The Australian figures would imply a life of eight years if the bike were used for travelling a 10 km round trip each day, which does not sound too unrealistic.

We could make a bicycle out of wood. Wood grows naturally, whereas steel has to be made in a factory, so maybe a wooden bicycle would be a lot better? Our bike could have a wooden frame and wooden wheels,[65] so maybe 75% of the 15 kg could be in wood, perhaps ash treated to make it rot proof. A typical embodied energy figure for wood might be 13.6 MJ/kg (this is the value for glue laminated timber, probably the most suitable type of wood for bicycle manufacture).[66] So if 75% of our bike is made of wood with an embodied energy of 13.6 MJ/kg, and 25% is in steel and other materials that have an embodied energy of 100 MJ/kg (the figure used above in the discussion of the car), the total would come to 528 MJ, compared to 1,500 MJ for the normal metal bike. This reduces the embodied energy of the whole bicycle to effectively a third of the original, or 0.03 MJ for each km travelled, provided of course that a wooden bicycle lasts as long as a metal one.

At present, cycling requires a helmet in many countries simply because cyclists have to share the road with much faster-flowing and less vulnerable motor traffic. In countries where cyclists dominate and cycling is relatively sedate, as it used to be in many parts of China, there is no need to wear a helmet. Helmets normally have an inner core of expanded polystyrene, and ideally this should be factored into the embodied energy of cycling. The embodied energy of polystyrene is 44.3 MJ/kg[67] and a lightweight helmet might weigh 300 g. This would give an embodied energy of 13.3 MJ for the helmet, which when considered over the 20,000 km life of the cycle results in a negligible impact. Organic alternatives to polystyrene are cork and end-grain balsa wood, although it is not yet possible to buy helmets of this type.[68] In sum, we probably do not need to worry about the environmental impact of making our cycle helmet.

We do, however, probably need to think about the embodied energy of shoes. A website devoted to walking suggests that a pair of shoes needs to be replaced after walking about 500 miles (800 km),[69] and many websites concerned with running suggest that shoes will last between 800 and 1,200 km. If we assume an average life of 1,000 km, a pair of shoes will have only a twentieth the life of a bike in terms of distance travelled. The walking website states that shoes will cost the equivalent of 12 Euro cents per mile (based on the conversion rate at the time of writing). However, although we can find the life of shoes and the cost, it is not so easy to work out the embodied energy of making a pair of shoes. One way round this problem might be to look at the cost of a car, compare it with the cost of a pair of shoes, and then use that ratio to find the embodied energy of the shoes. The costs of depreciation and finance for a 1.6 litre car in Ireland are 27.6 Euro cents per mile based on 10,000 miles per year.[70] This figure, which is based on the initial purchase and not the operating costs of a car, is therefore comparable to the cost of shoes. Very roughly, this suggests that the impact of making a car is just over twice the impact of making shoes. We already know from Table 2 that the embodied energy of a 1.6 litre Volkswagen Golf is around 0.5 MJ/km, so if a pair of shoes costs 12 Euro cents per mile, and a car costs 27.6 Euro cents per mile, the embodied energy of the shoes could be assumed to be 12 ÷ 27.6 × 0.5, which is 0.22 MJ/km. This is a lot more than that of a bicycle.

We can check this another way. In the UK, a basic bicycle costs around £200 and, according to the Australian figures we used earlier, will last for 20,000 km. This means that it costs £0.01 per km. A basic pair of shoes, on the other hand, costs around £40 and lasts for, say, 1,000 km, working out at £0.04 per km. If embodied energy is related to cost, as has been proposed by Craig Langston of Deakin University in Australia,[71] and if shoes cost four times as much as a bicycle per km, then the embodied energy of shoes is going to be around four times that of a bicycle per kilometre travelled. This would make the embodied energy of a pair of shoes around 0.3 MJ/km. This is fairly close to the figure worked out in relation to the cost of a car, so we can reasonably propose that the figure for shoes might lie between 0.2 MJ/km and 0.3 MJ/km. Of course, a cyclist wears shoes too, but the saddle is carrying his or her weight, so cycling shoes are likely to last a lot longer than those used for walking. This is borne out by cycling colleagues, one of whom says his cycling shoes have lasted for 15 years.[72] For the purposes of this comparison, the cycling shoes have been ignored.

We can use these figures in Table 18, which shows very roughly the embodied energy of a range of transport options compared with that of a smallish car. None of these values is large in comparison with the energy actually used to operate the transport.

Table 18: Estimated embodied energy of some modes of transport

mode	principal material	embodied energy (MJ/km)
bicycle	wood	0.03
bicycle	steel	0.08
shoes	leather	0.25
1.6 litre car	steel	0.50

FOOD AS FUEL

Now we come to another vexed question. The food required to fuel the walker and cyclist has not yet been factored in. Just as the pathway used for cycling and for walking can be ignored when we compare one with another, it could be argued that the food we need to pedal a bicycle or to walk is part of our daily intake, required to keep the body healthy, since exercise is a necessary part of being human. Sitting in a car is not part of one's necessary daily exercise routine. However, in order to be fair to the motorist, perhaps we need to work out the extra food the walker or cyclist needs compared to the driver. The West Virginia Dietetic Association says that our 190 lb (86 kg) man needs the following number of calories per day, depending on his age.

Table 19: Daily energy requirement for a 190 lb (86 kg) man[73]

activity level	cals/day*		cals/hour	
	age 25	age 50	age 25	age 50
sedentary	2,492	2,280	104	95
light activity	2,592	2,371	108	99
moderate activity	2,991	2,736	125	114
very active	3,389	3,100	141	129

* These figures are slightly different from those given by the FAO and used in Chapter 1.

So if our man is sedentary, and depending on his age, he is using around 100 calories an hour. Table 20 shows the extra food energy needed by our motoring couch potato if he is going to walk or cycle.

But this is not the whole story: food, like all fuels, has its own embodied energy, and to understand its full impact we have to take this into account. For example, a piece of sliced wholemeal bread contains around 80 kcal – a figure you can read on the label of the bag it comes in. So when you eat it, it provides you with 0.33 MJ of food energy, which will power you for nearly 3.3 km of gentle cycling. However, it is recognized that the total energy that goes into making a sliced loaf can be five or more times the food energy it contains.[74] This extra energy is used in all the processes that go into making, and marketing, a loaf of bread:

Table 20: Energy consumption of various forms of exercise compared with sedentary state

activity	total energy (cal/hour)	extra energy above sedentary (cal/hour)	(MJ/hour)	(MJ/km)
walking	302	202	0.85	0.18
cycling (light effort)	518	418	1.75	0.10
cycling (vigorous effort)	863	763	3.20	0.13

- growing (fuel for the tractor and to make the fertilizers and pesticides)

- harvesting (fuel for the combine harvester)

- transporting (fuel to transport the grain to the mill)

- milling and packing (energy to run the mill and to make the bags for the flour)

- transporting (fuel to transport the flour to the bakery)

- baking and packaging (energy to run the mixer, to bake the loaves, to slice them and to make the packaging)

- transporting (fuel to transport the loaves to the shop)

- sales (fuel to heat and light the shop)

The food energy embodied in a slice of bread needs to be multiplied by five, to become 1.65 MJ. This can be compared with the 7.2 multiplier that was the embodied energy coefficient for all food (see Chapter 1) and shows that bread is a lower embodied energy food. The extra food energy needed by the walker and the cyclist can then be calculated, on the premise that they are fuelled by sliced bread. The results are shown in Table 21 (overleaf).

What if you don't eat sliced bread? Perhaps you might eat a hamburger. According to the people at McDonald's, one of their 4 oz (114 g) cheeseburgers contains 300 calories.[75] This is equal to 1.26 MJ, so as food it would provide enough fuel for 10 km of gentle cycling or 5 km on foot. However, according to research,[76] a typical cheeseburger has an embodied

Table 21: Extra energy needed for travel, assuming the consumption of sliced bread for walking and cycling, and of petrol for the car

activity	total energy consumption (MJ/km)
cycling (light effort)	0.50
cycling (vigorous effort)	0.65
walking	0.90
1.6 litre car	3.19*

* The embodied energy of the petrol has been taken into account to make the comparison fair. The embodied energy multiplier for refining oil into petrol is 1.25.[77]

energy of between 7.3 MJ and 20 MJ (depending on exactly where and how the various ingredients were grown), giving an average figure of 13.7 MJ. The embodied energy of the cheeseburger is therefore more than ten times its food energy, again demonstrating that the more processed and packaged foods are the ones to avoid. Table 22 shows the effect of eating cheeseburgers on the total extra energy used for autonomous and car travel.

The cyclist who eats a cheeseburger is using 1.09 MJ/km, and the cheeseburger-powered walker is using 1.96 MJ/km, which is not a lot better than the car. In fact, two people driving to work in a 1.6 litre car would use less energy per person at 1.85 MJ/person/km than walking (see the figures in Table 24) if they relied on cheeseburgers to provide the extra energy they needed for the exercise. Driving to work in the most fuel-efficient car (a Honda Insight hybrid, which uses only 3.9 l/100 km in city driving), you

Table 22: Extra energy demand for travel, assuming cheeseburger for walking and cycling, and petrol for the car

activity	total energy consumption (MJ/km)
cycling (light effort)	1.09
cycling (vigorous effort)	1.42
walking	1.96
1.6 litre car	3.19

would consume only 1.67 MJ/km, even allowing for the embodied energy of petrol,[78] which is lower than the figure for one cheeseburger-powered walker. However, the Insight went out of production in 2006, which is probably a pity.

DIGGING FOR VICTORY

To reduce the embodied energy of food, you could grow it at home. Potatoes grown at home could supply the fuel you need for walking and cycling with little embodied energy, especially if seed potatoes are saved from a previous year's crop and possibly swapped with a neighbour to avoid growing the same stock year after year. These practices were common two generations back, and some organizations, such as the Henry Doubleday Research Association in the UK[79] and the Seed Savers Exchange in the US,[80] are devoted to seed-swapping in order to maintain supplies of plants and vegetables that have been deleted from the seed catalogues. When boiled, a 100 g potato will give about 100 cal,[81] so a serving of four boiled spuds could provide the extra energy for around 17 km of gentle cycling.

A Canadian pressure-cooker supplier states that to bring 1.5 l of water to the boil takes 190 Wh, or 290 Wh if you have a warped-bottom pan on an electric hob.[82] But let's assume that you have the right pan, and that your potatoes are going to take at least 200 Wh per day to cook. However, the fuel you use to cook them also has embodied energy, which depends not only on the type of fuel (gas, electricity, coal, etc.), but also on where you are. For example, Alcorn gives a figure of 1.53 MJ of fuel used for every 1 MJ of electricity generated and distributed in New Zealand.[83] This is because to make electricity other fuels have to be extracted, transported and burned to raise steam, and all of these processes are less than 100% efficient. This figure is for all of New Zealand's electricity, including the hydro-electric component that amounts to about 65–70% of the total. This is the figure that has been used for the present calculations because it reflects the generation of electricity with a component of renewable energy – the direction in which many countries are moving. Thus it would be reasonable to multiply the 200 Wh used to boil the water by 1.5 to allow for the embodied energy of the cooking fuel. If we cook with gas, the overall energy used to get the fuel to the stove is low, but combustion is not 100% efficient, so for our admittedly

Table 23: Cooking energy expressed in MJ/km

activity	distance covered on 400 g boiled potatoes (km)	energy consumption of cooking potatoes (MJ/km)
cycling (light effort)	17	0.06
cycling (vigorous effort)	13	0.08
walking	9	0.12

rough calculations the same factor applies. We can thus calculate that cooking the potatoes uses 300 Wh per day, or 1.08 MJ. Since this represents the food's only non-renewable energy input, we can work out the energy used for cooking per km. In the bread and cheeseburger calculations above, the cooking energy formed part of the embodied energy of the food, but because our potatoes are grown at home the cooking energy needs to be factored in (Table 23).

Now we know how much energy it takes to make a pair of shoes, a bicycle and a car; how much energy it takes to travel 1 km on foot, by bike and by car; and how much energy it takes to feed us while we are travelling that distance. All these figures have been fed into Table 24.

We can see that choosing a low-impact mode of travel all depends on what we eat. If you are addicted to take-away food, walking to work may not be the option with the lowest environmental impact. However, this does not mean we should all rush out thinking that we can drive to work with a clear conscience. All we can say with confidence is that 'some types of driving could be better in some ways than some types of walking', and that cheeseburger-eating drivers are still the worst. The point here is to show that making just one change, such as walking to work rather than driving, may not be enough. Our whole lifestyle needs to be reconsidered.

ENERGY FOR SHOWERS

As we mentioned above, another aspect should be factored in here: the fact that cyclists tend to get sweaty and often want to have a shower when they get to work. Indeed, the Green Building Council of Australia's Green Star environmental rating tool for office buildings (Office Design v2) recommends

Table 24: Energy used in different ways of travelling to work (*MJ/person/km*)

mode of travel	speed	using	embodied energy	fuel	cook	total
bicycle (wood)	slow	potatoes	0.03	nil	0.06	0.09
bicycle (wood)	fast	potatoes	0.03	nil	0.08	0.11
walking (barefoot)		potatoes	nil	nil	0.12	0.12
bicycle (steel)	slow	potatoes	0.08	nil	0.06	0.14
bicycle (steel)	fast	potatoes	0.08	nil	0.08	0.16
walking (shoes)		potatoes	0.25	nil	0.12	0.37
bicycle (wood)	slow	bread	0.03	0.50	nil	0.53
bicycle (steel)	slow	bread	0.08	0.50	nil	0.58
bicycle (wood)	fast	bread	0.03	0.65	nil	0.69
bicycle (steel)	fast	bread	0.08	0.65	nil	0.73
walking (barefoot)		bread	nil	0.90	nil	0.90
walking (shoes)		bread	0.25	0.90	nil	1.15
bicycle (wood)	slow	burger	0.03	1.09	nil	1.12
bicycle (steel)	slow	burger	0.08	1.09	nil	1.17
bicycle (wood)	fast	burger	0.03	1.42	nil	1.45
bicycle (steel)	fast	burger	0.08	1.42	nil	1.50
walking (barefoot)		burger	nil	1.96	nil	1.96
walking (shoes)		burger	0.25	1.96	nil	2.21
car (1.6 litre, 4 people)		petrol	0.50	3.19	nil	0.92
car (Insight, 2 people)		petrol	0.80*	1.67	nil	1.24
car (1.6 litre, 2 people)		petrol	0.50	3.19	nil	1.85
car (Insight, 1 person)		petrol	0.80*	1.67	nil	2.47
car (1.6 litre, 1 person)		petrol	0.50	3.19	nil	3.69

* A higher embodied energy value has been used for the Insight than for the conventional car because, although small and light, it uses aluminium and hybrid technology. Aluminium takes more energy to make than steel.

the provision of showers and changing facilities for cyclists in offices to encourage cycling to work.[84] But they may not have thought this process through sufficiently. In Australia, where they like vigorous showers, an inefficient shower head can use 'more than 20 litres of water a minute', whereas one with an AAA water consumption rating (the best currently available) will use only 9 l per minute.[85] A Brazilian study of 49 flats found that a typical shower lasted 7.85 minutes.[86] So, depending on the shower head and the strength of its flow, an average shower might use between about 70 and 160 l of water. It is also possible to shower more quickly: a 5-minute shower using an AAA-rated head would use only 45 l of water, or 100 l with an inefficient shower head. So we have a range of values between 45 l for an efficient 5-minute shower, and 200 l for an inefficient 10-minute one. But what do these figures mean in practice?

The specific heat of water is 4,186 J/litre °C,[87] so to heat your shower water from, say, 15 °C to 45 °C will take 0.126 MJ/l (35 Wh/l). Thus your daily shower might consume between 1.6 kWh and 7 kWh depending on the shower head and how long you like to stand under the hot water. We are ignoring for the moment heat losses from the hot water cylinder, which could add 20% to these figures. So if you cycle to work every day, and you get four weeks of holiday a year, you will need between 384 and 1,680 kWh a year just for your showers at work. If your commuting distance is a 10 km round trip, the amount of energy used by your daily shower in the office means adding between 0.57 MJ/km and 2.52 MJ/km to your travel, so the energy you need for your cycling is likely to be more than the energy you would need for walking (pedestrians tend not to shower when they get to work).

From these results we can appreciate the complexity of the simple question 'What is the best way to get to work?' Table 25 makes several things clear, and shows us what we need to worry about and what is trivial. It appears that cycling can be better for the environment than walking, and walking is certainly better than driving, but the result depends much less on what you do and much more on how you do it. The items in Table 25 with big ranges of values are the ones that make a big difference. So cycling sedately, for example – as they generally do in China, where it is still a means of transport rather than a sport – is better than cycling fast in terms of energy

Table 25: Range of energy values relating to different aspects of travel, and range of total values (*MJ/km*)

mode	embodied energy	food/fuel	shower	total
walking	0.25	0.12–1.96	no shower	0.37–2.21
cycling	0.03–0.08	0.06–1.42	no shower	0.09–1.50
cycling (shower)	0.03–0.08	0.06–1.42	0.57–2.52	0.60–4.02
driving (ave.)	0.50	3.19	no shower	3.69*

* The value for average driving is included as a comparison.

expenditure; it also means you will not arrive at work all sweaty and needing a shower. It really does not matter what your bicycle is made of, or what sort of shoes you wear: the important matters are what you eat and whether you shower when you get to work. So if you want to minimize the environmental impact of your commuting, get a bike, ride slowly, and dig up the garden to grow veggies. If you really feel the need to shower when you arrive at work, don't have a shower at home when you get up.

COMMUTING BY OTHER MEANS

Of course, many people do not walk, cycle or drive to work: they catch the bus or the train, the tram or the ferry. How do these modes of transport measure up? We saw in the discussion above that it is quite difficult to say 'a car uses this much fuel', because so much depends on the type of car, the number of people it is carrying, the driving style, and so on. To calculate the energy used by public transport is even harder: all of the same factors apply as for cars, but people get on and off the bus at different points, so the number of people it carries varies continuously throughout the trip. Occupancy also varies throughout the day: rush-hour buses are full, but daytime ones are often quite empty. The same applies to all the other forms of public transport. Table 26 (overleaf) gives some figures for the energy used in commuting on public transport in the United States.

The figures in Table 26 are derived from actual passenger and fuel-use data, so they represent a reasonably accurate picture of what happens

Table 26: Energy use for modes of commuter travel in the United States (not including embodied energy of fuel) [88]

mode	MJ/passenger-km	
	average	range
electric commuter train	0.59	0.45–1.94
tram/light rail	0.76	0.42–6.33
trolleybus	0.87	0.75–1.70
city bus	2.80	0.72–23.18
ferry boat	7.25	2.94–45.30

in the real world; they also take into account all the variables of passenger occupancy and time of day discussed above. One of the more interesting aspects that emerges is the range in values: some types of transport, such as the trolleybus and the electric train, have quite a small range, but buses and ferries seem to vary very widely in the amount of energy consumed per passenger.

We can now compare walking and cycling directly with powered vehicles, but to make a fairer comparison we need to modify the values from Table 26 to include the embodied energy of the fuels. This is relatively easy for the oil-powered vehicles (the bus and the ferry), because we saw when we were looking at cars that the embodied energy of petroleum fuels was about 1.25 MJ per MJ of fuel. The calculation is harder for the electric vehicles (the train, the tram and the trolleybus), because so much depends on how the electricity is generated. In New Zealand in 2005, 293 PJ of primary energy used in electricity generation resulted in 132 PJ supplied to consumers.[89] This means that the overall energy overhead for electricity was 2.22, since it took 2.22 MJ of primary energy to supply 1 MJ of electricity to a consumer – somewhat larger than the earlier figure given by Alcorn of 1.53 MJ/MJ, but the proportion of electricity generated from hydro-electric sources has been falling in recent years in New Zealand. For countries where most electricity comes from non-renewable sources, the overhead might be 3 or more. To make a fair comparison with our earlier calculations for walking and cycling, the energy values for oil-powered

Table 27: Range of values for commuting (*MJ/passenger-km*)

mode	food	shower	total
bicycle (slow, bread)	0.50	none	0.50
electric commuter train (renewable)	–	–	0.59*
bicycle (fast, bread)	0.65	none	0.65
diesel commuter train	–	–	0.74*
tram/light rail (renewable)	–	–	0.76
driving (4 people, 1.6 litre car)	–	–	0.80
trolleybus (renewable)	–	–	0.87
walking (shoes, bread)	0.90	–	0.90
electric commuter train (non-renewable)	–	–	1.77*
bicycle (slow, bread)	0.50	1.55	2.05
bicycle (fast, bread)	0.65	1.55	2.20
tram/light rail (non-renewable)	–	–	2.28
trolleybus (non-renewable)	–	–	2.61
driving (1 person, 1.6 litre car)	–	–	3.19
city bus (diesel)	–	–	3.50
ferry boat	–	–	9.06

* Commuter train values were calculated using the 'heavy rail' value from Bradley et al.,[88] of 0.59 MJ/passenger-km to represent an electric train running on renewable electricity, multiplying this by 1.25 to allow for the embodied energy of diesel fuel to get a diesel train value, and multiplying it by 3 for a non-renewable electricity value.

vehicles in Table 27 have been multiplied by 1.25, and those for electric vehicles by 3. Values have been included for electric vehicles powered by renewable energy as well, so an overhead of nil is assumed, to show the range of possible figures. Average values for walking and cycling from Table 24 have been used, and the embodied energy of vehicles (and shoes) has not been counted.

Buses appear to come out badly in Table 27, but to some extent this is because the values are measured over a whole day. Just to show how variable the figures can be, Table 28 (overleaf) gives a range of values for buses, calculated from a variety of sources.

Table 28: Energy use of buses, compiled from a variety of sources (includes embodied energy of fuel)

type of bus	MJ/passenger-km	source of data
rush-hour bus	0.32	(Vale, calculated @ 65% occupancy)[90]
buses	0.50	(Boyapati et al.)[91]
average bus	1.01	(Vale, calculated @ 20% occupancy)
private bus*	1.19	(Lenzen 1999)[92]
peak-time urban bus	1.91	(Apelbaum 1997)[93]
urban bus	2.09	(Lenzen 1999)
off-peak urban bus	2.88	(Apelbaum 1997)

* This is not defined, but we assume it means a private bus taking people to work.

It is very clear from Table 28 that the amount of fuel used by a bus, or by any other public transport vehicle, is highly dependent on the time of day, because during the rush hour the vehicles are more likely to be full. The values used in Table 27 are the average values for public transport over a whole day. We can conclude that commuting to work, school or university by public transport is always worthwhile.

FOLLOW THE YELLOW BRICK ROAD

When it comes to the infrastructure that supports mobility, it is obvious that, while walking can be done almost anywhere, cycling normally requires a smooth surface of some form, even though mountain bikes are designed for rough terrain. Cars and buses, however, need roads. Because of the use of oil for transport in the last 100 years, roads have become a very noticeable part of the built environment all over the world. There is evidence to suggest that the materials, energy and water that go into constucting the roads form only a small part of the total energy consumed in travelling by private car. At the end of an assumed 40-year life for a road and the cars and lorries travelling over it, a life-cycle analysis showed that the energy that operated the vehicles accounted for 62% of the total; that used in making and maintaining the vehicles spread over a 40-year lifespan amounted to 28% of the total; and

only 10% of the life-cycle energy went into road construction and maintenance.[94] This suggests that to ignore the energy built into the road and
footpath infrastructure, as done in the calculations above, is probably per-
missible, since 90% of the energy is used in vehicles and their operation –
or, as we have assumed, in the travellers and their food when they are
walking or cycling.

The problem with roads is that they are impermeable, so as more land
is given over to them, more water pours into the drains every time it rains,
taking pollutants from the vehicles with it. In addition, conflicts can occur
when the same road is used for vehicles and for cycling, and even, at times,
for walking. To avoid such problems, even more 'roads' in the form of
devoted cycle tracks and pathways are created as safe places for these slower
modes of travel. Even allowing for these problems, the materials and the
energy footprint represented by these networks are shown to be less significant overall than other factors.

LONG-DISTANCE TRAVEL

As we saw earlier, electric cars run on batteries seem to be the most efficient
of the powered transport options. They could be used confidently for round
trips of up to 100 km, so a distance of 50 km might be considered the point
at which other methods of longer-distance travel begin to enter the discussion. The sort of long-distance trips that you might make by car now could
still be made in a more sustainable future, but by bus or train. Longer-
distance trips made by air will be more of a problem.

The energy efficiency of longer-distance modes of transport can vary
widely, as can be seen in Table 29 (overleaf), which shows data from three
sources, adjusted in the same way as Table 27 to allow for the embodied
energy of fuels.

Perhaps the biggest surprise in Table 29 is the energy associated with
running ferries, which exceeds the energy needed for
domestic air travel, although obviously the
scale is somewhat different, with
aircraft travelling further. This is
discussed in more detail below.

Table 29: Energy demand (including embodied energy) for a range of longer-distance transport modes, from three sources (*MJ/passenger-km*)

mode	Bradley[88] (ave.)	Lenzen[92]	Bell et al.[95]
motor coach	0.61	1.25	0.36 (65%)
trolleybus (renewable)	0.87	–	–
InterCity 125 diesel train	–	–	0.99 (50%)
InterCity 225 electric train (renewable)	–	–	1.04 (50%)
electric intercity rail (renewable)	1.38	1.20	–
diesel intercity rail	1.73	1.50	–
trolleybus (non-renewable)	2.61	–	–
domestic air travel	2.69	3.88	4.36 (65%)
InterCity electric train (non-renewable)	–	–	3.12 (50%)
ferry boat	9.06	5.38	–

Note: Bradley values are averaged from the data given in the original reference. Percentages under Bell et al. are the passenger occupancies assumed in that reference.

'ELECTRIC, INDEED!'

Most transport is currently powered by liquid fuels made from petroleum. We have seen, in the earlier discussion of cars, that making sustainable liquid fuels to replace petroleum is possible, but that it needs a lot of land that might otherwise be used for growing food. Similarly, making hydrogen from renewable energy needs much more generating capacity than using electricity directly in vehicles. So, ideally, it would seem that longer-distance transport should be electrically powered. It is also very clear from Table 27 that the electricity should come from renewable sources.

The present state of battery technology makes the possibility of battery storage for long-distance electric vehicles seem unlikely, although from the end of the 19th century the German railways used battery railcars and continued developing them for a long time. The streamlined ETA 176 railcars, introduced by Deutsche Bundesbahn in 1952 and known as the 'Limburg cigars', had 72 seats and pulled a trailer with space for a further 96 passengers, making 168 in total; one reference says they could cover a range of up to 400 km. Their battery capacity was 398 kWh.[96] This seems a lot of transport for not much energy. To check whether this original figure is reliable or just incorrect, we can compare it with a two-car battery railcar used experimentally by British Railways on the Aberdeen to Ballater line, which carried 117 passengers and had a total of 471 kWh of battery capacity.[97] However, this vehicle ran on a route of only 43 miles (69 km). According to another part of the same website, the German vehicles covered only 100 to 150 miles (161 to 241 km) between charges.[98] Using the figure of 240 km per charge, the energy consumption of the 'Limburg cigars' can be calculated, allowing for 85% efficiency of the battery-charging process,[99] as a very impressive 0.04 MJ/passenger-km for a full train.

We do not have to use batteries. Some of the modes of transport in Table 27 are electrically powered, notably the electric rail options and the trolleybus, both of which receive electricity through overhead wires. It is not too hard to electrify existing railway lines. The city of Perth in Western Australia electrified its suburban trains in 1991, achieving a 300% increase in passenger use by 1997,[100] and then sold its old diesel trains to Auckland. It is, however, expensive to construct new railway lines. The new Perth–Currambine line

> was opened in March of 1993. The total cost of building the new rail line and electrifying the other three was $400 million – the biggest single capital investment by the government at that time in its term of office.[101]

The Perth lines are conventional railways, but even light railway systems – the modern equivalent of tramways – cost between US$10 million and $20 million per km, according to US studies cited by Transport Canada, the Canadian ministry of transport.[102] However, providing for an electric trolleybus is much cheaper, at only US$1 million per km for installing the overhead cables for a two-way system.[103] At first sight, this seems hardly relevant, since the trolleybus is not generally viewed as a long-distance mode of transport, but perhaps it should be. The longest trolleybus route in the world runs in the Crimean peninsula, from the port of Simferopol to Yalta. It covers 86 km and takes two-and-a-half hours for the scenic journey over the

Crimean Mountains.[104] One could imagine a future transport system in which all existing railway lines were electrified and in which places not on the railway network would be served by trolleybuses connecting with the railway stations. This would be the cheapest way to provide a basic passenger transport system that could be powered by renewable electricity. Freight that needs to travel longer distances could be carried by rail and then distributed either in electric trucks that also used the trolley wires or in trailers attached to the back of the trolleybuses.

TRAIN OR PLANE?

Much travel currently undertaken by air could be undertaken on existing railway lines. Many countries in Europe have had large railway networks since the 19th century: one thinks of the railways in England and Wales, which by the turn of the 20th century constituted a very extensive and well-connected public transport network. The system has decreased in size since then through the closure of many routes in the 1960s. The reason air travel has become so popular is that it can be quicker than rail travel, and it is often, perversely, much cheaper, even though its impact on the environment is greater. However, if reliance on oil is constrained by price, shortage and climate concerns, this may change. In many countries, such as Germany, the railway network inherited from the past has not been significantly reduced; it will still be there to do the job of moving people longer distances.

Throughout the world many places still have good railway access. In 2002 there were thought to be 1 million kilometres of railway in the world, and it has been estimated that, if this were spread out evenly across the world, the furthest you would be from a railway line would be 65 km.[105] Looking at the 19th-century railway maps, it is easy to see why Sherlock Holmes and Dr Watson always seemed able to get to their cases, even when they were in apparently remote parts of the country. Most places were no more than an hour or two's walk from a railway station. In the past, when New Zealand's railways were controlled by the government (and in fact they were renationalized in 2008), there was an attempt to ensure that the more energy-efficient railways were used for long-distance transport. The Transport Licensing Act of 1936 required that any shipment of goods over

48 km had to be carried by rail, since rail transport uses less fuel for the carriage of goods over long distances, as discussed below. In 1962 this distance was increased to 64 km, and in 1977 increased again to 150 km. The Act was repealed in 1982, opening the railways up to road competition. This gave greater freedom of choice, but at the same time greatly reduced sustainability in transport.[106]

GETTING UP STEAM

Would it be worth going back to earlier technologies for our transport? If we are looking at rail travel, should we also consider steam trains? Maybe it would make more sense to burn coal in a locomotive rather than in a power station to make electricity to drive an electric train. It is not easy to find out how much fuel is used by a steam train. According to the *Eagle Book of Trains*, 'The biggest British tenders hold from 9 to 10 tons of coal, which in normal conditions is more than enough for a run of 400 miles.'[107] The best coal, anthracite, has an energy density of 27–30 GJ per tonne.[108] If we take as an example a train with 11 coaches and assume that 3 are occupied by the kitchen, first- and third-class restaurants and a buffet, there will be 8 coaches for passengers. Corridor coaches with 8 compartments, each with 6 seats, would make 48 passengers per coach, and 8 coaches give a total of 384 passengers.[109] Assuming that the coal used is the best (anthracite) and that the average consumption for a trip of 400 miles (640 km) is 9 tonnes, total energy consumption for the trip will be 9 × 30 = 270 GJ, or 0.42 GJ per km. This gives a total energy consumption of 1.1 MJ/passenger-km for a fully occupied steam express train. The energy used to mine coal is quite small, with a multiplier of 1.02 MJ/MJ.[110] We can now construct a table of trains (Table 30).

The 1950s technologies perform quite well in this table, especially the battery railcar, which comes out top no matter whether it is charged with renewable or non-renewable electricity. The performance of the steam train is also interesting, not least because it could be fuelled with wood, making it a bio-fuelled train; wood has about half the energy density of coal, however, so the train would have to stop to refuel more often than its coal-burning equivalent.

Table 30: Energy demand (including embodied energy) for a range of trains

train	MJ/passenger-km
Limburg cigar battery railcar (renewable)	0.04 (full)
Limburg cigar battery railcar (renewable)	0.08 (50% full)
Limburg cigar battery railcar (non-renewable)	0.12 (full)
Limburg cigar battery railcar (non-renewable)	0.24 (50% full)
InterCity 125 diesel train	0.50 (full)
InterCity 225 electric train (renewable)	0.52 (full)
InterCity 125 diesel train	1.00 (50% full)
InterCity 225 electric train (renewable)	1.04 (50% full)
1950s steam express	1.12 (full)
electric intercity rail (renewable)	1.38
InterCity 225 electric train (non-renewable)	1.56 (full)
diesel intercity rail	1.73
1950s steam express	2.24 (50% full)
InterCity 225 electric train (non-renewable)	3.12 (50% full)

GOING ABROAD

For international travel, particularly to places not connected by land, aircraft have become the norm because sea travel is slow. In 1939 it took around 85 days, or 12 weeks, to sail from Liverpool to South Australia in a four-masted barque, powered by the wind, and longer to come back.[111] Nowadays the same trip on a container ship might take about 4 or 5 weeks, allowing for stops at various ports en route. In the early 1960s it took 4 weeks to travel by sea in a passenger liner from New Zealand to England – the longest single voyage that could be made.[112] Freight ships are very low energy users. According to the international Marine Environment Protection Committee, although ships are responsible for transporting 80% of world trade by volume, they account for less than 2% of total CO_2 emissions.[113] In contrast, passenger ships appear to use a lot of fuel per passenger-km, with estimates ranging from 2 MJ/passenger-km to 20 MJ.[114] On this basis a passenger ship could be no more efficient, at best, than an average American car. This may be easier to understand when you consider that a passenger liner carries a much lower weight than a container ship. For example, the P&O liner *Oriana* (42,000 gross tons), which provided sailings between Southampton and Sydney back in the 1960s, carried 2,134 passengers served by 903 crew.[115] Taking the average weight of a passenger and their luggage as 100 kg, this is a total load of less than 220 tonnes, not counting the crew. In contrast, the cargo capacity of a freighter is much higher:

> *In 1950, an average commercial vessel could carry 10,000 tons at a speed of 16 knots. With container shipping, the average commercial vessel carried 40,000 tons at a speed of 23 knots … The numbers are even larger today. A vessel capable of carrying 6,600 20-foot containers can carry 77,000 tons at up to 24.8 knots.*[116]

Most of the energy is used to move the ship, not the passengers. Some modern container ships carry a few passengers. For example, the 24,000-ton dead weight *Hansa Rendsburg* can take six passengers from Los Angeles to Australia and New Zealand,[117] but because they make up such a small part of the ship's total load ship, this could be said to be as close as possible to zero-emission transport: the passengers are merely piggybacking on the ship's main purpose. A container ship uses 0.12 MJ/tonne-km,[118] so if we assume that a passenger and his or her luggage weigh 100 kg, the energy to move them is only 0.012 MJ/km. On the other hand, if a typical container ship carries 40,000 tonnes, it uses a total of $40,000 \times 0.12 = 4,800$ MJ/km. If we assume that a passenger liner's fuel consumption is similar to that of a freighter, then it is carrying around 2,000 passengers for that amount of fuel, giving a figure of at least 2.4 MJ/passenger-km. In earlier decades, the 'cargo–passenger liner' was a common form of ship: a freighter with some passenger accommodation. Examples of such ships are shown in Table 31 (overleaf).

Even the larger examples of such ships carried only 25 tonnes of passengers, making the cargo far more important in terms of energy. It would thus make good sense to revive the cargo–passenger liner as a means of long-distance travel, although it would need to be redesigned (the advent of containerization has made the earlier designs with their general cargo holds mostly obsolete).

Table 31: Some cargo–passenger liners[119]

name of ship	owner	route	no. of passengers
City of Port Elizabeth	Ellerman	London–South/East Africa	100
Parthia	Cunard	Liverpool–New York	251
Caledonien	Messageries Maritimes	Marseilles–Australia	241

BUT WHAT IF YOU ARE IN A HURRY?

Travelling by sea is a very leisurely way to cross the world. It would be quicker to go by airship rather than by ship, as one would expect, because the airship's engines have to provide only propulsion and not lift, and thus use less fuel than an airliner. We could look, for example, at the *Hindenburg*, the largest airship ever built, which ran a regular transatlantic service in the 1930s until its famous fiery crash. The *Hindenburg* had 242.2 tons (US) of gross lift, 112.1 tons of useful lift and a hydrogen volume of 211,890 m³. It was powered by four 1,200 hp (895 kW) Daimler Benz diesel engines and flew at 135 km/h.[120] Expressed in metric units, these figures give a carrying capacity of 102 tonnes with a gross take-off weight of 220 tonnes. The *Hindenburg* carried 50 passengers. How does this compare with an airliner?

A Boeing 747-400 consists of 66,150 kg of high-strength aluminium. Flying a distance of 5,630 km and carrying 56,700 kg of fuel, it will consume an average of 11.8 l/km.[121] Maximum take-off weight of the 747-400 is around 397 tonnes. It can carry 416 passengers and 30 tonnes of freight and luggage.[122] The passengers will weigh about 33 tonnes at 85 kg each, and their luggage will be around 8 tonnes.

Table 32 lists the specific fuel consumption (SFC), in grams of fuel per hour per kW, of diesel aero-engines similar to those used on the *Hindenburg*. It seems that the fuel used by the *Hindenburg* in an hour, if it were going flat out, would be 0.210 kg × 895 kW × 4 engines = 752 kg of diesel fuel per hour. Diesel has an energy content of 42.8 GJ/tonne,[123] so the energy content of this amount of fuel is 42.8 × 0.752 = 32.2 GJ per hour. We can assume that the engines might, in cruising flight, be running at 70% of their maximum

Table 32: Specific fuel consumption (SFC) of diesel aero-engines[124]

power	date	engine type	SFC (g/kWh)
550 kW	1931	Junkers Jumo 204 turbocharged diesel	210
2,340 kW	1949	Napier Nomad diesel-compound	210

capacity, so the figure should be adjusted to 22.5 GJ per hour. If the airship is cruising at 135 km/h, it will use 166.7 MJ/km. For a full load of 50 passengers, the fuel consumption per person will be 3.3 MJ/passenger-km. How does this compare with a modern airliner? Jet A fuel has an energy content of 35,000 MJ/m^3,[125] or 35 MJ/l. The Boeing 747-400 uses 11.8 l/km, so each kilometre flown will consume 35 × 11.8 = 413 MJ. With 416 passengers on board, the energy per passenger is almost exactly 1 MJ/km. At first sight this makes no sense, because the airship uses so much less power (4 × 895 kW = 3,580 kW) compared with the airliner. A 747 has a total cruising engine power of 44,700 kW.[126] However, the airship takes ten times longer to make the trip, and the jet airliner carries nearly ten times more people. In fact, the engine power provided per passenger is remarkably similar: the *Hindenburg* used 72 kW per person, and the 747 uses 107 kW per person.

These results are put together in Table 33. Once again, we can see that we may need to think about returning to past modes of transport if we want to travel long distances, but we have to be very careful about how we do so. It is not, for example, just a case of choosing to travel by sea. The

Table 33: Energy use (including embodied energy) in MJ/passenger-km and time required for a one-way trip between the UK and Australia

mode	MJ/passenger-km	time required
sailing ship	?	85 days
cargo–passenger liner	0.015	30 days
Boeing 747 (full)	1.25	1 day
passenger liner	3.00	30 days
Zeppelin (full)	4.13	10 days

cargo–passenger liner of the 1950s, like the modern container ship, was a very low-energy means of travel, but, as Table 33 shows, the passenger ocean liner and the airship appear to be energy disasters.

We can now introduce our figures for long-distance transport into the table of commuting travel to produce Table 34. This comparison shows that it might seem to make sense to go to work in a Boeing 747, but probably only if you are able to walk between home and airport, airport and office.

Table 34: Energy consumption for different modes of transport, including embodied energy of fuel but not embodied energy of vehicles or shoes (*MJ/passenger-km*)

mode	total
cargo–passenger liner	0.015
bicycle (slow, bread)	0.50
electric commuter train (renewable)	0.59
bicycle (fast, bread)	0.65
diesel commuter train	0.74
tram/light rail (renewable)	0.76
driving (4 people, 1.6 litre car)	0.80
trolleybus (renewable)	0.87
walking (bread)	0.90
Boeing 747 (full)	1.25
electric commuter train (non-renewable)	1.77
bicycle (slow, bread, shower)	2.05
bicycle (fast, bread, shower)	2.20
tram/light rail (non-renewable)	2.28
trolleybus (non-renewable)	2.61
passenger liner	3.00
driving (1 person, 1.6 litre car)	3.19
horse (organic feed)	3.30
city bus (diesel)	3.50
Zeppelin (full)	4.13
ferry boat	9.06

However, all is not quite as obvious as it seems. If we take an average motorist in an average car, travelling, say, 13,000 km a year, their year's motoring will use about 41.5 GJ. On the other hand, if they decide to take a holiday and travel from London to Sydney and back, it would be useful to know how much fuel they use. London to Sydney by sea is 11,507 nautical miles (21,311 km),[127] whereas London to Sydney by air is 17,009 km.[128] Table 35 shows the energy used for the round trip.

The modern airliner looks quite promising in terms of fuel economy, but because we go such long distances by air the impact is high. One single long-haul holiday is equal to a year's motoring. For a family of four, one long-haul holiday will use four times the energy they use for the family car. There are not many ways round this, because long-distance travel cannot use renewable electricity, which, as we saw, is one way to reduce the environmental impact of transport. Biofuels are being proposed for airliners, but manufacturers are aware of the potential conflict between biofuels and food production. A paper from Boeing cites US Department of Energy research showing that algae could be used to produce aviation fuel, which have a yield of 10,000 to 20,000 US gallons per acre (or 234,650 to 469,300 l/ha) per year.[129] This yield is said to be 150 to 300 times better than that of oil from soya beans, and would mean that the entire world supply of aviation fuel could be grown on 3.4 million hectares of land – about the size of the state of Maryland.

In the 1980s scientists at Lockheed in the United States looked into using hydrogen as a fuel for airliners.[130] The Tupolev design bureau in the

Table 35: Energy used for a London–Sydney return trip, including embodied energy

mode	MJ/passenger-km	total for London–Sydney round trip (GJ)
cargo–passenger liner	0.015	0.64
Boeing 747 (full)	1.25	42.52
passenger liner	3.00	127.87
Zeppelin (full)	4.13	140.49
annual motoring (1.6 litre car)	3.19	41.50 GJ per year

Soviet Union also worked on hydrogen, and a Tupolev Tu-154 that had one of its three engines modified to run on hydrogen was first flown on 15 April 1988 as the Tu-155.[131] The European Union's LAPCAT project (sadly not a scheme to provide warm felines to help heat homes in winter; it stands for Long-Term Advanced Propulsion Concepts and Technologies) is working with Reaction Engines Ltd., a British company, on designs for a hypersonic (Mach5+) airliner that will fly from Brussels to Sydney in two to four hours.[132] This airliner, which is considerably longer than the huge double-deck Airbus 380, is intended to use hydrogen as fuel. Allowing for a 10% margin of safety, it will consume about 9.5 kg of fuel per km. The energy value of hydrogen is around 120 MJ/kg,[133] so the LAPCAT aircraft will use 1,140 MJ/km compared with 413 MJ/km for the familiar 747. This means that a full LAPCAT with 300 passengers on board will use 3.8 MJ/passenger-km, not much different from the hydrogen-filled Zeppelin except a lot faster. The intention is that the LAPCAT aircraft's fuel will be made from electrolysis of water using renewable energy, and on this basis a ticket is estimated to cost the same as the current business class fare.[134] So it could be that, as in the past, long-distance air travel will become the province of the wealthy. Table 36 shows the one-way fares for London to Sydney being offered by a cheap flights website in January 2008.

Projects like LAPCAT demonstrate that there are really two very different worldviews about a sustainable future. One – the standpoint generally taken in this book – holds that things are going to get increasingly difficult; that life for most people will change radically, and that we will get by through a process of making our lives simpler. The other view is that technological progress will continue unabated and that a rising world population will be able to have more and more material goods and services from a finite

Table 36: Cost comparison of an airline ticket from London to Sydney[135]

airline	tariff	fare (GBP)
Asiana	lowest	£575
Virgin	premium economy	£1,723
Korean Air	business class	£2,198

environment. The LAPCAT project, even if it is powered by hydrogen gener-ated by using renewable wind energy to electrolyse water (and, worryingly, the Reaction Engines website states that the ticket price would be reduced by roughly half if the hydrogen were produced from steam reforming of natural gas, which would not be at all sustainable), will consume far more fuel per passenger-km because it is a high-speed aircraft. The same quantity of hydrogen fuel could allow many more people to travel if it were used in highly efficient subsonic aircraft. The European Union's Cryoplane project is aimed at developing hydrogen-powered conventional subsonic aircraft,[136] very similar to the designs proposed in the 1980s, with the bulky, but light, hydrogen fuel contained in fat fuselage tanks. This line of research seems in many ways more appropriate to the future than a hypersonic airliner developed for the wealthy. So perhaps some aviation could continue to be a possibility for some people, or for many people very occasionally, in a more sustainable and oil-less future.

DISCUSSION

No one is suggesting that a sustainable future will not involve transport, either personal or public. People have always moved, from the journeymen tradesmen of the medieval period to Regency tourists undertaking the 'Grand Tour' through continental Europe. What is at risk is the very easy access to transport that we enjoy today. Most people in the West have access to cars; they can jump into the car parked outside the house and drive two streets away to the shop to collect the morning paper or buy a carton of milk. This makes no environmental sense at all if the journey can be made on foot. At present, however, there is little financial penalty for silly journeys like these, just as air travel is often much cheaper for short-haul trips than making the same journey by train, even though the environmental impact of the former is greater. In fact, short-haul flights have worse energy con-sumption per km than long-haul flights because it is take off and landing that consume the most fuel. At present, cost is no indicator of environmen-tal impact when it comes to travel. The much-vaunted free market does not appear to offer any encouragement for more sustainable behaviour. To give an example: towards the end of 2007, the authors' daughter wanted to travel from Newcastle-upon-Tyne, in the north-east of England, to London. The cheapest rail fare was £200 return, whereas the air fare was only £50. Out of interest, she checked the first-class return rail fare and found that this was £800.[137]

What also matters in a society that walks and cycles more – supposedly the environmentally friendly means of travel – is the type of diet that provides the additional energy needed for the exercise. This may come as a surprise, but in the world of ecology 'there's no such thing as a free lunch': there will always be some price to pay for travel. Walking is good exercise, and also fast. In the past, people covered prodigious distances by walking perhaps 20 miles a day. The problem with walking is that the modern built environment is not designed to encourage it, and most pedestrians are left feeling like second-class citizens as they wait for lights to change to let them cross the road. Cyclists also suffer, unless they are in some European countries like the Netherlands and Germany where residential environments are designed with sensible, sedate cycling in mind. At present, countries like China can safely support this type of cycling simply because there are far fewer cars per head of population, although car ownership is now rising fast.

Perhaps the best attitude to take when it comes to thinking about transport in a sustainable society is the old World War II slogan 'Is your journey really necessary?' In future, transport may well become more of a privilege than a right. Here are some options to consider:

- Walk short distances or cycle sedately and eat a wholesome diet to fuel these activities.

- Commute to work and school using public transport if you cannot walk or cycle.

- Drive when you can take lots of people.

- Enjoy holidays in your own country.

- Treat air travel as a very occasional luxury.

- Give up eating cheeseburgers.

3
BUILDINGS

It is often said that buildings account for 50% of all the energy used in the world. This book has tried to show that the consumption of energy and resources is as much down to the choices we make as it is to the objects themselves. Without the demand for golf, no resources would be tied up in the annual loss of golf balls (see Chapter 5), and without the need to work there would be no need to worry about the environmental impact of how we get there (see Chapter 2). In the same way, a building will take energy and resources to make it, but the building exists only because the client wanted it to exist or because a developer saw the building as a way to make money. A building also takes energy and resources because of the activities that go on inside it, and different activities will create different demands. A warehouse will not need much energy to keep it warm, whereas an office building will. Those who work in the warehouse expect it to be at outside temperature and dress accordingly, but office workers expect not to have to wear outside clothes indoors, and so energy will be needed to keep them warm in winter. And almost certainly the building will require some form of lighting, since it is always darker inside than outside.

What this section aims to do is ask questions about our current buildings and to consider how their environmental impact could be reduced through our behaviour and choices. Much has been written about the design of buildings that are more energy efficient, that consume zero energy, or are energy productive: there are buildings that demonstrate all of these technical approaches, some of which we have even designed ourselves.[1] The purpose of this book, however, is to consider behaviour, so buildings will not be discussed as technical problems in themselves, but as spaces in which people live, work and perform other activities.

NO BUILDINGS

Why do we have buildings at all? Shelter is always seen as a basic need, along with food and water. Shelter gives protection from the natural world, with all its associated hazards. From the time the cave was first used for protection or huts of leaves and branches were created, nature has been modified by the hand of man. However, this creation of shelter to avoid the unpleasant aspects of the natural world is a long way from the creation of buildings today. In the past, the minimum was done to provide protection, and most of life would be spent in the open air. The shelter was a retreat in which one could sleep safely. The opposite is now true: many buildings house activities that once might have been done in 'no buildings'. At Plato's Academy lessons were held in the open, but how many modern university classes are conducted out of doors? In many climates this could be done, but although the spoken word can be heard by a small group of students out of doors, today's large classes – a result of the principles of the modern economic model being applied to education – would just not be able to hear in a noisy modern environment. This suggests that modern buildings often exist to protect one group of users from the users next door – that is, to protect them from other people rather than from the natural world.

Architecture has been called 'the mistress of the arts', and the creation of buildings could be seen as an artistic endeavour rather than a utilitarian escape from inhospitable surroundings. It could be that mankind cannot help but make buildings as an artistic outlet just as we cannot help but sing and make music. However, it could be argued that few buildings in the modern world are put up purely as artistic endeavours, as happened in the past. Most modern buildings have budgets and deadlines, and any artistry is applied within these constraints. It is doubtful whether the huge timber temples in China or the vast stone Gothic cathedrals would have been built within the modern economic framework. They were constructed for reasons that were not based in economics, and because they represented the best artistry of their time. On a smaller scale, most vernacular societies had buildings that stood for the community's artistic endeavours, be they the carved and symbolically rich meeting houses of the Maori or the communal houses of Vietnamese villages. These were buildings rather than 'no buildings', but at the same time they were much more, since they repre-sented the aspirations, hopes and dreams of the people who created and used them.

So to what extent would doing without buildings, or having fewer of them, help reduce the resources that go into their construction and maintenance?

SIZE MATTERS

Perhaps the first option to consider is having smaller buildings, or more buildings with shared facilities, so that the resources that go into them can be used as much as possible throughout their life. Many office buildings in the West, for example, stand empty most weekends, and on working days are fully occupied for fewer than 12 hours out of 24, despite often having lights on throughout the night. The homes of office workers, on the other hand, are empty 12 out of 24 hours on working days. This is a long way from the medieval model of the shop, in which work was carried out at the front of the building on the street, the living quarters were behind, and the garden behind that.

SHARE NICELY

Where space is limited, timetabling has always been an option. In fact, on English naval vessels in the time of Nelson – now familiar to us through the novels of Patrick O'Brian – the crew was divided into watches of 4 hours each, making a total of 6 watches in one day. But one of these was split further, to make 2 watches of 2 hours each (the 'dog watches'). This meant an odd number of total watches, so they were rotated throughout the crew. On account of the timetabling system, while some men were on watch, manning the ship, others had more room in which to sleep. Ships also had different functions taking place within the same space, so that the place where the men ate together was also where they hung their hammocks. A caravan could be considered another example of timetabling: the same space is used for eating and later, when the table and benches have been converted into a bed, also for sleeping. Where movement or transport is involved, timetabled use of space is common.

Another common example is the use of school buildings for after-hours activities like adult education or community group meetings. In this way the resources that go into a building are used for as many people as possible. The one requirement for this approach to work successfully is good storage, so that equipment to support activities can be safe and secure when not required. We live more happily when boundaries are clear and there is no chance of one group consuming another's coffee and biscuits.

The effect of occupancy levels on the environment has been recognized in some building environmental assessment systems such as the Australian NABERS (National Australian Built Environment Rating System), in which the number of people living in a house is partly used to assess its impact.[2]

In the past, both in the West and in other cultures, multiple use of space was traditional. The shophouse that was common to most Asian cities allowed for trading in working hours, but at night goods were put away and tables and chairs brought out onto the street edge for family relaxation. This implies that the space needed per person in any given situation is small – exactly counter to what is happening in many Western countries, where private space, especially the house, is growing in size. According to the 2006 Demographia International Housing Affordability Survey,[3] in many parts of the Western world houses are getting bigger. They are moving away from timetabled use of space and towards separate spaces for separate functions. The figures quoted show that, in Australia and the US, the average new house is 2,200 ft² (204 m²), in Canada and New Zealand it is 1,900 ft² (177 m²), in the UK it is 815 ft² (76 m²), and in Ireland the figure is 930 ft² (86 m²). In part, these averages should reflect an increase in the number of single-person households and thus the smaller types of housing in which they live; but since this demographic phenomenon is happening also in New Zealand, it seems irrational that the average new house there should be so much larger. So what accounts for the extra space in these bigger houses?

The living room of the early 20th-century house in the UK contained the stove for cooking, with preparation and wet work being done in the adjacent scullery. It was also the place where family meals were eaten and where they relaxed, taking advantage of the warmth of the stove, just as in the shophouse tradition described above people enjoyed the cooler night air outside in a time before air conditioning. The bathroom used to be a single space, catering for timetabled use, but now there is an increased number of bathrooms within a single dwelling, each one getting used even less than the last.

Instead of a single living space with timetabled activities, the modern house may have a kitchen for cooking, a dining room for eating, and a living room for living. The latter may be split yet further into a formal living room for special occasions, a family room for everyday living, and a separate study. Instead of a space as small as 3×4 m = 12 m² for a minimum of four people in an early 20th-century house, the new super-size houses have multiple living spaces and multiple bathrooms. In the Melbourne 'Eco Home',[4] which is 281 m² in total, there is an area of 8×3 m = 24 m² for dining/kitchen, a 4×4 = 16 m² family room downstairs, a 3×3.5 m = 10.5 m² lounge, and a 3×3.5 m = 10.5 m² family room upstairs, making a total of 61 m². The 'Eco Home' has four bedrooms, whereas the typical house at the turn of the 20th century had three. However, even if one assumes that there was a family of four in the old house and a family of five in the Melbourne one, this gives a living area for various family activities of 3 m²/person in the older house and just over 12 m²/person a century later. This is all space that will need some form of energy to make it comfortable, and it is all space that requires energy and resources to make it. If being 'Eco' means worrying about where the resources and the energy are coming from, building large does not seem the obvious starting point.

Aspirations in the UK may well indicate a desire for a bigger house, even if the statistics show that new houses in 2006 were smaller than they were in the past, with a 30% drop in size from 1920.[5] Looking at a UK firm that offers timber-frame kits for self-builders, their smallest house is 133 m² and has two living rooms, a kitchen big enough to dine in, three bedrooms, a bathroom and a utility room,[6] whereas their 231 m² house (a little larger than the US and Australian average) has a large living room and kitchen/dining room, study, four bedrooms, four bathrooms (three en-suite), and a utility room.[7] The popularity of television shows like *Grand Designs*, which follows the construction or renovation of unconventional houses, would seem to suggest that large homes are desirable, even if not generally available, in the UK. Of the four houses featured in the latest series, one had 5 bedrooms, two had 4 bedrooms, and the one 3-bedroom house had additional spaces such as a study and children's playroom.[8] It has also been said that the average size of a self-build house is 200 m².[9] It appears we have moved from an ability to timetable functions in the home to a world where big is equated with good. This will have an impact on the consumption of energy and of resources, and hence will affect the impact of the home on the environment. It follows that a small house will have a lower impact on the planet.

WARM AND SNUG

To explore this idea further, it would be useful to compare 'average-sized' houses and the energy it takes to run them in different countries. In Table 1, energy use covers only space heating and cooling. A big house will obviously take more energy to heat it to the same level as a small house, but as houses get larger their lighting loads and demand for hot water may also rise. In New Zealand, larger houses – unsurprisingly – use more energy per m² than smaller ones.[10] The purpose of this table is to show where in the world large houses have a very large impact on the environment in terms of the energy it takes to make them comfortable. Because census data do not usually include household area (it is thought to be too difficult for those filling in the forms), we have taken the areas and relative sizes of daytime living areas from available plans. Obviously these plans will be indicative only of the overall situation, because they represent particular examples rather than an average, but they do allow us to make some comparisons.

One obvious fact to emerge from this comparison is that the houses in the US and Australia have a larger proportion of the floor area given over to living space as the house sizes increase. The example from New Zealand shows that the living rooms (two: a living room and dining room/kitchen) did not increase in size, although both these living rooms and the bedrooms were larger than, say, their equivalents in the UK. Since it is single-storey, as the average New Zealand house increases in size there is more circulation space. The smaller houses in the UK show a similar trend, with the living area remaining about the same. So where there is a fashion for larger houses, it would be interesting to know how this extra space is being used, and why.

Even from the limited data in Table 1, it is clear that the relationship between size and energy use is a simple one: the bigger the house, the more

Table 1: Comparison of energy used in the heating and cooling of related living spaces in different countries

country	total floor area of house (m²)	living areas (approx., m²)	average heating/ cooling energy use (MJ/m²)	house annual energy use (MJ)	annual heating/ cooling energy use for living spaces (MJ)
Australia (Victoria)	204	121[11]	400[12]	81,600	48,400
US (2001 average)	204	99[13]	250[14] (heating) + 57[15] (cooling)	62,628	30,393
New Zealand	177	67[16]	115[17]	20,355	7,705
Canada before R-2000 programme	177	99[18]	650[19]	115,050	64,350
Canada after R-2000 programme[20]	177	99	530[21]	93,810	52,470
UK average, old regulations	76	37[22]	504[23]	38,304	18,648
UK developer's house to old regulations[24]	96	37.5	504	48,384	18,900
UK theoretical self-build house to old regulations	200	100	504	100,800	50,400
UK average house to new building regulations	76	37	212[25]	16,112	7,844

energy it uses. The exception is New Zealand, where houses tend to be under-heated. Relying on national data for energy use blurs the differences in climate that exist across large countries like the US and Canada (in fact, no such data could be found for the whole of Australia, so we used figures based on a house in the state of Victoria instead). However, since large houses are built everywhere, in both the hot and cold parts of a country, we can still make a useful comparison. Furthermore, it is apparent from Table 1 that 'big is bad', and that places like the UK where houses are small benefit greatly from energy savings. National policy should discourage people from moving to bigger houses, and the media should accept some responsibility for fostering the notion of big houses as a desirable goal.

Why should an average family in Australia need so much more living space than an average family in the UK – especially when the Australian climate is conducive to outdoor living for more of the year (see the discussion below)? If you live in a small house in which activities in your living space are timetabled, you should congratulate yourself on doing your bit to save the planet. If your house is large, it should require zero energy in operation to compensate, since it will have needed more resources to make it in the first place, and more resources to fit it out with more furniture. What these extra resources mean when compared to the energy used to run the house is explored below.

BRICKS AND MORTAR

Bigger houses require more construction materials and also use up more land. This land, were it not covered by the floor of your house, might be used in a more productive way as a garden for fruit and vegetables, or for planting native species to encourage biodiversity. This gives us two different aspects to investigate: the energy embodied in materials, including all the energy needed for their extraction, processing, transport, use and (ideally) disposal; and the area of land taken up by the house, which is partly dependent on whether it has one floor or two.

Embodied energy coefficients vary from country to country according to what processes are used to extract and manufacture materials, so for a better comparison we need to find what the values for the different countries are. According to the Commonwealth Scientific and Industrial Research Organisation (CSIRO), the embodied energy of new Australian houses is about 5 GJ/m².[26] A 1991 study by the Canadian Mortgage and Housing Corporation gives the embodied energy of a standard Canadian house of 350m² as 1,310 GJ,[27] making 3.7 GJ/m², but this is an old figure and may not include energy for maintenance and repair over the years. A UK building materials site states that the embodied energy of a house ranges from 4.5–5.5 GJ/m², depending on the types of materials used and the number of storeys,[28] but no reference is given for this data. Generally, timber-framed and timber-clad houses will have a lower initial embodied energy than brick and tile houses on concrete slabs. The life-cycle embodied energy for New Zealand houses, including materials for maintenance and repairs, has been calculated as 4.5 GJ/m² for standard lightweight construction and 4.3 GJ/m² for heavy construction where the timber frame has a brick veneer cladding. The lower life-cycle value comes partly from not having to paint the cladding.[29] Given both the closeness of these values and also the fact there is still much debate and research on the boundaries for calculating embodied energy, Table 2 sets out the house sizes we used above but assumes different lifetime values of 4.5 GJ/m² and 5.5 GJ/m² for the embodied energy.

What it shows is that the quickest way to reduce embodied energy is not to worry about calculating it accurately or to try to use materials that have low energy, but quite simply to live in smaller houses. The difference

Table 2: House size, embodied energy and heating/cooling energy over 50 years

country	floor area (m²)	embodied energy at 4.5 GJ/m²	embodied energy at 5.5 GJ/m²	total heating/cooling energy use over 50 years (GJ)
Australia (Victoria)	204	918	1,122	4,080
US (2001 average)	204	918	1,122	3,131
New Zealand	177	797	974	1,018
Canada before R-2000 programme	177	797	974	5,753
Canada after R-2000 programme	177	797	974	4,691
UK average, old regulations	76	342	418	1,900
UK developer's house to old regulations	96	432	528	2,400
UK theoretical self-build to old regulations	200	900	1,100	5,050
UK average, new building regulations	76	342	418	800

between high and low values for a 204 m² house is 204 GJ, whereas the difference between even a lower embodied energy house of 204 m² and one of 96 m² is over twice as much at 486 GJ.

To explore this further, hypothetical UK houses of 100 m² and 200 m² are used in Table 3, which sets out the difference for various levels of embodied energy as a percentage of the total heating and materials life-cycle energy for 50 years. A hypothetical low value for embodied energy of 3.5 GJ/m² is taken to represent a deliberate attempt to choose only low embodied energy materials. In fact, energy-efficient houses – in other words, those being built following the changes to UK building regulations in 2000 – might be expected to have higher embodied energy values since they will contain more insulation and better window specifications. But insulation materials, apart from some plastics, generally have low embodied energy coefficients, so for the purpose of this broad comparison these effects are ignored.

A further column in the table sets out the energy footprint for heating and for materials as the land area required each year to supply this energy in a sustainable way. According to Wackernagel and Rees, the amount of land required to absorb the carbon dioxide from burning conventional fuels is the land energy footprint. It turns out that 1 ha will absorb the CO_2 given off by burning 100 GJ of fossil fuels annually, giving a land energy footprint of 100 GJ/ha.[30] However, to grow energy from wood in a sustainable way is another story. Matthews states the world's forests could grow a sustainable 10 m³/ha/year of wood.[31] This would amount to about 70 GJ/ha given 100% conversion efficiency. Hence it might be better to assume a more conservative 50 GJ/ha from forests. To compare this to the energy crops looked at in the previous chapter, the 1,212 l/ha of olive oil works out at 41 GJ/ha, and 6,679 l of ethanol from sugar beet yields 57 GJ/ha. Only avocados come close to the Wackenagel and Rees figure of 100 GJ/ha, with a yield of 90 GJ/ha, although this does seem an awful waste of the best food in the world. In another study Wackernagel and Rees have calculated that a hectare of land can yield 120–50 GJ of energy.[32] There is evidence to support this larger claim. Flavell states that US switchgrass lignocellulose, a dedicated energy crop, has an average yield of 135 GJ/ha,[33] but goes on to say that this figure could increase with crops bred especially for energy rather than food.

Table 3: Comparison of the impact of heating and materials over a 50-year life cycle for different levels of embodied energy and house size

house type and size	embodied energy (GJ)	heating energy over 50 years (GJ)	total energy (GJ)	ecological footprint of house (ha/year)	embodied energy as % of total
UK existing 100 m² EE 5.5 GJ/m²	550	2,520	3,070	0.45	18
UK existing 100 m² EE 4.5 GJ/m²	450	2,520	2,970	0.44	15
UK existing 100 m² EE 3.5 GJ/m²	350	2,520	2,870	0.42	12
UK existing 200 m² EE 5.5 GJ/m²	1,100	5,040	6,140	0.91	18
UK existing 200 m² EE 4.5 GJ/m²	900	5,040	5,940	0.88	15
UK existing 200 m² EE 3.5 GJ/m²	700	5,040	5,740	0.85	12
UK 2000 regulations 100 m² EE 5.5 GJ/m²	550	1,060	1,610	0.24	34
UK 2000 regulations 100 m² EE 4.5 GJ/m²	450	1,060	1,510	0.22	30
UK 2000 regulations 100 m² EE 3.5 GJ/m²	350	1,060	1,410	0.21	25
UK 2000 regulations 200 m² EE 5.5 GJ/m²	1,100	2,120	3,320	0.48	34
UK 2000 regulations 200 m² EE 4.5 GJ/m²	900	2,120	3,020	0.45	30
UK 2000 regulations 200 m² EE 3.5 GJ/m²	700	2,120	2,820	0.42	25

In 2004, Moriera analysed world biomass potential for the Expert Workshop on Greenhouse Gas Emissions and Abrupt Climate Change, noting that it was greater in tropical and subtropical climates than in temperate ones.[34] He stated that world average sugar cane yields were 650 GJ/ha, and that the average for eucalyptus plantations in Aracruz, Brazil (his country of origin), was 450 GJ/ha. He compared these figures with the US forest average of under 100 GJ/ha and 430 GJ/ha for Alamo switchgrass, which is much higher than the previous reference. From this it seems that there is the potential for much higher yields than we have at present, although, since they come from tropical climates, it raises serious concerns about the fate of tropical rainforests and other types of forest. It would be all too easy to destroy them in a search for cheap biomass energy as we run out of oil. Because of this, we have used a value of 135 GJ/ha, which may seem conservative in the light of Moriera's figures but is perhaps more realistic if we want a world in which there are still orang utans, gorillas and other close relatives. With current practice this 135 GJ/ha remains an optimistic figure, but we are optimistic people (we would not otherwise be doing all this work on sustainable lifestyle). If you wish to depress yourself even further, you could double all our energy footprint figures to reflect what can easily be achieved in temperate climates, which would equate to yields of 67.5 GJ/ha.

In the tables that follow, we have generally given energy footprints in ha/year. Sometimes footprints are small and it is easier to express them in m² (a hectare contains 10,000 m², so your fair earthshare is 18,000 m²·) but the way of calculating them is the same.

Once again, the figures tell us that size matters. All the energy-efficient houses show lifetime savings over the energy used in existing houses, demonstrating the benefit of renovating existing houses to save energy, even if that increases their lifetime embodied energy. However, the bigger the house, the more energy it uses, even if it is a low-energy house. This suggests that, rather than undertaking extensive research into making embodied energy figures more and more accurate, we should concentrate on showing how small houses can be beautiful and wonderful spaces for families to live in. If you want to do your best for the environment, then make sure your next house is a small, energy-efficient one.

MAKE IT AT HOME

Two other advantages of small houses are that they take up less land and they cost less. Table 4 sets out our hypothetical houses of 100 m² and 200 m² on the same plot measuring 350 m², and considers the effect of both single-storey designs, such as are common in Australia and New Zealand, and two-storey designs, more familiar in the UK. The plot size equates to just over one twelfth of an acre, which is the minimum recommended site area for building a 4-bedroom home in the UK of 1,800 ft² (167 m²).[35] It is also an increasingly common plot size in Australia and New Zealand, as existing larger plots in cities are subdivided in an attempt to increase density. Rough comparative costs are also given, based on a UK contractor-built standard plan house that cost £700/m².[36]

Table 4: Implications of house size on a plot of 350 m² in the UK, in terms of cost and available land area

house type	plot cover (%)	available garden area (m²)	cost (GBP)
single-storey 200 m²	57	150	£140,000
single-storey 100 m²	29	250	£70,000
two-storey 200 m²	29	250	£140,000
two-storey 100 m²	14	300	£70,000

These figures show that, if you can afford a large house in the UK but in the interests of the environment opt to have a small house, you will have £70,000 to spend on making the house produce rather than consume energy. You also have a larger garden and more space in which to grow fruit and vegetables. If you took these steps, what would happen to the ecological footprint of the house?

The simplest way to produce energy is to install photovoltaic panels (PVs) on the roof of your house, positioning them so that they face the sun and have minimal over-shading. At present, PVs cost around £8,000/kW (usually written kWp, where the 'p' stands for 'peak', meaning the peak power that the system can produce). This 1 kWp would occupy an area of roughly 10 m². Because panels do not produce their peak output at all times, it is best to base a system's output on recorded data. In the UK, output is around 800 kWh for every 1 kWp installed. The side of a gable roof of a two-storey house, 5 × 10 m in size and facing the sun, would have an area of around 30 m² for a 30° pitch. A 3 kW system could be installed for a cost of £24,000. The energy produced from this would be 2,400 kWh/year, or 8,640 MJ/year. The negative footprint from producing energy at home would be 8.6 ÷ 135 = 0.06 ha/year.

The PV panels also take energy and resources to make. According to a study by the University of Bologna, the lifetime environmental impact of making PV panels – the total energy they embody – is recovered in just under two years of operation in a medium-sunshine climate like Northern Italy.[37] One square metre of monocrystalline panels (the ones that look like a series of black squares behind glass) saved 4,400 kWh over a 25-year life, or 176 kWh/m²/year. This means that a 10 m² PV system in Northern Italy generates 1,760 kWh/year, which is roughly double what you would get for the same system in the UK. In New Zealand we measured an output of 1,200 kWh/year from 1 kW of panels. The total annual sunshine hours for these three places are 2,500 for Florence (the nearest city for which data were available), 2,050 for Auckland and 1,500 for London.[38] So the amount of time it takes to pay off the energy that goes into making PVs is related to where they are and how much sun they get. The problem is further complicated by the fact that there is a whole range of values given for the embodied and life-cycle impacts. A number of studies by the University of Bath on this issue give an average value for the embodied energy of monocrystalline PV panels for the UK as 4,752 MJ/m² (1,320 kWh/m²) (they ranged from 2,592 to 8,640 MJ/m², or 720–2,400 kWh/m²).[39] The expected life of silicon crystal panels is 25 years, according to the Bologna study. These figures from Bath show that a 10 m² system with 13,200 kWh of embodied energy that in the UK will generate 800 × 25 = 20,000 kWh over its lifetime will have to run for 16.5 years to pay off the energy used to make the system (assuming the average embodied energy value of 4,752 MJ/m²). In Northern Italy, the same system would have to run for 7.5 years, and for 11 years in New Zealand.

The age of the data also has an impact on the results. A recent paper by Fthenakis and Alsema[40] states that much data on the embodied energy and efficiency of PV systems are based on 15-year-old systems and old manufacturers' figures, leading to PV systems appearing to have higher greenhouse gas emissions per kWh than electricity generated from natural gas. Over time, manufacturing processes have become more efficient in response to the challenges of climate change and peak oil, which means that using old data can give misleading results. Fthenakis and Alsema recalculated the life-cycle energy of PV systems using recent data from manufacturers and found that for Southern Europe, with its insolation level of 1,700 kWh/m²/year, the energy payback was 2.7 years for monocrystalline silicon panels. This is closer to the Bologna estimate than the figures from Bath. If, therefore, it takes 2.7 years of generation in Northern Italy to payback the embodied energy, the same system will take (2.7 × 1,760) ÷ 1,200 = 4 years in New Zealand, and (2.7 × 1,760) ÷ 800 = 6 years in the UK. It is this figure we have used in Table 6 below.

For the theoretical house comparison in Table 6, we have allocated the first 6 years of generation to paying back the energy involved in the making and disposing of the panels, leaving 19 years of the panels' lifespan to produce energy. Over 19 years the energy generated by a 3 kW system is (800 × 3) × 19 = 45,600 kWh, or 164 GJ. If the panels have to be replaced after 25 years, then the total cost over an assumed life of 50 years will be £48,000, and the total energy generated will be 164 × 2 = 328 GJ. This has a negative ecological footprint of (328 ÷ 135) ÷ 50 = 0.05 ha/year for 2 PV systems over 50 years.

Having a small house will also mean that more land can be given over to a productive garden. A plot of 270 m² will supply all the fruit and vegetables for a family (see Chapter 5), with a reduction in ecological footprint of 0.1 ha. A two-storey house of 100 m² needs 50 m² of land space; to this is added an extra 10% to cover drives and pathways is usually added, making a total of 55 m² of built area. Subtracted from our initial area of 350 m², this leaves 295 m², meaning that 100% of a family's fruit and vegetables could be grown at home, with some land left over for flowers or ornamental plants. For the single-storey 100 m² house, the built area is 110 m², so 240 m² of space is left over, and 240 ÷ 270 × 100 = 89% of fruit and vegetables can be grown at home. This would have a negative ecological footprint of 0.1 × 0.89 = 0.09 ha. Table 5 (overleaf) sets out our hypothetical houses, the size of their gardens and the potential yields.

Table 5: Productive garden areas and negative ecological footprint values for various houses

house type, meeting UK 2000 regulations	area of land covered by house, driveway and paths (m²)	available garden area (m²)	negative ecological footprint of a garden used for fruit and vegetables (ha/year)
single-storey 200 m²	220	130	0.05
single-storey 100 m²	110	240	0.09
two-storey 200 m²	110	240	0.09
two-storey 100 m²	55	295	0.1+

Table 6, on the other hand, sets out the footprints per year over the course of 50 years of having a small, productive house as opposed to a large, relatively unproductive one; all figures are based on a lifetime embodied energy of 4.5 GJ/m². The cost in the final column is related to the choice of house in the first column, so other combinations are possible.

The results seem like a win-win situation: for less money – £22,000 less, in fact – buying a smaller house can reduce your household footprint

Table 6: Footprints for the productive house

house type, meeting UK 2000 regulations	footprint life-cycle house energy (ha/year)	footprint energy production (ha/year)	footprint food grown (ha/year)	total footprint for categories considered (ha/year)	cost (GBP)
single-storey 200 m²	0.45	0	(–0.05)	0.40	£140,000
single-storey 100 m², 2 PV systems	0.22	(–0.05)	(–0.09)	0.11	£118,000
two-storey 200 m²	0.45	0	(–0.09)	0.36	£140,000
two-storey 100 m², 2 PV systems	0.22	(–0.05)	(–0.10)	0.07	£118,000

from a worst-case 0.4 ha for a single-storey 200 m² house to 0.07 ha – an 83% reduction. This is also £22,000 you don't have to borrow. Alternatively, if you have won the lottery and have the cash in hand, you could spend it not on a new car but on a 1.5 kW PV system that you could install on a roof somewhere else, and on replacing it after a 25-year life. The idea of using rooftops other than your own has caught on in Freiberg in southern Germany, where a power company has installed its own PV panels on the roof of a local brewery. If you did this rather than have a large unproductive house for roughly the same money, your small house would have a footprint of 0.22 (the basic footprint of a 100 m² house) less 0.1 (for growing your own food), minus (0.05 × 1.5) = 0.045 ha. The main worry is that large houses are put forward as desirable rather than small ones. If sustainability is our goal, this has to change: we should be aiming for the house with the smallest footprint, not the one with the largest number of bathrooms (see below).

'I'LL HUFF AND I'LL PUFF'

The argument above is based on three levels of embodied energy, but it could be argued that a real sustainable house would make use of much lower embodied energy materials like straw bales and earth (adobe) for the walls; if this were done, some of the figures above might not apply. Baled straw has an embodied energy coefficient of 0.24 MJ/kg, and that for straw and stabilized earth block is 0.47 MJ/kg, whereas bricks are 2.5 MJ/kg.[41] All these materials can be used for making load-bearing walls. A study by Geiger suggests that using straw bale for the wall material in a conventional house that also has concrete slab and foundations, timber-frame interior walls, synthetic carpet, steel roof trusses, plywood sheathing, aluminium joinery (in window and door frames) and so, as is common in the US, would save only about 10% of initial embodied energy.[42] Of course, straw bales are insulating, so there would also be a saving on operating energy over the life of the building. Mithraratne looked at embodied energy for New Zealand houses, and, for a house with concrete foundations and slab, timber-frame walls with brick veneer, timber roof with concrete tiles and aluminium joinery, the walls for a standard 94 m² house represented 31% of the total initial embodied energy. This is quite a small house by today's standards, so the percentage is higher than the figure given by Geiger, who based his analysis on a 200 m² house that would have bigger rooms and proportionally less wall.

Table 7 sets out a comparison of houses containing walls of various materials, some with low embodied energy but with other components kept constant. So we have a timber roof with corrugated-steel roofing, aluminium joinery, slab and foundations of concrete. Two houses are considered, one of 100 m² (7 × 14.3 m) and one of 200 m² (10 × 20 m). According to Mithraratne's study, the area taken up by doors and windows in the smaller of the houses is 24.2 m².[43] Using a proportion based on the length of the perimeter walls to allow for more rooms and windows, we arrive at an area of 34 m² for the 200 m² house. The strip foundation is also adjusted using the same proportions. All other elements are assumed to be proportional to the floor area, such as roof, plumbing, electrical work, and so on. Although foundations for straw bale walls would have to be bigger to accommodate the width of the bales, this has been ignored for the present analysis.

The calculation of the embodied energy of the straw bales is based on a bale 18 × 14 × 36 in. (45 × 36 × 91 cm) weighing 50–60 lb (22.7–27.2 kg).[44] Thus every square metre of stacked bale wall requires 3.1 bales with a total weight of 3.1 × 25 = 77.5 kg, and has an embodied energy of 0.24 × 77.5 = 18.6 MJ. The perimeter walls of the 100 m² house have an area of 82.3 m², so if these are of straw bale they will have an energy intensity of 82.3 × 18.6 = 1.5 GJ. To this must be added the internal walls. It is reasonable to assume that they are equivalent in length to the external walls, giving a total figure for the walls' embodied energy of 3 GJ. The insulation properties of straw bale walls vary, but a study by the US Heschong Mahone Group states they are at least three times better than ordinary timber stud walls.[45] In New Zealand, it has been suggested the energy lost through the walls of a house is 24% of the total.[46] The average space-heating energy in the New Zealand houses in Table 1 is 115 MJ/m², and 24% of this is 28 MJ/m². This is for all houses, whether insulated or not, but for the moment we can assume that having straw bale walls will reduce this figure by a factor of three, to give 28 ÷ 3 = 9 MJ/m². This will give a value for space heating for the straw bale house of 115 − 28 + 9 = 96 MJ/m². From the figures used in Table 1, total energy use in New Zealand houses is calculated to be 344 MJ/m², so the total energy use for the straw bale house will be 344 − 115 + 96 = 325 MJ/m².

Adobe blocks, on the other hand, are normally 36 × 10 × 28 cm,[47] meaning that it takes 28 of them to make 1 m² of wall. They have a thermal resistance level (R-value) of 0.6 m² °C/W.[48] The density of an adobe block is similar to that of a brick,[49] which is about 2,400 kg/m³. One adobe block weighs 24.2 kg and therefore has an embodied energy of 24.2 × 0.47 = 11.4 MJ. This means 1 m² of wall has an embodied energy of 28 × 11.4 = 319 MJ. The energy contained in the external walls of the 100 m² house can therefore be calculated as 319 × 82.3 = 26 GJ. As before, this is doubled to take account of internal walls, making 52 GJ. An adobe wall, because of its thermal mass and ability to absorb and retain solar energy, will meet the building code in New Zealand, even though the R-value is low.[50] For the purposes of this comparison, therefore, it is assumed that having the adobe wall makes no difference to the operating energy requirement. Table 7 sets out the embodied energy in GJ for the building components of a 100 m² and

Table 7: Embodied energy in conventional and more sustainable house construction scenarios (*GJ*)

building element	100 m² house, timber frame, brick veneer	100 m² house, straw bale	100 m² house, straw stabilized adobe block	200 m² house, timber frame, brick veneer	200 m² house, straw bale	200 m² house, straw stabilized adobe block
foundation	8	8	8	11	11	11
floor	74	74	74	148	148	148
walls	82	3	52	116	4	73
roof	34	34	34	68	68	68
joinery	23	23	23	32	32	32
electrics	10	10	10	20	20	20
plumbing	17	17	17	34	34	34
finishes	16	16	16	32	32	32
total	264	185	234	461	349	418
annual operating energy	34	33	34	69	66	69

200 m² house, together with the amount of energy needed to operate every-thing in the house for a year (not just the space heating, as before).

As expected, having a large house with straw bale walls is still not better for the environment than an ordinary house half the size. However, to get a true picture we should look at the life-cycle energy of the house over 50 years, which is shown in Table 8. For this simple comparison, it is assumed that all building elements will last for 50 years.

These figures show that having an adobe block wall does not make much difference whatever size the house is, so it can hardly be claimed to contribute to sustainability. The straw bale does a little better but not much. Because life-cycle energy is dominated by operating energy, having straw bale walls would give an even smaller reduction in overall energy use in a colder climate like Canada or the UK, where space-heating energy is higher. To really lower the embodied energy, it would be necessary to change much more of the building specification. It would be possible to have beaten earth floors, recycled timber windows and doors, and a roof of recycled timbers clad in thatch. Plumbing and electrical work could be kept to a minimum and recycled materials used wherever possible. However, the final product would be much closer to the hippie commune ideal of the late 1960s than

Table 8: Energy comparison of houses with different wall materials over a 50-year life-cycle

house type	embodied energy (GJ)	operating energy over 50 years (GJ)	life-cycle energy over 50 years (GJ)	footprint (ha/year)
100 m² house, timber frame, brick veneer	264	1,700	1,964	0.29
100 m² house, straw bale	185	1,650	1,635	0.27
100 m² house, straw stabilized adobe block	234	1,700	1,934	0.29
200 m² house, timber frame, brick veneer	461	3,450	3,911	0.58
200 m² house, straw bale	349	3,300	3,749	0.56
200 m² house, straw stabilized adobe block	418	3,450	3,868	0.57

the grand designs in seamless glass and cladding presently put forward by much of the media. If we want to keep our modern comforts and aesthetics, the message is that we need to think small.

AND SO TO BEDS

Thus far we have considered only the energy used to make and operate the building. However, the bigger the house, the more furniture is needed to make it into a home rather than a warehouse. The fact that there are more floor coverings and more bathrooms will have been accounted for in the embodied energy figures already considered, because we have used published generic figures. A study by Fay showed that furniture accounted for 10% of the life-cycle energy of a typical suburban house in Australia over a 100-year period,[51] whereas it accounted for 6% of the initial embodied energy.[52] The embodied energy of appliances such as the cooker, fridge, etc. and the heating and hot water systems accounted for 13% of life-cycle energy after 100 years[53] and 5% at the start.[54] A more recent study of life-cycle energy in New Zealand houses quotes furniture and appliances as representing 27% of total life-cycle energy for all operating and embodied energy after 100 years.[55] Both studies indicate that the figure is significant, accounting for 23–27% of all the energy for making the house, its furniture and appliances, having hot water and comfortable temperatures inside, lighting, and running items like the fridge and freezer. The energy for furniture is significant because furniture is usually seen as replaceable – not necessarily when something wears out but because fashions change. Obviously, if you equip your house with furniture that you then maintain and repair as necessary, you can reduce this impact. This is probably more easily accomplished with furniture than with appliances, which are sold as virtually disposable items in today's society.

Table 9 (overleaf) explores the consequences of having a bigger house on the lifetime energy incorporated in the additional furniture and appliances it requires. It also looks at the potential savings from making a conscious effort not to replace furniture and appliances.

What the table shows is that, if you have a 200 m² house in Australia, with its annual heating and cooling load of 81.6 GJ (see Table 1), the energy embodied in the extra furniture and appliances you need to furnish it is akin to having to provide an extra 1.7 years of heating and cooling. For a

Table 9: Impact of house size and the rate at which furniture and appliances are replaced (*GJ*)

house type	energy embodied in furniture and appliances, normal replacement rates*	energy embodied in furniture and appliances, careful maintenance †	total embodied energy	saving in furniture and appliances from having a smaller house	saving in furniture and appliances from reducing replacement rates
200 m² EE 5.5 GJ/m²	275	138	1,100	–	137
100 m² EE 5.5 GJ/m²	138	69	550	137	69
200 m² EE 3.5 GJ/m²	175	88	700	–	87
100 m² EE 3.5 GJ/m²	88	44	350	87	44

* Based on 25% of total embodied energy, assuming the same percentage as for life-cycle energy.
† Based on 12.5% of total embodied energy.

theoretical 200 m² house in the UK, built to the current building regulations and with an annual heating load of 42.4 GJ (see Table 3), the extra furniture and appliances would add the equivalent of 3.2 years. As houses come to use less energy for heating and cooling, having a big house and more stuff in it becomes more of a problem.

DISCUSSION

This whole section began with the idea of 'timetabling' the use of built space. This entails having furniture that can be moved, put away and rearranged as necessary, such as the familiar ironing board or stacking stools. In the past, items like gate-leg tables that can be folded away against a wall (they appear often in many photographs of cottages and houses in the Arts and Crafts style) allowed for buildings to be both functional and moderately uncluttered. The built-in approach often favoured by the Modern Movement is, paradoxically, less flexible both for everyday use and over the life of the building, when different users and different tastes often lead to things being thrown away before their useful life is over. There is a big difference between being functional in the sense of every thing or space within a building having a defined function, and being functional in the way spaces are designed and equipped so that different functions (human activities) can happen within them. The first approach uses 'function' as a label, but the second sees function as being a response to human needs. However, what has emerged from this research is that, for anyone interested in sustainability, their home should be a small house or flat. At the moment most Western societies are going in the opposite direction, with larger and larger houses being built, even though changing demographics and an ageing population mean that the size of the average household is falling.[56] What is needed is for small, beautifully designed, flexible houses to become objects of desire.

WET, WET, WET

Instead of the whole house, this section will single out one particular room – the bathroom – for more detailed analysis. How this room is used is often a big timetabling issue within buildings. In fact it gets relatively little use, but most of it occurs at the same time. In the past, large families and a single bathroom led to a difficult juggling act in the morning, although families would develop a routine to cope. However, choosing to have numerous bathrooms may be taking things too far in the opposite direction.

> Mr. Simms [the architect] *said that if they really meant it, they could have this for very close to their figure, if they'd cut out two of the bathrooms, which ran into money in a dozen different ways, many of them remote from the eye, like the size of the hot-water heater in the cellar, or the septic tank in the flower-strewn fields ... 'I will not hazard the children's health in a house with three bathrooms,' said Mrs. Blandings.*[57]

There are two issues to examine here: the environmental impact of how much bathrooms are used, their size and their number; and what actually happens in the bathroom, so that we can see how behaviour can have an impact, particularly on water use.

TOO MANY BATHROOMS?

Our current house has one bathroom with a shower, a toilet and a wash-basin, and the two of us together (but normally separately) spend 50 minutes in it each day we work at home and a bit less when we go into the university. It measures just under 2 × 2 m (4 m²) and would be considered a small bath-room in New Zealand but a reasonably sized one in the UK, where houses are smaller. The bathroom in the house we are currently moving to has the same type and number of fittings but a larger floor area of 2.2 × 2.5 m (5.5 m²). However, some new houses in New Zealand have much larger bathrooms, with 'his and hers' washbasins, freestanding baths, and so on. The bathroom attached to the master bedroom on the Rangiora Eco Village showhouse plan – one of two bathrooms – measures 2 × 4.5 m (9 m²), which would be the size of a bedroom in a UK house.[58] The question is, does having

Table 10: Embodied energy of bathroom fittings

element	mass (kg)	embodied energy (MJ)
14 m copper pipe	11 (0.8 kg/m)	26.4*
bath, pressed steel and white enamel	55	1,760.0
shower over bath	3	96.0
glass screen (toughened)	20	520.0
vanity basin, vitreous china	12	30.0
toilet pan, vitreous china	17	42.5
cistern, vitreous china	17	42.5
plastic seat and accessories	3	309.0
taps and valves for bath, basin and shower	5 (1.5 kg/set)	310.0
heated towel rail	6	192.0
toilet-paper holder	0.1	3.0
mains-pressure 135 l hot water cylinder in steel	14	448.0
total		3,779.0

* Based on recycled copper.

more bathrooms or bigger bathrooms matter when it comes to making houses more sustainable?

Table 10 lists the weight of materials and fittings associated with a typical bathroom of 4 m² or larger, and shows their calculated embodied energy values.[59]

All these fittings, apart from (possibly) the cylinder, would appear in either a small or a large bathroom. The bigger the number of bathrooms, the larger the cylinder would have to be, and some houses with multiple bathrooms will have more than one cylinder. The table shows that, for each bathroom, about 4 GJ should be added for the fittings. However, there are also the walls, the ceiling and the floor covering to consider, as well as the heating. Multiple bathrooms used by one person still have to be heated,

Table 11: Embodied and operating energy of different-sized bathrooms, excluding fittings

element	quantity (m²)	embodied energy* (MJ)	operating energy† for 1 year (MJ)
tiled floor (6 mm thick ceramic tiles)	2.8	888 (floor) + 882 (tiles) = 1,770	
timber frame walls, plastered and painted	7.0	3,150	
tiled walls around bath	6.2	2,790 (walls) + 1,953 (tiles) = 4,743	
timber frame ceiling, plastered and painted	4.0	1,600	
window	1.0	230	
timber door	1.8	414	
electrical work including lighting		400	
total 4 m² bathroom		**12,307**	**1,307**
total 5.5 m² bathroom		**16,922**	**1,892**
total 9 m² bathroom		**27,691**	**3,096**

* Based on initial embodied energy values for New Zealand light construction.[60]
† Using 344 MJ/m² as an average for all house and energy use in New Zealand.[61]

whereas a single bathroom used by the whole family will need less energy to keep it warm, since the general activity in it will help. Table 11 sets out the energy involved for these items in the small 4 m² bathroom described above. A window of 1 m² is assumed in all bathrooms, as well as an internal door plus an electric light. Proportional values are given for the larger bathrooms at the end.

The next stage is to put Tables 10 and 11 together in order to find out whether size or the number of bathrooms is more critical. To arrive at this point we must look at the energy involved over a 50-year life. The life of the

Table 12: Life-cycle energy of different-sized bathrooms over 50 years (GJ)

bathroom size	embodied energy of fittings over 50 years	embodied energy of bathroom over 50 years	operating energy over 50 years	total energy over 50 years
4 m² (small)	7.6	12.3	68.4	88.3
5.5 m² (medium)	7.6	16.9	94.6	119.1
9 m² (large)	7.6	27.7	154.8	190.9

Table 13: Comparison of size and number of bathrooms

size and number of bathrooms	time spent in each bathroom (hours/year)	life-cycle energy over 50 years (GJ)	life-cycle energy for 1 year (MJ)	energy per hour of use (MJ/hour)	footprint (m²/hour)
1 small bathroom	730	88.3	1,766	2.4	0.2
1 medium bathroom	730	119.1	2,382	3.3	0.2
1 large bathroom	730	190.1	3,802	5.2	0.4
2 small bathrooms	365	176.6	3,532	9.7	0.7
1 large and 1 small bathroom	365	278.4	5,568	15.3	1.1
1 large and 2 small bathrooms	243	366.7	7,334	30.2	2.2

hot water supply and the cylinder might be 12.5–30 years; the copper pipe should last 50 years, along with the walls, the electrical work and so forth; and the sanitary fittings should have a life of 20–40 years.[62] To simplify matters it is assumed that all the fittings in Table 10 are replaced once during the 50-year period. This gives Table 12: a life-cycle comparison for three different sizes of bathroom.

Using these values, we can now compare some hypothetical situations for a 4-person household, assuming each person spends 30 minutes a day in the bathroom (Table 13).

SIZE DOESN'T MATTER

Size of bathroom is clearly not as important in terms of impact on the environment as the number of bathrooms. Having only one bathroom, whatever its size, reduces the environmental impact just because facilities are shared. Whatever their size, the more bathrooms you have, the greater the impact. You might argue, however, that the comparison is unrealistic because your fourth bathroom is never used, being reserved for guests, and thus mostly unheated. But the values used here are for total energy including hot water and lighting, and the same level of energy use has been applied to all bathrooms in the table above to give a clear comparison. Since these are average New Zealand energy values, the level of heating will not be very high anyway since most New Zealanders heat their houses only morning and evening, and heat the bathroom only when it is in use. The table also shows that the serious sustainable house should have only one bathroom, and that if the bathroom is small, the house will be more sustainable and have a lesser impact on the environment.

It might also be argued that having a large and beautiful bathroom means that you spend more time in it than the rather meagre 30 minutes a day assumed here. This raises the issue of whether such luxury is something to be enjoyed every day at home or whether it should be reserved for holidays (something you have every day is no longer a luxury). When we lived in the Autonomous House in Southwell in the UK, we only took showers so that we could live within our water allowance (we collected all water from the roof in an area of relatively low rainfall for the UK). Showering keeps you clean, but going on holiday meant enjoying a bath as an occasional luxury and something different from home. Home is where we live within our resources, but holidays can provide a contrasting experience. The problem now is that what used to be an occasional luxury has become normal, with consequent problems for the environment.

WATER, WATER EVERYWHERE...

Water is a resource that is in increasingly short supply in many parts of the world. Some experts suggest that one way to preserve this resource is to install low-flow shower heads and taps that save both water and energy, so that you use less hot water for each shower. The Australian government's guide to environmentally sustainable homes (and Australia is a country short of water) suggests five ways to minimize water use: fitting water-efficient outlets and appliances; avoiding planting grass and other garden plants that need water; washing the car on the lawn so that you water the grass at the same time; sweeping paths rather than using a hose; and reusing waste water where possible.[63] Surprisingly, behaviour within the bathroom is not mentioned. The question is, what is the most effective way to save water in a building? Should we fit water-saving fixtures and appliances, or should we change our behaviour?

An efficient shower head with an AAA rating uses water at the rate of 9 l/minute (see the previous chapter), whereas an older type might use 20 l/minute. How long you stay under the shower will also determine how much water you use. If you have an efficient shower just 5 minutes long, you use 45 l, which is less than half of the 25 gallons (95 l) you would use in a bath.[64] This means having the water about 10 cm deep in a tub that measures about 70 × 170 cm – the classic bath of the World War II period, when the UK government urged people not to use more than 5 in. (12.5 cm) of water.[65] However, if you spend 20 minutes in your efficient shower, you use 180 l of water, or about two baths' worth. Showers are generally thought to be more water-saving than baths, but we can see that this may not be the case depending on the time you spend in the shower. Table 14 compares the effectiveness of water-saving features with a change in behaviour. A Brazilian

Table 14: Environmental impact of a daily shower or bath per person

bathroom activity	water use (l)	water use footprint* (m²)	energy use† (MJ)	energy use footprint (m²)	total footprint (m²)	annual footprint‡ (m²)
20-minute old-type shower	400	0.32	5.6	0.41	0.73	266
Brazilian old-type shower	157	0.13	2.2	0.16	0.29	106
5-minute old-type shower	100	0.08	1.4	0.10	0.18	66
20-minute low-flow shower	180	0.14	2.5	0.19	0.33	121
Brazilian low-flow shower	71	0.06	1.0	0.07	0.13	48
5-minute low-flow shower	45	0.04	0.6	0.04	0.08	29
bath (economical)	95	0.08	1.3	0.10	0.18	66
bath with a friend	48	0.04	0.7	0.05	0.09	33

* Based on 0.08 m²/100 l.[66]
† Based on 35 Wh/l (see Chapter 2), with 10% added for cylinder losses to give 39 Wh/l.
‡ Assumes one shower or bath a day.

study of 49 apartments found that a typical shower lasted 7.85 minutes,[67] so this has been entered as a further comparison.

The table shows that behaviour change, rather than a change in technology, can make a significant difference – and incidentally costs nothing. Even with an old, water-hungry shower, a 5-minute shower will have a smaller footprint than spending 20 minutes in the most efficient shower, and the impact is about the same if you choose to have 10-minute showers using your low-flow shower head – or, in fact, a relatively modest bath in terms of the water used. So the message is as follows: if you like the feel of lots of water on your skin, you are better off running a shallow bath than having a long shower. A short, efficient shower has the lowest impact, but having a bath with a friend is about the same, and the advantage of having two people in the bath is that the same amount of water feels like a lot more, thanks to Archimedes' Principle.

FLUSHED WITH PRIDE

A similar change in behaviour can be applied to flushing the toilet. An old-style cistern will use 11 l/flush,[68] whereas some of the latest water-saving devices use 6 or 3 l/flush, depending on what you are flushing. It is possible to put something in an old cistern to reduce the amount of water used; the New Zealand government recommends a filled 1 l or 1.5 l plastic milk bottle.[69] However, changing your behaviour can also help reduce water use. There is a saying, 'If it's yellow, let it mellow; if it's brown, flush it down' – a maxim that can simply reduce the number of flushes. Like sharing a bath, sharing a flush is another way of reducing water use without changing anything.

Table 15 looks at the amount of water saved by taking these different approaches. The average number of flushes a day is assumed to be 1.5 (brown) and 5 (yellow).[70]

Once more, the results show that behaviour rather than technology is the key to saving water. The low-flush toilet does save water and performs much better than the advice to put something in the cistern, but still is not as good as simple behaviour change. If you don't have the money to install a

Table 15: Impact of using the toilet in different ways (data for one person)

approach	embodied energy (MJ/year)	embodied energy footprint (m²/year)	water use/day (l)	water use/year (l)	water footprint (m²)	total annual footprint (m²)
no change in behaviour, old cistern	n/a	0	72	26,280	21	21
fit a new 3/6 l flush toilet	4.3*	0.3	24	8,760	7	7
place a filled 1.5 l container in cistern	n/a	0	62	22,630	18	18
use 'yellow mellow, brown down' method	n/a	0	17	6,205	5	5

* Based on Table 10 and on a 20-year life.

new toilet pan and/or cistern, you can save water with any old toilet by observing the 'yellow mellow, brown down' rule. This works well at home but may be more problematic at work and in public toilets (perhaps a matter for debate).

The other point worth noting is that the number of bathrooms has no effect on the figures above: it is people who use water, not bathrooms. The one caveat is that having several bathrooms multiplies the risk of having a leaking toilet cistern, and a cistern that leaks can use a lot of water: up to 16,000 l/year.[71]

... NOR ANY DROP TO DRINK

Apart from changing our behaviour, another approach is to collect rainwater off the roof and use it in place of mains water, whether for everything or for selected activities like toilet flushing and watering the garden. Research in New Zealand has shown that collecting and using rainwater at home has a smaller overall footprint than using mains water. Over a lifespan of 100 years, a rainwater system that uses a concrete tank for all water supply, such as we had at our house in Auckland before moving to Wellington (and after 11 years of drinking untreated rainwater we are still alive), shows an 18% energy saving over mains supply with no change in water use, and a 3% saving over mains use with water-saving practices.[72] In Table 16 (overleaf), this value is compared with the behaviour changes discussed above for a house supplied with mains water. The basic water use is taken as 227 l/person/day.[73] The figures for life-cycle energy for mains and concrete tank systems are taken from a bar chart from the same source. It is assumed that mains water life-cycle energy is proportional to the amount of water supplied, so it falls as demand falls.

This table suggests that the many words written about rainwater collection in pursuit of the sustainable house (and we are guilty of some of them) would be better spent exhorting people to change their behaviour in ordinary houses. Given that mains water supplies exist and are sized to deliver the normal amount of water rather than to meet reduced consumption, the savings might not be proportional as assumed, but they do accord with the New Zealand findings that mains supply with demand management gave the lowest life-cycle energy at 100 years.[74] Given rising populations

Table 16: Relative effectiveness of water-saving strategies

approach to water use	mains water use (l/person/ day)	water use (l/person/ year)	saving (l)	saving as % of typical use	life-cycle energy over 100 years (GJ)
no change	227	82,855	0	n/a	49
concrete rain tank for all water	n/a	n/a	n/a	100	41
old fittings but 5-minute shower*	170	62,050	20,805	25	37
old fittings and 'yellow mellow' method	172	62,780	20,075	24	37
old fittings, 5-minute shower and 'yellow mellow' method	115	41,975	40,880	49	25

* Compared with the Brazilian average of 7.85 minutes, this shows a saving of 57 l/shower.

in cities and the pressures on water supplies, serious water-saving with a mains supply does seem a reasonable solution. More importantly, this is a way all of us can start saving water now.

INDOOR AIR QUALITY

Another favourite topic in any discussion of sustainable buildings is indoor air quality. Many materials, particularly those of a petrochemical origin, give off gases when new, putting chemicals into the air that you would probably rather not breathe. The smell of a new car or of the new carpet at work are typical of such 'off-gassing'. The US Environmental Protection Agency (EPA) states that homes may contain two to five times the levels of some organic chemicals compared with the outside air.[75] Part of the problem comes from the reduced levels of ventilation in houses, which ought to allow us to be comfortable at the same as saving energy, be it for heating or cooling. Greater levels of ventilation mean that the pollutants are diluted in the indoor air. However, the increasing use of chemical solvents, glues and other materials has contributed to the problem, leading to a demand for natural materials in buildings to improve indoor air quality.

Concern about indoor air quality must start with personal behaviour, however. If you smoke indoors, it is no use worrying about whether the materials of your house are damaging the indoor air quality. This section will deal first with issues related to behavioural and personal choices, and then move on to issues related to buildings.

CLEANLINESS IS NEXT TO GODLINESS

The quality of the air inside buildings is also affected by how we behave. The market for personal care products, including things like shampoos, cosmetics, hair-styling products, etc., is growing. The women's beauty market is said to be growing at the rate of US$202 billion a year.[76] Many deodorants and anti-perspirants contain chemicals we would probably rather not use if we read the small print. These chemicals also get washed down the drain every time we shower, adding their impact to the natural environment. At a time when there is also much talk of indoor air quality in both homes and workplaces, it is amusing to find that a study on the new Ministry of the Environment building in Wellington found that the biggest indoor pollutants were deodorants and other chemicals workers applied to themselves so they would smell sweet.[77] Maybe it's a case of one person's perfume being another person's poison. This much is recognized in Canada, where you can opt for a scent-free policy for your workspace.[78]

Most of the fragrances used in personal hygiene products, perfumes, aftershaves and indoor air fresheners are chemicals derived from oil – 95% of them, according to the Canadian Lung Association.[79] As these chemicals vaporize, they stick to skin and hair and can be absorbed through the skin as well as breathed in. There is also a worry that long-term exposure to low levels of these types of chemicals may be as dangerous as short-time high exposure that would not be permitted in the workplace.[80] Buying products labelled as 'fragrance free' is not a simple answer, since although no fragrances may have been added to these products, chemicals may have been added to mask unwanted smells.[81] The same Canadian source states that one perfume may contain up to 500 chemicals. This is one instance where our personal choices in not buying and using such products can immediately improve indoor air quality irrespective of how 'natural' the building materials are in either house or workplace. So what alternatives to chemical products are available?

For many years, soap has been made from two waste products: wood ash, the source of alkali, and a fat, such as tallow or olive oil. Washing in water, possibly with the addition of soap, has been the basic way of keeping clean for centuries.[82] It still seems a good way, and is much easier now that we have houses with running hot and cold water, with no need to take clothes down to the well or to the stream to wash them. However, just when personal hygiene should be so easy, we are perversely spending a lot of money on additional products that interfere with indoor air quality. This is probably the result of companies wishing to sell us products. 'BO', standing for body odour, was a concept created by Lever Brothers as part of a campaign to sell a brand of soap.[83] We are being sold the idea that how we naturally smell, even when we wash every day, is unpleasant. This is not difficult to do, since our sense of smell is linked directly to emotion and to memory.[84] If we are told that a particular smell is unpleasant, when we smell it we automatically associate it with unpleasantness.

Perhaps the first rule to reduce impact of personal hygiene products should be to use what you buy, finishing each bottle before starting the next.[85] This also stops you from cluttering up bathroom cupboards with half-finished bottles of this and that. If you can't face using only unscented soap and water and retraining your smell–emotion relationships, then choose products with an Environmental Choice label (this is from New Zealand, but similar systems exist in many countries), which will have met specified green standards. The Australian equivalent for shampoos and bodily cleaning products,[86] although only voluntary, guarantees that a certain portion of ingredients is biodegradable and that cancer-causing chemicals have not been used. Fragrances are also regulated. However, the only universally available guide to potential difference in environmental impact is cost. A quick visit to any pharmacy will show that a bar of unscented soap wrapped in paper might cost NZ$2, while a plastic bottle of shower gel can cost NZ$6–14 depending on the type. Both will do the same job and last for about the same amount of time but, going on its cost alone, the soap will probably have much less of an impact – at least two-thirds less, in fact. Giving Mum an unscented bar of soap for Mother's Day may not be much fun but, again, this is an area where perhaps a distinction can be made between what we use every day (the product with the least environmental impact) and what we use occasionally (the more luxurious gift). The point is that the simple soap product will not significantly affect indoor air quality in the way that many modern replacement products do. Concern about indoor air quality must start with personal behaviour.

DOING THE DISHES

When she was a child, Brenda can recall the washing up being done in soap flakes, whereas Robert remembers his family using a new Shell product known as 'Teepol'. This was the first oil-based organic chemical manufactured in Europe[87] and remains the oldest brand of detergent in the world.[88] As with personal hygiene products, there has been a move from the simple to the complex, as liquid detergents for washing up now come in the fragrance of your choice. However, there is another issue related to washing up: the relative environmental merits of using a dishwasher compared with doing it by hand. Using a dishwasher is said to use less water, energy and detergent than washing by hand.[89] The opposite view is also found,[90] but most analyses show that a dishwasher washing one full load a day is better than washing up done by hand in small batches after every meal. Given that our Mums are not alive to read this, we can happily say that we generally let the dirties pile up and do one large load by hand at the end of each day, just like a dishwasher. However, it may be useful to look at this issue in more detail.

Given that the kitchen will have a sink whether or not it has a dishwasher, the embodied energy of the sink can be ignored. To choose an example, the double DishDrawer dishwasher has a stainless steel outside and a plastic inside; in the absence of a manufacturer's figure, we can assume that it weighs 20 kg. If this is made up of 50% stainless steel and 50% polythene, it would have an embodied energy of 10×74.8 (stainless steel)[91] + 10×51 (plastic) $= 748 + 510 = 1{,}258$ MJ. Fay gives the useful life of a dishwasher as 13 years,[92] so $1{,}258 \div 13 = 97$ MJ/year, which is a footprint of 7.2 m². If only one drawer is used, this value can be halved.

(Although the top drawer has a larger stainless steel front, both drawers have the same capacity.)

The manufacturers state that the DishDrawer uses 2.4 US gallons (9.1 l) on average for each wash.[93] Another site gives the usage as 2 US gallons for each drawer in use.[94] A source in the US also gives energy use for a single drawer as 157 kWh/year.[95] This means that running each drawer over a year will consume 565 MJ/year, equivalent to a footprint of 41.9 m²/year. We measured our own washing up and reckon that it too uses around 9 l per wash. This water will be heated from, say, 15 °C to 45 °C using 0.126 MJ/l (see the previous chapter). Over a year, assuming one washing up session each day, this amounts to 9 × 0.126 × 365 = 414 MJ. Our water is heated instantaneously so there are no standing losses, making a footprint of 30.7 m². If the hot water came from a cylinder, we would add 10% to cover lost heat, giving a footprint of 33.7 m². In winter this lost heat might be useful, providing the cylinder is not outside your house (which is normal practice in Australia), but in summer it is unwanted. Given that standing losses are normally 20%, we have halved this figure for our calculations. The footprint of tap water is 0.08 m²/100 l, so in a year the water footprint of washing up by hand can be calculated as 0.08 ÷ 100 × 9 × 365 = 2.6 m². The footprint for using a single DishDrawer is 2.7 m².

These values can now be combined so that we can compare various ways of doing the washing up (Table 17). From the results, it might be possible to conclude that dishwashers are better for the environment than washing up by hand. Using the single DishDrawer, which takes six place settings, once a day is better than doing three lots of washing up by hand. However, it is not better than doing a single load of washing up by hand once a day, which shows a reduction in impact of about 25%. Of course, using both drawers of the dishwasher once a day will have a much greater impact, so once again it all comes down to behaviour.

Several points have been ignored in this analysis. The first is the tea towel: after you have done it by hand, you can leave your washing up to

Table 17: Environmental impact of various ways of washing up over the course of a year

washing up strategy	footprint, embodied energy (m²/year)	footprint, operating energy (m²/year)	water footprint (m²/year)	total annual footprint (m²)
one DishDrawer load a day	3.6	41.9	2.7	48.2
two DishDrawer loads a day*	7.2	83.8	5.4	96.4
washing up by hand once a day, instantaneous water heating	0	30.7	2.6	33.3
washing up by hand once a day, hot water cylinder	0	33.7	2.6	36.3
washing up by hand three times a day, instantaneous water heating†	0	51.2	4.4	55.6
washing up by hand three times a day, hot water cylinder†	0	56.2	4.4	60.6

* In terms of capacity, this is the equivalent of a full load in a conventional dishwasher.
† Each load is assumed to use a smaller 5 l of water.

air-dry, meaning that tea towels are not needed; and in the limited experience we have had of using a dishwasher, you also need to use a tea towel to dry at least some items properly when the machine has finished. For these reasons we have ignored the impact of using tea towels in our figures. Another factor we have not considered are the detergents. We have included this analysis in our discussion of indoor air quality because of the effect modern cleaning chemicals, including detergents, can have on it. As we stated earlier, it is quite possible to wash up with ordinary soap – something that does not work with a modern dishwasher. So if you are interested in reducing the chemical load in your home, you can wash dishes by hand knowing that a dishwasher is not going to be better for the environment. Finally, the overall energy balance could change depending on how you heat your water. Dishwashers normally heat from cold, but washing up can be done by hand in solar-heated water – as we have done for many years.

'CAN I DO YOU NOW?'

What has been said about personal hygiene products applies also to many cleaning products used in the home. They add low levels of oil-based chemicals to the indoor air and affect its quality. Many of these products can be replaced with simpler ones: soap can be employed in place of more complex detergents; both vinegar and baking soda can be used separately and together to replace off-the-shelf products; and many other suggestions can be found.[96] But some finishes, like carpet, are harder to clean without the help of more modern technology.

The Modernist architect Le Corbusier claimed that we should 'demand a vacuum cleaner',[97] as if this machine were essential to living in the modern house. The original version was a hand-operated affair designed to suck up dust while being pumped, and was an alternative to the broom and the dustpan and brush. The broom is a very old human invention found in many different cultures. Local plant materials, such as twigs or leaves, were fastened to a handle using other fibres in order to make a device to remove dust and dirt from inside to outside. This simple 'machine' has now become mechanized and uses energy for the same task for the sake of convenience.

To some extent the use of a machine – the vacuum cleaner – in place of a broom is related to the type of floor covering. When floors were hard and mats were portable (and men were real men ...), the mats would be picked up and taken outside to have the dust beaten out of them. This had the advantage of exposing the mats to direct sunlight with its sterilizing effect. The floor could be swept and washed down to remove dust and dirt. There were strategies for the 'wet dusting' of carpets in situ, such as brushing damp tea leaves over them to remove dust,[98] but the main cleaning process involved removal. Even stair carpets were fixed in such a way that they could be taken out; their position was also adjusted to even out wear since the most vulnerable part was where the carpet was stretched over the stair nosing. A particular type of carpet, the Kidderminster, was woven with no pile, which allowed it to be turned over; the pattern was visible in opposing colours on both faces.[99] But fitted carpets put an end to all this. We need to consider the environmental impact of having a fitted carpet compared with a solid floor, a wooden floor or a sheet flooring material such as linoleum. In addition, we should look at the impact of different sorts of cleaning.

Table 18 (overleaf) shows the embodied energy for the basic structural floor, and its finish, of a typical small living room measuring 4.0 m × 3.5 m, or 14 m². How the values are calculated is explained in detail below. Any insulation applied to the floor is ignored for the purpose of this comparison. Because the amount of energy to make products like floorboards and carpets varies between manufacturers and between countries because of how the energy is generated, we have used figures from New Zealand for this calculation. Another country would give different values, but the relative values between the floor and its cleaning should remain the same. Where it has been impossible to get data for New Zealand, other figures have been introduced.

The timber floor for the 3.5 m × 4 m room is assumed to have seven 50 × 150 joists, giving a total length of timber of 7 × 3.5 = 24.5 m that would need treating with a CCA (copper, chrome and arsenic) preservative. The total volume of timber is 24.5 × 0.05 × 0.15 = 0.18 m³. This would give an embodied energy of 0.18 × 4,060 = 731 MJ, assuming that the timber is kiln-dried, gas-fired, dressed and CCA-treated,[100] with an embodied energy of 4,060 MJ/m³. This will last at least 50 years. If the floor has a particle board covering, this will have a volume of 0.28 m³ and an embodied energy[101] of 4,400 MJ/m³, which adds 0.28 × 4,400 = 1,232 MJ, giving a total value of 1,963 MJ. It is assumed the particle board will also last for 50 years.

Varnishing this floor with a solvent-based product and coverage of approximately 16 m² to 1 l[102] gives an additional 384 MJ for a three-coat finish, using an embodied energy value of 128 MJ/l for a solvent paint.[103] It is assumed that sanding and revarnishing will take place every 10–20 years,[104] giving two revarnishings over the course of the 50-year period, but the energy required to sand the floor has been ignored.

For the next comparison it is assumed that the floor is not varnished but carpeted using wool carpet with a rubber underlay. Underlay weighing 1,799 g/m² is guaranteed for 8 years.[105] Applying this to the room for the first time would add 1,700 MJ to the floor covering, if we use a value for rubber of 67.5 MJ/kg.[106] If a felt underlay is used, guaranteed to last as long as the carpet and weighing 847.7 g/m²,[107] the initial embodied energy for the underlay becomes 221 MJ, although one New Zealand supplier suggests that felt underlay is seldom used nowadays.[108] Finding the total final weight of a

Table 18: Embodied energy comparison of a living room floor and finishes over 50 years

floor type for 14 m² living room	(1) embodied energy at start (MJ/m²)	(2) embodied energy at start for whole room (MJ)	finish replacement cycle (years)	embodied energy over 50-year life (MJ)	embodied energy at end (MJ/m²)
timber construction, particle board	140	1,963	–	1,963	140
timber construction, varnished particle board	168	2,347	10–20 (varnish only)	3,115	223
timber construction, particle board and fitted wool carpet on rubber underlay	474	6,631	12	20,635	1,474
timber construction, particle board with lino glued down	530 (high) 302 (low)	7,420 (high) 4,228 (low)	50	7,420 (high) 4,228 (low)	530 (high) 302 (low)
timber construction with varnished softwood boards	135	1,886	10–20 (varnish only)	2,654	190
timber construction with ceramic tiles on lining	627	8,773	50	8,773	627
concrete floor, power-floated and polished	253	3,546	50	3,546	253
concrete floor with ceramic tiles	592	8,288	50	8,288	592
concrete floor with carpet	568	7,958	12	21,962	1,569

Note: Value (1) is derived from value (2). See the discussion on pp. 165–66.

wool carpet is difficult since carpet is usually rated by the weight of the pile per square yard or square metre. For this calculation it has been assumed that the wool carpet pile, glue and backing together weigh 2 kg/m², noting that Tretford cord carpet, which is 80% goat hair and which does not require a backing but is glued direct to the floor, weighs 2.75 kg/m².[109] This would give an initial embodied energy value of 2,968 MJ for the fitted wool carpet. The average life of a carpet is 12 years,[110] so we can assume that the carpet will be replaced three times in the 50-year period, along with the underlay with its 8-year guarantee. Since the carpet is wool, it is assumed to be biodegradable at the end of its life. (In fact, ground-up carpet can be used as a fertilizer.[111]) Taken together, this gives a figure of 1,963 (floor) + 4,668 (four lots of carpet and underlay) = 20,635 MJ over a 50-year lifespan.

On the same basis a fireside rug measuring 1.5 × 3 m would have an embodied energy of 954 MJ. It could be assumed that the rug will be replaced every 12 years like carpet, to give an embodied energy over 50 years of 2,862 MJ.

Linoleum, although not as soft and warm as carpet, is often heralded as a more environmentally responsible floor covering choice and has attracted an eco-label.[112] It is a product that has been manufactured for over 100 years and is made of linseed oil and wood flour or cork dust pressed onto a canvas backing, so all the materials are grown. Pigments are added for colour, and the product can also be safely incinerated at the end of its life, with the CO_2 released being balanced by the CO_2 taken up in growing the raw materials.[113] A timber floor with particle board covered in lino would have an embodied energy of 1,963 MJ for the basic floor. A New Zealand figure for lino of 116 MJ/kg[114] contrasts with a Canadian value of only 40 MJ/kg.[115] This could be because linoleum is made in Europe and the US and has to be imported to New Zealand over long distances. In response to an enquiry an Australian firm said that all of their linoleum was made in Italy.[116] A flooring supplier gives flooring lino as 2.5 mm thick with a weight of 3 kg/m²,[117] but the 2.5 mm thickness would be for very heavy commercial or industrial use (it is called 'battleship lino', because that is where it was once used).[118] A thickness of less than 2.25 mm is recommended for domestic use.[119] If a heavy-duty lino is used for this domestic example, it should last the full 50 years given that the life of heavy-duty lino in commercial situations is

30–40 years.[120] This means that 1 m² of 2.5 mm lino has an embodied energy of between 3 × 116 MJ (the New Zealand figure) and 3 × 40 MJ (the Canadian figure), giving between 348 and 120 MJ/m². It also has to be stuck to the floor using a contact adhesive. A Canadian source gives the embodied energy value for flooring adhesive as 97 MJ/kg.[121] A flooring supplier states that an adhesive suitable for linoleum has coverage of 3 m²/l and a density of 1.3 kg/l.[122] The energy embodied in the glue for 1 m² of floor is therefore 97 × 1.3 ÷ 3 MJ, giving an embodied energy of 42 MJ/m². Total values for timber floor, lino and adhesive are shown in Table 18 above.

The same timber floor construction could be finished with varnished timber floorboards rather than with particle board. Kiln-dried dressed soft-wood has an embodied energy[123] of 2,204 MJ/m³, and if 25 mm boards are used each board has a volume of 3.5 × 0.15 × 0.025 m³. A total of 27 such boards will be needed for the floor. This gives a total volume of 0.35 m³ and an embodied energy for the boards for the whole floor of 771 MJ. Using the same figures of 731 MJ for the floor structure and 384 MJ for the three-coat varnish, and adding 771 MJ for the boards, the embodied energy for the boarded floor is 135 MJ/m².

A structural timber floor with particle board (total embodied energy 1,963 MJ) could be finished with a cement-based board and with ceramic tiles. According to a New Zealand manufacturer, the cement-based board is glued to the particle-board floor underneath, and the tiles are then glued to the cement-based board.[124] The cement board recommended for floors is 6 mm thick, and a sheet 1,500 mm × 900 mm × 6 mm weighs 12.5 kg, giving a total weight of 9.3 kg/m². The embodied energy of fibre cement-based board is 9.4 MJ/kg,[125] so for the area in the room under consideration the total embodied energy is 14 × 9.3 × 9.4 = 1,224 MJ. Using the value in Table 11, ceramic tiles 6 mm thick have an embodied energy of 315 MJ/m², making 14 × 315 = 4,410 MJ for the room. As for the linoleum, glue is assumed to have a value of 42 MJ/m², and 28 m² are needed as described above. The embodied energy for the glue is therefore 28 × 42 = 1,176 MJ. Thus the whole floor is 1,963 (timber floor) + 1,224 (cement-based board) + 4,410 (tiles) + 1,176 (glue) = 8,773 MJ. The floor finish should last 50 years.

Floors can also be made in concrete. The simplest finish is to power-float the slab when it is poured so that it is smooth and level, and then apply sealer to the concrete to stop any dust. Ready-mix concrete has an embodied energy of 2,350 MJ/m³.[126] A 100 mm thick concrete slab for a 14 m² room will have an embodied energy of 14 × 0.1 × 2,350 = 3,290 MJ. The number of coats of sealer depends on the porosity of the concrete,[127] and it is recommended that the sealer should be touched up in high-traffic areas, such as commercial environments.[128] For this comparison it is assumed that two coats are applied with an embodied energy equivalent to the varnish above, of 128 × 2 = 256 MJ, and that the floor finish lasts for 50 years. This gives a total value for the sealed concrete floor of 3,290 + 256 = 3,546 MJ.

A concrete slab with ceramic tiles would last 50 years and have an embodied energy over this time of 3,290 (concrete slab) + 4,410 (tiles) + 588 (glue) = 8,288 MJ. A concrete slab with carpet on the same basis would give 3,290 (concrete slab) + 18,672 (four lots of carpet and underlay) = 21,962 MJ. The starting embodied energy is 7,958 MJ.

Before moving on to the effect of cleaning over the floor's lifespan, it is worth reflecting on what Table 18 can tell us. The floors with the lowest embodied energy after 50 years are the hard floors, not the carpeted ones. The importance of considering the lifespan of a floor and its covering is also clear, since replacement cycles can have a big influence on the final outcome, as with carpet. Carpet has also been linked to poor indoor air quality because of the problem of dust mites. Mattresses harbour the most dust mites in a house, but dust (human skin cells) gets trapped in carpet fibres and provides the mites with a food source. As Hasselar notes, the temperature of the carpet is important: higher humidity, such as occurs in thick carpets on cold floors, favours the proliferation of dust mites.[129] For this reason some people advocate not having carpet in cold, damp houses.[130] The problem is that is the very situation where we want to use carpets: as an insulation material for the feet when floors are cold. Some also argue that carpets trap other allergens in their fibres, and that it is these fine dust particles that are more likely to cause asthma.[131] Without knowing whether the houses studied were warm or cold, all we can say is that hard floors have less impact on the environment. The other point about living with hard floors is that the build-up of dust and dirt is immediately apparent, so the floors tend to get cleaned regularly. Carpet can look good even when there is dust trapped between the fibres.

CLEANING SUCKS

A floor with carpet has to be cleaned with a vacuum cleaner. A discussion paper by the French Centre Scientifique et Technique du Bâtiment (CSTB) on the environmental labelling of vacuum cleaners for the European Commission[132] suggests that, to achieve an eco-label, a vacuum cleaner should have an embodied energy content of no more than 700 MJ and a lifetime of no less than 550 hours, spare parts should be available for at least 10 years after production has stopped, and the energy to clean 10 m² of carpet, assuming 5 strokes over each part, should be not more than 250 Wh. If an eco-label represents an efficient vacuum cleaner with a reduced environmental impact, it would seem appropriate to use these figures when considering the cleaning of a carpeted floor over its lifespan.

If a vacuum cleaner should last 10 years, we can say that over a 50-year lifespan the embodied energy of cleaning would be 5 × 700, or 3,500 MJ, since five cleaners will be needed. The energy to vacuum the 14 m² living room once will be 350 Wh. The Carpet and Rug Institute recommends vacuuming twice a week – if not the whole house, then at least high-traffic areas.[133] *Good Housekeeping* magazine recommends cleaning high-traffic areas every day, using 7 strokes over each piece of carpet, but acknowledges that once or twice a week is more realistic, and that 3 to 4 strokes are adequate for lightly used areas.[134] Generally, the more a carpet is vacuumed and providing the 'no shoes worn in the house' rule is applied, the better it will look for longer. Assuming, therefore, that the living room is vacuumed twice a week, the annual energy use for cleaning will be 350 × 2 × 52 Wh, or 36.4 kWh/year. Over the 50-year life this would work out at 6,552 MJ. Significantly, both the energy for cleaning and the energy embodied in the vacuum cleaner are less than the energy that goes into having the carpeted floor. The operating energy of the vacuum cleaners is less than twice their embodied energy.

Although a floor covered with lino can also be vacuumed, there are other ways of keeping it clean, such as sweeping and washing; indeed, dry, non-chemical cleaning methods are seen as one of the environmental advantages of using lino over other floorings.[135] It is also possible to buy a broom with a lifetime guarantee.[136] The embodied energy of a broom is around 1 MJ (assuming softwood that has been air-dried and dressed).[137] It could be argued that a lino floor would be washed over the course of its lifespan to remove scuff marks, but a carpet might also be washed regularly, so for this first analysis only 'dry' cleaning methods are considered. It is assumed that a bamboo carpet-beater has an embodied energy similar to a broom. A rug can be removed and taken outside for beating to remove dust, but this is obviously not possible with a fitted carpet.

To bring all this together, Table 19 sets out the environmental impact of the choice of floor, its maintenance and renewal over the life of the building, and the cleaning required for a typical living room measuring 4.0 m × 3.5 m over the building's 50-year life.

Table 19: Embodied and cleaning energy for a living room floor over 50 years (*MJ*)

floor construction	floor covering	embodied energy of floor and covering	embodied energy of cleaning tools	operational energy of cleaning	total energy after 50 years
timber	fitted carpet on particle board	20,635	3,500	6,552	30,687
timber	lino on particle board	7,420 (high)* 4,228 (low)*	1 (sweeping only)	0	7,421 (high)* 4,229 (low)
timber	floorboards with varnish and fireside rug	4,748	2 (floor swept and rug beaten outside)	0	4,750
timber	ceramic tile floor on lining, with fireside rug	11,635	2 (floor swept and rug beaten outside)	0	11,637
concrete	polished power-floated concrete with fireside rug	6,408	2 (floor swept and rug beaten outside)	0	6,410
concrete	tiled floor with fireside rug	11,150	2 (floor swept and rug beaten outside)	0	11,152

* High and low energy values for lino are taken from Table 18 and the related discussion on pp. 165–66.

What Table 19 shows us is that choosing a hard floor over a fitted carpet is always better in terms of life-cycle energy, even when a wool rug is included. The cleaning is simpler because it can be done by hand with minimal tools. However, even if the highest-energy floor – the timber floor with ceramic tiles – is cleaned with a vacuum cleaner, its life-cycle energy is 29% less than that of a fitted carpet. Obviously it could be argued that carpet could last longer, but an old carpet may well be a problem when it comes to indoor air quality because of the potential build up of allergens within it. The old wisdom was that solid floors were better for someone with a health problem like asthma;[138] they are certainly also the route to take if you are trying to reduce your environmental impact.

KEEPING THINGS SWEET

If you want good indoor air quality, you will also need to be careful what you do inside your house. It is not simply a question of using natural materials and finishes or those that give off lower gas emissions, though it would obviously be sensible to choose paints that don't use chemical solvents, such as those that have various environmental labels.[139] The following statement, from a Dutch study into the allergy-free house, is pertinent:

> The house is smoke-free, without air fresheners, perfumed candles or a wood-burning stove, a fireplace or a heater without connection to a flue-gas exhaust pipe. In the house, no pets with hairs and feathers are allowed and no excrement of other pets are [sic] found. Laundry is dried outside or with exhaust of damp air directly into the ambient environment and never into the house ... The flooring is hard, with washable carpets only. Interior decorations are kept dust-free and free of irritating emissions.[140]

Behaviour issues come first, and those to do with the building and its materials are lower down the list. In many ways, the air quality in buildings is as much up to us as it is to designers.

This brings the discussion back to where we started – the question of why we put so many resources into buildings at all. Right from the start, we encourage our children to play outside in both summer and winter (suitably dressed, of course). It is the school holidays as we write this at home, and we can hear the boy in the garden next door at a time when the outside temperature is around 11 °C. It is estimated that people in the West today spend almost 90% of their time in buildings,[141] breathing the air indoors whatever its quality rather than outdoor air, and being heated or cooled in the process, with all its attendant energy consumption. Why is there one rule for children and another for adults? Of course, not all outdoor air is automatically good air, especially in urban areas where pollutants from vehicles can build up. High-density city developments make it harder for winds to blow through and disperse these pollutants, meaning that the air brought into buildings already contains carbon monoxide and other chemicals that are not good for you. To these are added the chemicals that are already present within the building. Some will come from the building materials and finishes, but some will also come from you, as discussed above. All this suggests that the air inside buildings is likely to be more heavily loaded with contaminants than air outside buildings, so it might be better to spend more time outside.

USING THE EDGE

Using the terms 'indoor' and 'outdoor' eliminates a third category of built space: the building edge. By this we mean structures like arcades, verandas and covered pavements – all elements that provide shelter but that are effectively outside and need no energy to run. They are also generally lovely spaces to be in. The covered open-air market remains a popular place to shop compared to the air-conditioned mall, the modern alternative.

Table 20 on p. 176 compares a local market with a local supermarket in terms of environmental impact. Some assumptions have had to be made. The first is that a neighbourhood supermarket is 500 m², and that storage and loading facilities occupy 30% of the space,[142] resulting in 350 m² of conditioned space where you actually shop. The second assumption is that a market selling a similar range of everyday goods occupies an area of the same size. The market is made up of freestanding stalls, and the traders' vans are the on-site storage. Some open-air markets are also temporary, so that the market square can have secondary uses or host different types of market on different days, but this requires some permanent storage for the stalls. For this comparison, it is assumed that the outdoor market is permanent. The embodied energy for the supermarket is based on 4 GJ/m² for the basic concrete structure,[143] which accords with both Australian and New Zealand studies for commercial buildings, although these are rather old. These theoretical studies were for buildings with three to five storeys, over ten times the size of the supermarket considered here, and the smaller the building, the greater the embodied energy of the envelope compared to the volume of space enclosed. However, since the embodied energy values are similar to the figures for smaller residential spaces quoted earlier, in Table 2, they will be used here. (This is an area where further research would be useful.) To the basic value is added 1 GJ/m² for the finishes, which are generally much less lavish than for an office-type building, to give a total of 5 GJ/m².

The market stalls are assumed to be made of wood and together occupy the same 350 m² selling space. The same source quoted above for the energy of a simple concrete structure gives a three-storey wooden building an average embodied energy value of around 1 GJ/m². An investigation of the energy embodied in the materials of a home-made dog kennel (to be considered later, in Chapter 5) produced a value of 250 MJ for a 0.5 m² kennel, or 0.5 GJ/m². Assuming that wooden market stalls are more like a dog kennel than a three-storey building, we have taken a value of 0.5 GJ/m². Parking space for the traders' vans must also be found, so an extra 100 m² is added. To find the embodied energy of the car park, we need to know its construction. Finnish research shows conventional road construction to be 160 mm of asphalt over 250 mm of crushed stone, 250 mm of gravel and 250 mm of sand.[144] If the construction uses a geo-textile membrane on top of the subsoil, the surface could consist of 100 mm of asphalt over 350 mm of crushed stone.[145] Using the latter specification gives the embodied energy for 1 m² as 714 (asphalt[146] at 7,140 MJ/m³) + 662 (local stone at 1,890 MJ/m³) + 100 (membrane) = 1,476 MJ, or 1.5 GJ/m². This works out at 150 GJ for the whole car park. This same value will be used for the market place itself, which covers 500 m², so the total is (500 × 1.5) + 150 = 900 GJ.

The basic structure of the supermarket will probably last 100 years. How long the internal finishes might last is hard to guess, but for this study we have assumed a major refit every 25 years. Over 50 years this would give a total embodied energy of 4 × 500 (structure) + 1 × 500 × 2 (finishes/fit-out), or 2,000 + 1,000 = 3,000 GJ. Wooden market stalls are assumed to last

12.5 years, so over 50 years they would be replaced four times. This makes their embodied energy $350 \times 0.5 \times 4 = 700$ GJ. To this figure we must add the market place and the traders' car park, to give a total of 1,600 GJ.

Supermarkets use a lot of refrigeration equipment, with their freezers and chiller cabinets. Open markets use much less, though it would be fair to factor in some use of portable refrigeration systems. To do this, we first have to know something about energy use in supermarkets. It has been claimed they are the most energy-intensive commercial buildings of all, consuming 3–5% of all electricity use in industrialized countries.[147] In supermarkets about half the energy used is for refrigeration,[148] although a US Environmental Protection Agency (EPA) study quotes a figure of 35% for grocery stores,[149] which might be more representative of the small super-market under discussion here. Lighting also accounts for a significant amount of energy use, since most supermarkets are large boxes with little, if any, natural daylight. The EPA study also gives average energy use as 213.1 kBtu/ft^2 (2,500 MJ/m^2), while a Vietnamese study found that supermarkets used 2,987 MJ/m^2.[150] Using the lower figure, we can work out that 2,500 × 0.35 = 875 MJ/m^2 is consumed by refrigeration in supermarkets. Since items that are chilled in supermarkets, like cheese, fruit and vegetables, may well be sold at external temperatures in open markets, a lower value of 200 MJ/m^2 has been used for portable refrigeration.

The Energy Star programme in the US reports that one supermarket chain awarded the Energy Star Sustained Excellence Award four times cut its total energy use across all of its stores by more than 27%[151] while still expanding the number of stores. The EPA study showed that 15% of a supermarket's operating energy could be saved through the implementation of an energy efficiency strategy.[152] A Sainsbury's low-energy supermarket in Greenwich, London, was designed to save 50% of the energy of a conventional supermar-ket by powering the lights through renewable energy systems.[153] For the comparison in Table 20 (overleaf), two different 'low-energy' supermarkets are included: one achieved a 15% reduction by taking energy efficiency meas-ures such as better refrigeration equipment, better lighting and better management of energy use with no change in embodied energy; and one had a 50% reduction but saw an increase in embodied energy of 10% on account of the renewable energy equipment and other low-energy measures.

Table 20: Footprints for supermarket and open-air market shopping

	embodied energy over 50 years (GJ)	operating energy (GJ/year)	operating energy over 50 years (GJ)	total energy (GJ/year)	footprint (ha/year)
neighbourhood supermarket	3,000	1,250	62,500	1,310	9.7
low-energy supermarket (energy-efficient)	3,000	1,063	53,150	1,123	8.3
low-energy supermarket (energy-generating)	3,300	625	31,250	691	5.1
local open-air market	1,600	70	3,500	102	0.8

Perhaps the first thing to note is that shoppers' journeys to and from both market and supermarket have been ignored. Both the market and the supermarket are assumed to be local and equally accessible on foot. The comparison has assumed equal areas for both: in fact, the market could well be smaller because there will be less choice. Markets sell what traders have, whereas supermarkets stock a range of products that will all do the same job (they often give us customers more choice than we want). How small a supermarket could be if it offered less choice and what this would do to annual running costs are areas for more research. Of course, we have been taught over the years that to have a choice between twenty identical products is a fundamental freedom, but it does come at a price, as we see here.

As we expected, Table 20 shows that the market has a very much lower footprint than even the best supermarket, even though it serves the same purpose. Having a market outside means that there is no need to worry about indoor air quality, which is where this discussion began. Markets can also be temporary, so that the market place and the traders' car park, for example, could be used for other purposes at other times of the day or week. In contrast, a supermarket is dedicated space, and part of the reason they have such a high operating energy is the fact that they are open for very long hours. This is a behaviour problem. If we didn't want to shop at 9 or 10 pm at night, they would not stay open for us. The message is this:

if you are interested in reducing your personal impact on the environment, you should shop at your local market whenever possible. It is an activity with a much lower footprint than its alternative, and at the same time you will be getting yourself out of buildings and into the outdoor air. The economic impact on local shops of a new supermarket opening in the vicinity has been much debated,[154] but perhaps the environmental implications should also be added to the discussion.

EDGE SPACE AND HOUSES

Given that outdoor air quality is normally better than that indoors, what is the effect of having more 'edge space' around houses? In Wellington, New Zealand, Stan Swan has built his family a 5 m × 5 m × 2.5 m enclosure that is used for table tennis and other play activities, for drying the washing, and for growing plants that prefer more sheltered and sunny conditions.[155] The structure originally had walls of softwood trellis with a PVC roof on an existing concrete foundation. The open trellis was later backed with Vivak thermoplastic sheet[156] to make it more wind- and waterproof and hence more suitable for use all year round. The 1 mm thick plastic was fixed to the softwood trellis in panels and screwed onto a softwood timber frame, so the structure is effectively 'temporary'. Such a structure might be compared to the 'rumpus room': a games or recreation room made by filling the space under a raised timber house (quite common in New Zealand). But whereas this room is normally used only for play, an outdoor enclosure like Stan's has other uses, not least as a support for productive plants like runner beans or, in kinder climates, even grapes.

For the purposes of our comparison below, we have assumed that the outdoor shelter and the rumpus room both have a concrete slab, so what matters is the materials used for the walls and the roof or ceiling. We can assume that both structures also have softwood framing, so that too can be ignored. There will need to be a ceiling light in the more finished space of the rumpus room; the levels of light in the outside shelter will be generally higher, but it will not be so suitable for use at night. We will ignore the electrical work here, however. Both rooms will require some kind of door for access, so we have assumed double doors (as in Swan's example) that measure $2.0 \times 1.8 = 3.6 \text{ m}^2$.

The inside walls of the rumpus room will be finished in painted plasterboard. There will also have to be windows to let in the light: using the old rule of 10% of the floor area, we arrive at a window area of 2.5 m². This gives an internal wall area of 4 × (5 × 2.5) − 3.6 (doors) − 2.5 (window) = 43.9 m². The walls will need external cladding, for which we will use painted cement fibre board. The ceiling of painted plasterboard for the rumpus room has an area of 25 m², the same as the roof of the garden shelter. Operating energy has been added, since it is likely that the rumpus room will have some heat and light at certain times of the year; over one year we have assumed an average use of 5 kWh/day. The garden shelter is warm when the sun comes out but is otherwise unheated. From these dimensions and assumptions the following table (Table 21) has been constructed, allowing us to compare the embodied energy of two types of edge building.

We can draw a number of useful observations from Table 21. Because the rumpus room is heated and lit, the operating energy component has the greatest influence on the total 50-year energy comparison. Without operating energy the garden shelter (enclosed version) at 751 MJ/m² after 50 years is still 37% better than the rumpus room under the house in terms of the energy of its elements. However, whereas an unheated garden shelter will be warmed and dried by the sun, an unheated rumpus room under a house – unless it is permanently well ventilated (in which case you might as well be outside!) – could suffer from mould problems because of a build up of damp air. The lightweight, more temporary solutions work better in this instance because they rely on the weather outside: they are warm when the sun comes out and colder when it goes in. Because its roof is translucent, the way the shelter faces is not critical, whereas a conventional building would have to have its windows facing the sun in order to get any benefit from solar gain.

The embodied energy values of plastic are high, but because the plastic used here is thin (1 mm thick), they do not increase the total significantly. In the more conventional building, it is painting the walls both inside and out that increases the embodied energy of the materials over the structure's lifespan. The garden shelter lacks this type of finish, as would many edge buildings, meaning that their total impact will be reduced.

Do we need to spend so much time in buildings that are finished to conventional specifications, or could we spend more time every day in a

Table 21: Comparison of dissimilar elements of a rumpus room (conventional building) and a garden shelter (edge building)

RUMPUS ROOM ELEMENTS	area (m²)	embodied energy coefficient[157]	replacement cycle (years)	total at start (MJ/m²)	total at 50 years (MJ/m²)
12.5 mm plasterboard	43.9 (walls) 25.0 (ceiling)	5,890 MJ/m³	50	203	203
paint	68.9	115 MJ/l	10	63*	232†
fibre cement cladding	43.9	9.4 MJ/kg	50	408‡	408
paint	43.9	128 MJ/l	15	15	120
window	2.5	230 MJ/m² floor area[158]	50	230	230
total (no operating energy)				919	1,193
operating energy	25.0	6,667 MJ/year		0	13,334
total				919	14,527
GARDEN SHELTER ELEMENTS					
trellis	46.4	2,277 MJ/m³§	50	15	15
PVC roofing	25.0	93,620 MJ/m³	25	187	374
total (original, without plastic sheet)				202	389
plastic sheet	46.4	97,340 MJ/m³	25	181	362
total (revised design)				383	751

* Based on 3 coats at start and coverage of 15 m²/l.
† Based on 2 coats every 10 years.
‡ Based on 9.3 kg/m² for 6 mm thick sheet.
§ Value for kiln-dried, average, dressed, with 73 MJ/m³ added for CCA treatment. Trellis of treated softwood 25 mm × 12.5 mm × 12 m/m², making 0.0036 m³/m².

shelter that is not heated or cooled? Because such a structure is regarded as outside rather than inside space, it is more likely to be made of materials and finishes that have less embodied energy over the course of its lifespan.

However, we also come up against the fact that the real estate industry will probably view the seemingly more permanent rumpus room as adding value to the house, and therefore as a better investment. Once again, the notion of cost effectiveness is working against a more sustainable solution.

OLD IS BEAUTIFUL

The analyses above have assumed a life for buildings of either 50 or 100 years. Many buildings last much longer than this, but they still need to be maintained. Older structures can be renovated and repaired to extend their life, but once more this requires both material resources and energy. The question arises whether it is better to reuse old buildings or to invest in new ones. This is a very complex question, especially when the price of land is brought into the equation. Johnstone has undertaken research into the resource flows in New Zealand housing and found that the typical timber-frame house in New Zealand has a useful life of 90 years, at which point it is better to demolish it and start again.[159] In China, the period of 50 years is used for life-cycle assessment,[160] but there is also evidence that the rising cost of land there means that apartment buildings have been demolished after only 30 years, well before their useful life is over.[161]

A very useful study by the Empty Homes Agency in the UK compared carbon dioxide emissions over 50 years for six houses. Three were new-build: two to UK 2002 building regulations and one with measures beyond this. The other three were refurbishments, two of them with energy-saving features such as external insulation of solid walls or the installation of renewable energy equipment.[162] The study's conclusion is thought-provoking:

The study shows quite remarkably that despite very different approaches taken to producing new homes, the total CO$_2$ emissions for each [of the six houses] *were very similar.*

Broadly speaking, the new houses did have much lower operating energy, but their initial embodied energy, a large proportion of which was lodged in the new brickwork, was much higher than for the refurbishments, whose original brickwork was retained. The refurbished properties had slightly higher CO_2 emissions from operating energy, but over the 50-year life of the analysis there was little difference. A period of 50 years was chosen as the point at which most houses are likely to receive a major refit, such as having the windows replaced. However, this was a study of CO_2 emissions rather than footprint, and emissions will depend on the type of energy used in the manufacture of the various materials. These findings contrast with a 2007 theoretical study of the same issue by the Environmental Change Institute at the University of Oxford, who reported the following:

> From an energy perspective, there is ample evidence to support the assertion that there are long-term environmental advantages to be gained from replacing old, inefficient dwellings with super-insulated, airtight ones.[163]

What we can say is that refurbishing existing houses rather than demolishing them and building new ones could have the advantage of retaining urban continuity, in terms of both social community and physical appearance. But would this position change if new houses had zero operating energy, or even generated energy? We would have to compare them with the adjustments required to make existing houses just as efficient.

TO BUILD OR NOT TO BUILD...

Table 6 looked at the environmental footprints of making productive houses. Table 22 (below) combines these figures with information from the Empty Homes Agency report. The analysis was based on a period of 50 years. Three levels of performance are assumed for the refurbished house: extra insulation to reduce heating requirements; upgrading so that no heating is needed; and zero heating plus on-site renewable energy generation. The first level, insulation, could achieve a 50% reduction in space heating. This should be a simple step: we added insulation to our first refurbished house with solid brick walls in 1976 and measured an 80% reduction in space heating costs. The cost of the insulation at that time was the same as installing a central heating system, but the insulated house could be heated with a small wood-burner and from the heat given off by the solid-fuel cooker. Since the costs were the same, this thermal upgrading was effectively achieved at no extra cost. The money – and embodied energy – that would be put into a major refurbishment went instead into an energy-saving refit. It is assumed that the costs of achieving a 50% energy saving could be met by specifying a smaller or simpler heating system.

The EHA report states that the houses studied each contained an average of 33 tonnes of brick. Using a value of 3 MJ/kg,[164] we can work out an embodied energy of 3 × 33 × 1,000 = 99,000 MJ = 99 GJ. The Oxford report states that a new house incorporates 90 MWh of embodied energy, or 324 GJ. If we deduct the first figure, which represents the starting embodied energy, the balance would be 324 − 99 = 225 GJ for all other materials, making the brickwork 31% of the total. Mithraratne found that the embodied energy in the timber-frame walls of a house of about 100 m² was 25% of the total, and 31% for a brick-veneer timber-frame house.[165] The Baggeridge brick calculator estimates that a two-storey 100 m² house would need 10,800 bricks,[166] and Midland Brick gives the average weight of a brick as 2.8 kg,[167] making just over 30 tonnes of brick for the external walls. Table 22 uses the figure of 33 tonnes from the EHA report for the preserved portion of a refurbished house. For the moment, any additional embodied energy connected with regular repair and maintenance has been ignored. The Oxford report assumed, without calculation, that the embodied energy of a zero-energy house such as the BedZED[168] development could be 180 MWh (648 GJ). With Roger Fay we did an embodied energy assessment of the Melbourne Green Home in Australia and the zero-energy Hockerton Housing Project in the UK.[169] The initial embodied energy of the Green Home was calculated to be 2,026 GJ (16 GJ/m²). The figure for the Hockerton house was 2,866 GJ (17 GJ/m²). However, this included all floor coverings (ceramic tile), appliances and furniture. While the Green Home had a lower initial embodied energy, over a period of 100 years, which allows for maintenance, the Hockerton house had a lower embodied energy (29 GJ/m² compared with the Green Home's 36 GJ/m²). By year 20, the Hockerton house had a lower lifetime embodied energy than the Green Home because less maintenance in the form of

Table 22: Initial embodied energy and operating energy for different types of house over 50 years (all 100 m²)

house type	initial embodied energy (GJ)	energy generated (GJ)	operational energy, space heating over 50 years (GJ)	footprint (ha/year)
existing house, 50% energy reduction	225 (balance*) (99 for existing brickwork)		2,980	0.5
new house, 2002 UK regulations	99 brickwork 225 (balance)		1,060	0.2
existing house, zero operating energy	1,414 (balance*) (99 for existing brickwork)		0	0.2
new house, zero operating energy	1,513		0	0.2
existing house, 50% reduction, with generation	225	(−164†)	2,816	0.5
new house, 2002 UK regulations, with generation	324	(−328)	732	0.2
existing zero-energy house with generation	1,414	(−164)	0	0.2
new zero-energy house with generation	1,513	(−328)	0	0.175

* A value of 99 has been deducted to account for existing brick walls.
† Generation is through PVs on the roof; we have used the method shown in Table 6 to account for the energy used in their initial production. Although a new house can be given a favourable aspect, existing houses cannot, so values for generation from Table 6 are halved, assuming that an average 50% of existing houses have a favourable aspect.

painting and replacing internal finishes was required. The total annual energy requirement of the Hockerton house was 0.09 GJ/m², but this was all energy for cooking, lights, appliances and hot water. Space heating was effectively zero. Taking Hockerton as a 'zero-energy' standard, the embodied energy of a 100 m² house would be 1,700 GJ. Most of this energy is accounted for by the concrete used in the structure, which also acts to store heat. Losing 11% for furniture and appliances at the start makes a total of 1,513 GJ.

The figure for space heating energy is taken from the modern house in Table 2. According to the Resurgence home energy audit calculator, an unimproved 120 m² semi-detached house in the UK uses 39,703 kWh/year for heating, which works out at 1,191 MJ/m². A saving of 50% would reduce this figure to 596 MJ/m².

The table agrees with other UK reports in showing that new houses can be good for the environment. Yet there are problems with the comparisons. The first problem is that only initial embodied energy is compared with the operating energy for 50 years. As we have pointed out above, although it has a high initial embodied energy, a thoroughly insulated house such as Hockerton needs less maintenance, so if this were included we could well see a difference. Another difficulty with this table is the fact that the Hockerton figures have been calculated using an Australian hybrid method developed by Treloar,[170] which is much more inclusive and gives higher results, meaning that the figures quoted here for zero-energy houses may be overestimated. As with all work on embodied energy, it is very hard to compare data from different sources. However, the key message is that maybe we should stop arguing about what we should do and start to improve the energy performance of our houses. Whatever we choose to do will reduce their environmental impact.

Because zero-energy houses for a cold climate like the UK often include lots of mass in the form of insulated masonry and concrete, they do – as Fay's study shows – tend to have reduced embodied energy in the long term because of reduced replacement and maintenance cycles. Table 23 considers the same energy data as Table 22 but measures its impact over a 100-year life. Once again, it ignores the effect of lower maintenance for the zero-energy solutions. At 50 years, ordinary houses are assumed to be stripped back to the shell and renovated, so this same value for the energy involved in upgrading joinery and services is applied also to the zero-energy houses.

Both tables show that, when it comes to reducing environmental impact, the critical issue is not so much new build versus the refurbishment of existing houses as longevity. If houses are designed and built to last 100 years, they should be built in such a way that they need no space heating, even if this raises the initial embodied energy significantly. So if we really want low-energy buildings, the key is zero space heating (or zero space cooling, depending on the climate) combined with a long life – not worrying about embodied energy. Long life also brings responsibility. A long-life building has to be well mannered (like a Georgian townhouse) rather than flamboyant, so that it does not date; it needs to be flexible in how it can be used; and it should also be built in such a way that materials are protected and the whole is easy to maintain. These are not the concerns of many designers and architects today.

However, like the reports discussed above, the analyses in Tables 22 and 23 are based only on the energy needed for space heating. Figures from

Table 23: Comparison of initial embodied energy, 50-year renovation embodied energy and operating energy over 100 years (all houses 100 m²)

house type	embodied energy at start (GJ)	embodied energy over 100 years (GJ)	operating energy, space heating over 100 years (GJ)	total embodied and space-heating energy (GJ)	footprint (ha/year)
existing house, 50% energy reduction	225	450	5,960	6,410	0.5
new house, 2002 UK regulations	324	549	2,120	2,669	0.2
existing house, zero operating energy	1,414	1,639	0	1,639	0.1
new house, zero operating energy	1,513	1,738	0	1,738	0.1
existing house, 50% reduction, with generation	225	450	5,632	6,082	0.5
new house, 2002 UK regulations, with generation	324	549	1,464	2,013	0.15
existing zero-energy house with generation	1,414	1,639	(−328)	1,311	0.1
new zero-energy house with generation	1,513	1,738	(−656)	1,082	0.08

British Gas[171] on the average UK expenditure for space heating, water heating, cooking, and lights and appliances show a split of 28%, 22%, 10% and 40% respectively. This means that buildings with zero space heating will have to start generating energy if they are to offset these other demands. The figure for lights and appliances is of course also connected to behaviour: the more electronic appliances we have in our homes, the more this type of consumption goes up. The larger our homes, the greater our demand for lighting and also, to some extent, for appliances. The model of the family sitting around one television in a sitting room has been replaced by family members viewing individual televisions in a number of rooms.

In many ways, the decision as to whether we have these sorts of buildings is up to us. We are in control of many of the replacement cycles of items inside the home. We can choose to have finishes and fittings that are going to weather well and be easy to repair. Melamine-faced chipboard – the stuff of most kitchen cupboards – is not easy to repair, whereas painted timber is. We can choose not to rip out a perfectly serviceable kitchen just because we have moved house and want a change (see below). We can choose to keep on top of home maintenance and repairs so that small jobs do not become big jobs.

A KITCHEN TO DIE FOR

The biggest problem with houses is that many people see them as investments rather than just somewhere to live for which one has to pay. Our earlier analysis of bathrooms showed that having one bathroom rather than several was better for the environment. But the investors' view is the opposite: in the US, building a second bathroom can add up to 20% to the value of your house when you come to sell it.[172] The same is true of kitchen renovation: a new kitchen is seen as a selling point. A study by Florida State University found that an extra bathroom added 24% to the house value, an island kitchen added 5.3% and a double oven nearly 9%.[173] A real estate agent in the US states that giving the average kitchen a total makeover costs US$15,000–20,000 before the purchase of new appliances, but that, if done correctly, it should give a return on the investment of 80–90%.[174] An Australian website claims that kitchen makeovers are among the most common home renovation projects, although it also advises that you should not spend more than 10–15% of the house's total value on your new kitchen.[175]

The problem is not so much actual values but the general perception that renovating a kitchen will add value to your house. Of course, there is also the environmental impact of all this activity to consider. To calculate this, certain assumptions will have to be made. The first is the type of kitchen, for which we will assume a simple galley kitchen against the long wall of a room 3.6 m × 2 m. If we assume a freestanding fridge at one end, and also a cooker and a dishwasher, each 60 cm wide (the washing machine will be in a separate utility room), we have a run of base cupboards 1.8 m long. There will also be a work top with a sink in it. Assuming there is a window over the sink, there will be room for a 1.4 m run of wall cupboards. Table 24 (overleaf) sets out the components of the kitchen and their embodied energy values.

The first point to note is that most of the kitchen items can last a long time, with the exception of paint finishes and then the appliances. Paint on most house walls and ceilings is easy to maintain, and most appliances can be replaced without ripping out the whole kitchen (the possible exception being built-in hobs and ovens). Within the new kitchen, the items with big embodied energy values are the appliances.

Finding out how often kitchens are replaced is difficult. Table 25 (overleaf) demonstrates the environmental impact of keeping the same basic kitchen over a period of 50 years, repairing and replacing items as necessary, compared with replacing the whole thing at intervals of 10 and 25 years. Even for a modest kitchen like the one analysed above, a strategy of repair and replacement as necessary gives a 35% reduction in footprint over renovation every 10 years. The big issue influencing the result is the short replacement cycle for appliances, so making them last as long as possible is good. What has not been factored in here is the fact that new energy-saving appliances will reduce the operating energy component, which in fact will be larger than the embodied energy. An old fridge might use two to three times the energy of a new, efficient model.[176] What we need most, however, are new energy-saving appliances that will also last a long time or that can be repaired to extend their life. The good news is that many manufacturers will take back old appliances for recycling, helped by projects such as the Appliance Recycling Centers of America[177] and a local government initiative in New Zealand.[178]

Table 24: Embodied energy of a new kitchen

kitchen component	size or quantity	embodied energy value (MJ)	potential lifetime (years)
base cupboards (chipboard, hardwood doors)	1.8 m run	290	25
wall cupboards (chipboard, hardwood doors)	1.4 m run	95	25
worktop (imported granite, 25 mm thick)	1.4 m²	616*	50+
sink (stainless steel) and taps		428	50+
flooring (ceramic tile)	4.2 m²	1,323	50+
cooker	1	1,258†	13+
refrigerator	1	2,516†	13
dishwasher	1	1,258	13
paint (three coats)	16 m²	345‡	10
total		7,634	

* Based on 17,610 MJ/m³ for imported stone.[179]
† Value based on the estimated figure for a dishwasher given earlier and doubled for a full-height refrigerator.
‡ Assumes 3 l at 115 MJ/l.

Table 25: Environmental impact of different renovation strategies for a small kitchen

strategy	embodied energy at start (GJ)	embodied energy at 10 years (GJ)	embodied energy at 25 years (GJ)	embodied energy at 50 years (GJ)	footprint based on 50 years (GJ/ha)
repair and replace as necessary	7.6	8.0	18.8*	24.5†	0.18
full replacement at 25 years, with repair and replace in between	7.6	8.0	18.8	32.1	0.24
full replacement every 10 years	7.6	15.2	22.8	38.0	0.28

* Based on two full sets of appliances by year 25.
† Based on one further set of appliances by year 50.

CONCLUSION

The message we can take away from this analysis of buildings is that, by concentrating on trying to improve design and building technologies and materials, we may have missed a very important point. To reduce our environmental impact in terms of footprint we need to have less, which means living in and using smaller buildings. Once we accept this fact, we will find that smaller buildings also cost less, so there will be money left over to invest in the more expensive renewable energy systems to further reduce our footprint. Also important is the fact that smaller buildings need fewer resources to go into them, not only at the start but over their lifetime. The longer a building lasts, the lower is its impact on the environment, providing it can be kept in good repair.

This is bad news for a design industry predicated on the idea that new and innovative is better. Long-lasting buildings cannot be fashionable otherwise they soon look dated, and designing for easy repair and long life tends to mean that trusted ways of doing things are preferred over the experimental and the daring. A sustainable built environment could have very different visual characteristics from what is currently displayed as good taste, and therefore desirable, in glossy design magazines.

It also emerges that current discussions surrounding the 'healthiness' of buildings focus largely on their materials, ignoring the influence of user behaviour. It is up to us not to pollute the indoor air of buildings, whether at home or at work, with unwanted chemicals that we have been persuaded to buy for one reason or another.

There are some simple lessons for us to take home:

- Small is more sustainable.

- Repair is vital, so that what you have can last a long time.

- Indoor air quality in the home is largely under your control.

- Using semi-built space and spending more time outdoors are both worth considering.

4
STUFF WE HAVE
AT HOME

CLOTHING

CUT YOUR SUIT ACCORDING TO YOUR CLOTH

The issue of clothing seems simple. We just need to replace fabrics that are not sustainable for whatever reason with fabrics that are. Fabrics are made of fibres woven or knitted together, while the fibres themselves can come from plants (cotton, linen, etc.), animals (wool) or insects (silk), or can be man-made (nylon, polyester, etc.). Cotton – although still very common, pleasant to wear and easy to wash – is known to have a high impact on the environment because of the fertilizer, water and pesticides that are needed to grow it. Looking just at pesticides, a WWF paper on the 46 chemicals used for killing mites and insects that form 90% of all pesticides bought in the cotton industry lists 5 as 'extremely hazardous', 8 as 'highly hazardous', and 28 as 'moderately hazardous'.[1] Not only are workers at risk, but the run-off can damage wildlife in surrounding ecosystems. There is also a worry that cotton pests are becoming resistant to the chemicals. So if cotton is a bad choice of fibre, what might we use as a substitute? Polar fleece can be made from recycled plastic bottles and can be made fluffy to retain body heat, so why not just substitute combed fluffy cotton with polar fleece? Dyersburg Corporation has done just that: having been the first to develop knitted fleece fabric in the 1930s, it moved away from the manufacture of combed-cotton gloves and long johns to become a leader in acrylic fleece production by the mid-1970s. It was the first to introduce polyester fleece made from recycled plastic bottles, in 1993.[2] At the same time the company changed from a family business to a New York-based corporation.

This last fact seems significant. Modern fabrics and clothing rely on large industries to grow, process and supply them to the consumer. It is hard to grow your own clothing ... or is it? You could have a sheep in the garden, just as President Woodrow Wilson had sheep grazing at the White House to keep the lawn trimmed.[3] For grazing purposes, 2–3 ewes could fit onto an acre of grass.[4] This would mean a pasture (or lawn) that measured 13 × 100 m for each sheep, or that the classic New Zealand quarter-acre section (the traditional house plot of just over 1,000 m²) could accommodate a single small sheep with a bit of supplementary feeding. However, this same area would represent the back gardens of 5 or 6 terraced houses in the UK. This small sheep might produce 3 kg of wool a year, which could be knitted into 4 adult sweaters, given that a hand-knitted sweater uses about 700–900 g of wool. Another common measure is the fact that a single fleece gives enough wool to make a man's suit. This shows us that one sheep between a family of four is not going to go very far unless you are very careful with your clothing and make it last.

Moreover, it takes a lot of time to make clothes at home from such raw resources. Spinning wool by hand – although a pleasure for some because of the soothing, repetitive actions – takes time. It could take 48 hours to spin the wool for your sweater, and not many people today are prepared to do this. It is hard to produce the raw materials for clothing at home sustainably, which is why most fabrics and items of clothing are produced by large corporations.

So what is the alternative? If we cannot produce the raw materials at home, maybe we can source them locally rather than globally and make them into clothes ourselves. Here the experience of Kelly Cobb at Philadelphia's Institute of Contemporary Art might be salutary. Her ambition was to make a suit of clothes from resources found within a 100-mile radius (161 km). She found that she needed three sheep fleeces (in this case from sustainably produced sheep called Sunny, Thunder and Magic) that could be spun into wool and used to knit socks and underpants or made into cloth for trousers, a shirt and a tie. The whole task took some 500 hours of labour and cost just under US$3,000. The final outfit (which even included shoes made from buckskin) also looked as if it had been hand-spun and hand-made, lacking the familiar professional finish of off-the-peg garments.[5]

The lesson we can drawn from this experiment is that it takes many human hours to turn raw materials into clothes by hand. We have cheap clothes simply because fossil fuels are used to run machines that do all this work in a much shorter time. We also have cheap labour in many developing parts of the world to make the process affordable. But what will run all these machines after peak oil? Where will cheap labour come from once the developing world has developed?

Land is also an issue, since land is required to grow the fibres, be they from animals or plants. Rayon, although a man-made fibre, is produced from the cellulose in trees, so land is still needed to grow the raw material. There seems to be a relationship between cost and the amount of land required to produce the fibre for a standard garment, as shown in Table 1, which uses a man's suit as an example. The table includes the land needed to grow the basic fibre, and, for man-made fibres, the amount of land that would be needed to the grow trees to produce the energy to make them. In fact, a certain amount of energy would also be required to process the fibres into the finished suit, depending on the fibres used, but this has been ignored for the purposes of this analysis. A discussion of how these values were arrived at can be found below.

THE SUIT ON YOUR BACK

COTTON

According to the Indian Ministry of Textiles – and India accounts for 27% of all the land that grows cotton – the average figure for world production is 560 kg/ha, whereas Indian production averages 300 kg/ha.[6] India, the US, China and Pakistan together dominate the world's production of cotton, accounting for about two-thirds of world output. Much cotton is both produced and consumed in the developing world, but despite this it remains a highly traded commodity, with approximately one-third being exported; the US is the dominant exporting nation.[7] So the cotton industry is complex and also highly variable in terms of productivity. Moreover, from the high use of pesticides and herbicides in the industry we can see that it is highly reliant on chemicals and hence on limited resources.[8] (The organic cotton industry is still in its infancy.) We have estimated that a cotton suit weighs 2 kg, so if we use the figure for world average production, an area of 0.0036 ha or 36 m² (the size of a GP's waiting room) would be required to produce the necessary fibre.

Table 1: Footprints of making a man's suit from different fabrics

fibre	land area (ha)	land area (m²)	other resources*	other products
wool (grass-eating pet)	0.13	1,300	TLC/sheep dip	mutton
wool (Australian farm)	0.08	800	supplementary feed/sheep dip	meat
cotton (2 kg suit)	0.0036	36	water/pesticides/ herbicides	short fibres
linen (2 kg suit)	0.002	20	water and possibly pesticides/herbicides	linseed/tow
hemp (2 kg suit)	0.001	10	water and possibly herbicides	hempseed/ hurd for paper pulp
bamboo (2 kg suit)	0.003	30	water and possibly pesticides/herbicides	not known
silk (2 kg suit)	0.03	300	not known	firewood/ local income
rayon (corn husks; 2 kg suit)	0.0055	55	water and chemicals	corn
rayon (wood, world average)	0.006	60	chemicals and water	n/a
rayon (eucalyptus pulp)	0.001	10	chemicals and water	n/a
nylon (1 kg suit)	0.002	20	'coal, water and air'	n/a
polyester (1 kg suit)	0.003	30	oil	n/a
polyester and cotton suit (1.5 kg)	0.00375	37.5		n/a
recycled polyester suit (1 kg)	0.001	10		n/a

* Fertilizer has been ignored in all categories. It is not needed for the single sheep kept at home, since the sheep provides all the fertilizer needed for the small area of land, but it would probably be required for all the other crops.

WOOL

The situation regarding wool is also very complex, since sheep give us two products: wool and meat. An Australian source gives an average wool yield from sheep farmers as 34 kg/ha, with variation between 15–69 kg/ha.[9] Even without the meat output, it is easy to see that wool is much less productive than cotton, even though it is potentially easier to grow at home and to make into clothes. In fact, wool is not a valued commodity at present and farmers are getting out of sheep rearing. Because it costs money to shear a sheep – often much more than the value of the fleece itself – wool production is frequently unprofitable. Skills are lost, and a fibre that could be raised in climates like that of the UK, where cotton cannot be grown, is supplanted by cheaper fibres imported from elsewhere. There is no plan in Europe to make the continent self-sufficient in fibre for clothing, even though history shows that parts of Europe became wealthy from raising sheep and exporting wool products.

LINEN

Linen, which has a much older history than cotton (Egyptian mummies have been found wrapped in linen), is made of fibres extracted from the flax plant. A Dutch source gives the output per hectare of flax plants harvested at the correct ripeness as follows: 1 ton (presumably 1 tonne) of long fibres between 60 and 90 cm in length, which can be spun; 1 ton of short fibres of 10–15 cm (called 'tow', which can also be spun into a rough cloth or used for stuffing cushions, or starting fires, as in the past); 3 tons of shiv (a woody waste that was once burned as a fuel but is now used for making chipboard); and 1 ton of linseed, which can be eaten by people and animals or from which linseed oil can be extracted.[10] Although in the past flax was processed by hand, the work is now done by machines; even the process of 'retting' – whereby the harvested plant is left for micro-organisms to break down the inner stalk, leaving the useful longer fibres that lie close to the surface – can be artificially controlled with enzymes or carried out with steam. From the figures above, it seems that flax would yield more fibre than cotton for the same area of land, so linen would be a good choice for clothing. However, the natural retting of flax, with the anaerobic decomposition it involves, can cause pollution problems.

HEMP

Hemp is often put forward as a more sustainable fibre, despite (or perhaps because of) the fact the best hemp fibre comes from the cannabis plant. In some countries a variety known as industrial hemp, which has a very low content of the psychoactive ingredient, is grown for pulping for paper-making, for cloth fibre and for its seed (valuable as a raw material in the production of oils and pharmaceuticals). The long bast fibres are attached to the outside of the pithy stem; the inner part is known as the 'hurd' and, as with linen, needs to be retted to break down the pectin that binds the long fibres and the stalk together. Canadian studies suggest that the yield of bast fibre is 2.9 t/ha/year, with 5.5 t/ha/year of hurd that can be used for making paper or as an ingredient of fibre board.[11] This is a higher production of bast fibre than for flax, and would mean that the 2 kg of fibre needed for a man's suit could be grown on 0.0007 ha. Another source suggests that hemp produces 2–3 times the amount of fibre for the same area as cotton,[12] which would mean that the fibre for the suit could be grown on approximately 0.001 ha. Hemp was an especially important fibre in the past, since most ships' sails were made from it. India is still a main centre of production, although at present most hemp cloth comes from China. Unlike cotton, the growing of hemp does not rely on pesticides.

RAYON

Rayon, an artificial fabric based on cellulose fibres, has to be made from virgin trees (i.e. trees grown just for this purpose). It is also known as viscose. As in paper-making, the fibres are extracted from wood pulp using chemicals. Globally, as much woven cloth is made from cellulose as from wool. However, since much of the world's rayon comes from countries like Indonesia, where there is no guarantee that sustainable forestry practices are being used, care should be taken in buying clothes made of these fabrics. The cellulose is not recycled, nor is it recyclable, although rayon is biodegradable. Some rayon fabrics, such as Tencel, are made from trees grown in a sustainable way on land that is not suitable for growing food, and Tencel is also produced in such a way that 99% of the solvent used in the processing is recovered.[13]

    In terms of wood production (the raw material for rayon), the average amount produced by the world's forests is 2 m³ of wood for every 1 ha.[14]

Some figures from Alaska state that it takes 5.6 m³ of pulpwood logs and chips to produce 1 tonne of wood pulp.[15] The average productivity figure given above would suggest that a 2 kg suit of rayon would be grown from a forest area of 0.0056 ha. However, productivity rises in plantations grown expressly for pulpwood. Barr and Cossalter quote a productivity figure of 10–20 m³/ha/year from eucalyptus plantations in southern China.[16] This would reduce the land area needed for the suit to 0.0007 ha.

To convert the cellulose into fibre takes energy. Allwood et al. state that it needs 33 MJ to produce the material for a blouse of 100% viscose; they also claim that 50% of this energy is renewable as it comes from wood.[17] Assuming a suit would require more than double the amount of material used in a blouse, we arrive at an energy use of approximately 70 MJ, which equates to an additional 5.2 m² of land (0.0005 ha) to grow wood for energy (using the conversion of 135 GJ/ha as before). This gives a figure of 0.006 ha for a suit, assuming the world average forest productivity level and 0.001 ha for eucalyptus pulp.

Waste products from plants can also be used to make rayon. A research scientist at the University of Nebraska has a patent for the production of cellulose, and hence rayon fibre, from corn husks; he has stated that 3 lb of husks produce enough fibre for a T-shirt 150 g in weight.[18] Since 26% of the corn is kernel,[19] and the average yield is 5 t/ha, 3.7 t/ha of waste is produced. A man's suit takes 40 lb of husks, or 18 kg. This much waste would be produced from 0.005 ha of planted corn. However, to this must be added the land needed to grow the energy to convert the husk to rayon, making 0.0055 ha in total.

BAMBOO

Although trees are the major source of cellulose fibres for the rayon family of fabrics, short fibres from cotton-growing are also used, and new fibres such as bamboo are being marketed as more sustainable products.[20] Bamboo fibres can be extracted by steaming and boiling, which requires energy, and through chemical processes to make bamboo viscose, in a similar way to the production of rayon or viscose from tree cellulose fibres. However, it still takes land to grow bamboo. A Chinese source gives a figure for pulp from bamboo for paper-making, showing that 1 tonne of pulp can be extracted from 4 tonnes of bamboo culms. Bamboo for pulping has a growth rate of 1–5 t/ha/year.[21] This suggests that a hectare will yield a tonne of pulp, which could be made into viscose.

SILK

Raw silk production is still a home-based industry in parts of the world such as India. The Indian Silk Board states that a family of three can be supported by rearing silkworm on a mulberry garden covering 0.75 acres (0.25 ha).[22] Because areas of vacant land can be given over to growing the mulberry trees that the silk worms feed on, the poorest in society can benefit from silk production. It is claimed that almost 57% of the gross value of the product goes back to the grower. From a reported figure of 30,000 Rupees/acre/year from silk production and from an average price for raw silk of 1,100 Rupees/kg,[23] we can estimate a production of 27 kg/acre/year, or 67.5 kg/ha/year. This means that a 2 kg silk suit would require 0.03 ha. If the silk were guaranteed to have come from local growers, it would represent a responsible choice of fabric. Although more land is involved, the mulberry cultivation is labour-intensive and benefits those who produce the fibre directly.

NYLON

All clothing has a footprint, in that land is required to produce the raw fibres, be they plant or animal. The one exception would appear to be man-made fibres, which originate from fossil fuels. Nylon was the original man-made fibre, first produced in 1935.[24] At a fair in 1939 in San Francisco, DuPont exhibited a machine that simulated the production of silk, with coal, water and air being fed in at one end and a pair of nylon stockings emerging at the other.[25] Because of the original drive to replace silk stockings with nylon ones, nylon is still a very important fibre for hosiery and seems to have become synonymous with it. The same source used here describes a survey in World War II asking women what they missed most. Some 20% missed men, but 40% of women missed nylons.

Allwood et al. state that the energy needed to produce the basic nylon fibre is 160 MJ/kg, whereas the energy needed to grow and process cotton fibre is only 50 MJ/kg.[26] The chemicals used in the production of nylon are derived from non-renewable sources, so finding a sustainable way to manufacture them is likely to be problematic. As a result, for the moment we will consider only the energy it takes to make a nylon suit, should anyone want such a thing. Since the fibre is light, a nylon suit will weigh 1 kg, so the 160 MJ required to produce the fibre would come from 0.001 ha of land. To make the table above more accurate, the energy used in production should be added for the other fibres too. Using the figure of 50 MJ/kg for cotton would add 0.0004 ha to the value for cotton, to give a total of 0.0054 ha, rounded to 0.005 ha for a 2 kg suit. This suggests that the processing energy for grown materials is small and can be ignored. However, growing crops for energy in a sustainable future could conflict with growing crops for raw chemical feed stocks that presently come from petroleum. Because of this, the energy value of nylon has been multiplied by 1.5 (see the discussion of polyester raw chemicals below) to allow for this land, giving a total of 0.0015 ha, or 0.002 ha when rounded up, for the suit.

POLYESTER

Polyester, which is petroleum-based, has supplanted nylon to become the most-used man-made fabric. Cotton and polyester – which are often combined in fabrics – together account for 65% of total world fabric usage. However, energy is required to convert petroleum into fabric and, since petroleum is itself limited, man-made fabrics are not a simple substitute. It takes 11,724.2 Btu (12 MJ) to make one polyester knit blouse weighing 0.119 lb (0.05 kg),[27] giving this type of polyester a value of 12 × 20 = 240 MJ/kg. This would equate to 0.002 ha to supply this energy in a sustainable way. The basic chemical for making polyester fibre – DMT – accounted for 42.3% of the polyester blouse's total energy. This suggests that adding a rough 50% to the energy footprint would be a suitable way to account for growing the raw chemicals. This would give a total of 0.003 ha for a 1 kg polyester suit. A pure polyester suit, weighing in at about 1 kg, might not be a desirable item, so we also included in the table a suit of cotton/polyester mix (50:50), which weighs in at 1.5 kg.

There are fabrics made from recycled polyester materials, such as the various polar fleece fabrics mentioned at the start of this section. The firm Patagonia, which makes recycled polyester, has a programme to recycle existing polyester fibre. Some virgin polyester is usually added to the recycled product, but significant energy savings can be made. Patagonia's investigation of the process showed that manufacturing the raw chemical for polyester (DMT) consumed 72 MJ/kg, but this could be reduced to 18 MJ/kg if old polyester garments were collected in the US and shipped to the recycling plant in Japan, and to only 12 MJ/kg if the old garments for recycling were collected locally.[28] A large portion of the US collection figure came from transport energy for collecting garments within the US. DMT formed 42.3% of the total energy that went into the polyester blouse discussed above; making the fibre from the raw chemical (DMT) accounted for a further 6.8%, and making the fabric from this a further 37.9%.[29] So fibre that is recycled locally would have a value of 18 (recycled DMT) + (240 × 0.58) (0.58 is the balance of making the fibre, if we deduct the 42% normally accounted for by DMT) = 18 + 139 = 157 MJ/kg. Some virgin fibre is added to the recycled mix, but for the moment this is ignored. The footprint of a 1 kg recycled polyester suit is therefore 0.001 ha.

From all this, it would seem that hemp should be our first choice for a natural fibre, together with rayon from eucalyptus pulp and recycled polyester for man-made fibre. The fact that, at present, the first product is found in shops only rarely is thought-provoking. In the past, when fibres had to be grown locally, flax and hemp were common in climates like that of the UK. Both were processed similarly, by retting in water to free the long fibres which were then spun and woven into cloth. Retting dykes or ponds were usually separated from rivers or water where cattle would drink, since the retting process was thought to poison the water; Henry VIII had made a law to that effect. However, more modern methods are now used to separate the fibres, such as retting by steam. Hemp made a coarser cloth than flax. In *A Midsummer Night's Dream*, one of Shakespeare's characters refers to Bottom and his fellow artisans as they create their play, asking 'What hempen homespuns have we swagg'ring here?'[30] Thus hemp has never been associated with fine living and fine clothes. It is also connected with cannabis – a banned drug in many countries – which may also be inhibiting its wider use.

Recycled fibre looks like a reasonable option for man-made fibres. However, the source of the recycled material needs to be considered. Recycled polyester clothes have a low footprint, but there is a slight nonsense in continuing to sell soft drinks in plastic bottles just so that the plastic can be recycled into so-called environmentally friendly fabrics.[31] (As it is, the whole concept of soft drinks being sold in bottles is hardly sustainable. On the whole, the drinks have no nutritional value and may well do harm if they have a high sugar content, both nutrionally and to our teeth. Water from the tap would be a far more sustainable substitute and requires no bottles for transport.)

The very rough averaged figures on which our table is based also disguise the fact that production rates vary considerably in different parts of the world. Moreover, a fibre like cotton is often grown in one country, spun in another, woven in a third, made into clothing in a fourth country, and worn in yet another. Local customs related to local industry and local production, which formed part of the traditional clothing industry in the past, no longer exist in the modern world

Another point to emerge from Table 1 is the similarity of the various fabrics in terms of land footprint. With one or two exceptions, such as wool and silk, the footprints are all of the same order of magnitude. In some ways this is to be expected in the current economic conditions. Since the market determines price, what is available are fabrics that all cost approximately the same, since they are competing with each other to do the same job. This suggests that, unless real alternatives like hemp and recycled cloth become available, we should not worry about the type of fibre but concentrate on buying quality fabrics so that the garments have a potentially long and useful life. There is a Mexican saying that those who are poor buy the most expensive goods.[32] Maybe buying fewer clothes for the same amount of money is the sustainable way of keeping a wardrobe. This is the opposite of the present situation: a market flooded by clothes so very cheap that they are seen as expendable commodities.

THE IMELDA MARCOS SYNDROME

The fashion industry has been blamed for having a bad impact on the environment by encouraging the idea that clothes are disposable. To an extent they are, since both general wear and exposure to the environment (sun, water, etc.) will begin to degrade fabric from the time a new garment is first put on. Slater suggests that the fashion industry has gained in importance since the Industrial Revolution, which produced the energy to run the machines that mass-manufactured textiles.[33] He also comments that clothes are a good way to display wealth and status in society, which is why the purchase of a new outfit by even the poorest is seen as important.

Allwood et al. give the UK consumption of textiles as about 35 kg/head,[34] about half of which is clothing. So each year a person consumes 17.5 kg of clothes. If they were all made of cotton, the area of land needed to grow the fibre would be 315 m². However, Allwood also gives a figure of 50 MJ/kg for the energy used in the production of cotton.[35] It would therefore take 0.875 GJ of energy to produce this weight of clothes. If this is converted to a measurement of the land needed to produce the energy, a further 0.006 ha, or 65 m², would be needed. Thus the total land required per person in the UK for their new clothes is about 380 m² a year. In 2005, 30.55% of all land in the UK was used for growing crops and forests and so could potentially be involved in the production of clothing.[36] This represents 7,274,750 ha. The population of the UK in 2005 was 60.2 million.[37] Thus for each person 0.12 ha, or 1,200 m², of land was available on a fair-share basis for all uses, including growing all food and energy in a sustainable way. To use virtually a third of this fair share for clothes does not seem a sensible thing to do. The current consumption of clothes in the UK thus appears a very long way from being sustainable, whatever basic fibres are used. The issue is one of consumption, not what our clothes are made of. So what might we call an acceptable wardrobe?

DON'T MENTION THE WAR (AGAIN)

During World War II, textiles were in short supply and were directed towards the war effort. This led the UK to introduce clothing rationing in 1941, along with a consideration of what a fair-share wardrobe might be and the amount of new textiles that could be consumed each year. In 1941 each adult was allowed 66 coupons a year, which was supposed to be the equivalent of one new outfit, including shoes (although the money still had to be found to buy the clothes). Growing children were allowed extra, and items like work clothing were exempt. Obviously some clothes would last longer than others, so a man's overcoat, which needed 16 coupons, was expected to last for 7 years. It was also better to make your own clothes, because 3 yards of woollen cloth for dressmaking (to give an example) could be had for 9 coupons, whereas a complete woollen dress was 11 coupons. Sewing thread and mending materials did not need coupons. To make some kind of comparison with the current UK situation, a pair of trousers for a man was 8 coupons and a jacket 13, which would equate to the 3 kg woollen suit discussed above. Very roughly, this means that the ration of 66 coupons represented 9 kg of clothing, about half the current UK consumption.

During the war, the buying and selling of second-hand clothes became important, as these were not on coupons. Swap shops, run by the Women's Royal Voluntary Service, were invaluable for mothers with growing children, since outgrown but serviceable clothes could be swapped. The recycling of clothes – by either reusing the fabric (making a woman's skirt from a pair of trousers, for example) or unpicking knitted woollens and reusing the wool – was also practised. Fashions were also geared to using little material and cutting it well. The Utility scheme of 1941 restricted both the amount of fabric that was used (so that men's trousers no longer had turn-ups) and the number of trimmings (so that a woman's jacket had only three buttons). However, even with such extreme measures Utility clothes were still elegant. Items that were not rationed were popular, such as wooden clogs. Prized pieces of clothing were handed round the family for use on special occasions.

Many of the initiatives listed above have been suggested as ways of making clothing more sustainable. Allwood et al. suggest that the leasing of clothing is one way of reducing environmental impact. Expensive items of clothing, like ball dresses, wedding dresses and formal suits, are already hired by many people since it offers an affordable way of dressing appropriately for a grand occasion. It is also better for the environment. Buying expensive clothes is also a good idea, since they will need no more fabric, are probably better made in the first place and, because they are expensive, they are less likely to be discarded so readily. Making clothes last longer by mending them seems so obvious that it is not worth commenting on, but the current fast-changing fashion industry means that clothes are being thrown away before they wear out, let alone before they need mending. Buying second-hand rather than new immediately limits environmental impact, and swapping rather than shopping is another suggestion that is often repeated. They are all ways of reducing our new consumption, and they would also means that many fewer perfectly serviceable garments will finish up in landfill (which accounts for 60% of all clothes disposal in the UK).[38]

ONE ON AND ONE IN THE WASH

If the life-cycle of a garment is examined, we see that the big issue is not the energy to make the clothes, transport them, retail them and dispose of them at the end of their life, but the energy required to wash them during their life, whether this is an estimated 25 or 40 washes.[39] Thus Allwood claims that 65% of the energy associated with a cotton T-shirt is in the use phase, since it is washed at 60 °C, tumble dried and ironed 25 times during its life.[40] Apart from the question of whether anybody really bothers to iron a T-shirt, this seems an old-fashioned washing regime in a world where cold washing powders work well, and clothes lines and pegs are still available in every supermarket. Moreover, you might expect there to be a correlation between wearing a T-shirt in warm weather and having warm weather outside in which to dry it.

The key point is not the impact of the individual garment, but the impact of washing all of one's clothes over the course of a year: however many clothes you possess, you will wash only the ones you actually wear. So what is the impact of laundering one's clothes and how does it compare with the impact of buying them?

We wash clothes to get them clean. Soiling comes from two sources: contact with the body (e.g. perspiration), and stains. Quite simply, this means that underclothes need to be washed frequently and top clothes need to be protected to prevent them from becoming unnecessarily dirty. If we look at the wardrobe of the average middle-class Victorian lady, this strategy is obvious. Undergarments were laundered weekly, but dresses were seldom washed, especially since washing a dress of complicated construction, with numerous trims of different fabrics, could require unpicking the garment and making it up again afterwards. Protective garments that were easy to launder, such as aprons and smocks (the latter worn especially by children), were also common. The aim was not to stain good clothes. Any stain is best dealt with immediately before it has time to set; this reduces the need to scrub, which is bad for the fabric and also harder work for the person doing the laundry by hand. This is a long way from our current practice of washing soiled clothes in a machine. Washing was avoided in the past because it was hard work, although the raw resources then consisted only of soap and water, and fuel to heat the water. Although they are better at getting clothes clean, today's detergents can add pollutants to the environment.

The following table, Table 2, shows the footprint of washing garments using the appropriate cycle in a machine, and washing by hand. It is assumed that a week's washing for one person consists of 1 skirt (or 1 pair of jeans), 4 shirts, with some being worn for more than one day, and sufficient underwear to have a new set every day. This forms a load of about 4 kg. This is equivalent to the 9 kg of clothing worn under rationing, as discussed above, which allowed for two full sets of clothes and a weekly wash ('one on and one in the wash'). Most washing machines will take a load of 5–6 kg, so it is assumed that a week's wash represents a full load, allowing space for additional clothing if a clean shirt every day is thought to be essential. To wash the same amount of clothes by hand would take two sessions using a sink full of water and detergent, followed by a sink full of cold water for rinsing, and it takes around 20 litres to fill the sink for an adequate wash. This means that 80 litres of water would be used per week to wash the same load of clothes by hand.

An A-rated washing machine in Europe is quoted as using 0.95 kWh and 55 l of water for the wash at 60 °C.[41] A cold-water wash in the same machine is given as taking 0.4 kWh. However, the washing machines coming onto the market continue to become more energy efficient, and the Australian rating system, which uses stars (the more stars a product has, the less energy it uses), lists a 5-star machine made in Slovenia that uses 0.4 kWh for each 6.5 kg load.[42] At the other end of the Australian scale, a 1-star machine uses 2.1 kWh for each warm wash of a 6.5 kg load, and 0.2 kWh on the cold cycle. This suggests that, whatever the star rating of the machine, if you wash in cold water all machines will perform much the same.

In order to compare the impact of washing clothes against that of providing clothes, Table 2 converts the energy used in doing the week's washing

Table 2: Ecological footprint of doing the laundry in different ways

appliance type	warm wash at 60 °C (energy)	warm wash at 60 °C (land)	cold wash (energy)	cold wash (land)	water use (l/year)
European A grade	49.4 kWh/year (0.18 GJ)	0.0036 ha (36 m²)	20.8 kWh/year (0.07 GJ)	0.0014 ha (14 m²)	2,860
Australia/NZ 5 star	20.8 kWh/year (0.07 GJ)*	0.0014 ha (14 m²)	?	?	2,725
Australia/NZ 1 star	109.2 kWh/year (0.39 GJ)	0.0078 ha (78 m²)	10.4 kWh/year (0.04 GJ)	0.0008 ha (8 m²)	5,610
hand washing	(0.17 GJ)†	0.0034 ha (34 m²)	0	0	4,160

* This appears to be a 40 °C wash.[43]
† This assumes that water is heated by 20 °C from delivery temperature using electricity or delivered energy at 100% efficiency of conversion, as would happen in a washing machine.

over the course of a year into the land required to supply the fuel for this on a sustainable basis. The data are taken from manufacturers' websites.

A number of points emerge. First, whatever machine is used, washing in cold water reduces the impact on the environment, so there is no need to rush out and buy a new machine – just an appropriate cold-water detergent. Secondly, hand washing in warm water is worse than washing in the best available washing machine, in terms of both energy and water use. Hand washing in cold water is better, but it uses more water than some efficient front-loading washing machines.

The third point is that the environmental impact of washing a weekly load of clothes is far less than that of buying a lot of new clothes each year. As we discussed above, the average UK wardrobe accounted for an annual footprint of 380 m². Even a reduced wardrobe of about 9 kg of clothing, or two sets to allow for 'one on and one in the wash' at any one time, would have a footprint of 158 m² if it were cotton, whereas the annual energy footprint of doing the weekly wash in warm water is 14–78 m² depending on the machine, or only 10–20 m² if a cold wash is used. This is one instance where the embodied energy of a product is greater than the annual operational energy required to use it. This is in contrast to the Allwood study, which found that the largest part of a T-shirt's life-cycle impact came from the laundry process. It is essential to link clothes back to user behaviour and how they are worn and washed rather than treat each garment as a separate item.

SOAP AND WATER

Energy is not the only way washing has an impact on the environment. Water and detergents are also required. Detergents have been associated with pollution of the environment, not least because they produce froth that can be seen in rivers and streams rather than in the laundry tub at home. Soap is the oldest type of detergent and for years was made at home. The function of the detergent is to reduce the surface tension of the water so that, rather than sitting as droplets on the surface of a material, it soaks in. The detergent also reduces the size of grease particles so that they can be washed out of the fabric easily. The detergent also keeps the dirt suspended in the water so it does not get into the clothes again. All this soap will do. A modern soap-based detergent will have 'builders' added, which in theory serve to make the clothes look 'white', to give lather – which is a disadvantage as lather must be rinsed out – and to stop the product going lumpy in the packet.[44] The use of whitener forms part of the history of laundry. In the past, whites were spread out over bushes and on grass to expose them to the sun, which stopped them going yellow;[45] anyone who has hung nappies out on the line to dry in the sun will appreciate the fact that sunshine soon removes any stains. 'Blue bag' was also used after the clothes had been rinsed: a small amount of blue pigment, such as Prussian blue, was added to the water and the clothes were then dipped in this for a short while before being hung out, again to stop whites going yellow.[46] Starch was also used frequently in the past (it is less common now), which had the important function of keeping clothes clean. The rinsed garments were dipped into a solution of starch before drying. As they dried, the starch filled the gaps in the fabric's weave, giving it a 'finish' but also stopping dust getting lodged, meaning that clothes would stay clean longer.[47]

Today, the processes that would have taken time have been replaced by the use of a detergent that contains a soap replacement, a bleach, and possibly an enzyme stain remover, so that all tasks can be done together in a machine, with clothes dried in a drier. Detergents have been blamed for adding nutrients to waterways through the phosphates they contain, leading to 'eutrophication' – excessive plant growth and decay that can upset the natural ecosystem, especially in confined waters such as lakes. Some detergent companies have become involved in cleaning up contaminated sites, such Barton Broad in Norfolk.[48] However, the eutrophication that comes from excess water nutrients in water courses is now thought to come largely from animal husbandry and sewage effluents rather than from detergents. An EU report states that a 70% reduction in phosphorus use is necessary to stop eutrophication, and in places where there is limited agriculture this requires both the removal of phosphates from detergents and better water-treatment practices to extract phosphorus from the effluent. In agricultural areas, good animal husbandry is also needed.[49] Most European detergents no longer contain phosphates as a builder.

As stated above, washing in cold water reduces environmental impact. Special detergents for cold-water washing are available, but even if they were not, a normal detergent could first be dissolved in hot water and this liquid used in a cold wash.[50] One potential problem of a cold wash is that, unlike in hot washes, germs are not killed. Adding the right amount of liquid chlorine bleach to a wash will disinfect it, but such chemicals are not ideal. Hanging clothes in the sunshine, the old way of killing germs, still remains the simplest.

Although the impact of detergents seems bad, a life-cycle analysis of a detergent found that most of the environmental impact of using a dose of modern detergent in the wash cycle came from the emissions associated with the electricity to heat the water in the washing machine, accounting for 80% of the total.[51] The detergents were assessed for acidification through the production of acid rain, for their toxicity to water and to humans, eutrophication, climate change (this would account for the emissions from water heating), ozone depletion and production of smog. The conclusions from this study were that compact powders had the least environmental impact, closely followed by compact liquids. However, because the wash phase is responsible for most of the impact, the advice remains that we should use cold-water detergents wherever possible. It is also advisable to use the exact dose of detergent required (as recommended in old books on laundry), since putting in more than necessary means that more rinsing is needed; soap left in the fabric will soon weaken it. This is another instance where lack of time may mean that we guess the amount of detergent rather than work it out correctly. The new single-dose detergents avoid the problem by doing the job for you, but they involve extra packaging to separate each dose. Again, to save time more resources are used.

It is also advisable to choose a detergent without chemical additives like perfumes. As we saw in Chapter 3, this type of chemical pollution is often overlooked.[52]

DRY CLEANING

In addition to the laundry done at home, some outer garments will, if normal behaviour patterns are followed, need dry cleaning, which will also have an environmental impact. The best way to avoid visits to the dry cleaner is to wear clothes that can be washed at home. To reduce our visits to dry cleaners, woollen outer garments like suits and jackets can be hung out to air between wearings; and clothes can be stored in dust-free cupboards with plenty of air circulation, not in plastic – all advice your great grandmother might have passed on.

Dry cleaning means using a solvent rather than water to remove stains from clothes. It is thought to be better for fabric because the solvents evaporate very quickly and the clothes remain wet for a shorter amount of time. In the early days solvents like paraffin and other petroleum-based products were used, but these have been replaced by chemicals which are less flammable.

The problem with dry cleaning is the use of perc, short for percholoethylene (also known as tetrachlorethylene). Perc is categorized as a Group 2A substance, which means that it is probably carcinogenic to humans. The concern is that it may enter drinking water supply if it leaches from disposal sites.[53] In 1998, 80% of dry cleaners in the US used perc, although the numbers had dropped and were expected to drop further as other systems were installed.[54] Alternatives to dry cleaning with perc do exist. One uses water and detergents, but in a method that involves little water and the careful control of the washing and drying processes. A method called GreenEarth uses a liquid silicone product (methyl siloxane) as the cleaning solvent for stains that are not water-soluble, although it does have a low flash point. Using liquid carbon dioxide in a revolving drum is another way of removing stains, as are petroleum-based solvents, although these also need handling with care.[55]

This suggests that we should ask dry cleaners what process they use and avoid the use of perc. In some places dry cleaners are listed according to the solvents they use – one such list is produced by the University of Minnesota – so consumers can make an informed choice.[56] The other objective is to avoid dry cleaning unless absolutely necessary. In the past, when there was no dry cleaning, clothes were organized so that the expensive outer wear – worn for self-expression and status as much then as now – was cleaned as seldom as possible. Undergarments between the body and the outer wear could be washed frequently, and easy-to-clean pinafores and aprons also offered some protection. The uniform is the logical extension of this approach, but whereas the uniform in many modern schools in places like the UK consists of outer wear (skirts, trousers, jackets and jumpers), in France and other European countries the tradition was that children should wear the same form of protective overalls over their own clothes. In France, the school smock,[57] worn by all children up to the age of 18, was abolished in 1968, although school uniforms continued in the UK. However, uniform protective wear still seems the best way to reduce the environmental impact of clothing, and protective overalls – still worn by all schoolchildren in Tunisia, for example – are cheaper than the school uniforms worn in the UK and New Zealand.[58] It seems that protective clothing has almost disappeared in modern society in favour of cheap clothing, washing machines and plentiful energy. In a sustainable future it may again become a common sight.

WRAP UP WARM

From all the discussion above, it may seem that the only sustainable thing to do is to take the path of nudism and wear no clothes at all. Yet in many places clothes have the important function of climate modification: without appropriate clothing it might not be possible to live there at all. However, as world population continues to increase, the human race will have to be less choosy about where it lives. Most of the ideal sites have already been occupied. So is it better to wear clothes or to heat or cool the space in which we live?

It is often stated that putting on an extra jumper is better than heating a building to a more comfortable temperature. A jumper is made from about 700–900 g of wool, which represents 0.02 ha of marginal land. However, sheep also emit methane, a greenhouse gas, so further land needs to be factored in for the absorption of the equivalent CO_2 emission. A UK study has found that sheep in a polythene tunnel emit 20.3 l of methane each per day.[59] This equates to 14.5 g/day, or 5.3 kg/year, though it was felt that this figure might be an underestimate. Sheep in colder environments might emit more because they eat more dry matter. Another source gives 36.1 ± 10.4 g/day, giving a range of 9.4–17.0 kg/year.[60] In New Zealand, however, it is estimated that one livestock unit gives off 11.5 kg methane per year, where a stock unit represents a 55 kg breeding ewe and the lambs she raises each year.[61]

Methane has a global warming potential over 100 years of 23,[62] meaning that 1 kg of methane is equivalent to 23 kg of CO_2 in terms of global warming potential. This means that one sheep giving off 11.5 kg of methane per year emits the equivalent of 265 kg of CO_2. Sheep can be used for both wool and meat production, although sheep bred for meat do not produce the best wool and vice versa, and fleece is produced every year and meat only when the animal is slaughtered. For this investigation it is assumed that all annual emissions are attributable to wool. If the sweater takes 800 g of wool, each year 3,000 ÷ 800 = 3.75 sweaters can be produced from one sheep. So a single sweater equates to an emission of 265 ÷ 3.75 = 71 kg of CO_2. As pasture that is not grazed will absorb CO_2 at the rate of 11 tonnes/ha,[63] this means that an area of 0.006 ha or 60 m² is required to sequester the emissions for producing an adult's sweater. Using the figure of wool production of 34 kg/ha (see above), the land required for the sweater is 0.02 ha. This gives a total of 0.02 + 0.006 = 0.026 ha, or 260 m².

Assuming someone puts on a sweater because they are cold, what sort of insulation does it represent? The insulation value of clothing is measured in something called the 'clo value', and the clo value of a long-sleeved heavy sweater is 0.37.[64] Markus states that the clo unit is equivalent to an

R-value of 0.155 m²-K/W,[65] which means that the insulation provided by the jumper has an R-value of 0.06 m²-K/W.

Looking at it another way, a school in Whistler in British Columbia had what was termed an 'Ice Age for a Day', in which the temperature was turned down by 3 °C and everyone wore an extra jumper and a hat. For senior grades the average class size is about 25.[66] We have assumed that a Canadian portable classroom was used for the experiment, and from the classroom's dimensions we have calculated the amount of heat that would have been lost (Table 3).[67] If the classroom is typically heated to 20 °C and the average outside temperature is 3.2 °C for the Howe Sound area in British Columbia, then to heat the classroom during the school day (8 hours) will take 216.8 × 16.8 × 8 = 29 kWh.

However, the children in the classroom will provide some of this energy from their own body heat. A child can be rated at 75% of an adult male.[68] The heat generated by the children will be 75% of 75 Watts, or 56 Watts. This ignores any heat coming through the window in the form of solar gain, and also heat from the lights. The heat coming from the children is 25 × 56 (W) × 8 (hours) = 11.2 kWh. This means that 29 − 11.2 = 17.8 kWh of energy is needed to heat the space.

If the same classroom has an internal temperature of 17 °C because the children are all wearing sweaters and hats on their 'Ice Age' day, the energy needed to heat the space will be 216.8 × 13.8 × 8 = 22.5 kWh. After taking away the heating effect of the children, we are left with 22.5 − 11.2 =

Table 3: Heat losses from a Canadian portable classroom

element	area (m²)	R-value (m²-K/W)	U-value (W/m²-K)	specific heat loss (W/K)
floor (6.93 × 9.55 m²)	66.2	2.70	0.37	24.5
roof	66.2	4.50	0.22	14.7
walls	63.1	2.70	0.37	23.3
windows (estimate)	16.0	0.15	6.67	106.7
ventilation	158.8 m³			47.6 (1 air change/hour)
total				216.8

11.3 kWh of heating. Thus the reduction in heating needed from wearing sweaters is $17.8 - 11.3 = 6.5$ kWh.

Assuming that the heating is electric in the portable classroom, and using an average figure for the CO_2 emissions related to electricity production of 0.5 kg/kWh,[69] the emissions saved per day will be $6.5 \times 0.5 = 3$ kg CO_2.

The emissions associated with 25 extra sweaters would be $71 \times 25 = 1,775$ kg, meaning that it would be better to heat the space rather than give every child an extra sweater for a single day. However, the picture changes if the 'Ice Age' is extended over the whole winter season.

Assuming there are 28 weeks of schooling for which heating has to be provided and that school occurs for 5 days a week, the emissions saved will be $6.5 \times 28 \times 5 \times 0.5 = 455$ kg. Thus, providing the children wear the same sweaters for four years, it would make sense to turn the thermostat down and wear extra jumpers.

What these calculations emphasize is that the implication of wearing extra clothes need to be taken into account. It could be argued the children already have the sweaters to wear, but if they wear them all day in school they will obviously wear out more quickly, and replacing them will mean growing more wool with all its attendant emissions. Will the balance change if there are fewer children in the classroom? Fewer children mean less heat gain. The results are shown in Table 4. Additional rows have been added to the table to explore the use of recycled fleece in place of woollen sweaters, assuming equal insulation values and 800 g of recycled fleece per garment, working out at 17.5 kg of CO_2 for each recycled fleece sweater.

Putting on an extra sweater may seem like an obvious solution, but it depends on what the sweater is made of and on the occupancy of the room. If you want to turn down the thermostat and all the children wear extra clothes of recycled fleece, then it might just be worthwhile in terms of CO_2 emissions. Under-occupancy of a space designed to hold a full class of children is responsible for significant emissions, whether the space is heated to a comfortable temperature or the children wear extra clothes. This can be compared to the discussion in Chapter 3 of the timetabled use of a single bathroom, which had a much lower environmental impact as a result. It seems that, in conventional buildings that require heating, the appropriate use of space may be important. In zero-energy buildings that make use of

Table 4: CO_2 emissions from heating compared with emissions from producing extra clothes for different numbers of children in a Canadian portable classroom

number of children	energy to heat to 20 °C over winter (kWh)	energy to heat to 17 °C over winter (kWh)	emissions for electric heating (kg CO_2)	emissions from extra clothes (kg CO_2)	total emissions (kg CO_2)
25	2,492		1,246	0	1,246
25 (wool sweaters)		1,582	791	1,775	2,566
25 (recycled fleece)		1,582	791	439	1,229
2	3,935		1,968		1,968
2 (wool sweaters)		3,025	1,513	142	1,655
2 (recycled fleece)		3,025	1,513	35	1,548

passive solar gain, high levels of insulation and mass, the situation will be very different, since the building will be at the same temperature whether it is occupied or not.

MEN IN SUITS

Some have claimed that having a dress code requiring men to wear suits even in hot weather, so that air conditioning is required, does not make energy sense. In Japan, air conditioning in government offices is to be turned down in summer to try to force a change in the formal dress code.[70] This move could reduce greenhouse emissions in three ways: from the change in dress code; from the reduction in fossil fuel energy use; and, if fewer air conditioning plants were installed, because there would be less leakage of refridgerant gas.[71]

To look at the relative importance of dress and cooling, Table 5 has been constructed. It assumes that UK offices also have air conditioning thermostats adjusted in summer for less cooling. In place of the woollen suit and the tie, the worker wears just a cotton shirt, trousers and tie. For a normal air conditioned office, the full wool suit is assumed to last one year. In the non-

Table 5: Typical energy use and CO_2 emissions per worker in various types of UK office

office space of 15 m²	good-practice standard air-conditioned office	typical standard air-conditioned office	good-practice prestige air-conditioned office	typical prestige air-conditioned office
energy use (kWh)	3,375	6,060	5,115	8,400
CO_2 emissions (kg)	1,080	1,939	1,637	2,688

Table 6: Reductions in CO_2 emissions per worker from change in dress code in UK offices

	good-practice standard air-conditioned office (kg CO₂/ year)	typical standard air-conditioned office (kg CO₂/ year)	good-practice prestige air-conditioned office (kg CO₂/ year)	typical prestige air-conditioned office (kg CO₂/ year)	clothing emissions (kg CO₂/ year)
normal dress code (wool suit all year)	1,080	1,939	1,637	2,688	265
new dress code	902	1,560	1,392	2,218	136

air conditioned office, the worker wears the full suit only in winter, thereby making it last twice as long, so it is assumed that both sets of summer and winter clothes will last for two years. Both offices are heated in the winter so this is ignored in the comparison. The worker occupies a space of 15 m².[72] The first table below contains the energy needed to run heating, lighting, equipment, etc. for two types of offices that are air conditioned: standard and prestige.[73] The energy values given are for the 15 m² needed by each worker. A conversion factor of 0.32 kg CO_2/kWh has been used.

Under the new code, all cooling and humidifying energy, and 50% of energy for running pumps, fans and controls, is removed because no air conditioning is required (Table 6).

Table 7: Saving in CO_2 emissions per worker from the new dress code and no cooling in UK offices

	good-practice standard air-conditioned office (kg CO_2/ year)	typical standard air-conditioned office (kg CO_2/ year)	good-practice prestige air-conditioned office (kg CO_2/ year)	typical prestige air-conditioned office (kg CO_2/ year)	saving in clothing emissions (kg CO_2/ year)
CO_2 emissions saved per worker by new dress code	307	508	374	599	129

What this table shows is that the emissions associated with office buildings are high, and that altering our clothing habits does not make a big difference. The change in dress code reduces personal emissions for the wearer, but office energy use, inclusive of equipment, lighting, hot water, etc., remains high even if cooling is not required as a result of the changed dress code. The difference between total energy use in a best-practice office and in a typical office is more significant than any effect brought about by clothing. However, if we consider only the CO_2 emissions that are saved (Table 7), changing the dress code looks like a very simple step, since the emissions are cumulative. It would seem that men in suits all the year round are not good for the environment.

DRESSED TO KILL

As so often in the West, it seems we can never have enough of a good thing. All forces are pushing us towards increased consumption, and this is true also of clothes. In the 19th century it was not uncommon to have one set of new clothes each year, often as a present at Christmas or for a birthday. Last year's clothes became the garments one wore everyday, and those from the year before were then worn for rough work. Of course, this was not true for the rich, and the real problem now is that we are all rich (relatively, in the wealthier nations) and behave accordingly. It seems that what we are is now conditioned not by what we do and how we behave, but by how we look.

Clothing plays a big part in this. It is, however, having an impact on the environment. In a future with less energy we will have fewer clothes, because there will be less energy to make them, transport them, sell them, and so on. We may find that we are making more clothes at home (see the next chapter) or swapping and remaking old clothes rather than going out and buying new, as we do now.

Another lesson to emerge from this discussion is that we may need to rethink our dress codes in the West. Greater use of protective clothing that is easy to wash could reduce the need for dry cleaning, and dressing according to the weather could help to reduce energy use in buildings. However, there is still more research to do into the balance between emissions and wearing more clothes and heating less.

The following points are offered as guidance.

- Buy less clothing.

- Repair your clothing so that it lasts as long as possible.

- Do the laundry in cold water only.

- Swap, don't shop.

WATTS GOING ON?

In the globalized economy we are all encouraged to have lots of personal possessions. We have considered appliances and furniture in Chapter 3, we have looked at clothes above, and we have even considered shoes in Chapter 2. Now we are turning the spotlight on MP3 players, cell phones and the like.

Some societies are changing very rapidly in terms of their possessions. This was highlighted on a visit to Beijing in May 2004. Standing in a big department store, a group of us watched a young boy playing on an electronic games console. One of the party, a Chinese woman in her twenties, commented, 'When I was his age, I was playing with mud.' The reason we have decided to focus on electronic goods is that the range of such items that appear in our homes is increasing rapidly, and they all use energy. A few years ago we were all 'playing with mud', in the sense that we had few electronic goods – maybe a radio and a television, and perhaps a record player – but this is changing very fast. The Energy Saving Trust (EST), a body in the

UK funded by government and industry to tackle climate change, has said in a recent report entitled *The Ampere Strikes Back* that, by 2020, consumer electronics will use 45% of the electricity in the home.[74] These devices are not insignificant consumers of power. A typical UK house in 2004 used around 60 GJ of gas a year and 25 GJ of electricity. Of the houses with central heating, 84% use gas,[75] so it can be assumed that the electricity consumption is mostly for lights, appliances, and of course for consumer electronics.

It also appears that we have more free time in which to use these devices. In 2005 the average person in a UK household did 30 minutes' less housework per day than they did in 2000, and they spent far more of their leisure time watching television and DVDs or listening to music than anything else. Out of a total of 309 minutes of leisure time a day, 158 minutes were spent watching television and DVDs or listening to music – over 50% of all free time. Men did more of this (and, unsurprisingly, far less housework) than women.[76] What this means is that leisure time that used to be non-energy using, because you were sitting by a window reading a book, or talking to friends or playing Monopoly or kicking a ball about, is now tied into energy consumption.

HOW MUCH DOES IT USE?

New devices are not necessarily more energy-intensive than the old ones, but they are either much bigger, in the case of televisions, or they are completely new – not so much replacing an old appliance as adding to the total of appliances. With television sets, for example, a detailed measured study in the United States found that both plasma and LCD televisions could be as good as, or lower than, traditional cathode ray tube (CRT) televisions in terms of their energy use per square inch of screen, but they use more just because they are bigger. A 20-inch LCD television might use only 130 kWh a year, but a big 55-inch plasma television could use 1,450 kWh a year for the same number of viewing hours. Indeed, it is not possible to make any rule about which type of television to buy, because within each type – CRT, LCD or plasma – some use more energy and some use less.[77] Looking at it from the point of view of energy consumption, these electronic entertainment appliances generally use more energy because we have more of them. The EST, for example, lists the equipment shown in Table 8 as typical of

Table 8: Annual energy use of the electronics in a teenager's bedroom in the UK (*kWh*)

PC and monitor	240
printer	20
scanner	41
PC speakers	24
computing total	**325**
VCR	89
14" CRT television	53
Freeview set-top box	49
television total	**191**
PlayStation 3	187
games total	**187**
compact hi-fi	69
digital radio	41
iPod	4
music total	**114**
mobile phone	4
communications total	**4**
overall total	**821 kWh (approx. 3 GJ)**
operating ecological footprint	222 m²

what one would find in a teenager's bedroom in the UK. It also gives the annual running costs of all these devices, which allows us to work out how much energy this stuff consumes if we assume an average electricity price of 12.3 pence per kWh.[78] The cost of electricity is much harder to work out now that the UK electricity market is deregulated, and there is a multitude of competing suppliers with different pricing plans and special deals, but the figure we have come up with will give at least an idea of the likely energy consumption.

Table 9: Annual energy use of electronics in a living room in the UK (*kWh*)

42" plasma television	703
Sky+ set-top box	134
DVD home theatre	65
television total	**902**
PC and monitor	240
printer	81
fax/scanner	61
broadband router	89
PC speakers	24
computing total	**495**
XBox	114
games total	**114**
digital radio	73
iPod	4
music total	**77**
2 mobile phones	8
personal organizer	4
communications total	**12**
overall total	**1,600 kWh (nearly 6 GJ)**
operating ecological footprint	444 m²

If you think this looks bad, and you are smugly thinking how awful these modern teenagers are, you have only to look in your living room to see that you may well be part of the problem, not part of the solution. Table 9 (also based on the findings of the EST) shows the equipment that might be in your living room alongside its energy consumption.

Of course, not all electronics make equal energy demands. Some of these items need quite insignificant amounts of electricity. You do not need to worry too much about iPods and mobile phones, for example, but computers and televisions are pretty serious. The EST says that a laptop typically has a 70% lower power consumption than a desktop computer, so you could buy a laptop and knock 168 kWh off your computing load; you could use headphones instead of speakers; you could play games on the laptop rather than on a separate games console; and you could replace your digital radio with a solar-powered or wind-up radio that uses no mains power at all. This would deduct 379 kWh from the total, and you could go further by turning things like printers and scanners off at the wall when they are not in use. There isn't much you can do about the big television, though, short of turning off the lights when you watch it, which would save some energy. If you have designed your house right, your TV could be all the heating you need in the winter.

STAND BY YOUR PLUGS

Some electronic devices – and this includes many kitchen appliances like microwave ovens and cooking stoves – consume power even when they are not in use. The glowing red and green lights, the illuminated digital clocks and the visual displays that greet you in many darkened rooms are all consuming electricity. Some sources say this is a relatively small amount: for example, the Energy Efficiency and Conservation Authority (EECA) in New Zealand states that 'standby power', as it is called, uses 5% of total household electricity consumption. This does not sound much, but they also point out that it represents NZ$100 million a year.[79] Given that the average New Zealand house uses around 10,000 kWh of electricity a year, the standby power accounts for 500 kWh a year. A figure of 5% for US residential electricity consumption is also quoted, along with 15% for Japan, Germany and the Netherlands.[80] These percentages are in some ways unhelpful, since we also need to know the actual average consumption. In New Zealand homes, electricity is widely used for space heating, cooking and heating water, whereas in Europe it is mostly used for lights and appliances, with the other tasks being powered by gas. So is 5% of a large annual electricity use, as in New Zealand, the equivalent of 15% of lower consumption elsewhere? A study of ten households carried out by students and scientists at the University of California, Berkeley, and the Lawrence Berkeley National Laboratory (LBNL) in 2001 found that the average standby power in each house amounted to 67 W.[81] Over a year this works out as 587 kWh, which would indeed be roughly 5% of the residential consumption in New Zealand, given the very broad assumption that New Zealanders use the same sort of mix of appliances as Americans. We can conclude that it really is worth turning devices off at the wall, not leaving them on standby.

WEEEEEE!

A further problem with electronics is what is called 'e-waste', or Waste Electrical and Electronic Equipment (WEEE). It is estimated that the average UK resident will throw out about 3 tonnes of WEEE in a lifetime. According to the Royal Society of Arts, who commissioned a sculpture called the 'WEEE Man' – a figure 7 metres high constructed from one person's lifetime electronic waste – WEEE is the fastest growing source of waste in the European Union. Each year every European citizen throws out about 14 kg of WEEE, or collectively 6.5 million tonnes a year.[82] WEEE is bad because discarded electronic equipment contains a variety of hazardous materials, including lead, cadmium, mercury, chromium, pvc and brominated fire retardants, which pose a threat to human health and to the environment. According to the Iowa Department of Natural Resources, WEEE accounts for 40% of the lead and 75% of the heavy metals found in landfills.[83] The embodied energy of computer equipment is 220 MJ/lb (485 MJ/kg).[84] If this is applied to the waste thrown out by the average European annually, we get $14 \times 485 = 6{,}790$ MJ, or 7 GJ.

In order to find out whether it is the number of electronic appliances, the electricity they use or the materials they are made of that should be of most concern, we have examined the appliances from the UK living room above in more detail. The embodied energy for each of these appliances has been calculated in Table 10. The values used are rough by necessity, since the embodied energy and operating energy performance of each device will vary from one model to the other.

To get a sense of what these figures mean, we can compare the average user, who has all the equipment in Table 9 and throws away the average 14 kg of WEEE each year, with a careful user. Table 11 shows the assumptions made for a careful user of electronic equipment, while Table 12 compares the two users of electronic equipment in the living room and shows their annual footprint.

Table 10: Embodied energy of electronic goods for the average user in a UK living room (assuming 485 MJ/kg for electronic equipment)

device	weight (kg)	total embodied energy (MJ)	life[85]	embodied energy per year (MJ)
42" plasma television	30.0[86]	14,550	10	1,455
Sky+ set-top box	4.4[87]	2,134	10	213
DVD home theatre	80.0[88]			
assumed electronics	20.0	9,700	10	970
assumed chipboard (loudspeakers)	60.0	480*	10	48
television total				2.69 GJ
PC and monitor	10.9[89]	5,287	5	1,057
printer	6.7[90]	3,250	5	650
fax/scanner	1.6[91]	776	5	155
broadband router	0.5*	243	5	49
PC speakers	0.5*	243	5	49
computing total				1.96 GJ
XBox	3.5[92]	1,698	5	340
games total				0.3 GJ
digital radio	1.0†	485	5	97
iPod	0.1†	49	5	10
music total				0.10 GJ
2 mobile phones	0.2†	98	5	10
personal organizer	0.1†	49	5	10
communications total				0.02 GJ
overall total				5.07 GJ

* Based on an embodied energy value for chipboard of 8 MJ/kg.[93]
† These are assumed weights rather than manufacturers' values, and include power units.

Table 11: Embodied energy of electronic goods for the careful user in a UK living room (assuming 485 MJ/kg for electronic equipment)

device	weight (kg)	total embodied energy (MJ)	life	embodied energy per year (MJ)
42" plasma television	30.0	14,550	10	1,455
Sky+ set-top box	4.4	2,134	10	213
television total				1.7 GJ
laptop and headphones*	2.4	1,164	5	233
printer	6.7	3,250	5	650
fax/scanner	1.6	776	5	155
broadband router	0.5	243	5	49
computing total				1.1 GJ
wind-up radio	1.0	485	10	49
iPod	0.1	49	5	10
music total				0.06 GJ
2 mobile phones	0.2	98	5	10
personal organizer	0.1	49	5	10
communications total				0.02 GJ
overall total				2.9 GJ

* Games are played on the laptop.

Table 12: Comparison of two ways of using electronic equipment in the UK living room

	normal user (GJ/year)	careful user (GJ/year)	normal user footprint (m²/year)	careful user footprint (m²/year)
operating energy	6	4	444	296
embodied energy	5	3	370	222
wastage rate*	7	4	519	296
total	18	11	1,333 (0.13 ha/year)	814 (0.08 ha/year)

* Wastage has been reduced in proportion to the reduction in embodied energy, to give 8.4 kg waste/year.

In Table 12, the operating energy for the laptop is assumed to be 60 kWh/year. Total operating energy for the careful user based on the consumption of appliances in Table 9 and the list in Table 11, combined with turning printers and so on off at the wall, is taken as 4 GJ/year.

By thinking carefully, it is possible to make a 39% reduction in total impact. Savings are made in all categories in about the same proportion. The only thing that may not be as good as the original is the wind-up radio, since it really needs broadcasters to reschedule programmes to allow for winding time every 20 minutes! However, even if an ordinary radio were added to the careful user scenario, the results would not change significantly.

The big problem with electronics as part of the waste stream is that they are designed to be used briefly and then thrown out as new technology is introduced that is seen in some way as an improvement. Even greater savings could be achieved in Table 12 if devices were kept for much longer, providing that they still worked. This constant replacement of the not-very-old with the new is either a glorious demonstration of the rapid rate of technological progress that is making our lives so much better every day, or else a cynical ploy to extract as much money from us as possible. Which you believe probably depends both on your point of view and on whether you can afford the latest desirable electronic devices. We see this obsolescence in many products. The video recorder is a good example. Originally there were three consumer tape formats: Video 2000, Betamax and VHS. VHS became dominant and the Video 2000 and Betamax machines had to be replaced. DVDs then appeared, and people who wanted to watch films threw out their video recorders and bought DVD players instead. DVD recorders came onto the market, so that you could record off-air; and now a new generation of higher-definition Blu-ray players is set to replace the old DVD format. All this has happened in the last thirty years or so, and must have produced quite a lot of e-waste. The trend with computers is similar, but it was not always the way things were done.

In the past, there were interesting examples of manufacturers of home entertainment equipment who did not require owners to throw out their old machines. For instance, in the early days of the recorded music industry the manufacturers of Edison phonographs (which played records in the form of grooved wax cylinders) introduced the 4-minute 'Amberol' records to replace the original 2-minute records. But they sold upgrade kits for each model of phonograph, which comprised an add-on gear box and a reproducer with a stylus of the correct size to play the narrower grooves of the new cylinders. Sadly, this was not enough to enable Edison to continue making the cylinder phonograph, which was ousted by the cheaper and less fragile disc records. We no longer have this upgrading option, but many of the old Edison machines and their fragile records are still in working order today.

Steps to take:

- Buy a laptop computer, not a desktop one.

- Try to make your electronic equipment do as many things as possible. For example, play games or record television programmes on the computer rather than using a separate games console or DVD recorder.

- Make your electronic equipment last as long as you can, and then recycle it properly rather than throwing it away.

- Switch devices off at the wall rather than just using the remote.

- Watch television with the lights off.

HEAVY PETTING

Arguably pets also count as 'stuff we have at home', since exercise for many people consists of taking the dog for a walk, and cleaning out the family rabbit or guinea pig is certainly a common activity for children (or for parents, once the magic of pet ownership has worn off). Pets offer companionship, especially in places where community life has broken down, such as some urban societies. To some extent, the primary function of having animals in the home has been obscured. Historically, animals had to work for a living: the cat was kept to deter vermin, and the dog was a guard or a hunting companion. Other animals were kept for food (see the section on 'Edible pets' below), but would still have been part of the household until the time came to eat them. A pair of breeding rabbits could be 'pets' while their offspring filled the pot. At this point some people will fling up their hands in horror at such a callous and insensitive view. Our response is to suggest that insensitivity comes from failing to appreciate the cyclical nature of existence: life and death, eat and be eaten, etc. Our lack of sensitivity to this situation, the result of our industrial and post-industrial way of life, has changed the way animals are kept at home. Rather than giving a food animal a good and stress-free life before it is eaten, animals now have a footprint of their own in terms of how they are cared for. This is explored below.

The pet food industry is vast. The United States is a net exporter of cat and dog food, with exports increasing from a value of US$21 million in 1997 to US$700 million in 2003.[94] By 2006 this figure had risen to US$965 million,[95] alongside imports of cat and dog food to the value of US$275 million.[96] This conjures up an unhappy picture (or a happy one, if you are an advocate of the benefits of any kind of trade) of a vast world trade in tins of cat and dog food – something that human beings never taste when they are deciding which brand to purchase. Let us consider the pet food industry in one country: New Zealand, which in 2000 had an estimated population of just over 3.8 million.[97] Using the figure of 0.275 cats per person (see below), the country also contained 1 million cats. These were fed 37,800 tonnes of food worth NZ$140 million, of which over half (NZ$75.3 million) was tinned.[98] This is a long way from the historical picture of the cat kept as a mouser, expected to earn his or her keep and catch at least some food. As recompense, the cat was given shelter and a guarantee of food in hard times, although it would have consisted of kitchen scraps rather than tinned pet food. Cats will hunt whether they hungry or not.

Nowadays most cats and dogs are fed meat that takes land to produce, and the tins in which it is sold also have to be manufactured. The same tins later become part of the waste stream, so disposing of them has an environmental cost. It could be argued that cats eat only the parts of cows and other animals killed for meat that people do not want. Conversely, in a world with an increasing population it could also be argued that, once again, we need to learn to eat all parts of an animal, including such 'delights' as tripe, sweetbreads, pigs' ears and trotters, and sheep's brains, since they are useful sources of protein and other nutrients.

The following is an investigation of several animals we recognize as pets (including the perennial favourites of cats and dogs), with an assessment of their environmental impacts and benefits. It should thus be possible to work out which type of pet will have the least impact on the environment. At this stage the impact of a visit to the vet has not been incorporated into the footprint; some pets like goldfish may never see a vet. Healthy pets probably see the vet once a year for their jabs, whereas others may need frequent visits because of chronic conditions. In general, the larger the pet, the more likely it is to visit the vet.

CATS

Cats – once considered sacred in many cultures, such as ancient Egypt – are very popular pets. Perhaps not surprisingly, the US has the largest cat population in the world: an estimated 76.5 million moggies in 2006,[99] which for a human population of 300 million[100] works out as 0.25 cats per American. According to AC Nielsen Research Pty Ltd,[101] in 2000 New Zealand had a slightly higher ownership, with a figure of 0.275 cats/person and 52% of all households having a cat. Surveys also showed that the number of households in Australia that owned a cat was declining, while the number of cats per cat-owning household remained steady at 1.47,[102] or 2.2 cats/person.[103] The UK, which ranks seventh in terms of world cat ownership, has just over 0.1 cats per person (7.7 million/60.7 million[104]), although another source quotes an official estimate of 9 million cats in the UK.[105] China has the second-largest number of cats, but ownership is only 53.1 million/1,330 million[106] = 0.04 moggies/person. This is not just because of the rumour that the Chinese eat cats (Robert was told at a dinner in Beijing that 'people in Bejing will eat anything with four legs except a table'). If cat is served as food, it will be expensive because the cat is a carnivore. Peter Huston claims to have eaten cat with snake in Canton, in a dish served as 'dragon and tiger',[107] but also feels that this was a rare delicacy. The meat people commonly eat in China, as elsewhere in the world, comes from herbivores like sheep and cows, and from the omnivorous pig. Pet ownership is likely to rise in China because it has a certain prestige among wealthy middle-class families. These new pet owners are more likely to live in urban areas and hence will use commercial pet food rather than table scraps.[108]

Given the large number of cats in the world, it would be useful to find out the environmental impact of keeping a cat against the pleasure they bring. We will look at the food they eat and also at the damage they do to biodiversity, from which it will be possible to measure the footprint (paw-print?) of the average domestic moggy.

'CATS PREFER ...?'

The average cat weighing 7–9 lb (3.2–4.1 kg) eats 0.5 lb (0.2 kg) of dry or semi-moist food a day, according to one manufacturer of cat food.[109] However, this figure seems high for dried food (see the discussion). A cat that eats dry food will consume more water than if it were eating tinned foods, but both are acceptable for feeding cats. If we assume that all the food is dried, what environmental impact would it have?

DRIED CAT FOOD

A study by the University of Missouri-Columbia states that dry cat food is 30–40% carbohydrates.[110] A manufacturer gives the protein content of their food as a minimum of 45%, with the next biggest ingredient being fat at 18%, and then moisture at 8%.[111] The chicken-and-rice dried food we used to feed our cat (Iggy) consisted of a minimum 34% protein, a minimum 13% fat, maximum 12% moisture and maximum 7% ash.[112] For the purpose of this calculation, an animal content of 50% (both protein and fat) is assumed, together with 35% carbohydrate content; the rest (moisture and other ingredients) has been ignored. The recommended daily intake of this food is 35–70 g for a small cat weighing 2–4 kg, and 70–106 g for a large cat of 4–6 kg. The assumption is that the cat eats 70 g of dried food each day. The footprint of chicken is 43.3 m²/kg, and that of cereals is 13.4 m²/kg (see Chapter 1). However, these are the footprints for whole chicken and whole cereals with their normal moisture content, whereas dried food has had some of the moisture removed. According to the United States Department of Agriculture, raw whole chicken is 66% moisture and cooked chicken is 60% moisture.[113] As noted above, the moisture content of dried cat food is 12%, which means that dried cat food is more concentrated than the raw chicken and the footprint will need to be adjusted. The 70 g of dried food works out at 35 g of dried animal meat and 24.5 g of dried cereals. This would equate to 175 g of whole chicken. Depending on the type of raw rice used, it could have a water content of between 14% and 29%.[114] Assuming an approximate water content of 20%, this would equate to 41 g of raw rice.

If fed only dry food, in a year a cat would consume $175 \div 1,000 \times 365 = 63.9$ kg of chicken and $41 \div 1,000 \times 365 = 15$ kg of rice. This gives the cat eating dried food a footprint of $(63.9 \times 43.3) + (15 \times 13.4) = 2,968$ m²/year, or 0.3 ha. A well-fed domestic cat will tend to have a garden for its territory, which it will defend against other cats,[115] although cats will share their territories and can exist at higher densities. A typical garden in the UK would be about 200 m² in size, so the footprint of cat food is 15 times the size of the cat's territory.

There will also be a footprint for the packaging. The type of dried food considered here comes in packs of 3.5 lb (1.6 kg).[116] Over a year, a domestic cat will need 16 bags of dried food. The bags are made of a layered product consisting of foil and plastic. The footprint of multi-layered packaging such as this is 0.0000057 ha/tonne (see Chapter 1), or 0.057 m²/tonne. The packaging from the 16 bags might weigh 600 g, so the footprint of the packaging is so small that it can be ignored.

Table 13 (overleaf) shows the footprint of giving dried food to all the cats of the world's top cat-owning countries,[117] along with other feeding options.

TINNED CAT FOOD

One source states that a can of cat food is typically 80% moisture.[118] It also gives the percentage of dry protein, fat and other ingredients contained in a range of cat foods available in the UK. A typical 400 g tin of meaty chunks in jelly (a favourite of Iggy's) had a dry weight of 80 g, of which 48.6% was protein (39 g) and 31.4% was fat (25 g). A supermarket brand is 45% protein and 25% fat by dry weight, whereas some other brands are over 50% protein. For this analysis we have assumed that a 400 g tin of cat food contains 80 g of dry matter, of which 80% is animal and the rest cereal. If this is high-quality tinned food of beef origin, the footprint could be 209.1 m²/kg (see Chapter 1). However, raw brisket beef has a water content of 71%, falling to 56% when cooked.[119] This would suggest that additional water is added to tinned cat food. The dry-matter animal content in a tin is $80 \times 0.8 = 64$ g of meat. This would equate to $64 \times 1.71 = 109$ g of raw meat. The footprint of the tin's meat content is therefore $109 \div 1,000 \times 209.1 = 22.8$ m². Assuming that the other 20% is cereal, this would add $16 \div 1,000 \times 13.4 = 0.2$ m². The total is therefore 23 m² per tin, or $23 \times 365 = 8,395$ m²/year (0.84 ha/year).

If, however, a footprint of 29.8 m²/kg is used for all the meats apart from beef, the total footprint would be reduced to (109 ÷ 1,000) × 29.8 + 16 ÷ 1,000 × 13.4 = 3.25 + 0.2 = 3.45 m²/tin, or 1,259 m²/year (0.13 ha/year). All this suggests that it is the footprint value selected that will have the biggest influence over the environmental impact of keeping a cat. For example, using the 'all other meats' footprint for dried food will change the impact to 2,047.7 m²/year (0.2 ha/year).

During the course of a year 365 × 400 g tins will be needed. The footprint of steel food tins is 18 m²/kg (see Chapter 1), or 1.8 ha/tonne. Assuming that a single tin weighs about 50 g (we have measured some examples), its footprint will be about 0.9 m². Since we are encouraged to recycle tins, this figure has been ignored in the table below.

Some say that cats prefer fish.[120] However, the footprint of all fish is again high, at 134.3 m²/kg. The same proportions we used for the tin of meat-based cat food above would give a footprint of (109 ÷ 1,000) × 134.3 + (16 ÷ 1,000) × 13.4 = 14.6 + 0.2 = 14.8 m²/tin, or 5,402 m²/year (0.54 ha/year). Values for tinned meat and tinned fish have been fed into Table 13 below.

FREEZE-DRIED CAT FOOD

An alternative to tinned cat food is freeze-dried food sold in bags. One recipe is 95% animal in origin – meat, offal and bones – with the remaining 5% consisting of vegetable, fruit and fish oil.[121] However, the high meat and fish content would just push the footprint even higher. This option has not been included in the table.

The footprint for dried cat food in these ten countries, calculated using high embodied energy figures, is equal to an area about six times the size of New Zealand (268,680 km²) or of Japan or Colorado.[122] The lower figure for tinned food would see the footprint reduced to a land area equal in size to New Zealand. These figures will probably represent an overestimate, since cat food is likely to be made of leftover pieces of animals and fish, and so lower values could be used. However, even with these low values, the impact on the environment of all the cats in the top 10 cat-owning countries is high. Perhaps there should be a policy of no more than one cat per household, and certainly it would be good to feed your cat on tinned food, which is

Table 13: Cat food footprint for the top 10 cat-owning nations of the world

country	estimated cat population	footprint dried food, high meat content (ha)	footprint dried food, low meat content (ha)	footprint tinned food, low meat content (ha)	footprint tinned food, fish (ha)
US	76,430,000	64,201,200	15,286,000	9,935,990	41,272,200
China	51,100,000	42,924,000	10,220,000	6,643,000	27,594,000
Russia	12,700,000	10,668,000	2,540,000	1,651,000	6,858,000
Brazil	12,466,000	10,471,440	2,493,200	1,620,580	6,731,640
France	9,600,000	8,064,000	1,920,000	1,248,000	5,184,000
Italy	9,400,000	7,520,000	1,880,000	1,222,000	5,076,000
UK	7,700,000	7,896,000	1,540,000	1,001,000	4,158,000
Ukraine	7,350,000	6,174,000	1,470,000	955,500	3,969,000
Japan	7,300,000	6,132,000	1,460,000	949,000	3,942,000
Germany	7,700,000*	6,468,000	1,540,000	1,001,000	4,158,000
total		170,518,640	40,349,200	26,227,070	108,942,840
total (km²)		1,705,186	403,492	262,271	1,089,428

* This is the value as it appears in the original table of cat populations, although it may be a mistake for 7,200,000. The larger value has been used here, since all values are in any case only estimates.

basically offal and leftover scraps. But in some parts of the world these leftovers would be fed to people and can be very nutritious. Brenda recalls going to Hong Kong some years ago and being taken out for 'junk food' at a noodle stall, which basically entailed eating all the leftover bits of the animal, such as ears, tripe and feet. Very good they were too.

It might be helpful if cat food companies printed the footprint of their product on the tin or packet to aid your choice. The advice to stick with poultry (rabbit, turkey and chicken) – 'Think feathers and long ears, not horns and fins'[123] – over meat and fish as a better diet for your cat would also be good for the environment. The other point to note is that the packaging is not important, so how you buy your cat food will not have an impact on the environment.

LET THEM EAT RATS

Perhaps the answer is to use packaged vermin as cat food. After all, cats are supposed to eat mice, and some will even kill rats. According to the UK Biomedical Research Education Trust, over a 70-year lifetime each of us is responsible for killing 3 mice and 1 rat for experimental purposes, and 8 mice and rats as vermin.[124] Given that UK cat ownership is around 0.1 cats/person and that a domestic cat lives for around 14 years,[125] obviously not enough vermin are being trapped to feed cats, not to mention that fact that poisoned vermin cannot be used as food. Perhaps there are enough rats but we just aren't catching them. One source suggests there is about one rat to each person in the UK.[126] Braintree District Council even suggests that there are now more rats than people in the UK, which in part it attributes to the litter of take-away food waste and packaging in public places.[127] Working on the figure of one rat per person and 0.1 cats, it should be possible, in the short term, to feed the UK cat population with 'natural' cat food by catching vermin, since an adult Norway rat weighs between 150 and 300 g.[128] However, catching the rats will lower the rat population. In some areas where rat populations are high – landfills, for instance, where the density of rats has been measured at 0.1–0.17/m² by Robitaille and Bovet[129] – it might be possible to devise a sideline business producing 'natural' cat food. A fur company in New Zealand traps brushtail possums – a species imported from Australia early in the 19th century that has now become a major pest, destroying native vegetation. As well as possum fur products, they sell 'Possyum' cat and dog food made from the marsupial.[130] (Iggy was very fond of it, but it was hard to get where we lived.) In the end, however, the only sensible environmental option is to have fewer cats in the world.

WHAT GOES IN MUST COME OUT

Apart from the impact of the food that goes into a cat, a litter tray will mean sending the faeces that come out, and the used litter, to landfill. Unfortunately, as gardeners know, it is not possible to compost cat and dog faeces because of the risk of spreading disease.[131] An article in the *San Francisco Chronicle* states that each year America's 73 million dogs produce about 10 million tons of faeces, and the cat population of 90 million creates 2 million tons of used cat litter.[132] Cat faeces left in the natural environment will find their way into drains and water courses, and this can also lead to problems. In San Francisco, 4% of what goes to landfill is pet faeces, about on a level with used nappies.[133] One current idea is that pet faeces could be disposed of in a methane digester. This simple technology is used in many sewage works where the waste is treated anaerobically – that is, without access to oxygen, unlike in a normal compost heap – at a suitable temperature, with the result that methane is produced. This gas can then be burned to power the sewage works. A new facility of this type near Coventry is said to be capable of producing electricity for 500 houses.[134] However, these systems are not under the control of the average pet owner, and there is still the problem of how to get the used cat litter to the anaerobic digester. Technology can come up with solutions, but the problem disappears if we just have fewer or communal cats (see below).

WHAT GOES OUT MUST COME IN

A long time ago we calculated that the gap around the average front door in the UK is like having a brick missing from your wall.[135] Providing access for pussy by installing a cat flap can also give rise to unwanted draughts, although most modern flaps no longer wave with the wind but have magnetic strips to hold them shut. However, it would be useful to see if the cat flap makes much difference to the overall cat-owning footprint. The perimeter of our cat flap (we don't now have a cat but the previous owner did) is 600 mm; assuming that the gap around it measures 1 mm, the area of the gap is 600 mm², or 0.0006 m². If there is a moderate breeze registering 4 on the Beaufort scale,[136] this would mean an airflow of 6–8 m/sec. Every second there would be $7 \times 0.0006 = 0.0042$ m³ of air entering the kitchen through the gap. Given that the specific heat of air is 1,300 J/m³ °C, and assuming that the temperature is 5 °C outside and 20 °C inside, $1{,}300 \times 0.0042 \times 15 = 81.9$ J/sec would be needed to warm it up from outside to inside temperature. This is a rate of 81.9 W of heat energy, as 1 watt equates to 1 joule per second. So, in terms of the energy being lost, having a draughty cat flap is like leaving a 90 W light bulb constantly on outside. However, a cat is a mammal and gives off heat, so this also needs to be taken into consideration. The combined heat output of a cat, from its direct heat (sensible heat) and from its breathing (latent heat), is given by the Chartered Institution of

Building Services Engineers (CIBSE) as 14.8 W for a cat weighing 3 kg,[137] which is on the small side.[138] To offset the energy loss from a draughty cat flap, you would need to have 5 small CIBSE cats, or maybe 4 somewhat larger moggies at 20 W each, kept in the house all the time, which rather defeats the object of having a cat flap. The sensible move would be to have a draught-sealed cat flap. At a guess, this would save about 75% of the energy that would otherwise be lost (you can never seal anything perfectly), which we can calculate as $82 \times 0.25 = 20.5$ W, or about one good-size cat's worth. So if Tiddles spends most of his time indoors with you, the heat he gives off balances the disadvantages of having the cat flap. If you have a cat that lives mostly outdoors, it might be good to have a double cat flap to provide a better energy seal.[139]

The actual footprint of the energy lost from a well-sealed cat flap is small: 0.32 GJ. This is worked out by taking 20.5 W (= J/sec) and multiplying it by the number of seconds in six months, which roughly corresponds to the period when heating is needed and heat loss occurs. The conversion factor of 135 GJ/ha gives a footprint of 0.002 ha, which for the minute is ignored, assuming the cat spends most of the time indoors.

'LET ME TELL YOU 'BOUT THE BIRDS ...'

Cats are predators. Studies of the wild cat population in Stewart Island (Rakiura) at the southern end of New Zealand have shown that, although the main food for the wild cat population is rats, they also eat birds, reptiles and invertebrates.[140] The same source suggests that the cats in Stewart Island have been responsible for the near extinction of the kakapo, or night parrot, and of the southern New Zealand dotterel. They also prey on little blue- and yellow-eyed penguins and on young kiwi. In the UK, a number of organizations are involved in establishing gardens that promote biodiversity through providing habitats for native animals, birds and insects.[141] Their advice is always to site bird-nesting boxes and feeding tables above cat-jumping height[142] (which is 1.8 m according to our local fenced wildlife reserve at Karori in Wellington); but no one seems to want to make the link to the obvious idea of not keeping cats if you want to encourage wildlife.

The only way to own a cat and make sure it does not eat the native fauna is to keep it indoors. This approach is promoted by the American Bird

Conservancy, an organization that states that a domestic cat allowed to roam freely can kill more than 100 animals a year, with some cats specializing in birds and some in small mammals.[143] Methods that calculate ecological footprint offer another way to look at the problem of the cat's impact on bio-diversity; they state that 12% of biologically productive areas should be set aside for biodiversity.[144] Accepting that cats both domestic and feral are bad for biodiversity, 12% will be added to the cat footprint in the pet comparison table below (Table 17). This would give a footprint for a cat fed on tinned 'other meats' of $0.13 \times 1.12 = 0.15$ ha.

SKIMBLESHANKS AND FRIENDS

We have owned cats in the past but don't have any pets at present. But we are friends with the cats in our street, and certainly on nodding acquaintance with many cats in the locality. Maybe the problem is not cats in themselves, but the fact they have been privatized. Historically, cats were more commu-nal. The ship's cat had a specific task – to tackle the rats on board ship – but it was also the pet of the whole crew. The railway cat belonged to the station, the theatre cat to the whole company, and more recently rest homes have rec-ognized the value of having a communal cat for all the residents.[145] It is not the pets that are the problem, but how we choose to manage them.

DOGS

Dogs were originally domesticated because of their usefulness – in herding animals, helping with hunting, or for security – but recent research by Professor Herzog at Western Carolina University has shown that the dog is now a consumer item, with people selecting a particular breed for a pet on account of what is perceived as being fashionable at the time.[146] For instance, he links the sudden rise in the popularity of the Dalmatian to a certain Disney film.

The working dog is still important: dogs can help people who have sensory impairments, and they sniff out explosives, drugs and other banned goods at border control. However, most are still kept as pets, and it is pet dogs that are of concern here. Again, the US heads the estimated top 10 pet dog-owning countries in the world, with a dog population of over 61 million[147] (still less than the US cat population, however). The UK does not feature among the top 10 dog-owning countries, and the Ukraine and Germany also disappear. Instead, South Africa comes in at number six with 9 million, Poland at number nine with 7.5 million, and Thailand at number ten with just under 7 million. The full list can be found in Table 14. The case of Thailand is of particular interest, since dogs are not so much owned (there being no system of dog registration) as adopted and fed leftover food. The temple will have a dog; food will go first to the monks, then to the temple children, and anything that is left over will go to the dog.[148] Thus in Thailand the dog is used as part of a waste disposal system.

DOGGY BAGS

Dogs are omnivores and, unlike cats, can live on human scraps,[149] although there are some human foods they should not be given, such as grapes and onions.[150] Most, however, are fed on purpose-made dog food that is a mixture of meat and vegetables. One way of working out the impact of owning a dog is to assume it is fed a human diet. The footprint of the Cardiff diet is 1.33 ha (see Chapter 1), which comes from the consumption of 675.5 kg of mixed foodstuffs a year. The average dog requires 30 cals per lb of bodyweight a day, with large dogs needing 20 and small dogs 40.[151] The average 30 cals/lb/day works out at 66.7 cals/kg/day. Examples of medium-size dogs might be a cocker spaniel, weighing in at 18–28 lb[152] (8.2–12.7 kg), or a Border Collie at 30–45 lb[153] (13.6–20.4 kg). Assuming it weighs an average 15 kg, the dog will have a daily requirement of just about 1,000 cals/day. This compares with 3,200 cals/day for a man and 2,300 cals/day for a woman. Assuming the population of Cardiff is split equally between men and women, the Cardiff footprint supplies an average 2,750 cals/day. This would give a proportional footprint for a 15 kg dog of 0.48 ha/year.

The makers of a dry weight-loss dog food sold in the UK state that it is made of 30% protein (minimum 23% chicken), 6% oil (fish oil), and a variety of cereals.[154] They also recommend that a medium dog should be given 300 g of the food a day to maintain its ideal weight.[155] The moisture content is not given but is assumed to be 12%, as in dried cat food. If we consider just the main ingredients, 300 g/day represents 90 g of dried chicken, assuming that all the protein is chicken, and 156 g of dried cereals (52% of the total). Using the same method as for calculating the footprint of dried cat food, this 300 g serving of dried food represents 150 g of whole fresh chicken, and the 156 g of dried cereals represents 261 g of fresh cereals. Over a year of eating this dried food, a medium dog consumes ($90 \div 1,000$) × 365 = 32.9 kg of chicken, and ($261 \div 1,000$) × 365 = 95.3 kg of cereals. This gives a footprint of (32.9 × 43.3) + (95.3 × 13.4) = 2,702 m²/year, or 0.27 ha. This suggests it would be better to feed a dog on dog food rather than on a typical Cardiff diet.

It might be useful also to look at the relative impact of small and large dogs. The recommended serving to maintain the weight of a toy dog such as a Chihuahua is 100 g/day, giving a proportional footprint of 0.09 ha. The serving for a small dog like a Scottish Terrier is 200 g/day, giving a proportional footprint of 0.18 ha. The recommendation for a large dog like an Alsatian, on the other hand, is 400 g/day, making a footprint of 0.36 ha.

Because packaging has such a small impact it has not been considered here. Table 14 shows the top 10 dog-owning nations and the impact on the environment if the dogs are fed a human diet and a dried dog food diet.

Table 14: Dog food footprint for the top 10 dog-owning nations of the world

country	dog population	footprint with appropriate human diet* (ha)	footprint with dried dog food (ha)
US	61,080,000	29,318,400	16,491,600
Brazil	30,051,000	14,424,480	8,113,770
China	22,908,000	10,995,840	6,185,160
Japan	9,650,000	4,632,000	2,605,500
Russia	9,600,000	4,608,000	2,592,000
South Africa	9,100,000	4,368,000	2,457,000
France	8,150,000	3,912,000	2,200,500
Italy	7,600,000	3,648,000	2,052,000
Poland	7,520,000	3,609,600	2,030,400
Thailand	6,900,000	3,312,000	1,863,000
total		82,828,320	46,590,930
total (km²)		828,283	465,909

* Without foodstuffs (such as grapes) that are harmful to dogs.

The footprint of 0.27 ha for the medium dog is used to represent the total dog population, large and small.

The table shows that we need another New Zealand just to feed the dogs of the top 10 dog-owning nations. It also suggests that countries with high dog and cat populations should be devoting significant portions of their land to feeding them. The islands of Japan have an area of 372,801 km² while the footprint for feeding their cats and dogs on the diets with the lowest impact works out at 35,545 km², or 9.5% of the total. Italy has an area of 301,230 km²,[156] and a dog and cat footprint of 32,740 km², or 11% of the total land area. At first sight this does not seem too bad. However, agricultural land in Italy accounted for 146,940 km² in 2005,[157] which means that 23% of the area under permanent crops would be needed to feed the country's cats and dogs. In Japan in 2000, agricultural land amounted to 49,100 km², or 13.5% of the total.[158] An earlier figure from 1992 states that 13.9% of all land is cultivated fields and 66.7% is forest. This suggests that the land area dedicated to agriculture is falling over time, with the result that 72% of all Japan's agricultural land would be needed to feed its cats and dogs if the food were grown domestically. As one academic colleague noted when he was told these figures, it is no wonder Japan is keen on catching whales.[159] The world obviously has some hard thinking to do when it comes to common pets.

IN THE DOG HOUSE

Unlike cats, which tend to sleep wherever they feel like it, dogs often come with a piece of dedicated equipment: the kennel. Does a kennel contribute significantly to the overall footprint of owning a dog?

A medium dog – a cocker spaniel or a beagle, say – would need a kennel with a floor plate of 635 × 838 mm.[160] A manufacturer shows one such kennel, made from 9 mm exterior ply, that could just about come out of one 1,200 × 2,400 sheet. The volume of the plywood is 1.2 × 2.4 × 0.009 = 0.026 m³. The embodied energy of plywood is 5,200 MJ/m³,[161] giving a total for the basic kennel of 0.026 × 5,200 = 135 MJ. The kennel will need painting to protect it, and a litre of water-based paint will add 115 MJ, giving the kennel total embodied energy of 250 MJ. Using the conversion of 135 GJ/ha, this would add 0.002 ha to the footprint of owning a dog. This value will need to be divided by the years a dog lives and so effectively can be ignored.

HAMSTERS

Smaller animals are kept as pets too. Hamsters have an advantage for those who work: since they are nocturnal, they sleep during the day and are active in the evening. They live for 2–3 years on average.[162] Hamsters are fed hamster mix, which contains cereals, seeds, rodent pellets and sometimes dried fruit and vegetables.[163] They can also be given small amounts of fresh fruit and vegetables. As they are omnivores, they can eat meat, and in the wild they would feed on worms, insects and even carrion if they came across it.[164] However, eating mainly cereals and being very small could give them some advantages in footprint terms. The hamster will also be content to live on its own provided it is given plenty of attention at times.[165]

A hamster typically eats a tablespoon of food a day plus some fresh fruit and vegetables.[166] A standard cup contains 16 tablespoons, or 0.237 l. Over a year, the hamster's consumption equates to $365 \div 16 = 22.8$ cups of hamster mix, or $22.8 \times 0.237 = 5.4$ l. One litre of cornflakes weighs around 4 oz (113 g) and a litre of seed mix weighs 24 oz (678 g). (Our kitchen scales are not metric.) Assuming that the density of the hamster mix is closer to that of seeds than cornflakes (oats are heavier than cornflakes, but there were not enough in the kitchen cupboard to weigh), the happy lone hamster eats $5.4 \times 500 = 2.7$ kg annually. This would have a footprint of $2.7 \times 13.4 = 36.2$ m²/year, or 0.004 ha. To this must be added the fresh fruit. Assuming a hamster eats the equivalent of two small apples a week, which together would weigh 4 oz (113 g), over a year this would make $52 \times (113 \div 1,000) = 5.9$ kg. The footprint of fresh fruit is 6.8 m²/kg, meaning the additional footprint is $5.9 \times 6.8 = 40.1$ m². Thus the total footprint for hamster food comes to 76.3 m² or 0.008 ha.

Hamsters also need a cage and litter. Hamster cages are now almost a fashion statement: it is possible to buy plastic 'pink palaces' for girls and cages with a 'jungle' theme for boys.[167] But for the purposes of this exercise, it is assumed that you will be making a cage out of wood, wire and Perspex. Wire is good for hamsters as it ensures they get plenty of air. They will gnaw the wood with time, and a wooden-framed cage will need cleaning out to prevent it getting soaked with urine, but this will apply to any type of hamster cage. A home-made cage should measure 500 × 350 mm. One design has the base and two sides made from wood, a front made from

Perspex and the top made from wire mesh, which is hinged for access.[168] Like the kennel, this cage could be constructed out of a sheet of plywood, though less than a quarter will be used. We have nonetheless assumed that a whole sheet has to be purchased, with an energy content of 135 MJ (see above). It would be unwise to treat the wood in case there is a risk of poisoning the hamster, but you have plenty of the sheet left over with which to renew parts if they rot. The embodied energy of acrylic used as glazing, which is the same as Perspex, is 1,456 MJ/m² for a 3 mm thick sheet.[169] This would probably be adequate for a cage of this size. Assuming that the front is as high as the cage is wide, the area of sheet required is 0.35 × 0.5 = 0.175 m², the embodied energy of which would be 1,456 × 0.175 = 255 MJ. Welded wire mesh, which would certainly keep the hamster in, weighs 1.01 lb/ft².[170] The cage lid is 0.175 m² (1.89 ft²) in area, and the mesh would weigh 0.86 kg (1.9 lb). The embodied energy of virgin steel is 32 MJ/kg,[171] so the embodied energy of the top would be 0.86 × 32 = 27.5 MJ. This gives a total value for the home-made hamster cage of 418 MJ, or 0.42 GJ. (It is probably worth noting that the plastic accounts for most of this energy.) If we use the conversion figure of 135 GJ/ha, the cage would add 0.003 ha to the footprint sover the life of the hamster. Given the hamster lives for two to three years, this would add 0.001–0.0015 ha to its annual footprint. The message here is not to buy, or indeed make, a plastic hamster cage, but to stick to wood and metal as lower embodied energy materials. Another option is not to buy or make a new cage at all, but to recycle one that belonged to a previous hamster owner. For the present analysis, however, we have stuck with the figure of 0.001 ha.

It is possible to buy hamster litter made from recycled paper that can be flushed down the loo.[172] We have never owned a hamster, so it is difficult to know how many packets would be needed for one year. Guessing that a 35 l bag would last a month, we can estimate a figure of 420 l/year. According to the Florida Agriculture Experiment Station, the density of shredded paper as bedding is 74 g/l.[173] The embodied energy of recycled paper is 23.4 MJ/kg.[174] In a year, therefore, the energy embodied in the bedding would be 420 × (74 ÷ 1,000) × 23.4 = 727 MJ (0.73 GJ). Using the conversion of 135 GJ/ha, we can calculate that the bedding would add 0.005 ha to the hamster's footprint.

Adding all these figures together gives a total of 0.008 (food) + 0.001 (home-made cage) + 0.005 (litter) = 0.014 ha. The food is still the most important component, but because the animal is very small other factors have become more significant in comparison. The figure of 0.014 ha has been used in our pet comparison table below (Table 17).

CANARIES

Birds are also common pets. The species of bird chosen is often governed by the level of commitment the putative owner wants to make, since some birds can live a very long time. A parrot can live for 50 years, a cockatoo for 65 years, and it has been suggested that small birds like budgerigars and canaries can live for 15 years in ideal conditions.[175] For the purposes of our comparison we will look at the footprint of keeping a canary, since these birds can be kept on their own, not being social, and should live for 10 years.[176] Like all the other pets considered here, they can also be kept at room temperature in a temperate climate.

Canaries were prized as singing pets in 16th-century Europe.[177] In the past, canaries have also been working birds, kept in mines to detect the presence of poisonous gases like carbon monoxide and methane. According to the US Department of Labor (Mine Safety and Health Administration), canaries were preferred over other animals that reacted to toxic gases, such as mice, because the canary falling off its perch was a more visible warning.[178] In the UK, the use of canaries in mines, which began in 1911, was finally phased out in 1986.[179]

Canaries are a type of finch and do not become tame in the home, unlike birds of the parrot family. They need to be kept in a cage, but they will also make a mess with their food, water and general feather drop-out. Here, however, we are more interested in the canary's diet and housing.

Canaries are seed-eaters. In the wild, their basic food is seed from the canary grass plant, but they will also eat seeds of flax (linseed), hemp, millet, rape and thistle,[180] all of which are commercially available as packaged mixtures. In addition, a canary will need some cuttlefish bone and fresh water. It has also been suggested that canaries should be given protein every day, such as chopped hard-boiled egg at the rate of 0.5 teaspoons/day.[181] Other people differ, saying that wild canaries eat not only seeds, but also leaves, insects and fruit, and most importantly are exposed to sunshine, which ensures they will form sufficient vitamin D.[182] A basic diet of seeds is what we will consider here, at the rate of 0.5 tablespoons of mixed seed/day.[183] Given that there are 67.6 US tablespoons in a litre, the canary will eat (0.5 ÷ 67.5) × 365 = 2.7 l/year. This will weigh 2.7 × 678 = 1,831 g, or 1.8 kg. The footprint of seeds is taken to be 13.4 m²/kg as for all other cereals, on the basis that cereals like rice are seeds. From this we can estimate that feeding a canary its seeds would have an annual footprint of 13.4 × 1.8 = 24.1 m². As for the other foods a canary might eat, the 0.5 teaspoons/day of chopped hard-boiled egg will also be taken into account. A hard-boiled egg can easily be divided into eight pieces each about the size of a teaspoon. Assuming, therefore, that the egg can be stored safely until it has been used up, we can suppose that the canary will eat 1 egg a week, or 52 in a year. An average egg weighs 58 g,[184] so in a year a canary would consume 52 × 58 = 3,016 g, or 3 kg. The footprint of eggs is 15.5 m²/kg (see Chapter 1), giving a footprint of 15.5 × 3 = 46.5 m². This makes a total annual footprint for feeding a canary of 24.1 + 46.5 = 70.6 m², or 0.007 ha.

One source recommends a minimum cage size of 20 × 12 × 16 in. (50 × 30 × 40 cm).[185] It is also useful to have a metal grate at the bottom of the cage over the droppings tray, to keep the bird from its droppings. According to a manufacturer of cockatiel cages, a cage 22 × 15 × 23 in. weighs 14.8 lb (6.4 kg).[186] This would also be suitable for a canary. Using an embodied energy of 32 MJ/kg for virgin steel (see the discussion of hamsters above) would give an embodied energy for the cage of 32 × 6.4 = 205 MJ, or 0.205 GJ, and a land footprint of 0.0015 ha. Assuming a 10-year life, the cage works out at 0.000 15 ha/year. This gives a total annual footprint for the canary of 0.007 ha, and the cage is so small that it can be ignored. This effectively means that two canaries are the equivalent of a hamster when it comes to their footprints.

GOLDFISH

In some parts of the world, such as Vietnam, the fish is the culturally preferred pet.[187] In the West, the common goldfish (known as the 'gold carp' in the Far East and as *hibuna* in Japan[188]) has a large following because it is robust, able to live both outdoors in ponds and indoors in unheated aquaria.

According to the American Goldfish Association's website, goldfish evolved from the crucian carp, a fish that is recorded in China in about AD 1000. The 'gold' would have appeared as a mutation, since the fish was originally a drab olive colour.[189] Since then, goldfish have been bred to encourage various characteristics, until it has become the common pet we recognize today.

The world population of goldfish is hard to find out, although the 2007 Singapore Goldfish Festival included 200 tanks of goldfish for judging, along with 120 tanks of guppy and 140 tanks of flowerhorn,[190] suggesting that the fish is popular among fanciers. A pet website states that goldfish are the most common household pet in the world.[191] The reason we have included it here is that it is popular in the West, it is vegetarian (almost), and it eats little in comparison with the other animals considered above. It does need a degree of equipment – a tank or bowl, for instance – and a supply of water.

Goldfish can be vegetarian but are mostly omnivores. They need protein, carbohydrates and vitamins,[192] which usually come in the form of fish food pellets or dried flakes. They can be given some fresh food like vegetables, and will eat water plants in their tank if these are supplied, but for the purpose of our analysis only the flaked fish food is considered. The general rule for fish is that they should be fed only what they can eat in three minutes.[193] Overfeeding will mean that food falls to the bottom and decomposes, taking up oxygen from the water; in extreme conditions the fish can die through lack of oxygen. Goldfish are greedy and will ask for more, so the temptation is to overfeed them, but two pinches of food a day are considered enough. They really do not eat much at all compared to other pets. Assuming that there are 40 pinches to a teaspoon,[194] and that a tablespoon (the volumetric equivalent of three teaspoons) of cornflour (taken as equivalent in density to fish food) weighs 14 g,[195] a goldfish will eat $14 \div 40 \times 14 \div 3 = 0.35 \times 4.7 = 1.6$ g in a week. Over a year this works out as $52 \times 1.6 = 83.2$ g, or approximately one medium-sized tub.[196] Using a footprint of 20 m²/kg to represent a mixture of cereals and meats (see Chapter 1), we come up with an annual food footprint of 1.7 m² for keeping a goldfish.

Like the carp they are related to, goldfish can exist in murky water. But any water with a fish living in it gradually fills up with toxins and will need changing, or the fish will die, as many children have found out over the years. Goldfish should have a minimum of 50 l of water per fish.[197] To remove the waste products, the same source suggests that 10–20% of the water should be changed weekly for fresh water. The top-up water added to the tank over a year measures (50 × 0.15) × 52 = 390 l. Obviously a full 50 l are needed at the start. If the goldfish lives for 10 years, which is a reasonable life, the water used for topping up would add a 5 l share of the set-up water to the yearly total, to make 395 l. As with all embodied energy calculations, the longer the fish lives, the less significant the top-up water becomes as a factor. One goldfish, which lived in Yorkshire, was 43 years old when it died (1956–99).[198] However, this record was broken not long after by a goldfish in Devon (1960–2005).[199] One source even states that the only way to kill a goldfish is with a gun,[200] but this may be stretching things too far. For this analysis, a 10-year lifespan will be assumed.[201] Using the UK footprint of cold tap water of 0.08 m²/100 l,[202] we can give the goldfish an annual footprint of 0.08 × 395 ÷ 100 = 0.3 m².

For a home, the fish needs a glass tank with some large, smooth gravel or stones at the bottom (some advise against gravel in case the fish should choke on it).[203] A tank measuring 0.7 × 0.3 × 0.3 m could hold 50 l of water and leave a gap at the top below the rim. Assuming that the tank is made from 6 mm glass,[204] the volume of glass in the tank will be (0.7 × 0.3 × 0.006 × 3) + (0.3 × 0.3 × 0.006 × 2) = 0.005 m³. If we use the value of 37,550 MJ/m³ for general glass,[205] the tank would have an embodied energy of 188 MJ. Over the fish's 10-year lifespan this would add 18.8 MJ to the footprint. Using the conversion of 135 GJ/ha, we arrive at a figure of 135,000 MJ ÷ 10,000, or 13.5 MJ/m². In land terms, the additional footprint is 18.8 ÷ 13.5 = 1.4 m². Obviously a glass tank is not worn out after 10 years, but for now this value will be used.

From these figures we can now work out the full footprint of keeping a goldfish: 1.7 (food) + 0.3 (water) + 1.4 (tank) = 3.4 m²/year, or 0.00034 ha. This value has been incorporated in Table 17 (below).

COMPARATIVE PETS

In the world there are dog people and there are cat people (and probably canary, hamster and goldfish people too), and all would say that there is no real comparison between their choice of pet and the others. But owning any

Table 15: Number of families that could own different pets for the same ecological footprint

for a footprint of 0.36 ha you can have:	
1 happy family	with an Alsatian
1.3 happy families	with a Border Collie
2 happy families	with a Scottie
2.4 happy families	with a cat
25.7 happy families	with a hamster
51.4 happy families	with a canary
1,059 happy families	with a goldfish

kind of pet brings responsibility, and as a result all pets give some meaning to the life of their owners because of this mutual dependence. For this reason, we have included all the pets we have considered in Table 15, to compare their relative footprints. Rather than present a direct comparison, we have taken the pet with the largest footprint – a big dog such as an Alsatian, with a footprint of 0.36 ha – as our base, and then worked out how many other pets would make up an equivalent footprint.

When the economist E. F. Schumacher coined the phrase 'small is beautiful', he was not necessarily thinking of pets, but it does turn out to be the case. If you want to teach your children about the responsibility of pet ownership and at the same time be kind to the environment, a goldfish is the answer (unless you want to consider owning an edible pet; see below). For households without children, pets are in fact a better option on purely environmental grounds, as children will have very much higher footprints. As we mentioned above, communal pets could also be a way to reduce environmental impact while still maintaining a relationship with animals; having a school pet may be better than each child having a pet at home.

EDIBLE PETS

To set out clearly our position with regard to edible pets, it would be good to begin with an anecdote. Many years ago we had friends who went back to live in the United States, leaving us with a Rhode Island Red rooster they had affectionately named 'Lenin' (well, he was a Red). In fact, this bird turned out to be very aggressive, maybe as a result of being abandoned by his former owners. One day we were aware of our two eldest children, then aged 6 and 3, screaming outside when they should have been playing happily. It transpired that they had been chased the length of the garden by Lenin, who was pecking at their heels. This being the last straw, Robert took his air rifle and shot the rooster, who was then drawn, plucked and roasted. The children always claimed that this was one of the best meals they had ever eaten.

For years animals have been given a good life and their company enjoyed, and then they have been eaten. Children are well able to cope with this situation if they know what is going on, and the process links them into the natural cycles of life and death. However, even with this background there are going to be some people who will never cope with the idea of eating their pets. Those, we suggest, should skip this section. For readers who don't mind knowing whom they are eating, the purpose of this next discussion is to see the environmental impact of raising animals at home for meat, and to find out whether edible pets could have a negative footprint.

RABBITS

Rabbits do make good pets, although they have one drawback: despite their soft fur and cuddly appearance, they do not particularly like being held.[206] But if you have the room, they can give children a sense of the responsibility of pet ownership, they are fun to keep, they will eat grass, and they do taste very good in a pie, as Peter Rabbit was warned. They also provide economic benefits to the household. According to a book entitled *The Domestic Rabbit*,

> *The home production of food will of course produce a much cheaper food supply than the purchase of the same food.*[207]

To raise rabbit meat, you need a breeding pair of rabbits, housing for them and for their offspring, and a supply of food and water. Although rabbits are also bred for their fur, only meat will be considered here. Rabbits come in many shapes and sizes, but here we have concentrated on the New Zealand White – a popular breed for meat production and one we have kept ourselves for this purpose, albeit some years ago now. The New Zealand White weighs

9–12 lb (4.1–5.4 kg) and has high growth rate when young: given the right feeding, a rabbit weighing 4–4.5 lb (1.8–2 kg) can be produced eight weeks from birth.[208] The same source suggests that the dressing loss, or carcass weight as percentage of live weight, is 50%,[209] meaning that around 1 kg of meat with bones is available at eight weeks. According to an American rabbit-breeder's website, a single doe the size of a New Zealand White can produce 320 lb (145 kg) of meat in a year, which is 145 young rabbits and more meat than a cow would provide in the same time.[210] The website suggests that 6 lb (2.7 kg) of rabbit meat can be produced for the same amount of food and water as would be needed for 1 lb (0.45 kg) of meat from a cow. Sandford, an older source, suggests that 50 youngsters a year would be a very high level of meat production: it would represent a minimum of 150 lb (68 kg) per doe rabbit per year,[211] and would mean that the doe would be remated as soon as each litter were weaned. However, all this information suggests that rabbits are prolific and do in fact breed like rabbits.

For this study, we have supposed that the breeding pair of rabbits will be remated every two months, giving six litters of six rabbits a year to be reared for meat (the aim is to keep rabbits as pets, but also to produce meat as a by-product). Thus housing will be required for eight rabbits at any one time. Simple hutches can be made from wood, although when we kept rabbits for meat many years ago we made some three-storey hutches from recycled wood (that is, wood we happened to have left over from other things) and recycled plastic sheeting 12.5 mm thick, constructing walls, roof and floors that turned out to be totally rabbit-proof. We also had a moveable triangular run of wood and chicken wire (a type of Morant hutch, for those that are technically minded) into which we put the growing rabbits so they could eat grass; this was moved every day.

Plans put out by Penn State College of Agricultural Sciences suggest that to house the rabbits in four separate hutches, two up and two down, would require the following amounts of wood: 18 m of 50 × 50 timber; 12 m of 100 × 25 timber; 16 m² of painted chipboard for the solid parts, including the solid doors that will give the rabbits shade; 2 m² of wire netting for the other doors; and all the necessary fixings.[212] The volume of wood is thus $(18 \times 0.05 \times 0.05) + (12 \times 0.1 \times 0.025) = (0.045 + 0.03) = 0.075$ m³. If we convert this figure using the value of 170 MJ/m³ for air-dried rough-sawn timber,[213] we have an energy content of 0.075 × 170 = 12.75 MJ. The same source gives the embodied energy of particle board as 4,400 MJ/m³. The volume of chipboard (12 mm thick) in the hutches is 16 × 0.012 = 0.192 m³, which gives an embodied energy figure of 4,400 × 0.192 = 845 MJ. The value for the wire netting we used in the hamster cage earlier would give us a figure of 314 MJ for 2 m² of netting. Last of all, the chipboard needs to be painted since it will rot if left unprotected from the rabbit urine.[214] A litre of water-based paint adds 115 MJ, as for the dog kennel above. This gives a total value for the hutches of 12.75 + 845 + 314 + 115 = 1,287 MJ. Assuming that the hutches last 10 years, this would work out as 128.7 MJ/year. For the moveable pen, we will assume that it is an equilateral triangle in section, with sides 1 m long made of softwood framing, and covered in 13 mm steel chicken wire. A single roll of wire mesh 1.2 m wide and 10 m long will supply enough for the sides and ends, and it weighs 4 kg.[215] This quantity of virgin steel would have an energy content of 32 × 4 = 128 MJ. Since the softwood has a very low embodied energy and there will be some mesh left over for other purposes, we have taken this figure, 128 MJ, to represent the total for the moveable run. If it lasts 10 years, the embodied energy will be 12.8 MJ/year. So to house the productive rabbits requires 128.7 + 12.8 = 141.5 MJ/year, giving a footprint of 0.001 ha.

The rabbits also have to be fed, especially if they are being reared for meat. According to Sandford, and if we use the Harper Adams diet adjusted for weight,[216] a 10 lb (4.5 kg) rabbit has a daily requirement of 1.2 oz (0.034 kg) of mash (40% maize and 40% ground oats), 0.9 oz (0.026 kg) of oats, 2.4 oz (0.068 kg) of hay, and 4.8–14.4 oz (0.136–0.408 kg) of leaves, grass and assorted green stuff or roots. When breeding and lactating, the female rabbit will require more nourishment, and feed for growing rabbits also tends to have higher cereal content. Given that there will be eight rabbits at any one time, for this analysis it is assumed that the two breeding rabbits will eat these rations, and that the six young rabbits will eat 50% of the recommended levels. Less food would be required in practice, as the young are killed at 2 kg. This gives the equivalent of five adult rabbits to feed.

The rations eaten by the five putative rabbits in a year are shown in Table 16. We have assumed that the rabbit food crops are grown in a temperate climate like that of the UK.

Table 16: Types of feed for raising rabbit meat at home

food	quantity (kg)	land area required (m²)
mash	62	142*
oats	48	120†
hay	124	310‡
green stuff and roots	248–745	0 (these can be grown at home or collected locally)
total		572 (0.06 ha)

* Based on 3 tonnes/ha for corn,[217] and oats as below.
† Based on 4 tonnes/ha for oats.[218]
‡ Based on 4 tonnes/ha.[219]

This table looks only at the land area needed to produce the crops, not the total footprint, which would include fertilizer and fuel for growing, transport, and so on. That said, the final footprints should be less than that of finished foods, since there is only limited packaging, and only local transport is involved. Nonetheless, to account for these other issues the land footprint has been doubled to give a total of 0.12 ha/year. This also allows for the land needed to grow the greens or roots, which might be 166 m², the size of many back gardens – a figure based on growing 500 kg and a yield of 30 tonnes/ha for carrots and cabbages.[220] Gardens are generally more productive than agricultural crops, so this area might be reduced; and green stuff can be gathered from other sources ('weeds' from the gardens of friends and neighbours, for example). We used to make nettle hay for our rabbits, from nettles we found under hedges – a good source of nutrition. The total footprint is thus 0.12, since the small 0.001 ha for the housing can be ignored.

The aim is to produce 36 young rabbits to be reared for meat and killed at 2 kg, thus giving 72 kg of meat a year. If the 72 kg of meat were purchased, it would have a footprint of 72 × 29.8 (the footprint for all other meats; see Chapter 1) = 0.21 ha. So feeding the rabbits the Harper Adams diet, with its bought-in foodstuffs, would result in a negative pet footprint of −0.09 ha (0.12 minus 0.21), because you can keep pets (the two breeding rabbits), but not have to buy in 72 kg of meat, with its higher footprint.

Sandford also suggests an alternative diet for a 4.5 kg rabbit, comprising a daily maintenance ration of 0.65 kg of only fresh green food.[221] This would work out at 1,186 kg a year for the system of raising rabbits discussed above, and the area of land needed to grow the food would come out at just under 400 m², giving a pet footprint of minus 0.21 ha because all food is grown at home.

At this point many people will raise objections to the whole idea of keeping rabbits in the back garden, perhaps worried about smell, vermin, and so on, even though they would probably not object to keeping a large dog there. Here it may be salutary to recount a story a colleague at work told us.[222] In a 'good' neighbourhood in Vancouver, Canada, there lived a man who was interested in DIY around the home, much to the chagrin of his neighbours, who overlooked his backyard and who gave him a hard time for lowering the tone of the neighbourhood. One night he built in the back garden a rabbit hutch on legs of old timber. Every morning and evening he would go down to the hutch. Soon the council started to receive complaints about a man who was keeping rabbits in his backyard, and especially about the smell they generated. The grumbles reached such a level that an officer called on the man for an explanation; he was taken into the backyard, only to be shown the 'virtual' rabbit, for there was no rabbit. This story illustrates succinctly what we have been trying to say in this book. It is up to all of us to make changes that can reduce our impact on the planet, both in what we choose to do and in what we choose to find acceptable.

CHICKENS

If you baulk at keeping rabbits for meat, keeping hens for eggs may be a more acceptable option. But in peasant cultures, hens were seen as useful for both: there are many recipes from different places for converting tough old hens into something nourishing, such as *coq au vin* in France and *caldo de gallina vieja* in the Dominican Republic. However, for this assessment of footprint, only egg production will be considered. Hens are not the cleverest of pets but, as one authority has pointed out, there are people who just like them, such as 'the farmer's wife and the smallholder who have always kept chickens and always will, irrespective of whether they are or are not profitable'.[223]

Just down the road from where we live, three free-range hens are usually kept confined at the end of the garden, although sometimes we meet them on the path on the way home from work in the evening. According to a backyard poultry keeper who had 18 hens in a fenced area 100 × 60 ft (30.5 × 18 m), his chickens produced 80 eggs a week.[224] This works out at 30.5 m²/hen and 4.4 eggs/hen/week. Keeping 3 hens would therefore give us 12–13 eggs/week, and the area required would be just over 90 m², or an area of land 5 × 18 m.

Very roughly, the footprints of a coop made from softwood and chicken wire and of a fence can be extrapolated from the figures for the rabbit hutch and run mentioned earlier. The footprint for housing the 8 rabbits was 0.001 ha or 10 m², so if we assume 3 hens we would have a foot-print of 3.75 m² – say 4 m². This gives us a total footprint for land, housing and a fence of 94 m².

Free-range hens will obtain some food from their environment, but for egg production they need to be fed grains in some form. The backyard poultry keeper, who lives in the UK, states that the hens eat a diet of mixed grain and layers' pellets, plus scraps from the kitchen (and from the local cricket club in the summer) and what they forage on site.[225] According to his website, the cost for the bought-in food works out at £0.80/hen/month. Since 40 kg of mixed grain and layers' pellets costs £11, this means that each month every hen eats just under 3 kg of bought-in food, or 36 kg a year. Layers' pellets usually contain fishmeal or animal protein of some sort – typically 16 or 17%[226] – which the hens need for egg production. (In the wild, it would come from insects and worms.) Assuming that the 36 kg is 17% animal protein, 4% vegetable oil and 79% mixed grains, the footprint conversion factors we used for food in Cardiff (see Chapter 1) would give us a footprint of $(36 \times 0.17 \times 29.8) + (36 \times 0.04 \times 52.7) + (36 \times 0.79 \times 13.4) = 606$ m². Our total footprint – food plus land and coop – thus works out at 700 m² for three hens, or 0.07 ha.

If we suppose that the hens produce 12.5 × 52 = 650 eggs a year, and that the average egg weighs 58 g,[227] we would benefit from 650 × (58 ÷ 1,000) = 38 kg of eggs. Buying these eggs would have a footprint of 38 × 15.5 = 589 m², or 0.06 ha. If we subtract this figure from the hens' total footprint of 700 m², we get a net footprint of 111 m² or 0.01 ha for three pet hens –

which is like keeping a single hamster, but then hamsters don't lay eggs. So although as pets hens don't have a negative footprint like rabbits, you do have both a pet and a source of fresh free-range eggs. It is likely that the Cardiff footprint for eggs is lower than the footprint for producing only free-range eggs, since general egg production is dominated by intensive systems in which the space given over to each hen is very small – about the size of a piece of A4 paper, according to one New Zealand MP.[228] The footprint for our pet hens, on the other hand, allows 30 m² per bird. But since a detailed footprint for free-range eggs is unavailable, we have used the average value from the Cardiff study (see Chapter 1) here for comparison.

If you ate the hens at the rate of one a year, you could reduce the footprint. An old hen, plucked and drawn, should give you a 2 kg carcass. Buying in the equivalent would have a footprint of 2 × 20.8 (the Cardiff value for uncooked poultry) = 41.6 m², so the annual footprint for the three pet hens reduces to 69 m², or 0.007 ha, which is the same as keeping a canary. You could say that keeping chickens as pets gives you more bird per buck.

DISCUSSION

The footprint for all pets is determined mostly by the food they eat and by the land it takes to grow this food. Only when we are dealing with small animals like hamsters and goldfish does the footprint of housing our pets have some significance. Table 17 sets out the footprints of all the pets we discussed above in descending order.

Your choices should be determined by the reason why you want to keep a pet. If the idea of having a pet is to teach children responsibility, there is much to be gained by having a productive pet, and, if you don't eat meat, keeping chickens for eggs is a good option. If you want a pet for companionship, the smaller it is, the better; maybe sharing a pet could be a good option in such circumstances. Our key suggestions are as follows:

- Don't have a pet.
- Have an edible pet.
- Share a pet.
- If you must have your own pet, get a small one.

Table 17: Ecological footprint of common pets

pet	footprint (m²/year)	footprint (ha/year)
large dog (Alsatian)	3,600	0.36
medium dog (Collie)	2,700	0.27
small dog (Scottie)	1,800	0.18
cat allowed to kill wildlife	1,500	0.15
indoor cat	1,300	0.13
toy dog (Chihuahua)	900	0.09
hamster	140	0.014
3 free-range hens, kept for eggs	100	0.01
3 free-range hens, kept for eggs and meat	70	0.007
canary	70	0.007
goldfish	3.4	0.00034
2 breeding rabbits kept for meat, bought-in food	(−900)	(−0.09)
2 breeding rabbits kept for meat, food grown on site	(−2,100)	(−0.21)

Although the topics investigated in detail in this chapter may seem arbitrary, they have been selected because they cover items most people would expect to find in a Western home. They also represent categories of things we need (clothes) or desire (electronics), and the living creatures with which we choose to share our immediate environment.

5
TIME TO SPARE

As we mentioned at the start of this book, land is one of the four 'givens' of the natural environment within which the human race has to find a way of organizing life and behaving in a sustainable way. However, the hope is that such a system will be able to go beyond the basic provision of food, water and shelter (buildings and clothing), to include room for interests that offer enrichment: the so-called 'leisure activities' that occupy our time when we are not working to secure the basics.

Many activities that are thought of as hobbies today – for example gardening, cooking, making clothes, knitting and house maintenance – would have been viewed in the past as essential, necessary for survival. These are dealt with later. This section, on the other hand, looks at the impact of activities whose only relevance to survival is the exercise involved. Some, like playing chess and stamp collecting, provide little physical exercise even if they require mental agility or provide social connectivity, but they are nonetheless included here. Most activities have some social component, since even solitary pastimes like building model railways and doing the crossword have clubs and societies that support them. In a sustainable society such activities will be as important for individual development and social cohesion as they were in the past. However, not all activities are equal; our aim here is to find out which activities are resource-hungry (and may not, therefore, form a significant part of a sustainable future), and which have less of an impact.

ANYONE FOR TENNIS?

There is a big difference between the impromptu game of football played in the car park during lunch break or in the street after school and the matches held in dedicated stadiums that form part of the global football industry. Both are associated with exercise and social connection, but the former makes use of timetabled space (which will be essential if all human demands are to be met from the land in the future), whereas the dedicated land of the football pitch is often underused. The first section of this comparison begins by looking at sports such as association football, golf, skiing, tennis and swimming, the land for which has a single use only. This will enable us to see whether there is a large difference between the sports in terms of the amount of land required and the numbers and types of people who use the facilities over a year. To make this comparison some individual sports have been selected for closer investigation. First we will consider them one by one, and then summarize relative land use in Table 1.

GOLF

The worldwide popularity of golf is well accepted. According to the Golf Research Group, there are 57 million golfers in the world and 32,000 courses, of which 59% are in North America, 19% in Europe and 12% in Asia.[1] On account of its swift economic development, the number of courses in China has been increasing. In 1994 Beijing had just 3 golf courses compared with around 40 today, and there are about 180 in China as a whole.[2] But the same source states that one Beijing course was built on landfill because of competition for land with farmers. The United Nations Environment Programme (UNEP) has also commented on the increasing popularity of golf in Asian countries and the accompanying environmental problems. It states that, each year, a typical course in a tropical country such as Thailand needs 1,500 kg of chemicals in the form of fertilizers, pesticides and herbicides, and consumes as much water as 60,000 rural villages.[3] Although Thailand is not short of water, there is a dry season, so villages are encouraged to use ponds for water storage to promote self-sufficiency.[4] During the dry season the water for golf courses will have to be extracted from somewhere, possibly in competition with other users such as farmers.

The Scottish Assessors Association (and golf began in Scotland, after all[5]) claims that, for rating valuation purposes, an 18-hole golf course covers an area of 35–45 ha, to allow for a round of golf with minimum interruption.[6] The SAA also notes that courses vary in quality from those that are minimally developed agricultural land to full championship courses that are longer, larger (in order to accommodate practice areas and spectator facilities) and very well maintained. Courses also vary in size, with 18 and 9 holes being the standards. Since no breakdown for world course lengths is available, we can estimate very roughly that the land area taken up by golf courses is $0.75 \times 40 \times 32,000 = 960,000$ ha, assuming a 50/50 split between 18-hole and 9-hole courses. Since the number of active golfers has been quoted as 57 million, this works out at 0.017 ha, or 170 m^2, per player.

In the US, the Organic Consumers Association states that the country has 18,000 courses – more than half the 35,000 courses in the world – covering an area of 1.7 million acres (0.7 million ha), which consume 4 billion US gallons (15.1 million m^3) of water every day, not to mention the pesticides and herbicides necessary to keep the grass green.[7] If, broadly speaking, this figure represents half the area of all the world's courses, this would give a global total of 1.4 million ha, equating to 0.02 ha, or 200 m^2, per player. The water used each year would be 0.27 m^3/player, or 270 l/player. The average water use for a house in Auckland is 240 m^3 each year.[8] Chambers et al. give the footprint of cold tap water in the UK as 0.08 m^2/100 l.[9] Applied to all players, this would give a footprint of 0.2 m^2/player for water – a small amount compared with the land requirement.

As we mentioned above, land area is not the only type of environmental impact associated with golf courses. The water, herbicides and pesticides needed to maintain the grass also have an impact on local water courses, water tables and water supplies. New golf courses are also seen as a good way to sell new housing developments, perhaps one reason for the sport's popularity. The strategy is an old one: the 1911 development at Gidea Park, 30 minutes by rail from the City of London, was marketed as being next to Romford Golf Course.[10] On the positive side, golf courses can act as corridors for wildlife, providing these are considered at the design stage; but the surface of trimmed grass does not form a native part of most habitats.

FOOTBALL

Football can be played on any piece of relatively flat ground with a minimum of equipment, All that is needed is a ball, and even this can be replaced by a tin can. In the professional sphere, land is kept aside for matches, and practice space is also required. Playing fields in schools, as well as those provided by local authorities, will be multi-purpose, used for football in the winter and for other sports like cricket and softball in the summer. The pitches of amateur football clubs may be used for practice or for other purposes according to the season. Trying to calculate exactly how much land is used for the sport is therefore quite problematic.

Soccer, or 'association football', is the most popular game in the world, even though most matches will be informal. It is played in at least 200 countries and has millions of fans.[11] For the purposes of this study we will consider only professional soccer. FIFA, the governing body of association football, describes the football pitch as 90–120 m long and 45–90 m wide, meaning that it is very flexible in size. Even international pitches can vary between 100 and 110 m in length, and from 64 to 75 m in width.[12] The simplest approach here would be to take the average size of a non-international pitch of 7,140 m² and divide it by 25 (22 players plus 1 referee and 2 linesmen) to give 286 m²/player. But professional teams will have more than the 22 players, the referee and the linesmen on and around the pitch at any one time, and a professional football pitch will also cover much more land than a basic playing surface because of facilities for spectators and suchlike. On the other hand, the same pitch will be timetabled for use by different teams.

In 2006, FIFA conducted a worldwide survey to see how many people were involved in football.[13] It came up with a total figure of 270 million: 265 million players, and the rest consisting of coaches, referees, and so on. Of these, 226 million were unregistered players, including school teams.[14] The total number of clubs – 301,000 – remained similar to that revealed by the 2002 census, and 1.7 million teams were counted, more per club than at the last count. Unfortunately, FIFA did not count the number of football pitches.

For our comparison we have assumed that each registered player has access to a pitch permanently dedicated to football, although some will be registered beach football players.[15] The number of registered players is 39 million. A proposed new stadium in Auckland, New Zealand, on the waterfront would have meant losing 4–5 ha of container storage at the port.[16] A similar stadium in Wellington, New Zealand, that covers 4.8 ha[17] is home to three teams: two rugby and one soccer.[18] If we suppose an area for a permanent stadium of 4.5 ha, and three permanent teams of 32 players each (the number in the current Sheffield Wednesday squad[19]), we can calculate an area per player of 45,000 ÷ (3 × 32) = 469 m²/player. Applying this same value to the 39 million professional players in world would suggest that professional football occupies 1.8 million ha of land, which, unlike golf courses, offers no type of habitat whatsoever. This is just under 7% of the total area of New Zealand (270,000 km²). The figure does not include the playing fields used by non-professional clubs (we should remember that registered players account for just over 14% of all footballers, but we do not know how many non-professional football grounds there are). Of course, these stadiums and grounds also cater for spectators, and many people derive enjoyment from watching the matches at home on television. In addition, many stadiums host exhibitions and trade shows, but these are usually confined to ancillary spaces, leaving the actual pitch just for games. A value of 375 m² per player, which is mid-way between the two figures we calculated above, will be used for Table 1.

TENNIS

According to International Tennis Federation Rules, a tennis court measures 36 × 78 ft (11 × 24 m),[20] and a manufacturer of court coatings suggests that the whole area that is tarmac'd and fenced in typically measures 60 × 120 ft (18 × 36 m).[21] Using the same rough calculation method that we worked out for the football pitch above, and allowing for an average three players per court (singles matches are for two players and doubles for four), together with an umpire and two ballboys or -girls, we arrive at an area per player of 648 ÷ 6 = 108 m². For most informal playing (and the greatest number of tennis games in the world will be of this type), there will be no umpire or ballboys/girls, whereas tournament matches will see a greater number of officials on court because of the presence of line umpires, a net umpire and more ball retrievers.

The Lower Hutt Tennis Club in Wellington, New Zealand, has 10 courts, a car park and a clubhouse, and in

2005 had 386 members.[22] An aerial photograph from their website indicates that the land occupied by the whole club is roughly equivalent to 12 courts with their surrounding space, or $648 \times 12 = 7{,}776$ m². This equates to 20 m²/player, which will be more representative of the games each court supports in a year. In the Wellington region, the Karori Club has the highest number of members – 600, who play on 3 courts.[23] Assuming that the courts and ancillary spaces at the Karori Club occupy an area in proportion to the Lower Hutt Club, we can use a value of $7{,}776 \div 4$ (it has 3 rather than 12 courts) $= 1{,}944$ m². This gives an area per player of 3 m². The people of Karori obviously understand about sharing resources. If we assume that the average area per tennis player lies between these values, we arrive at the figure of 11.5 m²/player.

According to *Tennis Magazine*, the total number of tennis players worldwide is not known but thought to be large: 144 countries are members of the International Tennis Federation,[24] meaning that tennis is played in 74% of the world. The magazine also quotes from a study by the United States Tennis Association (USTA) and the Tennis Industry Association, which found that there were nearly 25 million tennis players in the US alone. The same figures, quoted by another source, claim that there were 559 million tennis-playing occasions in the the the country.[25] At the start of 2005 the US population was 295,160,302,[26] and world population was then 6.45 billion. This means that 8.5% of people in the US were tennis players when the study was carried out. Allowing for the 26% of countries not registered with the International Tennis Federation, we can estimate that the number of tennis players in the world is around 6.45 billion $\times (0.085 \times 0.75) =$ approximately 0.4 billion. If we use the value of 11.5 m² of land per player, we can conclude that the area permanently occupied by tennis facilities would be 4.6 billion m², or 460,000 ha. This could be an overestimate, since the US might have more tennis players per head of population than other countries, and the USTA study did not indicate how active all the tennis players were. However, tennis is the only traditional sport in the US that is still growing.[27] In the UK, one ball-manufacturer reports that tennis playing has declined by 30% in the last decade.[28] This is another area where better statistics are required if we are to assess accurately the true impact of tennis on the environment.

SKIING

As a winter sport, skiing uses land that may not be suitable for other purposes or that may once have been used for agriculture in the summer. It
grew out of a simple method of transportation: a ski on each foot to keep the
traveller on top of the snow and allow for easy movement. The Norwegians
are credited with seeing the sporting possibilities of using this equipment in
the 1700s, developing ways of turning the skis to control their passage down
a hillside.[29] This led to the Nordic code of skiing, in which Alpine techniques
were developed to cope with ever steeper slopes. The popularity of skiing
spread to other countries in the early 1900s, and some have claimed it to be
the fastest non-motorized sport in the world.[30]

The 2010 Winter Olympics in Vancouver, based at the Whistler
Blackcomb ski resort, are expected to attract 5,000 athletes and officials for
all winter sports in February, and 1,700 more for the Para Winter Olympics
the following month.[31] In Whistler, which we assume to be representative of
other ski resorts, there were nearly 2 million visitors in 1999–2000: over
959,000 in winter (1 November – 30 April) and approximately 1.3 million in
summer (1 May – 31 October).[32] The brochure for the resort states that it has
3,036 ha of terrain that can be skied, of which Blackcomb Mountain has
1,382 ha and Whistler Mountain 1,925 ha. Since the two mountains are run
as a single resort, it is assumed that the visitor numbers refer to the combined Whistler Blackcomb complex. If we take it that the winter visitors are
skiing and snowboarding only, we arrive at an area per person of 0.003 ha,
or 30 m². However, given that the same mountain area is also used for
summer activities such as mountain biking, walking, river rafting and bear
viewing (according to the official website[33]), the total for outdoor activities in
the resort will be slightly less than half this figure. For the purposes of this
investigation, we have therefore assumed that all ski resorts are also used in
summer, which gives an approximate area per skier of 15 m².

In the 1998–99 season, according to Statistics Canada, the country's
ski resorts received approximately 17 million visitors.[34] This would suggest
that the ski resorts in all Canada cover an area of 51,000 ha. Canada is one of
fifteen member countries of the Fédération Internationale des Patrouilles de
Ski (Ski Patrol Federation).[35] Missing from this group are the countries long
associated with skiing, such as Austria, Switzerland, Germany, Norway and

Finland (Sweden is a member). If we add these five to the fifteen countries in the FIPS, we have a total of twenty skiing nations. Multiplied by the area of land occupied by resorts in Canada, which we are taking as representative, we reach an area of 51,000 × 20 = 1,020,000 ha.

It could be argued that, since land for skiing is not suitable for agriculture, it should not be compared with other sports like golf, where land taken up by courses could be farmed. Some land in ski resorts could be used for growing trees, although not all, and it might be easier to combine tree-growing with cross-country skiing than with events like downhill skiing. We have already taken account of the fact that land used by outdoor sports in winter is also used for recreation in summer, and could also be used for pasture. But skiing poses a challenge to pristine mountain habitat and brings with it development in the form of accommodation, restaurants, access roads, and so on. Of all the sports discussed so far, it is the one where most people will make a special journey to take part and will stay in the vicinity. An article by Chris Madigan in the *Guardian* newspaper suggests that no one is considering the real environmental impact of ski resorts, allowing their claims to be 'green' to go unchallenged.[36] Such assertions relate to how buildings are heated, or the fact that power to run ski lifts might come from renewable sources. Among the environmental impacts of skiing, the travel company Ski Europe lists land disturbance during the creation of runs; intensive water and energy consumption for making artificial snow; disturbance to wildlife from construction and from day-to-day operations; the influx of workers; and changes to local settlements through part-time occupation of properties.[37] Cross-country skiing is thought to be less environmentally damaging because it can use natural terrain. But a study by the UN Environmental Programme suggests that many low-lying ski resorts may no longer be viable because of global warming,[38] so it may be that skiing is a sport under threat rather than a growing one like golf.

SWIMMING

Swimming is another sport that, like football, does not necessarily require dedicated land: the sea, rivers and lakes all provide opportunities for swimming. Yet much of the world's population, especially in the developed world, will have learned how to swim in special pools. In the UK, the first

Everyday Swim conference in 2007 stated that swimming was the most popular activity for the general population after walking.[39] The UK has a policy, embedded in the national curriculum, that every child must be taught to swim, so that by the end of Key Stage 2 (ages 8 to 11) they can swim 25 m unaided.[40]

In order to find out how much land each swimmer takes up, we have taken the city of Cambridge as an example. Cambridge has four public pools (one outside) that are run on behalf of the local council.[41] From the dimensions available, it seems the pools themselves have a combined area of approximately 2,050 m². To allow for surrounding land and ancillary spaces, this figure could be doubled to give a total land area for public pools of 4,100 m². The population of Cambridge in mid-2006 was either 117,900 or 113,600, depending on how it was estimated, but this includes students living at their term-time addresses.[42] University students use the pool of the Leys School, which has a 200 m² area of water;[43] if we double this figure to allow for facilities and ancillary spaces, we arrive at a total figure for Cambridge pools of 4,500 m².

A *Half-time Report* produced by the Everyday Swim initiative in the UK states that 20 million people in England swim every year – a figure that has remained relatively constant for the last twenty years.[44] According to the Office for National Statistics,[45] the population of England in mid-2006 was 50,763,000, effectively meaning that 39% of the population were swimmers. Applying this figure to Cambridge (we have taken the population as 115,750) gives 45,143 swimmers and an area per swimmer of 0.1 m². Thus much less land (or equivalent water area) is used for swimming than for the other sports considered so far.

According to the directory of the Fédération Internationale de Natation, 166 countries have national swimming groups linked to the organization. This suggests that 86% of nations are involved in competitive swimming events, including water polo, that make use of pools. If this same percentage is applied to the world population, it would suggest that roughly 6.45 billion × 0.86 = 5.5 billion people live in countries that use swimming pools. Using the fact that 39% of all people in the UK are swimmers, we can work out an estimate of 2.1 billion swimmers worldwide, and a pro rata land area given over to swimming pools, both public and private, of 21,000 ha.

The environmental impact of swimming in pools rather than in natural water courses or the sea is due to the energy needed to heat the water and the chemicals used to combat infection. Although many sports have associated buildings – the golf club or the tennis clubhouse, for example – that might use energy for lighting and heating, swimming pools will use more of it, for heating the water and the space, for ventilattion to avoid condensation, and for running the pool filters. Energy targets drawn up for swimming pools in New Zealand suggest that 9.2 GJ/year is consumed for every square metre of pool surface.[46] Since each swimmer occupies an area of 0.1 m², this equates to 0.92 GJ/year/swimmer. Using the energy-to-land conversion figure of 135 GJ/ha, this amount of energy per swimmer would equate to 0.92 ÷ 135 = 0.007 ha, or 70 m². This gives a total equivalent energy footprint per swimmer in a heated pool of 70.1 m², mostly composed of the energy needed to run the pool. The swimmer in an unheated pool will be kept at 0.1 m²/swimmer for the purpose of comparison.

The land equivalent of the chemicals used in pools is even harder to account for. These chemicals have to be controlled carefully to avoid poisoning the users through overexposure.[47] There is already some concern about chlorine in mains water, and about our exposure to chlorine when we shower or wash the dishes.[48] The problem is that the chlorine used to disinfect the water reacts with natural organic matter in the water to form trihalomethanes, known as THMs. In high quantities these compounds have been linked to cancer and to reproductive problems. An Australian study suggests that swimming for 60 minutes in a chlorinated pool gives an exposure to THMs equal to taking 141 showers of 10 minutes' duration (another good reason for having shorter showers; see Chapter 3) or to drinking 2,240 glasses of chlorinated water.[49] Apart from its possible impact on human health, the presence of chlorine in swimming pool water means that it cannot be discharged directly into surface water drains, where it could come into contact with natural water courses. Instructions issued by the city of Burleson in Texas state that swimming pool water can be discharged to surface water drains only if there is no chlorine in it; in practice, the addition of chlorine has to stop some days before discharge, and the pH of the water has to be neutral.[50] UNEP also suggests that, in hotels, swimming pools are responsible for increased water comsumption, and for increased waste water production, both of which can be detrimental to the environment.[51] Because it has been impossible to quantify the effects of chemicals on the environment, they have been ignored in the comparison below.

DRAGON-BOAT RACING

In dragon-boat racing, teams of twenty-two people occupy boats between 10 and 15 m long. Twenty of them paddle, a drummer maintains rhythm, and someone steers.[52] Small boats with ten paddlers are also used, and boats with fifty paddlers are also found in cultural festivals. The International Dragon Boat Federation states that the sport spread after the staging of an international dragon-boat competition in the early 1970s in Hong Kong to publicize the city as a tourist destination. The sport's rise in popularity means that there are now 50 million participants in China, 300,000 in the UK and Europe, 90,000 in Canada and the US, and many thousands in Australia and New Zealand.[53] Dragon-boat racing takes place on rivers and lakes and in harbours over distances of 200–2,000 m, and thus requires no land except for enough access to get boats into the water and out again. Thus the 50.4 million participants worldwide have negligible impact. The numbers quoted above make the sport almost as popular as golf.

The results of these discussions are put together in Table 1.

Table 1: The global land take of various sports

sport	area/player (m²)	number of participants worldwide	total impact (ha)
golf	170	57 million	960,000
football (professional only)	375	39 million	1,462,500
tennis	11.5	0.4 billion	460,000
skiing	15	n/a	1,020,000
swimming (assuming 50/50 split between heated and unheated pools)	35.05	2.1 billion	7,360,500
dragon-boat racing	n/a	50.4 million	negligible

DISCUSSION

The popularity of swimming is not surprising, but the popularity of tennis probably is. Swimming has a high impact because swimming pools are often heated. Golf and skiing, which could be seen as land-hungry and possibly elitist sports, turn out to be exactly that, being eclipsed only by professional football. But golf has more than ten times the land take per participant than skiing. If all the 50 million dragon-boaters in China were to convert to golf as their exercise of choice, approximately 1 million ha, or 10,000 km^2, would need to be set aside for courses. China has a total area of 9,600,000 km^2,[54] so these theoretical golf courses would occupy 0.1% of the country. This might not seem a lot, but the land would then not be available for growing food or energy in a post-oil future. It would be better if more of the world's sporting enthusiasts turned to dragon-boating: it is claimed to be non-elitist, since all types of people can take part, and it also emphasizes teamwork.

BATS AND BALLS

Land use is not the only way sport has an impact on the enivornment. The equipment used in sports also consumes resources. It might also be useful to know which sport gives the best exercise for the least use of resources, including land. These factors are considered below, along with the accessibility of each sport and its value in terms of exercise.

Male Spartan runners exercised without any equipment, since men were allowed to run naked. Women had to wear a short tunic, as shown in bronze statuette of a girl runner from around 500 BC, probably made in Sparta and now in the British Museum.[55] Today's runners expect to wear both clothes and shoes; and other sports also require balls, bats and so on, as well as having specialized clothing. For this analysis, we will reconsider the sports we examined above to try to assess the environmental cost of the resources involved. Special clothing will not be considered, since nowadays clothes are considered essential if one is to participate. It is assumed that the resources that go into the manufacture of sports clothing will be offset by the savings in resources made by not wearing normal clothing and footwear.

Although they cannot be classified as equipment, there are buildings that are associated with our sports, such as the swimming pool and the golf and tennis clubs. These will vary in their impact. Apart from swimming pool facilities, special buildings have been ignored since we are concerned primarily with the land taken up by the sport, together with any equipment necessary to take part. To give an example, ski lifts are included here because it would be more difficult to undertake skiing without such equipment.

GOLF

According to a retailer of sporting goods, it is not possible to carry more than 14 clubs in a bag when playing a round of golf.[56] The best guess is that clubs and bag together weigh approximately 32.5 lb (14.7 kg).[57] If all the clubs were made of steel (the shaft is usually steel, though carbon fibre is also used), the embodied energy of a set would be roughly 461 MJ. Assuming that all players have such a basic set, golf clubs represent an energy investment of 461 × 57,000,000 = 26,277,000,000 MJ, or 26 PJ. Net electricity production in New Zealand for 2006 was about 150 PJ for a country of 4 million.[58] Even if it is assumed that recycled steel is used for golf clubs, which has an embodied energy one third that of virgin steel, the energy they represent is still very high, at 8–9 PJ. The better news is that, if looked after carefully, the set should last as long as the golfer, assuming that fashions in golf clubs do not change. If it is assumed that golfers are healthy because they exercise, that they live for 75 years with a playing life of 55 years, and that the number of golfers remains static at 57 million, then the energy required to support all those sets of golf clubs each year is 0.5 PJ. Looking at it another way, if all dragon-boaters in China took up golf, 23 PJ would be needed to supply each of them with a basic set of clubs. However, the energy locked away in a set of golf clubs for each player each year is 461 ÷ 55 = 8 MJ.

Golf also needs balls. The original golf balls were wooden, to be replaced by leather skins stuffed with goose feathers and then with gutta-percha, which is the resin of a Malaysian tree.[59] Today golf balls are made of synthetic rubber, usually consisting of two layers with a thermoplastic cover; they must not weigh more than 1.62 oz (46 g).[60] According to an article in *Golf Digest* magazine, 90 million dozen golf balls were produced in 1998.[61] Since then, the number of golfers has risen. This would suggest that each golfer is using about 2 dozen balls a year. According to a US consumer report, 27 million golfers in the US spent US$763 million on golf balls in

2005.[62] Each player thus spent an average of US$28. The golf balls cited in the report cost US$40–45 a dozen for professional balls, US$25–35 a dozen for mid-range balls and US$10–20 a dozen for bargain balls. If we suppose that more bargain balls were bought, because of the greater number of average players, then a golfer uses about 1.5 dozen balls a year. Using this lower figure and an embodied energy for a golf ball of 110 × 0.046 = 5 MJ (synthetic rubber has an embodied energy of 110 MJ/kg[63]), we arrive at the conclusion that the energy that goes into golf balls each year is 5 × 57,000,000 × 18 = 5,130,000,000 MJ = 5 PJ. This would be roughly enough energy to power a town of 150,000 people[64] – that is to say, slightly larger than Middlesborough in the UK[65] or Hamilton in New Zealand,[66] both of which have populations of around 130,000. This calculation does not take into account the recycled golf balls that are on sale; and there are firms that sell on lost golf balls that have been graded and cleaned, though this process also requires some resources.[67] To put his another way, a study conducted by *Golf Magazine* in 2001 suggested that 2.56 billion golf balls (2,560,000,000) were lost each year.[68] The discrepancy between this figure and the number of balls bought may be due to the balls that get recycled. The figure of 2.56 billion lost balls equates to an energy loss of 5 × 2,560,000,000 = 12,800,000,000 MJ, or 12.8 PJ. The earlier, lower figure is the one that has been used in the table below. Per golfer, this works out as 5 × 18 = 90 MJ per year for golf balls. The person who makes a golf ball that cannot ever be lost is going to save the world an awful lot of energy! If we add this figure to the value of the clubs, we get an annual embodied energy figure for golf equipment of 8 + 90 = 98 MJ/player.

The other piece of equipment that we might consider in relation to golf is the golf cart. Golf is meant to give you exercise (see Table 5), but some people prefer to drive around the course. According to the Golf Research Group, there are 923,000 golf carts in use globally. Of these, just over half in the US are electric (in Europe the figure is 31%), and the average age of a golf cart is 3.5 years.[69] A single-seat electric cart weighs about 300–400 lb (136–181 kg),[70] whereas a two-seater weighs 250 kg without batteries and has a kerb weight, including batteries, of 415 kg.[71] Golf carts can be bigger and heavier, but for our purposes we will assume that all carts weigh 400 kg. An average golf cart travels 3–4 miles for each game of golf, assuming it follows the course in a straight line (a golfer might well walk much further in pursuit of balls that go astray).[72] Using the Australian embodied energy figure of 100 MJ for manufacturing 1 kg of metals, plastics and so on for vehicles, be they cars or bicycles,[73] we can calculate that the embodied energy of one golf cart is 400 × 100 = 40,000 MJ. But since this is a two-seater, the figure will work out at 20,000 MJ (20 GJ) per motorized golfer. The embodied energy of the world's golf carts is thus 20,000 × 923,000 = 18,460,000,000 MJ, or 18.5 PJ. The cart could be assumed to last twice as long as a set of batteries, say, 10 years compared to the batteries' 5 years.[74] The weight of the batteries accounts for approximately half the total weight (see above), so the embodied energy for the two sets of batteries will be (40,000 ÷ 2) × 2 = 40,000 MJ, and for the cart will be 40,000 ÷ 2 = 20,000 MJ. Over the cart's 10-year life, the total embodied energy will be 60,000 MJ, or 6,000 MJ/year. Divided by 2 for our two-seater, this gives 3,000 MJ/ player/year.

The cart also needs energy to power it round the course. The E-Z-GO TXT two-seater golf cart has a 1.9 kW motor and a top speed of 21 kph, and it uses six Trojan T-105 batteries, giving a weight of 415 kg.[75] Trojan Batteries, who make traction batteries suitable for electric vehicles, state that their product is used on over 98% of the top courses in the US.[76] The same source states the that T-105 battery is 6 volts and 185AH capacity at the 5-hour rate, so the total energy available in the E-Z-GO golf cart is 6 × 6 × 185 = 6.7 kWh. According to a UK vendor,

> *Electric buggies require a minimal amount of maintenance due to fewer moving parts. With a reasonable amount of care, a set of batteries should last about five years with the ability to play 36 holes on a single charge.*[77]

A round of golf is 18 holes, and it is estimated that the golfer covers 4 miles,[78] or about 6.5 km. Thus 36 holes would equate to a total of 8 miles, or 13 km. Allowing for inefficiencies in the charge/discharge cycle, we can assume that the full battery capacity of 6.7 kWh is used to travel the 13 km, which means that each km uses roughly 0.5 kWh, or 1.85 MJ/km. If two people are on the golf cart, the figure for each will be 0.93 MJ/passenger-km, or 0.93 × 6.5 = 6 MJ/round/player.

The difficulty comes in knowing how many rounds are played each year. When 60 players were surveyed,[79] their average turned out to be 38 rounds per year. The energy used by a golf cart to do these 38 rounds would be $38 \times 6 = 228$ MJ. When this is added to the 3,000 MJ/year that represents embodied energy, the total comes to 3,228 MJ. With the clubs and balls, the total comes to $3,228 + 98 = 3,326$ MJ for the motorized golfer – or about 64 times the impact of the golfer who walks and carries his or her own clubs.

TENNIS

To play tennis, one needs both balls and a racquet. Until the 1970s tennis racquets were made of natural materials; the wooden frame and leather grip weighed about 13 oz,[80] and the racquet was strung with natural gut or nylon. Present-day racquets are made of composite materials like graphite and fibreglass, or of aluminium,[81] but natural gut is the preferred material for strings, especially in the professional game. This gut comes from a small part of the cow's intestine, the serosa, and about three cows are required to string one tennis racquet[82] (the animals are slaughtered for their meat). Modern strings are also made from Kevlar or polyester.

The weight of the racquet determines its characteristics. Heavier racquets of 11.5–13 oz are used for careful control by professional players, who can supply the power behind the shot, while the lighter racquets of 8–9.5 oz, with their larger heads, give more power to the shot. Weights in between share these characteristics.[83] A weight of 10.5 oz, or approximately 300 g, would give us an average value for embodied energy. Assuming that the racquet is aluminium and ignoring the strings would give an embodied energy of 15.2×0.3 MJ, or approximately 4.5 MJ (using a coefficient of 15.2 MJ/kg for extruded recycled aluminium with powder coat finish[84]). If the racquet were Kevlar, which is basically an oil-derived synthetic fibre involving sulphuric acid in its manufacture, its embodied energy would be higher, since synthetic fibres typically range from about 50 MJ/kg for polyester to 150 MJ/kg for nylon (these are the figures quoted for carpet manufacture[85]). If we suppose, therefore, that all racquets have the lower value for aluminium and that each player in the world has one racquet, we would arrive at an embodied energy figure for tennis racquets of $0.4 \times 10^9 \times 4.5 = 1.8 \times 10^9$ MJ, or 1.8 PJ. How many years a racquet lasts depends on the level and frequency of play, but if each racquet lasts an average of 10 years the annual embodied energy for all racquets in the world would be 0.18 PJ. This would work out as 0.45 MJ/year for each player. Strings and grips will be replaced within the lifetime of any racquet, but these are relatively small components. The record for the number of racquets used professionally in one season seems to be 22 – a slightly expensive habit in energy terms.[86]

Balls for lawn tennis were originally made from vulcanized rubber, and it was this product that enabled the game to move from indoors, where real tennis had been played with leather balls, to outside, since the rubber ball provided sufficient bounce on the level grass surface without damaging it.[87] Further developments included the flannel covering stitched around the rubber core, giving the tennis ball its classic fluffy appearance, and a hollow core within the rubber that was pressurized with gas.[88] Balls are now made in two halves that are welded together; the seams are vulcanized rubber, and the covering is Melton cloth, a woollen fabric.[89] Tennis balls are sold in a pressurized container and begin to lose their bounce as soon as this is opened. Some balls have solid rubber cores to avoid this problem and are aimed at people who play less often. They wear out only when the cloth on the outside rubs off.[90] A tennis ball weighs $2-2^{1}/_{6}$ oz,[91] or about 60 g. Assuming a value for vulcanized rubber of 19.4 kWh/kg,[92] or 70 MJ/kg, each ball embodies $0.06 \times 70 = 4.2$ MJ. Tennis balls are sold in packs of four and six, but we have not been able to find out how many are bought each year. Obviously, the higher the level of play, the more new balls will be used, with older balls used just for practice. Assuming, therefore, that every player has on average one new ball each year, the energy bound up in these balls will be 0.4 billion $\times 4.2 = 1.7$ PJ per year. The energy embodied in tennis equipment each year is therefore $0.18 + 1.7 = 1.25$ PJ. Each player with one racquet and one ball will use an annual embodied energy of $0.45 + 4.2 = 4.65$ MJ.

FOOTBALL

A soccer ball that meets current regulations will be a hollow pressurized sphere of leather or synthetic material 68–70 cm in circumference, and it will weigh between 410 and 450 g.[93] The ball has to be pumped up as pressure is lost over time. In the past, balls were made of inflated pigs' bladders, so that the size varied according to the pig, and vulcanized rubber balls were also used following Goodyear's development of the material.[94] The synthetic alternatives to natural leather are polyurethane and PVC.[95] The outer covering is either stitched with polyester thread onto an inner lining or, in the case of cheaper balls, glued on. This lining of polyester or poly-cotton material separates the outer skin from the bladder of butyl or natural latex, the part that is inflated. Assuming that the ball's weight of 420 g is split equally between the covering and the bladder, and ignoring the lining, we can work out an embodied energy for each ball of $(72 \times 0.21) + (67.5 \times 0.21) = 29$ MJ. This calculation uses the embodied energy values of 70 MJ/kg for PVC, 74 MJ/kg for polyurethane, and 67.5 MJ/kg for natural latex.[96] If each of the 226 million players[97] in the world has his or her own ball, the energy bound up in soccer balls will be 6,554,000,000 MJ, or 6.5 PJ. Given that soccer balls also last for several years, the energy for soccer equipment is less significant than for the other sports considered here.

SKIING

As with motorized golf, ski equipment is made up of two types: the kit you attach to yourself (the skis and poles), and the lift that takes you up to the ski runs. More than 2,000 years ago, skis were originally made of bone; the word 'ski' comes from a root that also means 'to split', referring to the fact that the bone was divided in two to get a ski for each foot.[98] Leather thongs were used to tie the ski to the foot, and originally no poles were used. Later, medieval skis were made of wood; skiers would attach the toes of their leather boots to the skis either with thongs or thin willow branches such as you would use for making baskets. Metal skis appeared later: at one stage, aluminium was wrapped around a wooden core, and plastic has also been used. The modern ski is a complex composite. It has a core, which can be made from a wood such as ash, or from foam polyurethane or honeycomb aluminium. The outer part can be made from fibreglass or carbon fibre, and the surface that comes in contact with the snow is usually polyethylene. The edges of the ski are steel.[99] The weight and length of a ski also vary according to the type of skiing it is designed for, with downhill skis being longer and heavier than other models, for greater speed.

A ski manufacturer lists a number of wood-core skis for back-country skiing that weigh from 8 to 9 lb (3.6 to 4.1 kg).[100] Let us assume that the ski is

50% wood and 50% plastics (a mixture of glass fibre and polyethylene): this would give, very roughly, an embodied energy for a pair of skis weighing 4 kg of $2 \times 2 = 4$ MJ for the timber, using an embodied energy coefficient of 2 MJ/kg for kiln-dried hardwood.[101] For the plastic part, we can estimate $2 \times 51 = 102$ MJ, using 51 MJ/kg for polyethylene[102] as representative of the whole. This gives a total for the skis of 106 MJ.

Ski poles are similarly complicated, consisting of the basic pole, which can be carbon fibre; the grip of cork or synthetic cork; and the basket – the part that digs into the snow – which is plastic with a carbide tip. Considering the poles' embodied energy from the bottom up, one Canadian manufacturer give a weight for the basket of between 9.4 and 13.5 g, with the lowest figure being the most popular and the heavier baskets for off-trail use.[103] Assumed values of 10 g for the basket and 64 MJ/km for polypropylene[104] would give an embodied energy of $0.01 \times 64 = 0.64$ MJ. Moving to the grip, the embodied energy of cork board is 4 MJ/kg.[105] Ordinary cork, as opposed to the high-density cork that is used for floor tiles, has a density of 13 lb/ft^3 (0.2 kg/m^3);[106] given their small size, the embodied energy of the handgrips can therefore be ignored. Ski poles were once made of bamboo and had leather straps with which to hold them, and bamboo (sometimes bamboo and leather) baskets.[107] Now carbon fibre or a composite of carbon fibre and glass fibre is preferred for the pole, in place of the aluminium of the more recent past.[108] For an adult, poles are typically 1.25 m in length. The same Canadian firm has carbon-fibre poles ranging in weight from 40–64 g/m,[109] but it has not been possible to find an embodied energy figure for carbon fibre. An aluminium walking pole can weigh 300 g,[110] so if aluminium skiing poles weighed the same we could estimate an embodied energy of $2 \times 0.3 \times 15.2 = 9.1$ MJ, using the figure for recycled powder-coated aluminium we employed for tennis racquets earlier. This would give a total for the poles of $9.1 + 0.64 = 10$ MJ, which when added to the value for skis gives a total for the equipment of 116 MJ. We then need to ask how long skis and poles last. One source states that a new pair of skis every year would be ideal,[111] whereas another suggests that skis can last a long time if you look after them and repair them.[112] In this case, a 10-year life will be assumed to give an annual embodied energy of 11.6 MJ/year.

It could be argued that ski clothing, especially the boots and bindings, is more complex than ordinary clothing, but for the present we have ignored this fact. For someone like Robert, who when he was at school in Germany many years ago used to go skiing with a vintage pair of pre-war wooden skis, the values calculated above would be the end of the story, since he and his friends would walk up a neighbouring hill and then ski down it. Most modern skiers, however, will take a ski lift up the mountainside, so this equipment should also be factored in.

'Ski lift' is a generic term that covers a number of ways of taking people up a mountain: a simple T-bar that you hold on to, typically in pairs, which pulls you up on your skis; the classic chair lift for two people, with a haul rope passing over the top of supporting towers; larger versions that have enclosed gondolas with a greater capacity; and what are called 'tram systems' that take considerable numbers of people up to the top.[113] The type of lift depends on the terrain and the popularity of the piste. Trams, for instance, are very efficient, but because the car going up is balanced by the car going down, their capacity in terms of skiers transported per hour may be limited, even though the individual cars are large. Trams are used where it is difficult to build a row of poles in a line.

One Canadian portable ski lift – to take the most basic option – is designed for use in a back garden (which can be very large in Canada) or to be shipped to a slope in the back of a lorry; it tows the skier up the slope on his or her skis and uses a Briggs and Stratton 5–5.5 hp petrol motor to make it capable of 150 liftings an hour.[114] The motor runs at variable speed, idling until a skier picks up the rope, when it picks up pace. Apart from the motor and drive unit, the pulley uses steel cable $1/8$th inch (3 mm, or 0.003 m) in diameter, and also an anchor and safety rope. The weight of the drive unit is given as 25 kg, which is assumed to include the motor; Briggs and Stratton engines of this type often form part of an outboard motor for boats, and a 5 hp outboard unit weighs a comparable 56 lb (25.5 kg).[115] Assuming the unit is all steel, it would have an embodied energy of $25 \times 21 = 525$ MJ, using values for 50% virgin and 50% recycled steel of 21 MJ/kg.[116] The volume of 100 m of steel cable would be $100 \times 0.003^2 \times 3.124\ (\pi) = 0.003$ m³. A figure of 96,544 MJ/m³ for steel wire rod[117] would give us an embodied energy for the cable of $0.003 \times 96,544 = 290$ MJ. There are other steel components too, such as the pulley and anchor, but for the present a value of $525 + 290 = 815$ MJ will be used. Given that the equipment will probably last 20 years, this gives an embodied energy of 41 MJ/year. Even if it only does 100 lifts in total in a season, this would give a figure of 0.4 MJ/skier for embodied energy. The 5 hp Briggs and Stratton engine uses petrol at a rate of 0.5 US gallons/hour (1.9 l/hour) at full throttle.[118] A conversion factor of 34.2 MJ/l of petrol[119] gives us an energy use of 1.9 × 34.2 = 65 MJ/hour, with the potential for undertaking 150 liftings an hour, according to the manufacturer. This would give a figure of 0.4 MJ/person/lift since the engine idles when not pulling skiers up the slope. One website suggests that the intention of people who are staying near ski slopes is to ski every week in winter when they first arrive, but this soon slips to 15–20 times a season, with the reality being closer to 2–3 ski sessions.[120] Assuming 10 ski sessions a year and 2 lift journeys for each session, the energy associated with this portable type of lift would be (0.4 × 20) + 0.4 = 8.4 MJ/skier/year. Obviously this calculation is based on a number of assumptions, but the key point is that the final figure is not large.

Lifts that operate continuously are common in organized ski resorts – the chair lift, for example. This type comprises the open metal chairs, the haul rope, the towers and their large concrete foundations, the motor, which is often electric, tensioning devices, back-up motors and so on.[121] The same source gives the current upper limit for the capacity of a two-person chair lift as 1,200 skiers/hour, or two people every 6 seconds. For a three-person chair lift this rises to 1,800 skiers/hour. It has not been possible to discover the size of the motor in such a lift, but although it uses more materials it also carries more people, so for the current comparison a figure of 8.4 MJ/skier/year will be used for the average energy to move the skier up to the top of the slope. Other equipment, such as snow guns to make artificial snow, is ignored. A total energy figure, for skiing equipment and lift transport, of 11.6 + 8.4 = 20 MJ will be used in Table 2.

SWIMMING

Apart from the classic inflatable rubber ring or arm bands that help young children stay afloat and gain in confidence, the beauty of swimming as a sport is that the equipment is built in. For this comparison zero equipment has been assumed.

DRAGON-BOAT RACING

Dragon boats are traditionally made of teak,[122] though modern boats are also made of aluminium or fibreglass resin. A team website states that a racing dragon boat for 22 people measures 11.7 m in length, is just over 1 m wide and weighs 700–800 lb (317–63 kg).[123] Another source gives the weight of a 22-person dragon boat with a hull made of glass-reinforced polyester (a variety of fibreglass) as 500 lb (227 kg).[124] Using the latter figure, since both the material and weight are known, assuming all material is fibreglass (except for seats in plywood) and using an embodied energy coefficient of 54 MJ/kg for polyester,[125] we can estimate the embodied energy of the boat as 227 × 54 = 12,258 MJ, or 557 MJ/crew member. In Hong Kong, a 40 ft (12 m) dragon boat of teak weighs over 2,000 lb (907 kg).[126] With a coefficient of 0.5 MJ/kg for air-dried hardwood,[127] its embodied energy would be 907 × 0.5 = 454 MJ or 20.6 MJ/crew member. Such a boat might last 100 years with proper maintenance, whereas a fibreglass hull might last 20 years because of recognized problems with porosity. These two estimated life-times would give figures of 28 MJ/crew member/year for the fibreglass hull, and 0.2 MJ/crew member/year for the teak boat. These figures have been included in Table 2.

Table 2 (overleaf) looks at the impact of these various sports in terms of the land and equipment used for each participant. The equipment and land values have been calculated above, but here the land value is converted to an energy equivalent, to represent the energy that could be produced if the land were used to grow energy crops like timber or biofuels rather than for sport. Association football has been omitted from this table since it has not been possible to calculate the land associated with each player, whether professional or casual.

DISCUSSION

Clearly, if golf is your sport, you are having a considerable impact on the planet – far more than if you are a dragon-boat racer or a cold-water swimmer. For all sports apart from dragon-boating, it is the land rather than the equipment that makes the most significant impact, the one exception being the golfer who drives rather than walks round the course. Fortunately there are 57 million golfers and only just under 1 million golf carts in the

Table 2: Total impact per player of land and equipment associated with various sports

sport	land area (m²)	energy equivalent of land (MJ/year)	embodied energy of equipment (MJ/year)	total impact (MJ/participant/year)
golf (walking golfer)	170	2,295	98	2,393
golf (driving golfer)	170	2,295	3,326	5,621
tennis	11.5	155	4.65	160
skiing (walking to the piste)	15	203	11.6	215
skiing (taking a chair-type ski lift)	15	203	20	223
swimming (unheated pool)	0.1	1.35	n/a	1.35
swimming (heated pool)	70.1	946	n/a	946
dragon-boat racing (teak boat)	n/a	0	0.2	0.2
dragon-boat racing (modern hull)	n/a	0	28	28

world. Of course, if swimming were only ever done in the sea, it would be a sport with zero impact. If one swam all year it might be necessary to have a wetsuit, but our investigation into the equipment of other sports suggests that the impact of a wetsuit would not be very significant.

The history of sport shows that equipment has moved from being made of natural materials, such as wood and leather, to man-made materials, with a consequent increase in environmental impact. This is clear from the obvious difference between traditional boats and those constructed in fibreglass, although whether all the teak comes from sustainable sources is another issue to be considered. The logging of virgin teak forests in South-East Asia, where the wood grows, was considered an unsustainable practice, but now both suppliers[128] and users[129] are taking steps to ensure that teak comes from managed plantations. The idea that all sports could once again use natural materials appears questionable, since this move would still have an impact. What seems more likely in a world short of resources is that people will move to sports that use a minimal amount of equipment per player, such as swimming in unheated pools, and that they would make their equipment last as long as possible.

To help us consider the global impact of sports, Table 3 sets out the energy embodied in the equipment, the land each sport takes up, and the energy that land could produce if it were not being used for sport. For skiing, the value of 135 GJ/ha, representing the equivalent in land area, has been halved because trees are the only crops that could be grown on ski slopes, and some slopes are above the tree line. In order to generate a value for ski equipment, the number of skiers has been inferred from the earlier discussion of land taken up by skiing and from an area per skier of 15 m².

Two more issues need to be considered to give a full picture. The first, which is connected to Chapter 2, is the impact of travelling to participate in the sport. The second is the benefit the sport provides in terms of exercise compared with its environmental impact.

Table 3: Global annual energy involved for selected sports

sport	total impact (ha)	energy equivalent of land (PJ/year)	energy involved in equipment (PJ/year)	total energy (PJ/year)
golf	960,000	129.6	8.8*	138.4
football (professional only)	1,462,500	197.4	1.1†	198.5
tennis	460,000	62.1	1.9	64
skiing	1,020,000	68.9	negligible	68.9
swimming	7,360,500‡	993.7	0	993.7
dragon-boat racing	negligible	0	0.7§	0.7

* Based on 56 million walking and 1 million driving.
† Based on all 39 million registered players having one new ball a year.
‡ Includes land/energy equivalent for 50% of swimmers using heated pools (see Table 1).
§ Based on half the boaters rowing teak boats and half fibreglass boats.

HOW YOU GET THERE

Of the sports we are considering, it is obvious that some, like skiing, will involve some travel for those who want to participate, while the prevalence of local tennis clubs and swimming pools means these sports are much more easily accessed. Some sports like football also involve the travel of spectators, but this kind of journey has not been considered here.

To give an idea of the importance of travelling to a sports venue, just tennis and skiing will be compared. They provide similar levels of exercise (see Table 5) and their environmental impacts per player are similar (see Table 2). However, one requires travel to find snow, while the other will probably involve a local journey, whether by foot or car. We will have to make some assumptions in order to compare the two: we have situated our participant in the middle of the UK and supposed that they will go skiing in Switzerland, and we have assumed that they have a tennis club a mile and a half (2.4 km) from their home. Our table will thus include the environmental impact of various ways of travelling to these venues alongside each sport's environmental impact as already calculated. All figures are based on our rather large man of 86 kg (190 lb). Further explanations are given below. Obviously, any exercise gained by skiing for a person based in the UK will be in the form of a holiday rather than sustained exercise each week. It is assumed that one skiing holiday is taken each year; this is compared with the equivalent number of tennis sessions needed in a year for the same level of exercise.

SKIING

At present in the UK it is cheaper to fly than to go by train, even though flying has a much greater environmental impact (see Chapter 2). If our man flies from a city in the middle of the UK, such as Birmingham, the distance travelled on a round trip to the ski resort will be approximately 1,127 miles,[130] or 1,814 km. For domestic air flights, which spend shorter time in the air relative to the number of take-offs and landings, the impact for both operating and embodied energy as given by Lenzen is 5.7 MJ/passenger-km.[131] Lenzen also give a figure for long-haul flights as 3.1 MJ/passenger-km, but the domestic figure has been used here. This gives the impact for flying to the ski resort as $1,814 \times 5.7 = 10,340$ MJ.

Rather than fly, it would be possible to go to Zurich by rail; according to Lenzen, the impact of rail travel is less, at 2.8 MJ/passenger-km. From Birmingham to London by rail is 113 miles.[132] This equates to 182 km, making 364 km for the round trip. Going from London to Paris on the Eurostar train has the advantage that Eurostar will offset the carbon emissions for you for free.[133] Taking high-speed trains, it takes 8 hours to go from London to Zurich.[134] and a high-speed train averages 200 kph.[135] This would give a rail distance of 1,600 km from London to Zurich, and 1,964 km for the whole rail journey. The environmental impact of using the train is therefore $1,964 \times 2.8 = 5,499$ MJ, which is about half the impact of flying. Although Eurostar claims that train travel reduces carbon dioxide emissions by a factor of 10,[136] here the difference is less because Lenzen's figures also include the embodied energy of the travel systems.

According to some employees of the Zurich financial services firm, who planned a charity cycle ride from Edgbaston in Birmingham to the firm's headquarters in Zurich, the drive to Zurich is a trip of 750 miles, including a ferry ride from Portsmouth to Caen.[137] This gives a round trip of 1,500 miles, or 2,414 km. The environmental impact of driving given by Lenzen is 4.4 MJ/passenger-km, making a total of $2,414 \times 4.4 = 10,622$ MJ. To this must be added the impact of the ferry trip. From a map, the ferry trip is 135 km,[138] so using Lenzen's value of 5.5 MJ/passenger-km we can work its impact as $270 \times 5.5 = 1,485$ MJ. The total for driving and the ferry trips combined is thus 12,107 MJ.

TENNIS

During the week of the skiing holiday, it is assumed that 4 hours each day are spent on the slopes, making 20 hours of intensive exercise. From Table 5, we see that tennis and skiing both consume 604 cals/hour. The skiing holiday would be equivalent to 20 tennis sessions each of one hour. The other assumption is that the tennis club is 1.5 miles (2.4 km) from home. This makes a round trip of 3 miles, or 4.8 km. Using figures from Chapter 2, we can estimate that the impact of walking to play tennis is 1.1 MJ/km, or 5.3 MJ for one trip, and 106 MJ for the 20 sessions outlined above. However, because you are walking to your tennis sessions, you are also getting exercise. Walking at 3 mph consumes 302 cals/hour.[139] This is a moderate pace, such as would be used for walking a dog. This effectively means that the hour spent walking to and from tennis gives you half the exercise of your one-hour tennis session. Thus, to get the equivalent exercise of the 20 hours spent skiing, you only need to play 13 hour-long sessions if you are also walking from home and back each time. (Strictly speaking, you need to play for slightly longer than one hour each time, since 20 ÷ 1.5 = 13.3.) The impact of making 13 trips to play tennis is 1.1 × 4.8 × 13 = 69 MJ; this value has been used in Table 4.

Using the same method, the impact of cycling to tennis would be 0.58 MJ/km, assuming a relatively slow speed and a steel bicycle. If you cycle at 10–12 mph, this will burn 518 cals/hour.[140] Making the 3-mile round trip at 10 mph will thus take 18 minutes and will burn 518 × (18 ÷ 60) = 155 cals, the equivalent of about 15 minutes spent playing tennis. In order to get the same amount of exercise, it will be necessary to play 16 one-hour sessions when bicycling to and from the court rather than 20 sessions of the same length. This would have an impact of 16 × 0.58 = 9.3 MJ.

To give us a complete picture, we should also consider the effect of driving the 3 mile (4.8 km) round trip. If we use the same value as driving to Switzerland for skiing, this method of travel would have an impact of 4.8 × 4.4 × 20 = 422 MJ.

The advice has to be that you should play sport locally if you want to reduce impact. If you must go on a skiing holiday, then go by train and try and make your journey count by combining it with business or visiting relatives. In all cases except for walking and cycling, the impact of the travel is greater then the impact (land and equipment) of the sport.

One other thing to note is that driving to play tennis does not save you time. The figures for travel worked out above show the exercise equivalents of 20 hours of tennis. If you walk to your tennis match, to get the same total amount of exercise you would need to do play 13 one-hour sessions of tennis; the walking takes one hour per session, making a total of 26 hours. On the same basis, if you bicycle, you would need to play 16 hours of tennis, and cycling both ways would take 4.8 hours, making a total of 20.8 hours. If you drive, you would have to play tennis for the full 20 hours and, assuming the round trip takes 9 minutes, by the time you have started and parked the car you will spend 3 hours travelling back and forth, making a total of 23 hours.

Table 4: Travel considered as part of the impact of playing tennis and skiing

sport and mode of travel	impact of travel (MJ/year)	impact of sport (MJ/year)	total environmental impact (MJ/year)
tennis (walking)	69	160	229
tennis (cycling)	9	160	169
tennis (driving)	422	160	582
skiing (travelling by train)	5,499	223	5,723
skiing (flying)	10,340	223	10,563
skiing (driving and catching ferry)	12,107	233	12,340

Thus cycling is not only better for the environment, but will also save you time. The wisdom "T'ain't what you do, it's the way that you do it"[141] seems to be perfectly true when it comes to sporting activities.

BANG PER BUCK

We undertake sporting activities for a variety of reasons, but the one aspect promoted by many governments in the West is health. A human being is not meant to be a sedentary animal, but many of us spend most of our waking hours sitting and staring at a computer screen, only to undertake some form of regular exercise to compensate. In contrast, a hunter-gatherer lifestyle would have us walking for most of the day at relatively low speeds, interspersed with periods of standing while harvesting and perhaps sitting to eat, with some people getting occasional bursts of vigorous exercise from the hunt. In Table 5, alongside the environmental impact of each sport, the amount of exercise it provides in terms of calories has also been quantified.

The amount of calories burned will vary according to body weight, metabolism, physical condition, and the intensity with which the exercise is undertaken.[142] Table 5 lists the sports we considered above and the calories burned in one hour of exercise, all taken from the same reference source. Again, we have assumed that the person doing the sport is a man weighing 86 kg (190 lb). In many cases average or general values have been used. The case of skiing is interesting: cross-country skiing, which is considered less environmentally damaging, burns many more calories than downhill skiing, with 690 cals per hour for a moderate cross-country pace rising to 1,423 for maximum effort. In contrast, moderate downhill skiing burns 518 cals/hour, rising to 690 for vigorous or racing effort. The general value for snow skiing is given as 604 cals/hour, and this is the figure we have used in the table. As mentioned in Chapter 2, a sedentary man of the same weight uses around 100 cals/hour. Hence it is possible to calculate the extra food required to meet the demands of exercise. In this instance food has been expressed as slices of bread, since each slice contains around 80 kcals (Table 5).

Different activities obviously take different lengths of time. A dragon-boat race might last around 2.5 minutes,[143] a game of tennis maybe 30 minutes to an hour, and a round of golf can take all morning. However, the point of the following table is to see how much land and energy (represented by the equipment) are required to deliver a certain amount of exercise, and hence which sport offers the best environmental 'bang per buck'. In this case, we have taken the value of 3 slices of bread/hour as the base unit, since this represents the energy needed to cycle at an ordinary pace for an hour. A study by scientists at Havard University suggested that heart disease was reduced

Table 5: The exercise value of selected sports

sport	cals/hour	food equivalent, approx. slices of bread per hour of exercise
golf (walking)	343	3.0
golf (using golf cart)	302	2.5
tennis	604	6.3
skiing	604	6.3
swimming (light/moderate effort)	690	7.4
dragon-boat racing (vigorous effort)*	1,035	11.7

* Canoeing is the closest type of activity to dragon-boat racing. Canoeing at a moderate pace uses 604 cals/hour, but, since dragon-boat racing is competitive and vigorous for short periods, higher values for competitive canoeing have been used here.

through vigorous exercise – walking or running at speeds of more than 3.5 mph, for example, which amounted to 1,000 cals/week.[144] The same study also stated that intensity of exercise is not as critical as the number of calories burned off through exercise each week. Table 6 therefore shows how many hours of sport per year are needed to burn 1,000 cals/week over and above the 100 cals/hour required to maintain the basal metabolic rate. The same values have also been plotted in Fig. 1, with revealing results.

Table 6: Time needed in various sports to benefit from their health-giving effects

sport	total environmental impact (MJ/participant/year)	time required for exercise to reduce risk of heart disease (hours/year)
golf (walking)	2,393	208.5
golf (driving)	5,621	254.8
tennis	160	103.0
skiing	219*	103.0
swimming	474*	87.9
dragon-boat racing	14.1*	55.6

* Averaged from Table 2.

Fig. 1: Footprint and hours of exercise per year

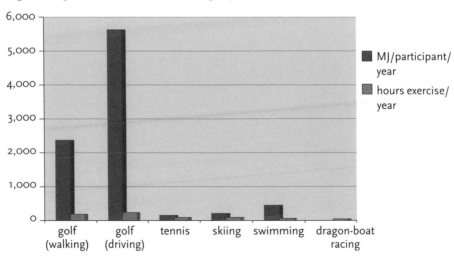

Quite simply, the sports with the higher footprints require more hours of exercise for health per year, while those with lower footprints require significantly less. This is a win–win situation if people change their behaviour and abandon land-hungry sports in favour of those that require very much less land and equipment. Sports that can be timetabled to share facilities should also be encouraged – playing fields, for example, can be used for different activities. However, one other issue could be factored in: the benefits that could be enjoyed in our day-to-day lives if exercise rather than convenience were our priority. This is considered in the next section.

SPORT IN THE HOME

Some sports like football and hockey can claim to go back thousands of years.[145] Since obtaining a supply of food was time-consuming, it could be argued that early sports provided social interaction and cohesion rather than exercise, since expenditure of energy meant that more food had to be taken in. The situation has been reversed in modern Western societies, where people deliberately exercise in order to burn off the surplus calories they have consumed. This suits capitalist society, since someone makes a profit from selling extra food, and someone else can make a profit from selling the exercise. However, one can also get exercise from ordinary activities. Table 7 expands on Table 6, setting out the time required to burn off 1,000 cals/week performing ordinary activities.

The first point to note is that there are no values for the environmental impact of these home-based activities, since it is assumed that they form part of ordinary life rather than an additional leisure activity. The second point worth noting is that mowing the lawn will give the recommended amount of exercise faster than a round of golf, and that the average person keeping their house clean gets all the exercise they need in a week. Finally, playing with small children instead of playing sports could benefit both adult and child. Perhaps the question to ask is: 'Is my sport really necessary?'

Table 7: Weekly activities and their effects on cardiac health

activity	environmental impact (MJ/participant/ year)	time required to reduce risk of heart disease (hours/year)	number of activity sessions per week
golf (walking)	2,393	208.5	1 round of 4 hours
golf (driving)	5,621	254.8	2 rounds of 2.5 hours each
tennis	160	103	2 matches of 1 hour each
skiing	219	103	60 downhill runs of 3 mins each[146]
swimming (unheated pool)	1.35	87.9	310 laps of 25 m[147]
dragon-boat racing	14.1	55.6	24 races
scrubbing floors on hands and knees (474 cals/hour)[148]*		139	2.7 hours of cleaning
playing with small children (216 cals/hour)		448	1.2 hours of play **per day** (8.6/week)
walking upstairs (619 cals/hour)		100	55 stair ascents **per day** (384/week)[149]
cleaning the house (302 cals/hour)		257	5 hours of cleaning
mowing the lawn (474 cals/hour)		139	2.7 hours of mowing

* All values for domestic activities are from the same reference source.

ADVICE

Given the high levels of participation in sporting activities, they are clearly valued. However, it is also clear from this discussion that not all sports are equal when it comes to environmental impact. If you want to reduce your personal footprint, you should first look at ways in which ordinary activities can give you the exercise you need. Housework can be as good as a workout and does not require any travelling – or time spent travelling. However, this rather solitary type of exercise may not suit everyone. When choosing a participatory sport, the advice is to look locally and to try to find an activity that you can walk or cycle to. Travelling any distance to take part is not good for the environment. Skiing should be left for those with easy access to snow; and it is good to remember that expensive sports like golf tend to have more of an environmental impact. Choosing a sport that is played on a field or other piece of land with multiple timetabled uses will also minimize impact. Exclusive uses of land tend to result in a higher impact. Although its impact is not high, making your equipment last, or even sharing it where possible, will help. It is also useful to remember that many people who do not live in the West take part in activities like tai chi, which can be done anywhere and often collectively in public places, thus offering valuable exercise and social interaction with no equipment and no special land take. All this can be boiled down to three points to consider:

- Ask yourself whether your sport is really necessary.
- Walk or bicycle to the sporting venue.
- Choose a sport that is not land-hungry.

COLLECTING

You can, of course, collect anything for a hobby. The largest items we know personally to have been collected are double-decker buses (as many as nineteen at one point), and the smallest are stamps and first-day covers. There is an obvious difference between these two types of collectible in terms of land take and hence environmental impact. It could be said that there is another type of collecting that relates to experience, such as recording train numbers, bird sightings, mountains climbed or countries visited.[150] Both satisfy that often overwhelming urge to take control of one's life – at least according to Freud, who links the desire to collect with poor toilet training[151] – by amassing a collection of something, however strange or ordinary that something might be. At one extreme, collecting – the collecting of art in particular – has become a multi-billion dollar industry,[152] while at the other it is represented by public libraries, which are available to anyone who can produce proof of residence in a particular place.

At first sight, the environmental impact of collecting items would seem to be higher than that of collecting experiences, but this section will examine whether this is really true. It starts by looking at the impact of collecting a variety of objects of different scales, and then goes on to discuss the impact of collecting selected experiences.

'SLIGHTLY FOXED BUT STILL DESIRABLE'

It is always good to start with what you know. We have a collection of books, almost all second-hand, the size of which has become a problem. The collection began when we were doing research into the UK Temporary Housing Programme, which produced the temporary houses known affectionately as 'prefabs'. A modest number of books on architecture that we had acquired as students took on a life of their own, and we now have two shelves of books just on the post-war prefab house. The problem is that this got us hooked on going into second-hand bookshops, which are always full of such interesting and often beautiful things. In a bookshop anything is possible. We have one book on taxidermy that starts with the topic of stuffing a mole and then moves directly on to stuffing a bear; can it really be that simple? The thrill of the chase is always with you, such as trying to find all the books in a particular sequence, such as the ten wonderful Penguin Illustrated Classics from 1938 (we were successful).[153] As this example demonstrates, one collects books not just to access the information they contain, but for the sake of owning them (this applies to collections of anything: objects are amassed for reasons beyond their immediate purpose). But what is the impact of collecting books, in this case second-hand copies?

One advantage to collecting second-hand stuff like books is that it has already been labelled as unwanted, and disposed of. So collecting second-hand books is interrupting the waste stream rather than relying on resources to make something new. We can work out the impact of brand new books if we look at their production; we have to be very careful here, since what you are reading is a book, although both we and our publisher hope that you have bought it in order to read about the environmental impact of living. If we take it that the average book uses half a ream of paper, this equates to 3% of a tree.[154] According to the Library and Information Statistics Unit, in 2004–5 there were 3,474 public libraries in England, which held a total of 264,826,000 books.[155] There were 279,923,000 issues (or lendings) of books for the same period, which equates very roughly to each book being read once that year. Obviously, some books are read a lot more times than others, but this figure represents an average. We can also assume that a trip to the library is similar to a trip to the bookshop, since public libraries are historically sited in town centres, so we can ignore the issue of transport here. A book sitting on a shelf at home also equates to a library book either in someone's house or in the library itself, so the impact of providing the building and the shelf has also been ignored. Over a period of, say, 10 years, a book you buy and read once would have been read 10 times if it were in a library. Indeed, a simple comparison shows that owning a book could be said to take 10 times more resources, in terms of trees for paper, than borrowing a library book. Looking at the issue another way, a tree converted to library books provides over 330 readings, whereas a tree converted to new books gives just 33 readings. Some books we have at home have been referred to many more than 10 times, and some have been read from cover to cover more often than that (well, how many times have you read *Harry Potter*?). And yet, at the risk of upsetting Thames & Hudson, communal use of a lending library is probably better for the environment than buying new books – assuming, that is, you read all your books less than once a year.

GUILT-FREE BOOK-BUYING

Since we are considering the book you are reading, it might be good to see what you would have to do to offset the environmental cost of owning it. A book is made of paper, so one could claim it to be carbon neutral: paper comes from trees and, when it is burned, the carbon it contains is returned to the atmosphere to be taken up by more trees as they grow. We are not, however, advocating book-burning, especially not in bonfires in the street where all the energy would go to waste.[156]

Trees are not the only ingredient of paper. Water is also important, as are certain chemicals. The environmental impact of paper can be worked out using the US Environmental Defense Fund paper footprint calculator.[157] If the book you are reading is a modern compact paperback, a 50 cm run of such books would weigh 15.7 kg.[158] Three modern paperbacks chosen at random in our office have a total spine width of 6 cm, making a total of 25 books in 50 cm, which would give each book a weight of 15.7 kg ÷ 25, or approximately 0.6 kg. Assuming a standard magazine paper, the environmental impact of this weight as worked out by the paper footprint calculator is 4 lb (1.8 kg) of CO_2 equivalent, 10 US gallons (37.9 l) of water and 2 lb (0.9 kg) of solid waste. To convert these quantities into a footprint, some assumptions will have to be made. First, we will assume that the paper is made in the UK using electricity. The CO_2 emission factor for electricity in the UK in 2005 was 0.46 kg/kWh,[159] so 1.8 kg of CO_2 equivalent emissions represents 1.8 ÷ 0.46 kWh = 3.9 kWh = 14 MJ = 0.014 GJ. With the conversion factor of 135 GJ/ha, this equates to a land area of 0.0001 ha, or 1 m². The second assumption is that tap water is used for making the paper. The UK footprint for tap water is 0.08 m²/100 l,[160] so this would add 0.03 m² to the footprint. The UK Carbon Trust states that municipal waste has a value of 2,639 kWh/tonne.[161] This waste could be reclaimed, for instance through incineration, in order to offset the use of other fuels; this would reduce the footprint. If the waste is reclaimed, 0.9 kg (0.0009 tonnes) would equate to 2.4 kWh, or 8.5 MJ, which would have a footprint of 0.6 m². However, if the waste is left to rot in landfill, we should perhaps add its value to the footprint. We have not considered the waste water that results from paper-making, but this decision is consistent with New Zealand's approach to emissions trading, which includes methane production from solid waste but not from waste water disposal.[162]

At worst, therefore, the footprint of this book would be 1 (paper) + 0.03 (water) + 0.6 (waste) = 1.6 m². But this accounts only for the raw materials, and not for the publishing house, retail facilities and so on that are also required to get the book into your hands. Without a detailed analysis of a book's footprint to draw on, we will once again have to make some assumptions. According to Oxford University Press Canada, the cost of paper accounts for over a third of the total manufacturing cost of a book.[163] If cost is taken as a guide to environmental impact, the footprint of the paper can be multiplied by three to give a footprint for the book of 1.6 × 3 = 4.8 m².

With this very rough footprint of 4.8 m², or 0.0005 ha, we can now work out what you, the reader, need to do to offset the environmental cost of purchasing this very worthy book. For slightly more than this footprint, you could eat not your dog, but two goldfish, with their estimated individual footprints of 0.00034 ha (see 'Pets' in the previous chapter). Less contentiously, you could go without drinking two pints of beer, or abstain from one bar of chocolate (100 g), or, if you don't want to give anything up, you could swap half a bottle of wine, with its high footprint, for a pint of beer; this would more than offset buying the book (see Chapter 1). Of course, if our book inspires you to more substantial life changes, such as walking to work or growing some food at home, it will be well worth its footprint, and we shall all be happy.

'I WOULDN'T GIVE IT HOUSE ROOM'

The impact of purchasing a second-hand book is different. No new trees have been destroyed to make paper, and a personal library of second-hand books will have less of an environmental impact than a collection of new volumes. What was potential landfill is now occupying space in a building. But this space, along with shelves for the books, still needs to be found, and it still needs to be heated.

If you take a room that is 2.4 m high, you could fit perhaps 7 shelves onto one wall, assuming that the books are approximately A4-size (297 mm high) and that the shelves are constructed of 25 mm timber. If this bookcase were 2 m wide, the whole wall of books would contain a total of $7 \times 2 \times 50 = 700$ books. With a depth of 200 mm, the shelves mark out a volume occupied by books of $0.2 \times 2.4 \times 2.0 = 0.96$ m³ – say 1 m³. A paper suggests that a UK house has an embodied energy of 9 MWh (324 GJ).[164] This is similar to the New Zealand figure of 268 GJ for a brick veneer house with a concrete floor of the same size.[165] If a house is assumed to have a 60-year life, the total embodied energy of 324 GJ works out at $324 \div 60 = 5.4$ GJ/year. The area occupied by the book collection is $2 \times 0.2 = 0.4$ m². Assuming that our house has a floor area of 96 m² (see Chapter 3), the embodied energy associated with the area covered by the book collection is therefore $5.4 \div 96 \times 0.4 = 0.02$ GJ. Using the conversion factor of 135 GJ/ha, this equates to a footprint of 0.00015 ha. To this must be added the embodied energy of the wood for the shelves. For a collection of 700 books, 14 m of 200 × 25 mm timber will be needed, plus 3 uprights of 2,000 × 200 × 25 mm to hold the shelves. The volume of timber is thus $(14 \times 0.2 \times 0.025) + (6 \times 0.2 \times 0.025) = 0.1$ m³.

Assuming that the timber is kiln-dried and dressed softwood, its embodied energy value[166] is 2,205 MJ/m³, giving a value for housing the books (ignoring any fixings) of 220 MJ, and a footprint of 0.0016 ha. However, the shelves should last as long as the house, so this figure has to be spread over 60 years, giving an annual footprint of 0.00003 ha. This effectively means that the embodied energy of housing a collection of 700 books in the UK is about 0.0002 ha.

If the house is heated, the book collection will be heated too. We could argue that, since the house is heated anyway, heating the books does not count; but we are trying to be scrupulously fair, so we will account for their share of the energy. According to the UK Energy Research Centre, in 2007 the average energy used for space heating in existing houses was 32.7 GJ, falling to 19.9 GJ for new UK houses.[167] This would add 32.7 ÷ 96 × 0.4 = 0.14 GJ, or 0.001 ha, for a book collection in an existing house, and 19.9 ÷ 96 × 0.4 = 0.08 GJ, or 0.0006 ha, for one in a new UK house. Since our books are in New Zealand, it would be worth comparing their footprint here with its equivalent in the UK (the amount of energy used for space heating is usually smaller in New Zealand). According to the Building Research Association of New Zealand (BRANZ), space heating accounts for 34% of energy use in the average New Zealand home,[168] and total average energy use was 46 GJ/house in 2001.[169] This means that space heating accounts for 15.6 GJ. In 1999, the average house size in New Zealand was 140 m²; although it has since risen, we will use this value since it is the closest in date to the energy figures.[170] Heating a collection of 700 books in New Zealand is, therefore, 15.6 ÷ 140 × 0.4 = 0.04 GJ, or 0.0003 ha, being half the value for the same collection in the UK. In fact, our own collection of second-hand books is somewhat larger, at an estimated 120 m of shelving, or 6,000 books. The footprint of such a collection in an existing house in the UK is 0.01 ha. Since we have at various times housed our books in an existing house in the UK, a newly built, very low-energy house in the UK, and in various types of house in New Zealand, we have collected the relevant figures in Table 8 (overleaf).

What the table shows is that collecting things does have a footprint. It also demonstrates that moving to New Zealand was good for us, since it reduced the footprint of our collection: the climate is better so less

Table 8: Footprint of a collection of second-hand books in three different locations

number of books in collection	UK existing house (annual footprint m²)	UK new house (annual footprint m²)	New Zealand existing house (annual footprint m²)
700	12	8	4*
6,000	100†	70	34

* This figure has been adjusted using an embodied energy value for a New Zealand house of 268 GJ.[171]
† Calculated from the hectare footprints and rounded.

energy is used for space heating, though it is also fair to say that houses are much colder in New Zealand in the winter than in the UK. Compared to other activities such as keeping pets – one thinks of the Alsatian's footprint of 3,600 m²/year (see 'Heavy Petting' in the previous chapter) – perhaps collecting second-hand books is not too bad. The books probably contain more useful information than the Alsatian, and are certainly easier to have in bed with you.

There is an argument that the heating of books should not be counted as they can help make a house more comfortable by storing energy in their thermal mass. A collection of 6,000 books amounts to 3,768 kg, or 3.7 tonnes, of mass. Let us assume that they are kept in a New Zealand house 140 m² in area, single storey (as is the New Zealand norm), and with a 100 mm concrete floor slab. The slab itself would represent 14 m³ of concrete, which at a density of 2,400 kg/m³ would have a mass of 34 tonnes. Thus the book collection cannot compare to the mass contained within the building envelope. Our house in New Zealand is two storeys, with a ground-floor concrete slab 76 m² in area. On the same basis, this equates to a mass of 18 tonnes, or about 5 times the mass of the book collection, so here the mass of the books is more significant. In a lightweight house that is all timber frame, with a timber frame floor, the book mass might be useful, storing some energy to even out temperature swings to a small degree. Since the effect is minimal, however, we have decided to ignore this factor in our calculation of the books' footprint.

In the past, books tended to be printed on thinner paper, which will have reduced their footprint. The Book Production War Economy standard is found on many of the books we own that were printed during and just after World War II. The standard was introduced in the face of paper shortages, so the pages are very thin. A return to this model could be another way of reducing the footprint of books, as well as the space they take up.

STAMPS

Although smaller than books, stamps can still be very big business. Stamp collecting is still very popular – perhaps one of the most popular hobbies in the world. It can also be seen from the discussion above that a few stamp albums are likely to have very little environmental impact, so all stamp collectors should be applauded.

TEA FOR TWO

The collecting of china is another popular pastime – and one with the advantage that china items are also potentially useful. (We plead guilty: Susie Cooper is particular weakness of Brenda's.) One branch of this hobby is the collection of novelty teapots, the subject of this investigation. A group of over 3,500 such pots can be visited at Teapot Island in Kent[172] – and in 2004, when it stood at 3,950, was the holder of a Guinness World Record. But what is the environmental impact of a novelty teapot?

A small bone china teapot might weigh 1 lb (0.45 kg), and a larger one 2.8 lb (1.3 kg).[173] A 2-pint earthenware teapot weighs in at just over 2 lb (0.9 kg).[174] Assuming that the average novelty teapot weighs 1 kg, it represents an embodied energy value of $1 \times 2.5 = 2.5$ MJ. The figure of 2.5 MJ/kg is for ceramic tiles,[175] the nearest we could find to glazed earthenware. A record-winning collection of 3,950 teapots would thus measure $3,950 \times 0.0025 = 9.9$ GJ if they were all new. A lot of collectible novelty teapots are indeed new, being made in limited editions.[176] The smaller the edition, the rarer and hence more valuable the teapot becomes after a space of time. But many examples are old, and, as with second-hand books, we can argue that once an object effectively enters the waste stream its embodied energy can be ignored. Not knowing the exact ratio of old to new teapots in the collection, we are using a 50:50 split for the present analysis. This would give an embodied energy of approximately 5 GJ. However, the collection will last a number of years (providing the pots are not dropped, that is). To work out the annual footprint of the collection, we need to know either how long the collection will last or the rate of collecting. If we assume that the collection lasts 60 years – the life we have allocated to the building that houses it (see below) – the annual energy would be 5 ÷ 60 = 0.08 GJ/year. We also know that between 1983 and the Guinness World Record in 2004 – a period of 21 years – 3,950 teapots were collected,[177] making the rate of collection 359 teapots a year, which would have a value of 359 × 0.0025 = 0.9 GJ. Given that between October 2004 and July 2005 a further 610 teapots were collected, this higher value seems more representative of collecting activity.

The teapots also need to be put on display. Judging by the ones we have on the dresser at home, it would be possible to show 7 teapots on a shelf 1.5 m in length. If the majority of the Teapot Island collection were on display, this would work out as 3,500 ÷ 7 × 1.5 = 750 m of shelving, plus a little space to house the rest of the collection in storage. In a room 4 × 4 m, it would be possible to fit a 130 m run of shelving, assuming 6 rows of shelves so that all the teapots are visible, a double-banked freestanding unit in the middle, and allowing a little space for a door. This would mean that the collection could be displayed in a building of 6 such rooms, covering a floor area of 96 m² – about the same as a UK house (see Chapter 3).

The teapots do not need to be kept warm to preserve them, so the only services required are lighting. In 1998, lighting in the UK worked out at 8.6 kWh/m²/year.[178] It has been stated that, despite the promotion of low-energy lightbulbs, the energy used for lighting in the UK has not decreased since the 1990s.[179] For this reason the value of 8.6 kWh will be used here, to give a total of 96 × 8.6 = 826 kWh/year, or 29,738 MJ or 29.7 GJ/year – about 6 times the energy embodied in the teapots themselves. To this figure must be added the energy it takes to make the space that houses the collec-tion. A photograph of Teapot Island shows a single-storey brick building with roof tiles probably of concrete and wooden window frames.[180] Using the UK embodied energy value for a house of 324 GJ, as above, and assum-ing a 60-year lifespan for the building would give the space housing the teapot collection an embodied energy figure of 324 ÷ 60 = 5.4 GJ/year, which is similar to the energy embodied in the current teapot collection. Strictly speaking, as the collection grew more space would have to be found, but for the moment this has been ignored. It has been assumed that more and more teapots will be kept in storage and that the display space will remain constant. Shelving has also been ignored, since the embodied energy figure is for a whole house, including fittings.

Adding the embodied energy values and the energy needed to light the collection on display suggests that the environmental cost of collecting the teapots is 0.9 (adding to the collection) + 5.4 (housing it) + 29.7 (lighting it) = 36 GJ/year. Using the conversion factor of 135 GJ/ha, this represents a land area of 0.27 ha, which is about the same as having a medium-sized dog like a Border Collie.

The owner of the collection at Teapot Island has also posted details of a 'teapot diary' for July to December 2005, detailing visits connected with teapots.[181] Two entries describe trips to Stoke and to Devon. From Teapot Island to Devon is about 230 miles (368 km), and to Stoke about 210 miles (336 km). If they travelled in a 1.6 litre car, the energy footprint of the journey would be 3.69 MJ/km (see Table 20 in Chapter 2), immaterial of how many people are travelling since the figure here is being used to consider collecting rather than people. So for these two journeys the total footprint will be $(368 \times 2 \times 3.69) + (336 \times 2 \times 3.69) = 5{,}196$ MJ, or 5.2 GJ. Assuming that similar trips related to collecting happen also in the other six months of the year, the annual travelling footprint will be 10.4 GJ, or 0.08 ha. The values of the different aspects of collecting novelty teapots are summarized in Table 9.

Table 9: Footprint of world record-holding novelty teapot collection

	footprint (GJ/year)	(footprint ha/year)
novelty teapot collection	0.9	0.007
housing the collection	5.4	0.040
lighting the collection	29.7	0.220
associated travel	10.4	0.080
total	54.5	0.350

At first sight this seems a big footprint, since it represents almost 20% of the fair earthshare footprint of 1.8 ha/year. Obviously this is a big collection and offers a lot of fun, as it is also open to the public.[182] But, to put this figure into perspective, the whole collection has the same footprint as keeping a large dog such as an Alsatian.

The point of this exercise is not at all to say that collecting teapots is a bad thing to do – and we have enjoyed finding out about novelty teapots to write this – but, rather, to discover the significant environmental costs associated with it. The actual collecting accounts for only 1.6% of the total footprint, whereas the biggest impacts come from lighting and travel. A very general figure for lighting has been used here, which could be reduced by using a low-energy lighting system. The travel associated with collecting could also be combined with other trips, such as visiting relatives, but the figures should signal a warning to collectors. You may be a stamp collector thinking that your hobby has a very low impact, but if you do a lot of driving about, going to swap meets and stamp fairs, your footprint could be much more significant. It is also worth noting that, in the case of a large collection open to the public, the travel footprint of visitors may also need to be considered.

CARS

About an hour's drive from Wellington, where we live, there is a private collection of cars that is now open to the public as the Southward Car Museum. This is claimed to be the largest private collection of veteran and vintage cars in the southern hemisphere,[183] consisting of some 250 vehicles, half of which are on display at any one time.[184] The collection was amassed by Sir Len and Lady Southward after they bought their first Ford Model T in 1956, was opened to the public in 1979,[185] and is now run as a charitable trust. As with the second-hand books, these are old cars that have been removed from the waste stream and so their embodied energy can be ignored. But they do occupy space – more space than, say, the teapots. This investigation will focus on the impacts of housing a collection that is open to the public and of the visitors who travel to see it.

The exhibition hall is a two-storey building of 6,000 m² in total, with sufficient natural light for indoor photography.[186] There also is a workshop, a restaurant, a shop and a theatre on the site, which covers some 6 hectares, and the museum caters for conferences and functions.[187] For our current purposes, we will take the 6,000 m² as the space that houses the collection. The building is made of pre-cast concrete, and some assumptions will have to be made about the car park. The British Cement Association states that buildings of reinforced concrete have an embodied energy of 417–695 kWh/m².[188] This works out at 1.5–2.5 GJ/m², which for a building of 6,000 m² gives an energy footprint of 6,000 × 2 = 12,000 GJ. For a 60-year lifespan this works out as an annual footprint of 200 GJ, or 1.48 ha. Since the building has two storeys, it actually occupies a ground area of 3,000 m², or 0.3 ha. A car park that will take 50 cars would add a further 500 m², giving total footprint of 1.48 + 0.3 + 0.05 = 1.83 ha.

Working out the number of visitors to the Southward Car Museum is more complicated. A chart of tourist visitors to the Wellington region shows that 23% of all international visitors go to a museum or gallery.[189] International visitor numbers are forecast to rise from 592,000 in 2002 to 875,900 in 2009. Domestic visitor numbers for the same period are due to rise from 2.15 million to 2.37 million.[190] Although many people come to the region to visit relatives, museum-going may also form part of their stay. Assuming a total of 3 million visitors to the region based on the figures above, 25% of whom go to a museum or gallery, out total would be 750,000 museum visits a year. To account for domestic visits this figure could be increased to around 1 million going to a gallery or a museum, although visitors may well visit more than one attraction. Statistics New Zealand published a survey of cultural experiences in New Zealand in 2003, which stated that an estimated 1.34 million New Zealanders over fifteen years of age had visited an art gallery or museum in the year before the survey date.[191] Wellington had the highest proportion of adults visiting galleries and museums, at around 70%, although this was perhaps influenced by free entry in Wellington and the presence of Te Papa, the national museum, in the city.[192]

The largest museum in the region, Te Papa, situated alongside the harbour, attracted 1,275,055 people in 2005–6, and 1,351,675 in 2006–7. The former figure was split between 46% international visitors, 22% from outside the region, and 32% from Wellington City and region.[193] According to the Wellington Museums Trust, during the same year of 2005–6 the

City Gallery attracted 236,406 visitors, and Plimmer's Ark – the remains of a ship that have been excavated and conserved beneath a central city building – 100,229 visitors. All of these attractions are in the centre of the city, unlike the Southward Car Museum, which is an hour's drive away. The Wellington Cable Car Museum also attracted nearly 200,000 visitors despite being shut part of the year; it is also only a 10-minute ride from the centre. This suggests that attractions related to transport are of interest to visitors, although their proximity to the city centre and the nature of the ride itself will also influence numbers.

From this discussion, we can assume that 50,000 people visit the Southward Car Museum each year. The distance between Wellington and the museum is about 60 km. We will use the figure of 3.69 MJ/passenger-km we employed in our consideration of teapot-related travel above, but this time we will assume that there are 3 people in each car. This decision is based on a report stating that the average number of people in a group visiting the Karori Wildlife Sanctuary in Wellington was 3, and that 88% of people go there by car.[194] Earlier data from 2001 suggested that the average car occupancy for holiday and leisure trips was 2.2 people.[195] Not all people will come from as far away as Wellington and, given that the Southward Car Museum is promoted by cruise liners, some visitors will come in mini buses and coaches, so an occupancy level of 3 people to a car seems reasonable. This will give a visitor travel impact to the collection of 60 × 2 × 1.23 × 50,000 = 7,380,000 MJ, or 7,380 GJ. Using the conversion factor of 135 GJ/ha, this would give a footprint of 54.7 ha.

As might be expected, the travel footprint is very much higher than the collection's footprint – about 30 times higher. The issue, then, is not collecting, but having the collection on display to the public. In fact, the railway line from Wellington runs right past the Southward Car Museum, but passenger services currently stop about 10 km to the south. However, there is a proposal to extend passenger services further north, so it would be possible to provide the museum with its own station. If this were done, the visitor footprint would reduce to 60 × 2 × 0.6 × 50,000 = 3,600,000 MJ = 3,600 GJ = 26.7 ha – a 50% reduction.

As a postscript, we would like to mention the donation to the Southward collection of a NZ$90,000 Ariel Atom sports car. The owner gave it to the museum as part of the International Day of Action on Climate Change at the end of 2007, saying that he used to think it was cool to drive fast cars, but now thought it was cool to ensure that the planet had some kind of future in the face of climate change.[196] This two-seater car has a fuel consumption of 29 mpg[197] (9.7l/100 km or 4.25 MJ/km, allowing for the embodied energy of petrol); because it weighs less than 500 kg with a full tank of fuel, its embodied energy will be around 0.2 MJ/km (see Chapter 2), making a total of 4.5 MJ/km. Swapping the Atom for an 'average' car that does 3.69 MJ/passenger-km and making the journey to see the sports car once a year would not seem much of a step forward. Perhaps he should ask for it back ...

eBAY

The popularity of eBay and similar companies illustrates our desire to collect things. Brenda has bought online – a poetry book with lithographed illustrations, for instance – but felt that not finding it in a shop was somehow cheating. Yet shops get fewer, and more and more desirable second-hand goods are sold on the internet. The question is: does online commerce have less of an impact on the environment than other forms?

As we saw above, it is the journeys associated with collecting that seem to have the greatest impact. We always try to combine visits to second-hand bookshops with other types of visit, as our family know well. Most people do not deliberately buy a computer to use eBay – the need to communicate with work and friends is a much more significant reason – so buying online to feed a collecting habit constitutes a secondary use, just as we combine family visits with searching for books. The impact of buying online, therefore, is mostly in the form of electricity (which is negligible for internet purchases) and postage, which should be compared with journeys made in person.

Assuming that a person visits a car boot or garage sale every other week, they might only drive 20 km there and back on average. This makes 26 visits in a year, the impact of which would be $26 \times 20 \times 3.6 = 1,872$ MJ, or 1.9 GJ. This represents a footprint of 0.014 ha. If parcels are bought off eBay they are likely to travel further. To compare the two we will need to make some assumptions. The first is that each parcel travels 200 km and weighs 2 kg. The second is that 12 parcels are bought each year, which is the same as if every other visit to a garage sale resulted in a purchase. We also need to know that freight transport uses 2.8 MJ/tonne-km (see Chapter 1). Each year, the impact of buying off the internet is 12 × 2 × 200 × 2.8 ÷ 1,000 = 13.4 MJ, or 0.0134 GJ, with a footprint of 0.0001 ha. This means that its impact is nearly 150 times less than travelling to support a collecting habit. So whatever the parcel postage costs, using the post rather than collecting things in person is very much better for the environment.

'I SPY WITH MY LITTLE EYE'

As we noted at the start of this section, not everyone collects *things*. Some people prefer to collect experiences. When we were children, we both had the series of 'I-Spy' books that listed objects to be ticked off as you saw them: things to do with the countryside, or the railways, or the seaside.[198] (Brenda never did find the grain store raised on stone legs that she can picture to this day.) Doubtless these little books now have collectors of their own. At that time, in the 1950s, the objects we were looking for could be found relatively locally and seen, if you were lucky, as you went about your normal life. Collecting these experiences was a local activity.

It is clear from the analyses above that where you go for your experience will be significant. If you are a birdwatcher (or 'twitcher') who travels long distances, usually by car, in order to see rare birds, then you are bad for the environment, and you are helping to bring about the demise of the very birds you go to see. If you aim to climb the highest mountains in the world and travel there by air, you are even worse. But walking around your locality looking for all the wildflowers that are supposed to be growing there seems a low-energy use of your time and enthusiasm that will also offer useful exercise.

CONCLUSION

As with pets, the bigger the item you collect, the bigger the impact of your hobby. Using eBay and other electronic services coupled with parcel post is a much better way to collect than seeking out objects personally, even if it is not as much fun. Collecting old things that have already been thrown away once is also a better way to go than collecting new stuff; but most significant of all for collecting as a hobby is the associated travel.

This raises a significant point not just for private collectors, but also for local and national collectors who open their collections to the public, whether they are local historical museums or internationally significant collections of cars. Museums and galleries need to be accessible by public transport in order to minimize environmental impact: indeed, this is the most important aspect of having a collection open to the public. Locating museums in the centres of towns and cities so that people who come to stay can walk to them is also a good option, but this is straying into planning territory and away from lifestyle considerations. Our recommendations can be summarized as follows:

- Collecting small objects or local experiences is best for the environment.

- Travel associated with collecting should be minimized.

- Public collections must be easily accessible on foot or by public transport.

PRODUCTIVE PASTIMES

Not all of the activities we undertake for pleasure or leisure have a negative effect on the environment. As we saw in the discussion of keeping rabbits for meat in the previous chapter, it is possible to reduce our footprints by doing things at home. The purpose of the following section is to consider some other pastimes that might have a positive impact.

In the past, the home was the site of production; and often objects were made there that could be sold for extra income. But this was before industrialization and the split between work and home. However, many of us still spend a lot of time producing things at home, such as the dolls' clothes a former schoolfriend made for her niece in New Zealand, over which many hours were spent while watching television.[199]

COOKING

At first sight it may seem odd to describe cooking as a productive pastime, but whereas for ordinary people in the mid-20th century most meals were cooked and eaten at home, the pattern is now very different. Restaurants and take-away food outlets have proliferated, as have cookery books and food programmes; and the popularity of cooking has been recognized by the UK government,[200] so it must still exist.

In 1999 the United States Department of Agriculture published *America's Eating Habits: Changes and Consequences*. This document claimed that national spending on eating out had increased from 25% of total food spending in 1970 to 40% in 1995. It also considered that this trend had an adverse affect on the country's diet.[201] From the UK National Food Survey of 1994, it appeared that an average of 12% of total food energy intake in the UK came from eating out (1 MJ/person, out of a total intake of 8.9 MJ). Those with higher incomes eat out more, and retired people the least.[202] The survey also mentioned that

> *Expenditure on all food and drink consumed outside the home accounted for 28 per cent of total expenditure on food and drink, which is a higher percentage than its contribution to nutrient intakes, given the necessarily higher cost of food eaten out.*[203]

What is worth nothing here is that eating out does not seem to be as good for us nutritionally as eating in. The US study found that fat density – the amount of fat expressed as a proportion of a serving – and saturated fat density had declined in foods prepared at home to a greater extent than in food eaten in restaurants or in fast food.[204] The Cardiff study of food-related footprints (see Chapter 1) showed that food eaten out of the home constituted one tenth of the total diet but one third of the total footprint. This would suggest that eating at home could reduce the Cardiff footprint from 1.3 ha/person to 1.0 ha/person – a 23% reduction – and would be very beneficial for the environment.

MAKING A PIZZA

To look at the question of cooking at home in more detail, the environmental impact of three pizzas will be assessed: one from an ordinary but nameless pizza chain, delivered to the door; the second from a 'green' pizza firm where 75% of ingredients are organic and delivery is by a hybrid car;[205] and the third a pizza made and eaten at home. First we need to work out the impact of the pizza, which can be adjusted according to whether it is made of organic or even home-grown ingredients. To this figure must be added the cost of running the retail outlet and the impact of delivering it to your door.

A pizza is a wheat-based bread dough base topped with tomatoes of some kind and then other vegetables, meat or fish. The big ingredients in a typical pizza are the flour (3 cups, or 390 g), oil (1 tablespoon, or 13 g) and yeast (1 tablespoon, or 13 g) in the base; 6 tomatoes, an onion and various herbs for the tomato sauce; and grated cheese (1 cup, or 100 g), chopped ham (0.5 cup, or 50 g) and mushrooms (0.5 cup, or 50 g) for the topping.[206]

The footprint for making this pizza at home could be assembled from the footprints of the various ingredients. One website gives the breakdown for a pizza as 50% crust, 25% cheese, 12.5% tomato sauce, 7.5% sausage (or ham) and 5% mushrooms,[207] which is roughly the same as the recipe we gave above. In a study of packaging material for pizzas, a takeaway pizza was given as 45% bread dough, 20% tomato paste and 35% mozzarella cheese, with the pizza cooked for two minutes at 300 °C.[208] A 410 g frozen pizza is described as enough for one (if piggy) but not enough for two.[209] From all this information we have decided on a recipe for our study: our 500 g pizza will be 45% bread dough, 35% cheese and 20% tomatoes. Using footprint conversion figures from the Cardiff study (see Chapter 1). the footprint of the ingredients will be $(0.5 \times 0.45 \times 6) + (0.5 \times 0.35 \times 148.8) + (0.5 \times 0.2 \times 6.8) = 1.35 + 26.04 + 0.68 = 28.1 \ m^2$, the cheese being the high-footprint ingredient. The pizza also has to be cooked. At home you might have the oven at 180 °C for 30–40 minutes. An oven is about 3 kW when on full, so assuming it needs 2 kW for 40 minutes, this is 1.3 kWh or 4.7 MJ – a footprint of 0.3 m^2. This shows that the ingredients are much more significant than the cooking.

If the pizza is made at home, all that remains is to serve it, eat it and wash the dishes afterwards. However, if the same pizza is made in a shop and then delivered to your door, there will be a box to put it in and the impact of driving. Pizza boxes are normally made of corrugated cardboard, and a standard size is 33 × 33 × 3 cm.[210] The area of cardboard involved is 0.3 m^2, and if we use the weight of 125 g/m^2 for corrugated sheet[211] we can estimate that it would weigh 37.5 g. Using the Environmental Defense Fund paper calculator[212] and assuming the box is made of bleached corrugated cardboard, the impact would be a very, very small part of a tree, 1,792 Btu

(1.9 MJ), 0.24 lb (0.1 kg) of CO_2 equivalent, 0.89 US gallons (3.4 l) of waste water, and 0.1 lb (0.05 kg) of solid waste. Using the figures for just the greenhouse gas emissions and the water, as we did in analysing the impact of this book (see 'Collecting'), and making the same assumptions, the impact will be (emissions) $0.1 \div 0.46 = 0.2$ kWh = 0.78 MJ, or 0.06 m², and (water) 0.08 $\div 100 \times 3.4 = 0.003$ m². As suggested in Chapter 1, the impact of packaging is not as significant as the ingredients, and the cardboard pizza box has a low footprint of 0.063 m². The problem is the total number of pizzas delivered. A US newspaper article from 2004 stated that Domino's expected to deliver 1.2 million pizzas on Superbowl Sunday – double the number of a normal Sunday.[213] From this figure of 0.6 million pizzas delivered on a normal Sunday, we can estimate 31.2 million delivered in a year. The impact of all those boxes is 1,965,600 m², which is 2 km² – and this is just for one chain that has an 8.4% share of the pizza market in the US alone. This is land devoted to packaging food that could easily be made at home.

A take-away pizza has to be delivered to your door. It has not been possible to find out the average number of pizzas delivered in any single trip, and obviously how many are carried will vary according to what has been ordered and where it has to be taken. However, we know that pizzas are commonly delivered by scooter, so for this analysis we will assume that 6 pizzas are delivered on a 10 km round trip. Our local outlet uses a new Toyota Yaris with a 1.5 l engine as its delivery vehicle. For a 10 km trip, this will use $10 \times 3.69 = 36.9$ MJ, assuming 1 person delivering 6 pizzas. The figure of 3.69 MJ/person-km is for a 1.6 l car (see Chapter 2). This comes to 0.037 GJ and a footprint of 2.7 m², or 0.5 m² for each delivered pizza. Thus the total footprint of one take-away pizza is 21.8 (ingredients) + 0.3 (cooking) + 0.5 (delivery) + 0.06 (packaging) = 22.7 m².

After writing this section at work, the only sensible course of action was to go home (on the bus) and make a pizza for supper. It took 35 minutes to prepare it for the oven, but this time included part-cooking the base (a quick version that does not require yeast but is very crisp), going down to the vegetable garden to pick tomatoes and basil for the topping, sorting out the recycling bins for collection, and preparing four stuffed baked apples to be cooked at the same time as the pizza. The pizza took 20 minutes in the oven, making a total time of 55 minutes (though not all this was spent on the pizza). In the UK the average delivery time for the Domino's pizza chain is 24 minutes,[214] so the home-made version takes twice as long. But the home-made product is eaten straight from the oven rather than being kept warm; the base is made of stoneground wholemeal flour from a windmill; the tomatoes are fresh; and the fat and salt content is limited because you are in control of how much cheese is in the topping, making a product that is probably better for you than the shop-bought variety.[215] The home-made product is also cheaper: the total cost of the wholemeal pizza with tomato, basil, anchovy, olive and cheese topping was under NZ$5, including the cost of cooking, whereas a comparable take-away pizza from an outlet in our suburb is NZ$15. Some take-away pizzas are cheaper, but this particular chain makes a type of pizza that tastes similar to home-made, so this is the value used here. Using cost as a guide, the footprint of the ingredients of home-made pizza could be assumed to be less than the bought one. These ingredients form $21.8 \div 22.7 \times 100 = 96\%$ of the total footprint of a take-away pizza, so in cost terms this is NZ$14.4. The home-made pizza costs about NZ$5 for ingredients, and the footprint of its maker can be ignored because we are considering cooking as a pastime in place of some other activity like watching television or playing football. Thus the footprint of the home-made pizza is $21.8 \times 5.0 \div 14.4 = 7.6$ m^2. Packaging and delivery are also avoided, so the total footprint works out as 7.6 (ingredients) + 0.3 (cooking) = 7.9 m^2 – a 65% reduction for an extra 25 minutes in the kitchen.

'Ah!', you will argue, 'I have to go to the shops by car to buy the ingredients just like the pizza has to be delivered to my door by car, so is the comparison fair?' In fact, the footprint figures include the delivery of raw ingredients both to the place where the food is cooked, when the food is consumed outside the home, and to the supermarket. Most people buy a range of products when they visit the supermarket and not just the ingredients for a single dish, and some people still do most of their shopping on foot. In the past, take-away meals like the traditional fish and chips were also collected on foot. The point of the pizza analysis is to show the relative impact of a product that can be easily made at home and how, if you enjoy home cooking, you will be reducing your impact on the environment at the same time.

Other advantages that come with being a home cook are increased knowledge and a control of resources.

Traditionally, the world over, the woman in a house has been known
as the 'keeper of the keys.' To hold the keys to the household, to its
storerooms, attics, chests, and cupboards, was a position of great
responsibility and, therefore, of great honour. In a season of
impoverishment, it was the woman's wise allocation of limited
supplies that would see the family through, and in times of plenty,
it was her foresight that provided for future needs.[216]

If you are a cook, you will know what ingredients you have in store
and in the garden; you will design meals around these items, the time you
have available, and the opportunity you will have to shop during the day or
on the way home from work. Most home cooks will use recipes in creative
ways, adjusting them to the resources that are available. This is not necessarily fine dining, but it is a way of creating wholesome and nutritious food
that also imparts an understanding of what working within available
resources means, and how creativity is part of resource limitation. Cooking
at home also gives a negative food footprint of 23–65%, according to the
brief investigation above. However, since much of the food in the Cardiff
diet we examined is cooked and eaten at home, for this comparison only
the smaller percentage will be considered. The average food footprint of
1.3 ha/person/year, worked out earlier, would be reduced to 1.0 ha, on
account of a negative footprint of −0.3 ha achieved through never eating out.
This is an area where more detailed research is needed, but it would seem
that, as a hobby, cooking is good for the environment.

GARDENING

We have already mentioned how housing environments in the past were
designed to allow a certain amount of food to be grown at home, and that
such productive activities were seen as normal. We once grew 75% of our
total diet, including meat and dairy products as well as fruit and vegetables,
on 0.7 ha of land, spending about 2 hours a day doing so. It never seemed a
chore, but rather something that made you feel good about living. This was
when we had a cow, pigs to consume the excess milk, hens, a sheep and a
hive of bees. When at the end of the 19th century George Cadbury set up his
new settlement of Bournville – designed not just for his factory workers but

for any citizen of Birmingham – the gardens were made large so that the father of the household could grow all its fruit and vegetables, thus keeping him productively engaged in the fresh air.[217] The gardens came complete with apple trees to encourage this home productivity.[218]

Home gardening also came into its own in World War II, when the citizens of many countries were encouraged to grow food at home. In New Zealand, Deputy Prime Minister Walter Nash said the following:

> *The reasons for the campaign to 'Dig for Victory' are so compelling that on behalf of the Government, I urge every citizen who has access to land to do everything in his power to supply his own family with vegetables ... warring in Europe is not only consuming current production but is exhausting seeds and parent stocks, imperilling the very sources of crops, herds and flocks of all kinds ... This makes it clear that vegetable growing in New Zealand will be a vital need for many years to come.*[219]

So how much could home gardening reduce your footprint? The New Zealand Heart Foundation recommends that at least 5 out of 14 servings of food each day should be fruit and vegetables.[220] They might take the form of a breakfast of cereal, toast and an apple (3 servings; 1 fruit), a lunch of bread and cheese with tomatoes followed by a yoghurt (4 servings; 1 vegetable) and a main meal in the evening consisting of meat, Yorkshire pudding, potatoes and carrots followed by rhubarb crumble and custard (6 servings; 2 vegetables and 1 fruit), making 13 servings of which 3 are vegetables and 2 fruit – ingredients that could be grown at home. The extra serving could be a snack mid-morning or afternoon. Thus 5 out of 14 servings, representing roughly 35% of the diet, could be home-produced. Taking 35% of an average food footprint of 1.3 ha (see Chapter 1) will give a new footprint of 0.85 ha, but this will not be very accurate since fruit and vegetables have a lower impact than other components of the diet like meat and dairy products (see Chapter 1). Using a rough average of 6 m²/kg for fresh fruit and vegetables from data in Table 5 in Chapter 1 and the fact that 675.5 kg of food is eaten annually, we can work out that the footprint for the 35% of your diet that can be grown at home is 675.5 × 0.35 × 6 = 1,419 m², or 0.14 ha. This is 0.14 ha that you are not consuming because you are growing your own food, so it becomes a negative footprint.

Against this must be set the actual land needed to grow the food. The 'Dig for Victory' plot for growing vegetables all year round was the size of a typical allotment, 90 × 30 ft (27 × 9 m).[221] The fruit trees in our garden – two apple trees, a plum tree, a pear tree, a lemon tree, and an unidentified citrus (it hasn't fruited yet) – occupy a space 9 × 3 m, making a total area of 30 × 9 m = 270 m², or 0.027 ha. This will reduce the negative footprint to 0.14 – 0.027 = 0.11 ha.

There is also the question of cooking to be considered. Cooking a serving of potatoes uses 1.08 MJ (see Chapter 2). Over the course of a year, we need to cook 3 servings of vegetables a day, assuming that most fruit is eaten raw and that the vegetables are cooked. The energy for cooking the home-grown part of our diet in a year is 3 × 1.08 × 365 = 1,182.6 MJ, or 1.2 GJ, which has a footprint of 0.009 ha. This may be an overestimate, as several vegetables can be steamed at the same time over a single burner or hot plate, and vegetables (roast potatoes, for instance) can also be cooked in the oven at the same time as meat. Including this level of cooking reduces the negative footprint insignificantly (by about 0.009 ha) to around –0.1 ha.

Another way to discover the amount of fruit and vegetables that can be grown at home is to use the annual consumption of the Cardiff diet discussed in Chapter 1. Although this is a measured diet, it may not represent the ideal shown above, but it will provide a comparison. Table 10 sets out the amount of food eaten and its footprint (all values are taken from Table 5 in Chapter 1).

The total weight of all the fruit and vegetables in this diet is 49.8 + 41.8 + 36.6 + 22.3 + 18.1 = 168.6 kg. This works out as 168.6 ÷ 675.5 × 100 = 24.9, or 25% of the weight of the diet. If they were all grown at home, the associated footprint reduction would be 354 (processed veg.) + 284 (fresh fruit) + 187 (fresh veg.) + 96 (fresh potatoes) + 78 (fresh green veg.) = 999 m², or 0.1 ha. To this we would have to add the footprint of cooking the fresh vegetables. But since this footprint does not represent an ideal diet from a nutritional point of view – merely the current average diet – for the moment the figures of 35% of fruit and vegetables grown at home and the – 0.1 ha footprint will be used here.

Of course, gardening also provides exercise. For a 190 lb (86 kg) man, one hour of gardening will burn 431 kcals[222] – the same as using a stationary exercise bike. If, rather than playing one round of golf for 4 hours, you spent

Table 10: Weight of food eaten in a year compared with its footprint

type of food	annual total (kg)	footprint (m²/kg)	footprint (m²)
skimmed milk	66.5	18.3	1,217
processed veg.	49.8	7.1	354
beer	46.7	6.1	285
fresh fruit	41.8	6.8	284
whole milk	37.3	18.0	671
other fresh veg. (not potatoes, green veg.)	36.6	5.1	187
bread	35.7	6.0	214
misc. meats	33.8	29.8	1,007
soft drinks	30.3	2.2	66
fresh potatoes	22.3	4.3	96
fruit juices	22.1	14.9	329
misc. cereals (not bread, flour products)	18.6	13.4	249
fresh green veg.	18.1	4.3	78
low cal. soft drinks	17.8	2.6	46
wine	17.5	29.0	508
sugar	12.8	8.9	114
biscuits	11.7	19.1	224
cakes	10.9	21.7	237
mineral water	10.4	1.7	18
poultry (uncooked)	9.9	20.8	206
misc. dairy (not milk, yoghurt, cheese, eggs)	9.3	22.9	213
spirits	9.1	54.0	496
yoghurt etc.	9.1	23.1	210
total fish	8.8	134.3	1,182
pork/ham/bacon	8.2	25.4	208
eggs	7.6	15.5	118
beef and veal	6.6	209.1	1,380
cheese	6.0	148.8	893
soft drinks	6.0	2.5	15

continued overleaf

Table 10 *continued*

type of food	annual total (kg)	footprint (m²/kg)	footprint (m²)
ice cream etc.	5.9	56.9	336
fruit (tinned)	5.8	6.7	39
chocolate	5.7	61.1	348
misc. foodstuffs	5.5	14.2	78
soups	4.2	15.5	65
mutton and lamb	3.4	100.6	342
confectionary (non-choc.)	3.4	12.6	43
flour	2.8	9.3	26
tea	2.5	47.6	119
preserves etc.	2.4	12.1	29
low-fat spreads etc.	2.2	90.0	198
poultry (cooked)	1.8	43.3	78
low cal. soft drinks (conc.)	1.8	2.2	4
cream	1.2	79.2	95
coffee	1.1	59.1	65
vegetable oils	1.1	52.7	58
butter	1.0	160.0	160
margarine	0.7	85.7	60
cocoa/drinking choc.	0.6	71.7	43
animal fats (not butter)	0.3	30.0	9
Horlicks etc.	0.3	23.3	7
total	**675.5**		**13,307**

Note: All categories and data are taken from Table 5 in Chapter 2.

2.3 hours a week gardening (see 'Golf'), you would get the same level of beneficial exercise. However, the impact of golf is 2,393 MJ/golfer/year (2.4 GJ), so changing from golf to gardening would reduce your footprint by 0.018 ha (2.4 ÷ 135 ha). Thus the total negative footprint for a converted golfer would be 0.1 (growing food at home) + 0.02 (gardening for exercise rather than playing golf) = 0.12 ha. Maybe the answer is that more informal business meetings should be conducted while digging over the office vegetable garden than on the golf course, as currently happens.

GREEN FINGERS

Many people's immediate objection to gardening is, 'I don't have the time.' But, as we have shown above, swapping from golf to gardening would give you extra time – an extra 1.7 hours a week – as well as reducing environmental impact. Another familiar objection is that growing vegetables is ugly and does not make for a proper leisure garden. Vegetables are often relegated to the back of the garden, preferably out of sight behind a hedge, giving the impression they are something we don't want to have there. However, as one friend commented to a non-gardener, a garden should have plants in it that *you* want or think look good[223] (thus echoing William Morris's maxim about having nothing in your house that you don't know to be useful or believe to be beautiful) – and never mind what books or other people tell you. If you are still worried, one book we have suggests a vegetable garden for children, consisting of marrows, squash or pumpkins on a mound at the back of the plot, then a row of potatoes, and then salad vegetables right at the front, since they look attractive.[224] The history of the cottage garden also suggests that vegetables grown between flowers and other decorative plants can also form part of an inclusive approach to gardening. Those who embrace 'permaculture', an abbreviation of 'permanent agriculture', set out to make a productive landscape where food is grown not just 'horizontally' but arranged vertically, so that shade-loving vegetables and herbs are planted under fruit and nut trees. These productive gardens are created along the principle of a natural eco-system.[225] We grow our vegetables in raised beds using ideas based on French intensive gardening,[226] but just because it suits us (probably because we don't have to bend down so much!). This particular method relies on the creation of good compost: another advantage of the productive garden is that wastes can be recycled on site rather than sent to landfill (see Chapter 1).

Anyone who has ever written about the chance sustainability offers us to be in better harmony with nature must be a productive gardener, since the home is the first place where this harmony is discovered: 'No mystery is involved in the making of a garden; only the learning of a few of Nature's laws, and the likes and dislikes of plants.'[227]

MAKING CLOTHES

Most people will tell you that it is not worth making your own clothes, either through sewing or knitting, because it is cheaper and less time-consuming to buy ready-made articles. When we were both children, however, it was normal that at least some of people's clothes were home-made. Making clothes at home was cheaper and also meant that garments would fit much better, since people are not as standardized as modern sizing systems would have us believe. The falling numbers of shops selling knitting wool and dress fabric would suggest that habits are changing. But do knitting and sewing at home reduce ecological impact?

KNITTING

To make a jumper or cardigan for a child takes 17 hours.[228] A Fair Isle sweater for an adult, knitted in many different colours and in complex patterns, takes over 100 hours.[229] One particular piece of information on this website is interesting: it states that the people who hand-knitted these jumpers were paid £100 a garment, out of which they had to cover the cost of the wool (over £30), making the selling of home knitting an uneconomic proposition. A new company now sells this type of sweater for £350, of which 65%, or £227.50, goes to the knitter. This price is for a top-quality all-woollen garment made using a traditional pattern, and from order to delivery it takes around 6–8 weeks. This suggests that, when labour and skill are taken into account, for complex hand-knitting materials constitute around 10% of the total cost. A single-coloured hand-knitted woollen cardigan and hat for a one-year-old child can be bought for NZ$38,[230] whereas just the wool to knit them would cost NZ$12, making the materials 32% of the total cost.

Knitting uses a minimum of equipment – normally two needles made of steel, aluminium or bamboo (bone in the past) – and once acquired they can last a lifetime. Because of their longevity and small size they have been ignored in this analysis. However, very few people knit as a sole occupation, and most will their knitting with watching television, talking to people or supervising children, meaning that the real cost of a garment resides in its raw materials. An all-wool child's cardigan for our granddaughter that I could have bought for NZ$40 in a shop cost NZ$20 for 5 oz (0.14 kg) of wool. What is saved is the footprint of manufacture and retail. If I knit the jumper myself, the room where I make it and the television I watch at the same time will be there whether or not I'm knitting. Unless I am spinning wool from my own sheep, I will have travelled to a shop to buy it; but wool will also have been shipped to the place where the bought garment was manufactured. In this part of the world, balls of wool from Australia or New Zealand probably travel to China and finished garments travel back again, so for the moment this issue is ignored.

A sheep provides about 3 kg of wool each year (see 'Clothing' in the previous chapter) – enough for 21 child-sized cardigans each knitted from 5 oz (0.14 kg) of wool. In our earlier discussion, the footprint for an adult sweater weighing 800 g worked out at 0.026 ha, or 260 m². This means that the footprint of the wool for a 0.14 kg cardigan will be $260 \div 0.8 \times 0.14 = 45.5$ m². Because the footprint of wool is high when methane emissions from sheep are taken into account (see 'Clothing'), it will not be possible to work out a saving for knitting at home based on cost. We could look at it another way instead, estimating that what has been saved is 17 hours of a person's time. Using an average Western lifestyle footprint of 3.5 ha/year, 17 hours represents 0.007 ha, or 70 m², which is getting on for twice the value of the wool. The saving to be gained from using your own time rather than the time, and hence the footprint, of someone else per 50 g ball of wool (the way wool is normally sold) is thus $70 \div 5 = 14$ m². So no matter whether you knit up a few balls of wool each year or a lot more, you can work out the saving that comes from having a productive hobby. A family of four making on average one new sweater or cardigan each every year and not buying any other knitwear would save around 14×60 balls (50 g each) $= 840$ m², or 0.08 ha.

Knitting is also one of those activities, like gardening, that are supposed to stave off memory problems associated with dementia and Alzheimer's,[231] so maybe the footprint calculation should include the resources saved because people who knit are more likely to stay well. Nonetheless, this is beyond the scope of the present investigation and has not been considered.

SEWING

Much of what has been said about knitting applies also to sewing clothes. Sewing is slightly different, however, in that it cannot be done while watching television and it normally involves more equipment in the form of a sewing machine.

It is often said that a simple pattern for a skirt should take about 2 hours to complete, though Brenda is somewhat slower and would suggest 4 hours as a better estimate, especially if you finish all the seams. The total fabric for a skirt could cost anything from a bargain NZ$10 to NZ$30, depending on what you choose. Buying a skirt could cost anything from a bargain NZ$20 to NZ$100, but, on the whole, more expensive fabric would equate with a more expensive purchased skirt. It would seem reasonable to assume that a fabric price of $NZ20 equates with a bought skirt of $NZ60. As with wool, we can suppose that a financial saving reflects a footprint saving, although the footprint will also depend on the type of fabric used. Assuming that the skirt is cotton, a value of 50 MJ/kg can be used (see 'Clothing' in the previous chapter). A cotton skirt requiring 3 metres of fabric weighs 12 oz (0.34 kg) on our kitchen scales, so the energy associated with the fabric is $50 \times 0.34 = 17$ MJ.

Brenda's sewing machine, which she has had for 20 years, weighs 8 kg. Assuming that its components are 50% plastic and 50% metal, it would have an embodied energy of $(4 \times 32) + (4 \times 111) = 128 + 444 = 572$ MJ, in which 32 MJ/kg is the value of virgin steel and 111 MJ/kg that of ABS plastic.[232] A lighter sewing machine would have more components in plastic, which has a higher embodied energy value, so the total value should work out about the same. Because the machine has been used for 20 years, the embodied energy works out at $572 \div 20 = 28.6$ MJ/year. Brenda's mother had 3 sewing machines in her life and spent over 60 years making clothes, so this seems reasonable. The machine will normally make more than 1 garment a year. Assuming Brenda makes 6 in a year (see Table 12), the footprint of the machine for each garment works out as $28.6 \div 6 = 4.8$ MJ/year.

The sewing machine motor is rated at 70 W. Supposing that half of the 4 hours needed to make up a skirt is spent using the machine, and the rest cutting out and pinning, the energy used by the machine works out at $70 \times 2 = 140$ Wh, or 0.5 MJ. The energy footprint of the skirt is therefore

17 (fabric) + 4.8 (machine) + 0.5 (energy to run the machine) = 22 MJ. If a bought skirt were 3 times the cost of the fabric, it would have an adjusted footprint of 66 MJ, and the energy saved through making it at home would therefore be 44 MJ, or 0.04 GJ, equating to 3.3 m². A cotton shirt also requires 3 metres of fabric and would thus show a similar saving.

If you sew, you might make 6 garments a year, with a total weight of 6 × 0.34 = 2 kg. (It is worth noting that the average consumption of clothes in the UK is 17.5 kg/person, which would include both knitted garments and heavier coats; see 'Clothing' in the previous chapter.) Obviously the footprint of each garment would differ with the type of fabric used, but from the value above we can calculate that the total saving over a year would be 6 × 3.3 = 20 m², or 0.002 ha.

Making clothing at home reduces our footprints because the labour is given for free. But several other advantages also need to be considered. Clothes made at home offer more choice in terms of style, material type and colour than garments in the shops; they are also likely to fit better. Home-made clothes can also be recycled, and hand-knitted items can be unpicked into a single thread; this cannot be done with machine-knitted items, which are cut out of knitted fabric and the seams sewn. In addition, because you are making clothes at home, you are likely to save accessories like buttons and trimmings for reuse (button boxes have always made wonderful toys for children). The most important factor, however, is the time it takes to make garments, since this helps us appreciate their true value; they may then seem more of an investment in resources than simply disposable items.

DIY

Cooking, knitting, sewing, and to some extent gardening are all hobbies perhaps associated more with women than with men, so we will now look at a 'male' activity such as do-it-yourself. Fortunately, we are in the process of moving house, and Robert has been making new kitchen cupboards to give us an excellent example to analyse.

A classic way to consume resources is to buy a house and then promptly refit the kitchen (see Chapter 3), often throwing away cupboards and worktops that would have given service for several more years. At first sight, it might thus seem perverse to discuss new kitchens. But the house we are moving to is a New Zealand Arts and Crafts-style cottage that, although dating from 1939, has a kitchen that looks as if it were designed just after World War I, with a free-standing cooker against the chimney breast and floor-to-ceiling cupboards in the recesses on either side. Previous owners had cut one of the original adzed wood cupboard doors in half and fitted a free-standing bench at right angles to the cupboard, thereby making almost half of it inaccessible. This bench we shall reuse in the scullery, where there was nothing, so it will not be wasted. We are making cupboards for either side of the cooker and reusing the remains of the original door, moving it forward. This creates a rather deep cupboard – in fact more of a priest hole – but makes it easier and safer to use the cooker.

Apart from time, the impact of DIY derives from the materials and the tools required. To make the sides, tops and bottoms of our cupboards, we have used softwood planks 25 × 200 mm dowelled together. The volume of timber used is 0.1 m³. Using an embodied energy for dressed kiln-dried softwood[233] of 2,204 MJ/m³, the wood has an energy content of 220 MJ. Because the original cupboards are painted white, another 115 MJ should be added to account for three coats of water-based paint,[234] giving a total of 335 MJ. The same cupboards if bought would have been made of melamine-faced chipboard. The chipboard is only 16 mm thick, so the volume used would be 0.06 m³, but it has an embodied energy[235] of 4,400 MJ/m³, making 4,400 × 0.06 = 264 MJ. Accounting for the melamine is difficult, so the value of 1 litre of solvent-based paint is used instead, adding 128 MJ to the total.[236] This gives the ready-made equivalent an embodied energy of 392 MJ.

Most people involved in DIY have a collection of tools, most of which are used only very occasionally. Most of our tools in New Zealand were acquired when we almost doubled the size of our first house here from 50 m² to 90 m², but only a limited selection is needed for making a cupboard. Probably the most critical tools are the two portable workbenches that weigh approximately 10 kg each and are mostly steel. Assuming that the saws, drill and so on make up another 10 kg of tools, again mostly metal, the total weight of 30 kg represents an embodied energy of 30 × 32 = 960 MJ, using 32 MJ/kg for the embodied energy of virgin steel.[237] However, some of these tools belonged to Robert's father, so it might be reasonable to assume a 50-year life for all of them, making 960 ÷ 50 = 19 MJ/year.

The total energy for the DIY cupboard is thus 335 + 19 = 354 MJ, or 0.35 GJ, giving a footprint of 0.35 ÷ 135 = 0.003 ha. To allow for the tools for the bought cupboard, a cost comparison will be necessary. The materials for the home-made cupboard cost just over NZ$200, making a cost of NZ$250 including the paint, and it took 10 hours to make. The equivalent cupboards in melamine-faced chipboard from a UK budget kitchen supplier cost £104.90,[238] which would convert to NZ$262. This gives a multiplier of 262 ÷ 250 = 1.05 for the energy in the bought product, which accounts for the labour, tools and so on involved in its manufacture. After taking this into account, the value for the bought cupboard is 392 × 1.05 = 412 MJ, or 0.41 GJ, with a footprint of 0.003 ha. Since in both cases materials or finished articles have to be brought to the site, travel has not been considered.

At first sight it might seem that the DIY cupboard is much the same as the bought version, since the home-produced example takes 0.35 GJ to make and the bought one 0.41 GJ. But this is not the whole story. The DIY cupboard is likely to last for at least one hundred years, because there is really nothing to go wrong with it and it is easy to repair. According to the British Standard for domestic kitchen units (BS 6222), a chipboard cupboard for general domestic use has a service life of 15 years.[239] This means that, over the life of the DIY cupboard, you would need at least 6 shop-bought equivalents, giving an embodied energy of 6 × 0.41 = 2.46 GJ. The home-made kitchen might get 6 recoatings of paint over the same period; this would require a total of 2 litres of paint and thus add a further 2 × 115 = 230 MJ, or 0.23 GJ, to the cupboard's initial embodied energy of 0.35 GJ, making a total of 0.58 GJ over its lifetime. So the energy saving over its life-span is 2.46 – 0.58 = 1.88 GJ, or a footprint of 139 m². This sounds good, but over 100 years it is only 1.4 m² a year. DIY also gives you exercise, but since this is sporadic rather than regular exercise like gardening it has not been taken into account.

In fact, like is not being compared with like here, as the home-made cupboards are of softwood and commercial versions tend to be made of chipboard. The home-made cupboard has also been built to fit the space, whereas a bought-in one would have to be adjusted on site, especially since old houses like ours are not regular in shape.

Apart from an appreciation of the time it takes to make something, DIY helps us understand what can be achieved when one works with one's own hands. The whole philosophy of the Arts and Crafts Movement was that items should be both artistically designed and should reflect the fact that they had been made by hand. With this type of finish, such items of furniture are very different from the seamless, perfect products that are often presented as the ideal for modern kitchens.[240] DIY could be a way of bringing the human touch back into the home environment.

HOBBIES AND THE ENVIRONMENT

Our discussion of selected productive hobbies above is really an analysis of what we choose to do with our time. Table 11 sets out the possible footprint reductions that can result from spending 10 hours (the time it took to make the kitchen cupboard) on the productive pastimes we have outlined here.

Perhaps the most significant point to emerge from this table is that all activities show a footprint saving. The saving for DIY is small, perhaps because of the example chosen (the kitchen cupboard): comparisons of home-made items with more expensive off-the-shelf equivalents might show better savings. With DIY, as with all productive hobbies, there is satisfaction both in the activity itself – in the 'doing' – and in the fact that the result will probably be of a better quality and more personal than what one

Table 11: Footprint savings from undertaking productive activities in the home

hobby	footprint saving from spending 10 hours on hobby (m²)
cooking	355*
gardening	100†
knitting	41‡
sewing	7§
DIY	1.4

* Based on 25 minutes to make one pizza, with its footprint saving of 14.8 m².
† Based on spending 2.3 hours/week productive gardening, for a saving of 0.1 ha/year.
‡ Based on 17 hours to knit up 250 g of wool.
§ Based on a cotton skirt taking 4 hours to make.

can buy in a shop. What productive pastimes do is change us from a society of passive consumers into a society of active producers. At the same time our skill level is improved. This kind of sustainability works against capitalism, which would prefer to see us as consumers – an issue discussed in more detail in the book's conclusion.

THE LEISURED CLASSES?

Obviously, the categories in this section are selective. They were chosen as representative of the ways we spend our leisure time in Western society, in an effort to determine whether some activities had more impact on the environment than others. Table 12 (overleaf) shows the results of this comparison and also includes other footprints, such as that associated with keeping a pet (see the previous chapter).

Putting these different activities together produces some surprises. Golf, a sport that seemed high in environmental impact, is not even in the same league as owning a large dog like an Alsatian. If you are a fit golfer who lives near the golf course and does not use a car to get there, your impact is only slightly greater than that of a hamster owner. Pets are bad news for the environment because of the food they eat, and will be increasingly so as food becomes more expensive. Productive pastimes are also good for the environment because of the goods we do not consume as a result. There is no need to go to the lengths of growing your own meat in the back garden, since significant reductions can be made in other activities. Productive hobbies such as gardening or working on DIY projects can also provide good exercise, thus offsetting the need to take part in a sport. Since these pastimes are connected to the home, they do not involve any travel, which again is beneficial.

All this discussion of leisure footprints has to be set against big-impact activities like driving. Table 12 shockingly illustrates that owning an Alsatian has the same impact as the annual motoring of the average New Zealander. In all the discussion of fuel-efficient and low-emission motoring, no one has yet done any research into the fuel-efficient (and low-emission) dog.

If you took part in all the productive activities discussed above (cooking, gardening, knitting, sewing and DIY) in a year you could hope to reduce your footprint by 0.3 (cooking) + 0.1 (gardening) + 0.2 (knitting one

Table 12: The footprints of various leisure activities compared

leisure activity	footprint per participant (ha/year)	footprint per participant (m²/year)
golf (walking to and round course)	0.018	180
tennis (driving to local court)	0.004	40
dragon-boat racing (walking to participate in teak boat)	0.00002	0.2
owning an Alsatian	0.36	3,600
owning a hamster	0.014	140
keeping rabbits for meat, with some food bought in	(–0.09)	(–900)
collecting books (6,000 in an existing house in New Zealand)	0.0034	34
sewing (6 garments a year)	(–0.002)	(–20)
DIY (8 projects equivalent to one kitchen cupboard a year)	(–0.0012)	(–12)
driving for a year (in New Zealand)*	0.38	3,827

* Based on 14,000 km/year[241] and 3.69 MJ/person-km, using a 1.6 litre car with one occupant (see Chapter 2).

sweater) + 0.004 (sewing) + 0.0012 (DIY) = 0.6 ha, or 6,000 m², which is a significant amount compared to a year's driving. Our suggestions are summarized below:

- Take up a productive hobby.

- Choose a hobby that gives you useful exercise for a low environmental impact (dog walking is out).

- Combine both of the above.

6
WORK

To a large extent, the environmental impact of our jobs depends on where we work and what policies are in place to try to reduce the environmental impact. Studies of how we work and how much energy we use, such as those undertaken by Andrew Alcorn, New Zealand's principal researcher into embodied energy, show that, over time, manufacturers are tending to use less energy to make building materials like bricks and cement. All kinds of manufacturers are becoming more energy efficient;[1] and products are also frequently labelled to show that they use less water or produce less waste, or even that they can be taken back by the manufacturer for recycling and final disposal (nylon carpets are a good example[2]). But this section is concerned principally with how our behaviour at work, rather than what we make at work, impacts on the environment.

WORKING LESS

The real problem with work is not what we do, how we travel to work, or the kind of buildings we do it in, but the fact that all of us in the West do too much of it trying to keep up with ever rising standards of living, which are judged only on our possessions. If we are to live a lifestyle that brings us anywhere near a fair share footprint, it will mean having fewer things, smaller houses and fewer holidays in distant destinations, and at the same time producing more at home and drastically reducing our levels of consumption overall. It doesn't take a trained economist to see that this means many people will have a lot less work to do in the future. The last time Western society came close to having a fair earthshare was probably in 1950s Europe. The following comment was made by a woman being interviewed about her experiences when she first came to New Zealand in 1952 after marrying a local. She had also travelled in Asia and had lived in Australia and England.

In a community where salaries are high, costs are often high, long hours of work are required, social expectations are high – 'keeping up with the Joneses' is demanding. These high salaries may be accompanied by very low incomes for a section of the community, so that housing, nutrition, health and education are quite inadequate. I am more comfortable where most people have enough for good development physically, educationally, morally and socially. New Zealand has done fairly well in this, which makes it a pleasant, friendly country.[3]

This quote sums up one of the issues connected with a move towards a sustainable future: that of equity. In this case 'equity' has been linked to the ownership of possessions. The interviewee's experiences suggested to her that a society based on equity and balance, where no one had too much but everyone had enough, could be a good place to live. This was just one view of New Zealand in the 1950s. At that time it could also be taken for granted that a family could be supported by one person working full time rather than the two it seems to take today. One website claims that US workers put in longer hours compared not just to their European counterparts or to US workers in the 1950s, but to medieval peasants.[4] The economists Ellen McGrattan and Richard Rogerson have examined this issue in more detail. Looking at all workers aged 25–64 in the US, they found an increase in average weekly working hours from around 25 in 1950 to 30 in 2005.[5] However, they go on to show that this disguises where the change is really taking place. Average weekly hours for both single men and women were about the same over the whole period, with single women working almost 95% of the hours of single men, but much greater changes were noticed in the working hours of married couples. The total average hours worked by a married household went up by 12 during the period in question; but whereas the number of hours worked by married men in a week decreased by 4, from 42 to 38, those for married women increased by about 16, from 8 to just under 25 according to the website's graph.[6] Furthermore, it appears that women's hours are longer in households where the husband is highly skilled, whether this is in terms of education or earning ability. This would suggest that women are not necessarily working to earn money that is essential for supporting the household; rather, because there is enough money to pay for things like childcare, they can earn extra money to support consumption – the 'keeping up with the Joneses' mentioned earlier.

The UK Labour Force Survey found that the number of workers opting to work more than an average 48 hours a week had risen from 12.8% of the workforce in 2006 to 13.1% in 2007.[7] Again, this supports the idea that in Western societies, where standards of living for the majority are already high, people are working more.

Trying to live sustainably means less consumption, which in turn means working less. If both men and women wish to work, this would mean both of them working part-time. The problem, as we have found out ourselves, is that the world is not set up for those who wish to share jobs or to work part-time on a permanent basis. Any government that is genuine in its aim of moving society towards sustainability needs to do some very serious thinking about this issue. But there are some decisions we can take about the way we work now.

WHERE SHOULD WE WORK?

How to commute in a way that minimizes environmental impact has been examined in Chapter 2, which arrived at the not unexpected conclusion that cycling, walking and public transport tend to have less of an impact. Of course some important workers, such as those in agriculture, work very much closer to home. But for most people in the West today, going to work – be it in the manufacturing, institutional (hospitals, schools, etc.) or service sectors – means leaving home in the morning and travelling somewhere else, reversing the journey at the end of the day. Even the trip to school can have these characteristics, since parents may choose a school further away from home. Gone are the days, envisaged by the US planner Clarence Arthur Perry in 1924,[8] when a neighbourhood could grow up around an elementary school so that children could walk there on foot, and when main roads formed its boundaries. Even though much of the physical environment we have inherited from the past contains such patterns, the decisions we take now ignore them.

In the UK, where such arrangements certainly exist, Hampshire County Council states that the number of journeys to school by car has doubled in the last 18 years, and that, nationally, car travel accounts for about 29% of all journeys to school.[9] They further state that, in Hampshire, 24% of journeys to and from school are for just one child, and a further 20% of children arrive by car with more than one school pupil in it. Not every child travels to school every day by car, but the figures represent an average for all journeys, and they still seem high for an activity – schooling – whose principal aim is the benefit of a local community. Research by the Central Research Unit of the Scottish government demonstrated that parents choose to drive children to school for a number of reasons, with safety and convenience being identified as key.[10] Their report shows a lower number of overall journeys to school by car, at 20% of pupil travel, but notes that car ownership is lower in Scotland than in Great Britain as a whole. It also found that 74% of children in Scotland live within one mile of school – a higher figure than the 63% of children in England and Wales, so obviously many children are still getting to school without a car. In terms of safety, a parental concern, the Scottish study noted that a child travelling to school by car is twice as likely to have an accident as a child who walks, and seven times as likely as a child travelling by bus to school. It seems that any interference by third parties is extremely rare and more likely to come from someone the child knows than from strangers.

The point of this discussion is to highlight the fact that choosing a certain type of transport on the basis of perceived rather than documented safety reasons means that we are moving away from being a society organized around walking to one where activities with a relatively high environmental impact are seen as normal. So should we, or could we, try to return to a time where work, like school, was a short distance from home?

OFFICE WORK

The importance of working in an office is shown in Table 1, which sets out the working environments of people in England and Wales based on 2001 census data.[11]

Occupations such as those in the construction and utility industries will involve office work as well as work on site. If we take the last five categories (ignoring 'other', which includes home workers) as representative of the number of people involved in office work, this gives a total of 42%. This

Table 1: Occupations in England and Wales based on 2001 census data

occupation	number of workers aged 16–74	% of all workers aged 16–74
agriculture; hunting and forestry	354,416	1.50
fishing	4,726	0.02
mining and quarrying	59,069	0.25
manufacturing	3,534,712	14.96
utilities	172,483	0.73
construction	1,599,599	6.77
wholesale and retail trade; vehicle repair	3,976,551	16.83
hotels and catering	1,124,681	4.76
transport; storage and communication	1,656,306	7.01
financial intermediation*	1,117,593	4.73
real estate; renting and business activities	3,064,520	12.97
public administration and defence	1,351,508	5.72
education	1,833,514	7.76
health and social work	2,554,160	10.81
other	1,223,918	5.18
total	23,627,756†	100.00

* The borrowing and lending of money.[12]
† Actual value given in source is 23,627,754; the total here has been rounded.

broadly matches the information in the *Columbia Encyclopedia*, which states that the number of white-collar workers in the US is almost 50% of the total.[13] This means that where we site office buildings and the amount of energy they use are critical when it comes to reducing the environmental impact of current working practices. The Energy Information Administration in the US defines commercial buildings as all those not related to transportation, manufacturing or residential use; most of the energy consumed in this sector goes towards maintaining the buildings' internal spaces and the services needed to support their commercial activities.[14] This is a wide definition that would include retail as well as office space. A rough analysis of retail premises can be found in Chapter 3, so here we will concentrate on office working.

An analysis of the life-cycle energy impact of working in offices showed that commuting was as significant as the energy they consumed; their initial and maintenance embodied energy, and associated business travel, were much smaller.[15] A study conducted in 1995 looked at energy use over a period of 60 years in offices in London and Manchester. Energy used inside the building was about 1 $GJ/m^2/year$ for both locations, but commuting in Manchester, where the private car was more important, was almost 1.3 $GJ/m^2/year$, while in London, with its better public transport system, it was under 0.7 $GJ/m^2/year$. Initial and recurring embodied energy (the energy in materials and equipment used for maintenance and repairs over the life of a building) in both cities was about 0.3 $GJ/m^2/year$, and business travel 0.5 $GJ/m^2/year$ in London, and 0.1 $GJ/m^2/year$ in Manchester. This led to the conclusion that where the office was located was more important than whether or not it was a low-energy commercial building. A more recent and more detailed study by Jurasovich[16] came to the same overall conclusion. His examination of 50-year energy and CO_2 emissions compared a typical tower in a central business district with a conventional low-rise suburban office such as you might find in a business park, a low-energy version of the same, and an office at home. The study was based on three locations in New Zealand (from north to south, Auckland, Wellington and Christchurch), to see if climate made a difference. In all locations the overall energy use was lowest in the home office. Working part of the week at home and part in an ordinary commercial office also showed a lower overall energy use than working full-time in a low-energy office. The results for Wellington are summarized in Table 2.[17]

The home office had a higher energy consumption and was equipped with all necessary items like a photocopier and fax machine, but because there was no energy required for transport and because it was not air conditioned, the impact of office work there was reduced by 82% compared to

Table 2: Footprint of various types of office work and commuting in Wellington, New Zealand

type of office	life-cycle energy (GJ/worker/year)	life-cycle CO$_2$ emissions (kg CO$_2$/worker/year)	footprint for commuting and office work (ha/year)
home office	5.6	270	0.04
some days at home and some days in low-energy office	11.1	639	0.08
some days at home and some days in low-rise suburban office	12.8	898	0.10
low-energy office	17.6	1,077	0.13
low-rise suburban office	22.0	1,825	0.16
tower in central business district	31.6	2,448	0.23

working in a conventional glass tower in the business district. The same results held true for all locations in New Zealand tested in the study. Jurasovich concluded that: 'In situations where working from home is not an option, the provision of convenient, clean, quiet and efficient low-cost public transport to naturally ventilated low energy suburban or business park offices appears to provide the next best solution.'[18]

This suggests that, rather than worrying about the creation of low-energy commercial buildings, we should be much more concerned about the pattern of work and where we do it. Technological advances and the rise in individual ownership of electronic equipment (see Chapter 4) mean that communication anywhere, at any time, is now extraordinarily easy. We no longer need to be tied to a desk and phone in an office. A study of IT workers for Microsoft showed that the vogue for open-plan offices between the mid-1970s and the mid-2000s paralleled an increase in working hours.[19] It is so far unclear whether this was because of pressure from peers and management, so that workers felt that they needed to be seen to be working;

or the result of better social interaction, making work a good place to be; or because people come early and stay late just to get their work done when there are continual interruptions from the open-plan layout. A survey by Durham University Business School found that working at home reduced stress but also led to people feeling overlooked and missing out when it came to promotion.[20]

The home office offers benefits apart from the elimination of commuting. It is likely that one works better in a space that is more readily closed off than open-plan. The psychologist Mihaly Csikszentmihalyi has written about the concept of 'flow' – a state reached when a person is immersed in what they are doing and time passes without them noticing. But this state – ideal for creativity and for problem-solving – is not reached immediately when one sits down to work, and first requires a period of uninterrupted concentration.[21] The worry is that open-plan offices in some types of work may be full of people never able to reach their full creative working potential, although it does mean the boss will be able to control them better. It would seem that allowing people to spend more time working at home would be better for them, result in greater productivity, and be much better for the environment.

TRAVEL AT WORK: CONFERENCES

In some types of work, such as academic work, it is usual to attend conferences. For many delegates this will involve overseas travel. We looked at the 2006 Passive and Low Energy Architecture (PLEA) Conference in Geneva,[22] and discovered that each delegate created an average 770 kg of CO_2. The total distance travelled by all delegates was 327,522 km for regional and domestic journeys, and 2,411,581 km for international travel. Using the value of 1 MJ/passenger-km (see Chapter 2), we can estimate that the energy tied up in all this travel was 2,412 GJ, or a footprint of 17.9 ha. There were 426 delegates at the conference, so this works out at an average footprint of 0.04 ha just for travel.

Table 3, based on these figures, gives the annual footprint for various modes of office working and commuting, and for levels of conference attendance each year. Using the average distances travelled to the Geneva

Table 3: Types of office work and various levels of conference attendance for Wellington, New Zealand

type of office	number of domestic conferences per year	number of international conferences per year	conference footprint (ha/year)	total footprint of work and conferences (ha/year)
home	0	0	0	0.04
low-energy office	0	0	0	0.13
tower in central business district	0	0	0	0.23
home	1	0	0.01	0.05
low-energy office	2	0	0.02	0.15
tower in central business district	3	0	0.03	0.26
home	0	1	0.14	0.18
low-energy office	0	1	0.14	0.27
tower in central business district	0	1	0.14	0.40
tower in central business district	2	2	0.3	0.53

conference as representative of conference travel in general, we worked out that domestic and regional flights averaged 1,321 km for each delegate for the round trip, and international travel was 18,409 km per delegate for the round trip. We took the domestic distance to be typical of travelling from Wellington to a national conference in New Zealand, or from somewhere in the UK to London by air, and the other value was used for international travel in general.

Even one international conference doubles the footprint of working in a naturally ventilated low-energy office building. Attending a national conference adds 25% to the footprint of a home office worker. If you are a high-flyer (literally) based in a tower in the business district and attend several conferences a year, you are bad news for the environment. This again raises the question why more conferences are not conducted electronically via video networks. A study in Japan suggests that using video conferencing in place of face-to-face business meetings reduces environmental impact by between 60 and 90%.[23] Perhaps we need to learn that what is considered fun on a mobile phone – sending pictures and exchanging information – can also be applied to work.

THE PAPERLESS OFFICE

When computers first arrived in offices, they were considered heralds of the 'paperless office'. In fact, a book published in the UK in 2001 claims that email alone increases paper consumption in offices by an average of 40%.[24] Its authors maintain that paper is important to people, and make a case for using electronics and paper sensibly. Research carried out in Canada in the 1980s found that reading from paper was faster than reading from computer screens, which was taken to explain the increasing use of paper in computerized offices. But a repeat of this research in 1991 came to a different conclusion.[25] The authors stated that reading from the computer screens available at that time was as good as reading from a book in terms of speed and comprehension, and screens have almost certainly improved since then. The book you are now reading was generated electronically and drafts of it were read on screen, even though it is still common in academic circles for pages to be printed out as a work progresses. A printed copy of the text will be used for final reading and correction, as it provides the closest experience to actually reading the book. This typescript will be used as an example in our discussion of paper use below.

About 500 words of this kind of text can be typed on a sheet of paper. This means that the whole typescript would take up 220 sheets of A4 paper printed one side only, which is just under half a ream (500 sheets is typical for a ream of A4 office paper). We have been writing this book for 11 months (there are only two of us, working half-time). As with most projects the rate of output has gone up towards the end, not least because we have by now established a consistent methodology, but had we been consistent we would have produced 22 finished pages a month, or approximately 5 pages a week. Assuming that we both had a copy of these 5 new pages to read through every week, we would have printed 440 pages in draft as we progressed. Given that we might be expected to take a holiday each year, and together are the equivalent of one full-time member of staff, this figure can represent the paper associated with drafts of the most important research work of one year. (We have been writing other things as well, but nothing nearly as large as this book.) In 2004 Victoria University, Wellington, had the equivalent of 697.5 full-time members of academic staff.[26] Using this information and the US Environmental Defense Fund paper footprint calculator,[27] the following table has been put together to show the comparative impact of different levels of paper use in an academic office. The paper used is assumed to weigh 80 g/m², and a ream of paper contains 30.132 m²,[28] giving a weight of 2.4 kg per ream. If each academic prints 660 sheets a year, all staff between them will consume a total of 921 reams, weighing 2.2 tonnes. The recycled paper included in Table 4 is assumed to be 100% post-consumer – that is, made from old paper that has been de-inked and had coatings removed to leave the basic paper fibres. In practice, most recycled papers have only partial post-consumer content, which will increase the impact of the recycled paper quoted below.

Printing everything on recycled paper reduces impact by only 43% compared with the conventional print-as-you-go strategy, because energy is needed to make recycled paper. Changing your behaviour by not printing

Table 4: Impact of different printing strategies for drafts of academic work

printing strategy	wood (tonnes/year)	energy (GJ/year)	waste water (l)	solid waste (kg)
print all drafts single-sided	8	88.6	58,855	2,273
print all drafts double-sided	4	44.3	29,429	1,137
print only final draft, single-sided	3	29.5	52,712	741
print all drafts on 100% recycled paper, single-sided	0	50.6	85,986	1,152
print only final draft on 100% recycled paper, double-sided	0	8.4	14,460	194

until you get to the final draft gives a reduction of 67%, even when using ordinary non-recycled paper. Printing double-sided is good, but when many members of staff share a printer – as is common practice in offices – it becomes much more difficult.

To look more carefully at the footprints of different ways of printing, Table 5 converts trees and energy to land. For the moment the impacts of waste water and solid waste, which includes disposal of the paper itself, are ignored. The number of trees per hectare depends on species, climate and soil, as well as on how far apart trees are planted. Trees spaced widely will grow more quickly because there is less competition for light and nutrients. The US Environmental Defense Fund calculator uses a mix of hardwood and softwood species that measure 150–200 mm in diameter and 12 m in height. These are 'thinnings' removed from between densely planted trees and sold for pulp. Trees planted at a density of over 1,000/ha might be thinned to half this at 3–4 years, and by half again at 5–6 years.[29] A paper on growing wood for energy in Florida gives yields of 32 green tons/acre/year (79 tons/ha/year) for eucalyptus, which could rise to 55 green tons/acre/year (136 tons/ha/year) with improved management, and 20.6 green tons/acre/year (51 tons/ha/year) for pine.[30] A website on sustainable crown

Table 5: Footprint of trees and energy for paper used in academic research over a year, per academic

printing strategy	land used for trees (ha)	energy use (ha/year)	wood and energy footprint (ha/year)
print all drafts single-sided	0.1 (53 trees)	0.7	0.8
print all drafts double-sided	0.05 (26 trees)	0.3	0.4
print only final draft, single-sided	0.04 (18 trees)	0.2	0.2
print all drafts on 100% recycled paper, single-sided	0	0.4	0.4
print only final draft on 100% recycled paper, double-sided	0	0.1	0.1

timber resources in Alberta, Canada, states that land can be cleared only if it delivers sufficient timber to be merchantable, which equates to a minimum of 35–40 tons/ha.[31] For the present analysis a yield of 75 tonnes/ha/year is assumed. The data relating to the number of trees come from the US Environmental Defense Fund calculator.

Including the land needed to grow the trees shows that changing your behaviour so that you print only your final draft halves the impact of behaving normally and printing as you go on recycled paper (a reduction from 0.4 ha to 0.2 ha/year), though printing less and only using recycled paper is still the best option. The amount of paper considered here – around a ream for each academic – is still only a very small portion of the total paper used in a typical university. Stamford University states that it uses an average 162,000 reams/year, or the equivalent of nearly 70,000 trees.[32] From the figures above, this would work out as a footprint of 98,181 ha/year for just one university. We currently live in Wellington, a city of 163,824 people according to the 2001 census, which occupies an area of 28,990 ha[33] – roughly one third of the land used by Stamford for paper. It is probable that most of this paper will end up in landfill, since much of the paper used in universities and offices has a relatively short life.

Stamford has a policy of using recycled paper to reduce its impact, but the analysis presented here shows that how we behave is as important as persuading management to use recycled paper. However much we love using paper, we have to learn to use a lot less of it.

ONE MAN'S WORK IS ANOTHER MAN'S FOOTPRINT

We began this chapter with the idea that using fewer resources and having less impact on the natural environment will mean that we work less, because we will need fewer possessions. This has a bearing on how we calculate footprints. Much analysis of resources is at least in part based on national statistics for resource and energy use. This makes sense, as all the energy and resources are then covered; but often statistics lump together categories that need to be separate if they are to be useful, as Baird et al. acknowledge.[34] Using this top-down approach means that all the energy that goes into making steel can be accounted for – not just the energy required to produce the metal, but also for such things as lighting the offices and transporting the ore. A second approach, also described by Baird et al., is to find out detailed information on energy use for each process by going directly to the manufacturers. This, however, can be time-consuming. Most methods for establishing embodied energy make use of a hybrid approach; this starts with a process analysis of the various components of a material until such time as each additional component does not significantly change the result. One then turns to national statistics to add data for the components not already accounted for.[35]

This hybrid approach is based on analysis undertaken by the International Federation of Institutes for Advanced Study,[36] who proposed that the energy used to make things can typically be broken down as follows: under 50% used directly in the manufacturing process; 40% used in extracting raw resources; seldom more than 10% for making the machines used for manufacturing the product; and very little energy for making the machines that make the machines. However, Treloar argued that values obtained were too low because they failed to take account of factors like insuring factories and the infrastructure needed to access them; as a result, his embodied energy coefficients are often higher than those of other analysts.[37] At the moment we are all living a Western lifestyle, and the insurance sector (for example) will show an energy use because its workers are housed in air-conditioned open-plan offices – not, as we have seen, the most efficient option in terms of overall energy consumption.

Most of the comparisons in this book are based on simple 'bottom-up' calculations of what resources go into our everyday lives, from feeding the cat to playing tennis. They have used embodied energy coefficients worked out using a hybrid method that, in order to find a footprint, looks at energy and then converts this figure into the amount of land required to generate that energy. The results have shown that most people in the West are living way beyond their fair earthshare, and this is further discussed in the Conclusion. Anyone in the West who tries hard to live within their fair earthshare will have little effect on the overall pattern because of the huge majority that don't. Even when a Western lifestyle is made efficient and low-energy, its footprint cannot be reduced to a fair earthshare.

A WWF study of Solihull, in the West Midlands of England, found that the normal footprint for a Solihull resident was 5.5 ha/year; this could be reduced, by a 'keen' household living in an energy-efficient house, to 3.0 ha/year.[38] The authors noted that 1.54 ha/year could not be changed, irrespective of what an individual chose to do. This is because it was bound up with medical and educational activities, and also with a concept commonly called 'gross fixed capital formation', which is defined as all the machines and infrastructure in place to support Western society. This gross fixed capital formation accounts for 18% of a normal Solihull resident's footprint – the same as their food footprint. A further 6% and 4% of the footprint comes from central and local governments respectively.[39] The new city of Dongtan[40] near Shanghai is designed to be run on renewable energy, to use electricity or hydrogen for transport and to grow food locally. It has a projected footprint of 2.2 ha/person,[41] which is still above the fair earthshare of 1.8 ha/person and still has to be verified in practice. What all this points to is the influence of the conventional structure of society on those who, as individuals, want to reduce their personal environmental impact.

To reduce this large part of the footprint we all need to change. The fact that we will have to work less in a sustainable society because there will be less consumption, fewer service industries to support that consumption, and fewer civil servants to monitor that consumption will change the nature of this infrastructure. To take educational buildings as an example, schools will serve a local community both during and after school hours, and access will be on foot or by bicycle. Subjects that a local school cannot supply will be pursued through distance teaching, perhaps on the model of the Correspondence School in New Zealand, which was developed along these lines to satisfy the needs of children in scattered rural communities.[42] Universities and other institutions increasingly making use of web-based teaching can be structured in a similar way to the Open University in the UK,[43] whereby study materials are sent to students whose learning is supported by some face-to-face contact at regional centres. There is still some travel associated with studying, but much less than travelling to and from university every day. Nor would there be the energy and environmental implications of having double households, such as happens in the UK where students live at university during term time. Health institutions may also see some changes if diet improves, as we discussed earlier. Growing more food locally and domestically, which means it will probably be organic, and cooking and eating it fresh at home, will improve the overall diet, with accompanying health benefits. More walking and cycling instead of driving would also be good for health. As far as the retail sector is concerned, apart from the basics there will be many fewer new items for sale, and many more outlets selling recycled and used goods. As we discussed earlier, temporary markets will take the place of shopping malls. Far fewer commercial buildings will be required. Some will undergo change of use, so that unwanted structures will be converted to zero-energy housing or energy-generating apartments. This will free up land for food and biofuel production that would otherwise have been taken up by new housing. Some buildings will be dismantled for their resources, which will be recycled into renewable energy equipment like wind turbines and solar panels. In addition, the supply of energy will have to rely not on fossil fuels but on renewable sources. When all this happens, the way that energy flows through society, as measured by national statistics, will change. As a result, embodied energy coefficients will also begin to fall. This in turn will start to reduce the footprints of materials and activities.

We will all have to change, and change at the same time, if there is going to be a move towards sustainability. If we do not, it will never be possible to live on the resources of just one planet.

The following are suggestions for what we can do now while we wait for major changes in the way we work and in society as a whole:

- Work at least one day a week at home.
- Use video conferencing facilities.
- Think before you print.

7
RITES OF PASSAGE

FOUR WEDDINGS TO A FUNERAL?

Family gatherings and rites of passage can be quite big occasions. According to Richard Markel, President of the Association for Wedding Professionals International, the average number of guests at a wedding in the United States is 149.[1] As far as that other large gathering at life's end is concerned, 'Clydebank crematorium will typically carry out 1,750 cremations per year, and an average funeral will have around sixty mourners.'[2] Weddings and funerals are also quite expensive. The UK's Department of Environment, Food and Rural Affairs (DEFRA) points out that the cost of an average funeral was £1,215 for a cremation and £2,048 for a burial.[3] According to the National Funeral Directors Association in July 2004, the average cost of a funeral in the United States was US$6,500,[4] and the average cost of a wedding in the US in 2008 was said to be between US$18,000 and US$21,000.[5] The average cost of a traditional wedding in the UK is given by one website as £11,000,[6] which in money terms equates to 9 cremations but only 5 burials. So 5 funerals equal 1 wedding (not the other way round). But what is their cost to the environment?

If the internet is to be believed, we are increasingly encouraged to consider 'greening' many of our family activities, including traditional weddings and funerals. Websites now offer 'green weddings', and there are 'wedding calculators' that allow you to offset the carbon emissions from your guests' travelling and from your own honeymoon.[7] If we imagine a wedding in England with 100 guests, each making a 300 km round trip by car, and a honeymoon in Australia, we would get the energy consumption outlined in Table 1 (overleaf).

So depending on how you choose to honeymoon, your wedding could result in the consumption of anything between 200 and 360 GJ. This is a lot

Table 1: Energy consumption of wedding-related travel (*GJ*)*

total consumption of guests, assuming each travels in a 1.6 litre car	111
honeymoon to Sydney, travelling by air in a full Boeing 747	86
honeymoon cruise to Sydney	256

* Values are taken from Chapter 2; the figure for travel by car (assuming 100 guests) comes from Table 24, and those for travel by air and cruise ship from Table 35.

of energy – maybe ten times the energy a modern house uses in a year (see Chapter 3). The honeymoon is the big contributor, but every guest adds about 1 GJ to the total.

A trawl through the internet looking at 'green funerals' suggests that people worry a lot about the disposal of their mortal remains once their life is over. Should the body be embalmed, which uses formaldehyde and other possibly undesirable chemicals? Should you opt for a traditional burial (using scarce land and perhaps polluting groundwater), or perhaps opt for a woodland burial in a cardboard coffin or wrapped in a simple winding sheet? Or should you be cremated so as not to take up any land at all, but in the process use fossil fuels and emit mercury into the atmosphere from your amalgam fillings?

Some of the emissions associated with funerals can even be quite significant on a national scale. For example, the DEFRA report shows that crematoria were responsible for 16% of all mercury emissions to the atmosphere in 2000.[8] Burials also have an environmental impact. According to statistics compiled by the Casket and Funeral Association of America, the Cremation Association of North America, Doric, Inc., The Rainforest Action Network, and Mary Woodsen of the Pre-Posthumous Society,[9] each year the 22,500 cemeteries across the United States bury approximately

- 30 million board-feet (70,000 m³) of hardwoods (caskets)

- 104,272 tons of steel (caskets 90,272, vaults 14,000)

- 2,700 tons of copper and bronze (caskets)

Table 2: Rough estimate of materials used per burial in the United States

material	quantity (m³)	total weight (tonnes)	weight per burial (kg)
hardwood	70,000	35,000*	21
steel		104,000	61
copper and bronze		2,700	2
reinforced concrete		1,636,000	962
embalming fluid	3,130	3,130†	2
total			1,048

* Assuming an average density of wood of 500 kg per m³.
† Assuming that embalming fluid weighs the same as water.

- 1,636,000 tons of reinforced concrete (vaults)

- 827,060 US gallons (3,130 m³) of embalming fluid

In the United States in 2003, 28.71% of a total of 2.42 million funerals were cremations.[10] This means that over 1.7 million bodies were buried. We can now calculate how much of each of the materials listed above is used per burial. We have converted 1 ton into 1 tonne, which is accurate enough for the rough calculations shown in Table 2.

So an average American interment involves burying roughly a tonne of assorted materials per body, with the largest component by far being, unexpectedly, reinforced concrete. The materials associated with the funeral weigh about ten times as much as the corpse, which perhaps should not surprise us for a society so keen on conspicuous consumption. To give a comparison, burial in a winding sheet would require a 6 m length of cloth 1 m wide. The embodied energy and footprint for both types of funeral are set out in Table 3 (overleaf). Transport to the place of burial in a hearse and use of a chapel beforehand for the funeral service are assumed to apply to both.

To the material's footprint we must add 4 m² of land for each burial plot (see below). A cemetery will have a certain amount of land to allow circulation around the marked graves, but there is also the likelihood that more than one body might be buried in the same plot, so an extra 4 m² has been

Table 3: Footprints of two types of burial

US-TYPE BURIAL	weight of material (kg)	embodied energy coefficient (MJ/kg)[11]	embodied energy of buried material (MJ)	total footprint of burial (m²)
hardwood	21	2.0 (kiln-dried)	42	
steel	61	10.1	616	
copper/bronze	2	2.4	5	
reinforced concrete	962	1	962	
embalming fluid	2	n/a	n/a	
total			3,250	241
WOODLAND BURIAL				
cotton	2	50*	100	7

* Taken from 'Clothing' in Chapter 4.

added to both totals. This gives 245 m² for the typical US burial and 11 m² for the alternative, which shows a 96% reduction in footprint.

SMOKE GETS IN YOUR EYES

Some of the impacts of a funeral are hard to see. For example, if formaldehyde from embalming fluid is leaching from a graveyard into the groundwater, it will not be noticed for some time. One of the more obvious environmental impacts of cremation results from the fuel used in the process. Early cremators burned coke in a furnace that looked, not unnaturally, something like the boiler of a steamship. It took 500 kg of coke to get the cremator up to operating temperature, and 250 kg for each cremation after that.[12] Today the most popular fuel for cremations in many countries is natural gas. A gas-fired cremation in the UK uses on average 285 kWh of natural gas and 15 kWh of electricity (for fans, etc.), according to one source.[13] TERI, the Energy and Resources Institute in India, states that a traditional cremation on an open-air funeral pyre requires 500 kg of firewood and takes many hours. Use of the TERI wood gasifier, which makes a combustible gas from the wood fuel, can get this down to 100 kg of wood and one hour to perform the cremation. TERI also reports that, in India, an electric cremator uses 165 kWh per cremation when it is operated round the clock so that it does not have to be warmed up (it deals with 8 bodies per day). Another alternative used in India, the diesel cremator, uses 25 l of diesel per cremation.[14]

From this information we can draw up a table showing the energy demands of different fuels and types of cremation (Table 4). This shows that the old-fashioned European coke-fired cremator used more energy than any other possible method and was less efficient than the traditional Indian funeral pyre. The Indian pyre uses half as much fuel, in terms of weight per body, as a modern American burial, and the wood fuel is potentially carbon-neutral if it comes from a managed plantation. An average 'modern' cremation (gas, diesel or electric) uses around 1 GJ, which is quite a lot of energy. If all the 6.6 billion people in the world were cremated at once, at least 6,600 PJ would be needed – about one seventh of total global energy consumption. The UK's Environment Agency states that the area of land used for burial is typically 2,500 graves per ha for people and 10,000 for pets,[15] so each grave uses 4 m² – a figure that suggests that little allowance has been made for paths, buildings, etc. The land-for-energy value used in ecological footprint calculations is 135 GJ/ha/year, or 13.5 MJ/m², so cremation

Table 4: Energy use for different cremation processes

fuel	amount required	MJ per unit	energy used per cremation (MJ)
coke	350 kg*	29.6 MJ/kg†	10,360
wood (traditional)	500 kg	16.0 MJ/kg‡	8,000
wood (using gasifier)	100 kg	16.0 MJ/kg	1,600
gas (plus electricity)	300 kWh	3.6 MJ/kWh	1,080
diesel	25 l	35.9 MJ/l§	898
electricity (India)	165 kWh	3.6 MJ/kWh	594

* Assuming that five cremations are carried out per day, the initial 500 kg of coke for warming up the furnace comes to 100 kg per cremation.
† Energy content of coke.[16]
‡ Energy content for air-dried firewood from Saddler et al.[17]
§ Energy content of diesel from EU.[18]

would allow only 135 funerals per ha, but it would preserve the land from the possible pollution associated with the decomposition of bodies.

A possible solution is the practice of 'woodland burial', which seems to be growing in popularity in the UK. The body is laid to rest in a woodland area and a tree is planted over the grave in place of a normal headstone. Looked at another way: if a tree was planted for each newborn baby, by the time the child reached the age of 30 the tree would be big enough to provide the 500 kg of air-dried wood necessary for cremation (given a lot of assumptions).[19] Perhaps this means that people who wanted to be buried could still be buried, using the tree as a marker, and those who wanted to be cremated could be cremated, relying on one fully-grown tree for the necessary fuel.

The option of a woodland burial plot sounds attractive: in some way, one's remains are helping biodiversity by encouraging the growth of a forest and all the living creatures it supports. Another type of body disposal good for biodiversity is that traditionally practised by the Parsi people, followers of the prophet Zarathustra, in India and elsewhere. To avoid any pollution of the ground or of the living, the dead are placed on top of stone towers where they are exposed to the sun and to vultures who strip the flesh from the bones within a couple of hours. Even the towers' drains are fitted with sand and charcoal filters to ensure that rainwater run-off does not pollute the ground.[20] This tradition has been practised by the Parsi for 3,000 years, but recently there has been a spectacular die-off of vultures: the three commonest species have declined by 97% over 12 years in India, and by 92% over only 5 years in Pakistan. This decline is attributed to the use of the anti-inflammatory drug diclofenac on cattle: the birds are poisoned when they feed on cattle remains.[21]

GET ME TO THE CHURCH ON TIME

A funeral, like a wedding, is one of those occasions when families get together. If a funeral is held in Scotland, with sixty people attending,[22] and if each of them drives an average of 50 km there and back, the total transport for the funeral will be 6,000 passenger-km. Even if each of the mourners drives in a smallish 1.6 litre car (3.69 MJ/km), the energy used will be over 22 GJ, which puts the 1 GJ consumed by the cremation into some sort of perspective. If the funeral is in America, you can probably double the travel distance and halve the fuel efficiency of the vehicles, so the impact would be 88 GJ – more energy than the deceased's home used in a year.

This business of getting the mourners (and the corpse) to the funeral was dealt with rather more efficiently in the past. The London Necropolis Company opened a cemetery at Brookwood in Surrey, 25 miles (40 km) outside London, in 1854. In partnership with the London and South Western Railway, it ran funeral trains between its own London terminus, next to Waterloo Station, and Brookwood, taking coffins and mourners to the funerals and bringing the mourners back again. The LSWR main line was used for most of the journey, but at Brookwood the funeral trains were backed onto a line that ran through the cemetery. The cemetery had its own stations, one for the Anglican section and a second for the Nonconformist area. This line was used up until World War II, after which it was dismantled.[23] Similar systems operated in Australia – between Sydney and the large Rookwood Cemetery, for example[24] – and a railway line also served Waikumete Cemetery in Auckland, New Zealand.

WHAT DOES IT ALL MEAN?

Alongside weddings and funerals we also need to think about divorces.[25] If you get divorced and once more live alone, you may have to establish a new home, with your own set of the appliances that you used to share with your beloved: fridge, stove, television, kettle, toaster, and so on. A study of sustainable Solihull in the UK states that someone living alone consumes on average 55% more electricity, 61% more gas, 38% more goods and 42% more packaging than the same person living in a four-person household.[26] Following a wedding that may have used as much energy as a house consumes in 10 years, your divorce could result in the creation of a second separate household and all the energy consumption that goes with it. Table 5 (overleaf) shows the possible impact of the divorce.

Table 5 does not paint an imaginary scenario. A Dutch study found that 'six to seven years after the divorce the extra demand for housing is about one-third of the number of divorces in any given year',[27] so not everyone who gets divorced finds a new partner. If you do get divorced and then remain single, you will, unfortunately, cause a lot more environmental damage. Divorce doubles your energy demand.

Table 5: The possible effect of divorce on lifetime energy demand (*GJ*)

(A) MARRIED 'TIL DEATH DO US PART	
wedding	200
sharing a house for 50 years at 30 GJ/year	1,500
funerals (2)	46
total energy	**1,746**
energy per person over a lifetime	**873**
(B) DIVORCED AFTER 10 YEARS	
wedding	200
sharing a house for 10 years at 30 GJ/year	300
2 people living alone for 40 years at 30 GJ/each	2,400
funerals (2)	46
total energy	**2,946**
energy per person over a lifetime	**1,743**

Things to do: Weddings

- Live in sin and don't get married.

- Have a very small-scale wedding, inviting only your closest family and local friends.

- Don't get divorced until you have found a new partner.

Things to do: Funerals

- Donate your body to a local medical school for educational purposes.

- Don't ask your family from Australia to attend your funeral in London.

- Have a very small funeral and choose a cemetery or crematorium on a bus route or railway line.

CONCLUSION

BACK TO DAN DARE

If you can remember that far back, you will recall that at the start of this book we talked about Dan Dare, Pilot of the Future. It is now time to relive his first adventure, which ran in weekly issues between 14 April to 28 September 1955.[1] The story is set in 1996: Earth is running out of food, and an expedition has been mounted to Venus, which is thought to be uninhabited, to see if it can be grown there. After a long series of adventures, the earth is invaded by the fierce Treens, who occupy one half of Venus and who are ruthless logical scientists bent on conquest of the universe under their cruel leader, the Mekon. Because of technological issues we need not go into, a situation arises in which no modern machinery, weaponry or explosives will function on Venus. Dan Dare's response is to organize an attack against the Treens using cavalry and archers delivered by parachute. The attacking force includes the Mounties, the Life Guards and Household Cavalry, the Indian Horse, the Cossacks, and a lot of civilian archery clubs. Without their advanced technology, the Treens are totally demoralized and flee in terror. A treaty is concluded, and in the end Earth gets its food and all live happily ever after.

The message of this story – that advanced technology will not necessarily solve all our future problems – is one we might all consider.

AIR, WATER, EARTH AND FIRE

Part of the problem with sustainability is prioritizing the huge range of issues, from air travel to plastic bags, with which we are assailed by the media every day. One way of doing this is to rank them in terms of their real importance to our survival. The Ancients used to believe that everything was made of the four elements of air, water, earth and fire, and in some ways this is a useful way of approaching the question of sustainability.

A programme called 'Scope', broadcast by RTÉ Television in Ireland, sought the advice of Traolach Sweeney, an outdoor survival expert who was in the Irish Defence Forces for 26 years. According to Sweeney, 'You can survive without air for three minutes, you can survive without water for about three days. You can survive without food for about 30 days.'[2] In some climates you can probably go without fuel and energy for even longer than you can go without food. If we assign the ancient element of fire to stand for fuel and energy, and the element of earth to represent food, we can arrange the four elements in the following order of importance: air, water, earth and fire.

AIR

If we do not have air, we will be dead quite quickly. A paper from the Air Resources Board in California suggests that an average rate of respiration is around 10 l per minute for adults.[3] This means that, if we live to be 80 years old, we will have breathed in over 4 million m³ of air; 80 years × 365 days × 24 hours × 60 minutes × 10 l = 4.2 million m³. This amount of air would fill a building as high as the Eiffel Tower (300 m) that measures 120 m on each side – a larger volume than the famous Vehicle Assembly Building at Cape Canaveral, which was built for the Apollo Program and contains only 3.7 million million m³ (itself twice the size of the Pentagon).[4]

How much air we breathe in a lifetime is important because we will take into our lungs whatever the air contains. For example, the US National Ambient Air Quality Standard for sulphur dioxide in the air is 0.03 parts per million (ppm) averaged over a year.[5] Over a lifetime you would have inhaled 120 l of this toxic gas. The Australian federal government's 'Substance Fact Sheet' for sulphur dioxide states that it can cause lung damage and possibly harm the reproductive system.[6] You would probably be better off not breathing in any pollutants, but the aim of air quality standards is to ensure that you are not exposed to levels of a substance that would kill you outright.

The breathable part of the earth's atmosphere is only about 5 km thick, which is why mountaineers often use oxygen when they attempt high peaks like Everest. The surface area of the earth is around 510 million km²,[7] so, very roughly, each of us has 350 km³ of available air. But what if we choose to count all the whales, elephants, rats, cows, beetles, bacteria, fishes and trees that also want to breathe? Luke Donev, a graduate student at Cornell University's Center for Materials Research, says on the centre's 'Ask a Scientist' website that the total mass of the earth is 6×10^{24} kg, and that the total biomass is roughly 0.00000003% of the mass of the earth.[8] This would mean that the total biomass weighs in the region of 180,000,000 million tonnes. (To give some sense of scale, if we assume 7 billion people on the planet, each weighing 50 kg, the entire human population will weigh only 350 million tonnes.) So the atmosphere has to be shared between lots of creatures. Over 90% of the earth's total biomass is composed of plants.[9] Plants both absorb and emit oxygen and carbon dioxide, but – luckily for us – they absorb more carbon dioxide than they emit, and they emit more oxygen than they consume.[10] In sum, they make the oxygen that we breathe, and they help to take carbon out of the atmosphere. As the human population grows and demands a 'higher standard of living', it uses more energy and emits more carbon dioxide; but at the same time areas of land covered in plants are being replaced by areas covered in concrete, so we are reducing the ability of the earth both to supply us with oxygen and to absorb our carbon emissions.

WATER

Without air we will die within minutes, but we can go for a few days without water (unlike the Bactrian camel – the two-hump model that, according to Alaska Zoo, can last for months without water[11]). The earth is 70% water, but most is ocean. Only 1% of the earth's water is usable by people, and of this 99% is groundwater. According to the US Geological Survey, it is sources of surface water such as rivers that are used most, and these constitute about 93,100 km^3, or roughly 0.0067% of the world's total water supply.[12] This means that we rely on a tiny part of the world's water resources. Nearly all this water is used to feed us: over 90% of the world's fresh water consumption goes into agriculture.[13] According to Traolach Sweeney, the Irish survival expert we quoted earlier, we need to drink 3 l of water a day, so over a whole lifetime we will consume 3 l × 365 days × 80 years ÷ 1,000 (to convert litres to cubic metres), which works out as just under 90 m^3, or roughly 1 m^3 each year. This equates to only 630 km^3 of drinking water for the whole population, but of course we use water in many other ways. Figures quoted by the Food and Agriculture Organization (FAO) of the United Nations show that the world's total water consumption in 2000 was 4,000 km³, and that it has risen steadily by 5% a year since 1940.[14] Groundwater sources are exploited to a high degree – more than 50% of the natural rate of recharge – in many countries in Europe, the Middle East, Africa, Asia and Cuba.[15] Water is yet another of those 'limitless' resources that turns out to have limits after all.

EARTH

The element of earth represents not only the food that we can grow, and without which we will die in maybe a month, but also the land we need to support all of our daily activities. The earth is all we have – the only way to provide all we want and need. This is why throughout the book we have used the area of land required for activities as a way of measuring their impact. Land is the ultimate non-renewable resource, and, as we saw above, it is ultimately the land that provides the air we breathe. We are currently covering more and more land with structures like houses, roads, car parks and supermarkets. To give one example, 4% of the whole state of Illinois is built up.[16] The more of us there are, and the more physical infrastructure we demand, the less land we have to feed us and to supply our air. No one has yet asked the question, 'What is the limit to physical change from natural to built environment?' The assumption has been that you can build what you like where you like. It is easy to see when roads and new housing encroach on land you used to walk through, or to see wind farms appearing on hills that formerly had only sheep, and to protest about it. What we can't see – the land needed to feed, clothe and shelter us in a sustainable way – is seldom considered, which is one of the reasons we set out to write this book. If we could see with our own eyes each burial in the US taking over 200 m² of land, we might soon start a 'less land for burial' campaign. Another often ignored fact is that the land we use to support our Western lifestyles is not ours. True, we pay for the privilege, but does this represent a fair exchange? The issue of equity between the developed and the developing world has not been discussed in any detail here, but every time a footprint exceeds what a nation can supply from its own land in a sustainable way we should all be concerned.

FIRE

Finally we come to fire, an element that here represents energy. We can survive for a lifetime without energy. The Aboriginal people of Australia lived on the land for 40,000 years[17] without the need for non-renewable energy, and they have a sophisticated ability to control fire, which forms part of their long-term land-management strategies.[18] We, on the other hand, seem to depend either on burning the remains of dead creatures (oil and gas) or fossilized trees (coal), or on pieces of radioactive rock. The world's current average energy consumption of 76 GJ per year (see Chapter 1) represents a continuous load of just over 2.4 kW, and the 2006 United States energy consumption of 334 million Btu per person (350 GJ)[19] represents a load of more than 11 kW. So for every American there is the equivalent of over a hundred lightbulbs burning continuously every day of their entire life. Put like this, the idea of running the whole world on renewable energy sounds quite challenging, which is another reason why we need to think about consuming less.

CHOICES

Throughout this book we have seen that sustainability depends on the choices we make in all areas of our daily lives. Every time we buy lunch, turn on the light, go out in the car, take a holiday or play a round of golf we make a choice. These choices can be more or less bad for the environment. We doubt very much that we can buy our way out of the problem, since everything that we choose to purchase, be it a large item like the latest hybrid car or the newest eco-house, or smaller things like hemp shopping bags or organic cotton jeans, still has an impact. Nothing that we buy has no effect. The more stuff that is sold to us, the bigger the impact on the environment.

The obvious conclusion to draw is not that we need to buy products that are more sustainable, but that we need not to buy at all. For the world to be sustainable we have to find ways to content ourselves with less. This may not be as big a problem as it might first appear, since research suggests that after a certain point we do not seem to be happier with more.[20] To give an example, researchers at Princeton University found that people with an above-average income were not only barely happier than others, but also tended to be more tense and did not, in fact, spend more time in very enjoyable activities.[21] So having less need not mean being miserable. We can have more happiness, more pleasure, more discussion, more belonging, more caring and sharing without needing to buy anything at all. If you want fewer possessions you can work less and have more time for a walk in the park, a chat with friends or an afternoon in bed.

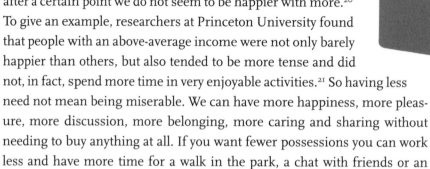

One often sees criticism of big business and its environmental records, but it is unfair criticism. We get the businesses that we support. A market, whether local or global, needs buyers and sellers. We are the buyers, and if we do not buy they cannot sell. Whether it is Shell oil or Starbucks coffee, we want what they offer: we have not (yet) got to the stage where we are tied down and forced to drink coffee or buy oil. But it is undeniably true that businesses and governments want us to buy – a bigger house, more processed foods, more clothes, a bigger car and a giant television – because it is good for industry, and 'what is good for General Motors is good for America'[22] (just as what is good for Sony is good for Japan). From a commercial point of view, it is a good idea to sell you so much food that you get fat, because then you can be sold new clothes to replace the ones that no longer fit, a slimming club membership and a gym subscription to help you get thin again. If you eat less and walk more, you are not what the market wants. Much of what we are expected to buy we used to provide for ourselves. In the past we would make clothes, knit jumpers, bake bread, grow vegetables and care for the children at home; but capitalism requires us to buy food, clothes and childcare services. We used to get together with neighbours to put on concerts and amateur theatricals; but capitalism would rather we bought DVDs and theatre tickets. Doing things for yourself is probably the most subversive course of action you can take in a modern market-based economy.

DANGER! ECONOMISTS!

We are dissuaded from doing things that will benefit us and the planet by economists, who emphasize issues like cost-effectiveness. Much is written about the fact that renewable energy technology is not cost-effective in comparison with conventional energy sources like coal and oil, which is a barrier to wider uptake. The cost of PV panels is such that the energy they generate, and which you will not have to buy, will not off-set the high cost of the installation. Typically the crossover point comes 20 years or even longer after installation, so PV systems are said to be not cost-effective.[23] However, golf is not cost-effective either, as we have shown, and yet many people choose to play it. Even if we assume that the costs of setting up a vegetable garden (the spade, fork, compost, etc.) are the same as preparing to play golf (clubs, balls and shoes), golf takes 1.7 hours a week longer than gardening to provide the recommended amount of exercise. Golf has a footprint of 0.02 ha/year if you walk from home to the golf course, whereas the amount of time spent gardening that would give the same exercise as golf (less time, in fact) has a footprint of – 0.1 ha/year (see Chapter 5). In addition, golf has running costs – green fees or club membership – that are higher than the price of seeds. True, it offers a certain camaraderie, as you contemplate your missed shots over a stiff drink in the clubhouse afterwards, but gardening can also provide companionship when you swap seeds, plants and advice with friends and neighbours.

So why do people choose to play golf when the more environment-friendly alternatives are cheaper and take up less time? Why do they choose the less cost-effective option? It is the same when people buy cars: if they can afford it, they will pick the larger, more expensive car over the smaller, cheaper model that would provide just as much transport. People don't care about cost-effectiveness when they really want something. Of course, in a free society we can choose to do what we like with our time and our money.

But it does seem that everyone who has enough cash to install a solar water-heating system or a PV system and who chooses not to, using the excuse that solar energy systems are not cost-effective, is really saying, 'I will not to spend my money on things that will reduce my footprint because I don't care about the environment or future generations. What I really want is a big house and a big car instead, because what I really care about is my image as a successful person.' They are effectively saying that they are happy to destroy the world. Of course, this comment does not apply to those who, through lack of money, do not have a choice; but almost everybody else picks the large house and the large car. As we have shown, it is possible to live in a smaller house and have enough money left over to put in solar hot-water and PV systems (see Chapter 3). It is not a question of cost-effectiveness but of selfish choices. Cost-effectiveness is just used as a convenient and plausible-sounding excuse.

Cost-effectiveness receives so much attention because the world is ruled by economists – quite literally in the case of the Czech Republic, whose economist president Václav Klaus has asserted that 'the freedom to have children without regulation and control is one of the undisputable human rights'. President Klaus made this comment as part of a speech on climate change in which he argued that to decrease CO_2 emissions we would have either to stop economic or population growth, or to make huge reductions in the emissions intensity of our activities.[24] He is probably right, but his answer is that we should do nothing about climate change and let things take their course. On the other hand, Sir Nicholas Stern, head of the UK Government Economic Service and also an economist, said in his 2006 report (HM Treasury's *The Stern Review on the Economics of Climate Change*) that we could not afford not to act, and that the cost of acting would be only 1% of global GDP each year.[25] In 2008 he was reported as saying that his original report had underestimated the seriousness of the climate change problem.[26] So which economist should we believe? It is tempting to listen to Václav Klaus, because he tells us not to worry; but if he is wrong and Sir Nicholas Stern is right, we are in big trouble. If Klaus is right and Stern is wrong, we will have lost only 1% of global GDP. But if Klaus is wrong, we will have lost the world.

MAKING THE DECKCHAIRS ON THE *TITANIC*

Klaus and Stern may disagree, but at least they see the nature and the scale of the problem. Most of what our leaders, governments, local councils and industrialists are saying about sustainability is a little like making sure the deckchairs on the *Titanic* are made from recycled timber – a good idea as far as it goes, but really missing the point.[27] This is obvious from the recent trend towards carbon offsetting. The idea is that you can pay towards projects that either absorb or reduce carbon emissions, such as the planting of trees or the building of wind farms, and that this then compensates for the carbon you emit in that flight to Australia. This service, the sale of indulgences, was offered by the Catholic Church in the Middle Ages. It has been understood as the payment of cash for the forgiveness of sins; the *Catholic Encyclopedia* quite reasonably points out that this was not its intended meaning, but the practice came to be abused by mercenary ecclesiastics, like the Pardoner satirized in Chaucer's *Canterbury Tales*.[28] The same sort of misuse is probably already taking place with carbon offsets, carbon credits and the other schemes that, in terms of modern consumption, are supposed to allow us to carry on sinning. Another problem with carbon offsets is that they allow you to feel you are winning without having to make a real difference. If you reduce your carbon footprint, you could still be totally reliant on ultimately unsustainable sources of energy. To give an example, people might change from coal-fired electric heating to gas-fired heating to reduce their carbon emission; but the gas-fired heating is ultimately just as unsustainable as coal, even though it is lower in carbon emissions, because it uses a non-renewable fuel. Carbon offsets permit 'business as usual' but with a greenish tinge. That is why we have used land as our standard measure – because we want to see what sustainability really means.

DEATH FROM CONSUMPTION

Many a young Victorian heroine is shown dying from the then incurable disease of consumption (tuberculosis). It is very tempting to draw parallels between this favourite illness of 19th-century writers and the consumption that features so large in the modern Western lifestyle. The only treatment for tuberculosis before modern drugs arrived was isolation in sanatoria, often in the mountains, where patients would spend many hours of the day wrapped up but outside in the fresh, clean open air. As will become clear from our discussion of alternative footprint below, it could be that we, who spend too much time inside buildings earning money for the purposes of consumption, would benefit from a similar remedy.

A recent study has shown that we could reduce carbon dioxide emissions by 6% by changing our lifestyles so that we buy fewer goods and consume more services (restaurants, concerts, etc.) instead.[29] But we will

Table 1: The breakdown of the ecological footprint of a Cardiff resident

INDIVIDUAL CHOICES		footprint (ha)	% of total
food and drink	(food eaten at home and away from home)	1.33	24
energy	(energy used in the home)	0.99	18
travel	(car, bus, train and air travel)	0.99	18
stuff	(clothes, computers, televisions, books, furniture, appliances)	0.64	11
housing	(house-building, maintenance and repairs)	0.16	3
holidays	(holidays abroad)	0.10	2
footprint related to individual behaviour and choices		**4.21**	**75***
COLLECTIVE CONTROL			
infrastructure	(motorways, railways, bridges, stadiums)	0.74	13
government	(consumables and durables for local and central govt.)	0.41	7
services	(water, phone, post, hospitals, education, finance, police, etc.)	0.26	5
footprint related to government and services		**1.41**	**25***
total footprint		**5.59**	

* Values have been rounded.

need to change on a much greater scale if we are to make a big difference. This is apparent from the current ecological footprint of a resident of Cardiff, shown in Table 1, which is compiled from the same source of information we used in Chapter 1.[30] Here we have reorganized the figures to make it clear which parts of the footprint we have some control over as individuals, and which parts are determined by government at local and national levels.

The current fair earthshare is around 1.89 ha. As we have seen, there is some flexibility in this figure, with different sources quoting different values, but what we do know is that the more the population grows, the smaller this figure becomes. We in the West live as we do because people elsewhere live with much less. It is not possible for the entire global population to enjoy the Western lifestyle without the world being entirely destroyed. We might manage for a while, but in the end the world would become uninhabitable for ourselves and for all the other species we share it with. We must get our individual footprints down to around 1.89 ha if we are to find a way of living that everyone in the world can share and that can continue into the future. Currently that part of our footprints over which we have direct control (not that related to government and infrastructure) is more than double the fair earthshare. And the total footprint needs to be reduced to around a third of its current level. Table 3 (overleaf) explores how this might be achieved.

For the categories in Table 3 that are based on individual choices and behaviour, the 'high' footprint (the one labelled 'I'll do what I damn well want') has been calculated on the basis that the current Cardiff footprint has been generated from all the city's residents, whether they consume lots of resources or, like some elderly people living on a pension, very few. Given that we had only average values to work with, we needed some way of determining what the footprint of a high consumer might be. To arrive at this estimate, we subtracted the lowest values we think are possible from the average value; whatever was left has been added back onto the average figure. For example, our analysis suggests that the food footprint of 1.33 ha/year/person could be reduced to 0.41 ha/year if people ate food that was organic and in season and avoided packaging. There will be some in Cardiff who already live like this, so the current average value of 1.33 ha/year must be influenced by others who eat lots of meat and dairy products and buy lots of take-away food (this has a higher footprint than fresh or home-grown food cooked at home, as we have seen). A high value for the food footprint is worked out by subtracting the lowest value we can calculate, 0.41 ha/year, from the current average of 1.33 ha/year, which gives 0.92 ha/year. This figure is then added to the average figure to give a high value for the food footprint of 2.25 ha/year. The method is very rough and ready, but it enables us to get a feel for how large some of these footprints are.

The low footprint for the 'house' category in Table 3 is based on an 80% lifecycle energy reduction (see Chapter 3, Table 22). The high value is a doubling of the existing average footprint – the result of having a large house rather than a small one (see Chapter 3, Table 3). For commuting travel, a footprint reduction of 96% is possible if you cycle slowly rather than drive to work (see Chapter 2, Table 24). If you decide to use the bus instead, a reduction of around one-third is possible (see Chapter 2, Table 28), although the impact of buses varies greatly from source to source.

The Cardiff average travel footprint of 0.99 ha/year represents all travel. The Scottish Government's *Household Survey: Travel Diary 2005/2006* gives a breakdown of reasons for travel;[31] of all the journeys undertaken, 23% are to and from work, of which 60% are made by car, meaning that commuting by car accounts for around 14% of all journeys. The figure of 60% corresponds with another study, which found that in the UK about 63% of people commute by car.[32] Returning to the Scottish study, 4% of all journeys were for business, of which 87% were by car, so in Table 2 we have assumed that all business travel is by car. The greatest category – 'personal journeys' – accounts for 64% of all trips; their exact purpose varies (including shopping, visiting friends, and so on), but around 40–50% of such journeys were by

Table 2: Possible reduction to the Cardiff car travel footprint

	% of total travel footprint	footprint (ha)	reduced footprint (ha)
business travel	4	0.04	0.004
commuting by car	14	0.14	0.014
personal journeys by car	30	0.3	0.03
total	48%	0.48	0.048

Table 3: Possible footprints resulting from different attitudes towards behaviour (*ha/year*)

	high ('I'll do what I damn well want')	average ('I don't know what I'm doing')	low ('I'll do as I would be done by')
food	2.25	1.33	0.41
house	2.30	1.15	0.23
travel	1.58	1.09	0.60
stuff	1.07	0.64	0.21
behaviour totals	7.20	4.21	1.45
infrastructure	0.74	0.74	0.74
government	0.41	0.41	0.41
services	0.26	0.26	0.26
full totals	8.61	5.62	2.86

car. In Table 2 we have assumed that around 45% of personal trips are by car, meaning that they represent roughly 30% of all trips. It applies the Scottish Government's breakdown of reasons for travel to the Cardiff footprint to see how the car travel component could be reduced. A footprint reduction of 90% is assumed for cycling and some walking.

Subtracting the existing car-based footprint of 0.48 ha/year from the travel footprint of 0.99 ha/year and then adding in the 0.048 for cycling and walking to replace driving gives a revised travel footprint of around 0.6 ha/year. It is assumed that the low-impact person will not travel overseas, making a total low-impact travel footprint of 0.6 ha/year. The difference between this figure and the average figure for all travel including holidays (1.09 ha/year) is used to generate the high value of 1.58 ha.

When it comes to possessions, the low-impact person has no pets and a low value for electronic goods, and also undertakes productive activities at home, like gardening, that provide exercise. The assumption is that this will reduce the footprint by two-thirds, to 0.21 ha/year. This gives the high-impact person a corresponding value of 1.07 ha/year (Table 3).

It might be possible to reduce the travel total further, by adopting and using more efficient forms of public transport – particularly for long-distance travel – and by avoiding domestic air travel (this unknown component is still included in the analysis above). As we discussed in Chapter 6, if a fundamental change in society really does result in reduced consumption levels, the way we work will also change, which in turn will affect those aspects of our footprint that remain unaltered in the table above – infrastructure, services and so on. The potential effect of this fundamental shift is shown in Table 4.

Table 4: The ecological footprint of sustainable living (*ha/year*)

INDIVIDUAL	now	goal	how do we do it?
food and drink	1.33	0.43	eat organic food and eliminate waste
domestic energy	0.99	0.33	save energy at home and turn down the heating
domestic travel	0.99	0.33	walk, cycle, use public transport and travel less
stuff	0.64	0.21	buy less, buy second-hand, and make things last
housing	0.16	0.05	build smaller houses, share more, renovate less
holidays	0.10	0.03	take more holidays at home
individual total	5.00	1.38	
COLLECTIVE			
infrastructure	0.74	0.24	make what we have last longer, build less
government	0.41	0.14	manage with less government
services	0.26	0.09	make do with fewer services
collective total		0.47	
total revised footprint		1.85	

TIME TO EAT THE DOG?

Remember that, if we are to achieve our goal of a sustainable standard of living, there is one big precondition: zero population growth, or perhaps even a reduction in population. If the world's population rises, we will all have to accept even less. In spite of President Klaus's belief in our absolute right to have as many as we want, if we keep having children we may end up with nothing. We have shown that the impact of having a pet is large, though it depends on the pet's size; but the impact of having a child in the West is potentially very much greater. Quite simply, this is because children don't just eat (unlike pets, whose footprints on the whole were determined by the food they consumed), but have a whole range of requirements, from shelter and clothes to possessions and travel.

We could choose to reduce our footprint further in some areas to maintain other aspects of our lifestyle at a higher level: we might want to maintain the existing level of services, for example, but that would mean less government, less infrastructure or, at a personal level, even less transport, fewer possessions and fewer holidays. Of course, services could also take steps to reduce their footprint, as in the example we discussed of universities cutting back their paper use.

The question is whether we recognize the importance of these issues and plan for a changed but sustainable future. If we accept that we need to take steps, we can metaphorically 'eat the dog' by not replacing our pet, as part of our plan to reduce our personal impact on the planet. If we do not take heed, we may find ourselves in an unplanned future of resource shortages and high prices when we may be forced to eat the dog to keep the family going.

Either way, it may not be a good time to be a dog.

NOTES

INTRODUCTION

1 Calculated from data in J. Trinnaman, *World Energy Council 2004 Survey of World Energy Resources* (Oxford: Elsevier, 2004), p. 295.

2 http://science.nasa.gov/headlines/y2000/ast01jun_1m.htm (viewed 19 March 2008).

3 http://www.atsnotes.com/other/glossary.html (viewed 3 April 2008).

4 V. O. Packard, *The Hidden Persuaders* (London: Longman, 1957).

5 http://www.iucn.org/themes/ssc/red_list_2004/Extinction_media_brief_2004.pdf (viewed 19 March 2008).

6 China's 'one child' policy has achieved what it set out to achieve; see http://today.uci.edu/news/release_detail.asp?key=1597 (viewed 9 April 2008).

7 'Long-term Global Demographic Trends: Reshaping the Geopolitical Landscape' (2001), Central Intelligence Agency, Washington, D.C., at https://www.cia.gov/library/reports/general-reports-1/Demo_Trends_For_Web.pdf (viewed 9 April 2008).

8 http://siteresources.worldbank.org/DATASTATISTICS/Resources/GDP.pdf (viewed 9 April 2008).

9 http://www.iucn.org/themes/ssc/red_list_2004/Extinction_media_brief_2004.pdf (viewed 19 March 2008).

10 http://www.pce.govt.nz/projects/topic4.shtml (viewed 19 March 2008).

11 http://www.stats.govt.nz/analytical-reports/monitoring-progress/economic-growth/default.htm (viewed 9 April 2008).

12 Fig. 37 in Energy Information Administration, 'Chapter 3: Petroleum and other liquid fuels', *International Energy Outlook 2007 Report #:DOE/EIA-0484(2007)* (2007), available at http://www.eia.doe.gov/oiaf/ieo/oil.html (viewed 6 April 2008).

13 L. V. Ludy, *Locomotive Boilers and Engines: A Practical Treatise on Locomotive Boiler and Engine Design, Construction and Operation* (Chicago: American Technical Society, 1920), p. 120.

14 http://inventors.about.com/library/inventors/blbenz.htm (viewed 6 April 2008).

15 http://www.hfmgv.org/exhibits/showroom/1908/model.t.html (viewed 6 April 2008).

16 Fig. 1 in Energy Information Administration, *Energy in the United States: 1635–2000* (2008), available at http://www.eia.doe.gov/emeu/aer/eh/intro.html (viewed 6 April 2008).

17 National Commission on Energy Policy, *NCEP Staff Background Paper: Unconventional Oil* (2004), at http://www.energycommission.org/files/finalReport/1.3.a%20-%20Unconventional%20Oil.pdf (viewed 6 April 2008).

18 'Fact Sheet 3: Solar water heating' (Wellington, NZ: Energy Efficiency and Conservation Authority, 2004), p. 4.

19 http://www.kitchenstudio.co.nz/how_to.php (viewed 7 April 2008).

20 http://www.ird.govt.nz/business-income-tax/depreciation/bit-depreciation-methods.html (viewed 31 March 2006).

21 A 1.8 litre Corolla sedan costs NZ$30,500: see http://www.toyota.co.nz/NewVehicles/Models/Passenger/Corolla (viewed 7 April 2008). A 1.8 litre C 200K Avantgarde sedan costs NZ$81,900: see http://www.mercedes-benz.co.nz/cars/emb/a_subarticle2.asp?aid=-890048048 (viewed 7 April 2008).

22 http://www.smh.com.au/news/global-warming/greenhouse-gas-cuts-will-cost-430b-costa/2008/04/03/1206851105550.html (viewed 7 April 2008).

23 F. Thompson, *Lark Rise to Candleford: A Trilogy* (London: Oxford University Press, 1945).

24 M. Wackernagel and W. Rees, *Our Ecological Footprint: Reducing Human Impact on the Earth* (Gabriola Island, British Columbia: New Society Publishers, 1996).

25 Cardiff Council, *Cardiff's Ecological Footprint* (2005), at http://www.cardiff.gov.uk/content.asp?Parent_Directory_id=2865&nav=2870,3148,4119 (viewed 4 February 2007).

26 The National Trust for Ireland and many other bodies quote a current figure of 1.8 ha: see http://www.antaisce.org/natural-environment/ecological-footprint/?searchterm=sustainability (viewed 10 April 2008).

27 http://www.britannica.com/eb/article-9044024/James-Prescott-Joule (viewed 19 March 2008).

28 http://www.britannica.com/eb/article-9044023/joule (viewed 19 March 2008).

29 http://www.research.noaa.gov/spotlite/archive/spot_maunaloa.html (viewed 19 March 2008).

30 http://www.worldwatch.org/node/82 (viewed 23 October 2007).

31 http://geography.about.com/od/obtainpopulationdata/a/worldpopulation.htm (viewed 23 October 2007).

32 http://www.netl.doe.gov/publications/others/pdf/Oil_Peaking_NETL.pdf (viewed 23 October 2007).

33 http://www.ipcc.ch (viewed 23 October 2007).

34 http://www.census.gov/statab/hist/HS-33.pdf (viewed 18 March 2008).

35 Per capita income trends in China and India 1972–2002 based on data from the Organisation for Economic Co-operation and Development: http://www.itls.usyd.edu.au/seminars/presentations/johnp.pdf (viewed 18 March 2008).

36 http://www.unep.org/Documents.Multilingual/Default.asp?DocumentID=97&ArticleID=1503 (viewed 23 October 2007).

37 World Commission on Environment and Development, *Our Common Future* (Oxford: Oxford University Press, 1987).

38 Ibid.

39 http://news.bbc.co.uk/2/hi/health/542205.stm (viewed 23 October 2008).

40 B. Braithwaite, N. Walsh and G. Davies, *The Home Front: The Best of Good Housekeeping 1939–1945* (London: Leopard Books, 1995), p. 162.

41 http://www.ww2poster.co.uk/posters/imagebank/isyourjourneyreallynecessary.htm (viewed 23 October 2008).

42 H. Hardin, 'The Tragedy of the Commons', *Science*, 162 (1968), pp. 1243–48.

43 http://www.transitiontowns.org (viewed 19 March 2008).

44 B. Commoner, *The Closing Circle: Nature, Man and Technology* (New York: Knopf, 1971).

45 http://www.pha.jhu.edu/~ldb/seminar/butterfly.html (viewed 23 October 2007).

46 http://www.conservative-resources.com/definition-of-capitalism.html (viewed 19 March 2008).

47 http://mw4.m-w.com/dictionary/democracy (viewed 19 March 2008).

CHAPTER 1: FOOD

1 Information from Dr Samir Bali of Miami University of Ohio, at http://www.cas.muohio.edu/%7Ebalis/182/ 182webpage.html (viewed 29 January 2008).

2 P. Fisher and A. Bender, *The Value of Food* (Oxford: Oxford University Press, 1975), p. 22.

3 British Nutrition Foundation, *Nutrient Requirements and Recommendations* (2004), at http://www.nutrition.org.uk/ upload/Nutritient%20Requirements%20and%20recomm endations%20pdf(1).pdf (viewed 15 September 2008).

4 N. Mithraratne, B. Vale and R. Vale, *Sustainable Living: The Role of Whole Life Costs and Values* (London: Butterworth-Heinemann, 2007), p. 140.

5 *The State of New Zealand's Environment* (Wellington, NZ: Ministry for the Environment, 1997), p. 3.17 and Table 3.2, pp. 3.5–3.7.

6 G. Leach, *Energy and Food Production* (London: International Institute for Environment and Development, 1975), p. 8.

7 Calculated from data in G. Treloar and R. Fay, 'The embodied energy of living', *Environment Design Guide*, GEN 20 (1998), The Royal Australian Institute of Architects, pp. 1–8.

8 *The State of New Zealand's Environment*, pp. 3, 21.

9 From Fig. 8, 'World marketed energy consumption 1980–2030', at http://www.eia.doe.gov/oiaf/ieo/ world.html (viewed 24 January 2008).

10 www.eia.doe.gov/pub/oiaf/1605/cdrom/pdf/gg-app-tables.pdf (viewed 24 January 2008).

11 http://www.census.gov/cgi-bin/ipc/idbagg (viewed 24 January 2008).

12 Derived from data given in *Key World Energy Statistics* (Paris: International Energy Agency, 2007), p. 6; population data from http://www.census.gov/ipc/www/idb/ worldpop.html (viewed 25 January 2008).

13 Data from *BP Statistical Review of World Energy* (London: BP plc, 2007), pp. 6, 22, 32.

14 http://www.iaea.org/NewsCenter/News/2006/ uranium_resources.html (viewed 29 January 2008).

15 *World Energy Outlook Executive Summary* (Paris: International Energy Agency, 2007), p. 5.

16 Cardiff Council, *Cardiff's Ecological Footprint* (2005), at http://www.cardiff.gov.uk/content.asp?Parent_Directory_id =2865&nav=2870,3148,4119 (viewed 4 February 2007), p. 2.

17 A. Collins, A. Flynn and A. Netherwood, *Reducing Cardiff's Ecological Footprint: A Resource Accounting Tool for Sustainable Consumption* (Cardiff: WWF Cymru, 2005), p. 12.

18 http://baltimorechronicle.com/ 080304ThomasWheeler.shtml (viewed 14 February 2008).

19 *Europe 2005: The Ecological Footprint* (Brussels: WWF International), p. 11.

20 See http://hdr.undp.org/en/humandev/hdi (viewed 10 April 2008).

21 Data from Table 1 at http://www.iisd.ca/consume/ mwfoot.html (viewed 17 December 2007).

22 Table 1 at http://www.iisd.ca/consume/mwfoot.html (viewed 17 December 2007).

23 Taken from Table 7 at http://www.steppingforward.org.uk/ ef/food.htm (viewed 17 December 2007).

24 Basic data for creating Table 6 from Collins et al., *Reducing Cardiff's Ecological Footprint*, pp. 33–35, Table 13. The rows in bold, and the values for % of diet, % of footprint and footprint in m²/kg, were calculated by us.

25 See, for example, C. Stancu and A. Smith, *Food Miles: The International Debate and Implications for New Zealand Exporters*, Business & Sustainability Series Briefing Paper 1 (Auckland: Manaaki Whenua Landcare Research, 2006).

26 Collins et al., *Reducing Cardiff's Ecological Footprint*, p. 26.

27 Basic data for creating Table 6 from Collins et al., *Reducing Cardiff's Ecological Footprint*, p. 32, Table 12.

28 Ibid., p. 28.

29 *International Shipping: Carrier of World Trade* (London: International Maritime Organization, 2005), p. 3. The unit of 1 megajoule per tonne-kilometre (MJ/tonne-km) is the amount of energy needed to transport 1 tonne of freight 1 kilometre.

30 Data from *Indicator Fact Sheet TERM 2002 27 EU: Overall energy efficiency and specific CO_2 emissions for passenger and freight transport (per passenger-km and per tonne-km and by mode)* (Brussels: European Environment Agency, 2002), p. 1, Fig. 2.

31 Calculated using figure of 1 million tonnes oil equivalent = 41.868 PJ, as given in http://astro.berkeley.edu/~wright/ fuel_energy.html (viewed 2 January 2008).

32 Data from New Zealand Ministry of Transport at http://www.transport.govt.nz/nrs-page-8 (viewed 21 February 2008).

33 It has proven very difficult to find reliable air-freight energy intensity figures. However, according to US data, an all-cargo aircraft in the year 2000 was estimated to use 14,037 Btu per ton-mile: M. Mintz and A. Vyas, *Forecast of Transportation Energy Demand through the Year 2010*, ANL/ESD-9, DE92 000222 (Argonne, Ill.: Argonne National Laboratory, Center for Transportation Research, 1990), p. 92.

34 From Table 2 in Worldwatch Institute, 'United States leads world meat stampede' (1998), at http://www.worldwatch.org/ node/1626 (viewed 24 January 2008).

35 http://www.worldwatch.org/node/1626 (viewed 24 January 2008).

36 Based on figures of 2,557 million for 1950 and 5,919 million for 1998, given at http://www.census.gov/ipc/ www/idb/worldpop.html (viewed 24 January 2008).

37 All data from http://www.essortment.com/family/ howdoyouknow_svkw.htm (viewed 4 February 2008).

38 Data from http://people.eku.edu/resorc/ Medieval_peasant_diet.htm (viewed 4 February 2008).

39 M. Rubner, 1908, quoted in C. Treitel, 'Food science/ food politics: Max Rubner and "rational nutrition" in fin-de-siècle Berlin', in P. J. Atkins, P. Lummel and D. J. Oddy, *Food and the City in Europe since 1800* (Aldershot: Ashgate, 2007).

40 Collins et al., *Reducing Cardiff's Ecological Footprint*, Table 15, p. 36.

41 C. Vasilikiotis, 'Can organic farming "feed the world"?', at http://www.cnr.berkeley.edu/~christos/articles/ cv_organic_farming.html (viewed 21 February 2008).

42 Collins et al., *Reducing Cardiff's Ecological Footprint*, Table 15, p. 160.

43 Based on data from ibid., pp. 53–54 and 69–71.
44 *The State of New Zealand's Environment*, p. 3.17 and Table 3.2, pp. 3.5–3.7.
45 Collins et al., *Reducing Cardiff's Ecological Footprint*, p. 29.
46 Ibid., p. 36.
47 http://www.wellington.govt.nz/services/environment/climate/carbon.html (viewed 10 April 2008).
48 http://www.wellington.govt.nz/aboutwgtn/glance/index.html (viewed 11 April 2008).
49 http://en.wikipedia.org/wiki/Ecology_of_Hong_Kong (viewed 10 December 2007).
50 http://earthtrends.wri.org/pdf_library/country_profiles/ene_cou_344.pdf) (viewed 17 December 2007).
51 *Wind Farm Basics Fact Sheet 1* (Wellington, NZ: New Zealand Wind Energy Association, 2005), p. 3.
52 Data from 'Wind Power Project Site Identification & Land Requirements: A Part of the NYSERDA Wind Power Toolkit' (2005), prepared for New York State Energy Research and Development Authority, pp. 5–6.
53 *Measuring Up 2005: The State of the Environment Report for the Wellington Region*, Table 9.1, p. 127, at http://www.gw.govt.nz/ section1768.cfm (viewed 10 April 2008).
54 Calculated from data provided at http://www.wellington.govt.nz/aboutwgtn/glance/index.html (viewed 10 April 2008).
55 F. H. King, *Farmers of Forty Centuries, Or Permanent Agriculture in China, Korea, and Japan* (Madison, Wis.: Mrs F. H. King, 1911).
56 D. Cadbury, *Seven Wonders of the Industrial World* (London: Harper Perennial, 2004).
57 http://www.perseus.tufts.edu/cgi-bin/ptext?doc=Perseus%3Atext%3A2000.01.0027;query=page%3D%23442;layout=;loc=449 (viewed 9 January 2008).
58 For example, through the 1905 Birkeland-Eyde arc furnace: see http://www.physics.ubc.ca/%7Ewaltham/d2098/paper/node3.html (viewed 6 January 2008).
59 http://www.tfi.org/factsandstats/fertilizer.cfm (viewed 6 January 2007).
60 T. L. Roberts and W. M. Stewart, 'Inorganic phosphorus and potassium production and reserves', *Better Crops*, 86:2 (2002), p. 6.
61 Table 1 in K. A. Barbarick and D. G. Westfall, *Biosolids Recycling*, fact sheet no. 0.547 (Fort Collins, Colo.: Colorado State University Extension – Agriculture, n.d.), available at http://www.ext.colostate.edu/pubs/Crops/00547.html (viewed 25 February 2008).
62 J. Jacobs, *The Economy of Cities* (New York: Random House, 1969).
63 M. Pritchard and R. Vale, 'How to save yourself (and possibly the world) on 20 minutes a day', paper presented at the Shaping the Sustainable Millennium conference, Queensland University of Technology, Brisbane, 5–7 July 2000. Paper no. BEE101 PDF on CD-ROM.
64 http://www.aucklandcity.govt.nz/auckland/introduction/people/population.asp (viewed 14 April 2008).
65 MetroWater, personal communication with Renee Shirley, 22 June 1999.
66 A. Twort, F. Law, F. Crowley and D. Ratnayaka, *Water Supply* (London: Arnold, 4th edn 1994), p. 9.
67 *Facts New Zealand* (Wellington, NZ: Statistics New Zealand, 1995),p. 96.
68 *IHVE Guide Book A 1970* (London: Institution of Heating and Ventilating Engineers, 1971), p. A2-24.

69 For details see B. Vale and R. Vale, *The New Autonomous House* (London: Thames & Hudson, 2000).
70 For example, M. Pritchard, *North Shore Recycling Survey: Sample Survey of 300 Households December 1990–May 1991* (Auckland Regional Council, 1992); B. Hammonds, *Domestic Waste Reduction: Promotion of Strategies at the Household Level*, MSc thesis (University of Auckland, 1996).
71 http://www.wrt.org.nz/wrt/composting.htm (viewed 15 April 2008).
72 G. Leach, *Energy and Food Production*, p. 8.
73 http://www.nzfsa.govt.nz/publications/food-focus/2007-08/page-16.htm (viewed 14 November 2007).
74 A. García-Contreras, D. Mota-Rojas, M. R. Becerril-Herrera, H. J. Herrera, C. Noriega and M. Alonso-Spilsbury, 'Feeding kitchen leftovers to fattening pigs: Effects on health and production performance', *Journal of Food Technology*, 3:3 (2005), pp. 356–60.
75 http://www.wc.adfg.state.ak.us/index.cfm?adfg=bears.bearpolicy (viewed 6 January 2008).
76 http://www.ccc.govt.nz/Waste/Composting/AGuideToWormComposting.pdf (viewed 14 November 2007).
77 http://www.arc.govt.nz/auckland/the-big-clean-up/reduce-your-rubbish/worm-composting.cfm (viewed 14 November 2007).
78 T. Evans, *Environmental Impact Study of Food Waste Disposers* (The County Surveyors' Society, Herefordshire Council and Worcestershire Council, n.d.), summary, p. 1 at http://www.insinkerator.com/pdfs/fwd_eis_summary.pdf (viewed 14 November 2007).
79 E. Emery, A. J. Griffiths and K. P. Williams, 'An in depth study of the effects of socio-economic conditions on household waste recycling practices', *Waste Management Research*, 21:3 (2003), p. 180.
80 W. F. Strutz, 'Life cycle comparison of five engineered systems for managing food waste' (1998), p. 2, at http://www.insinkerator.com/pdfs/uwstudy.pdf (viewed 14 November 2007).
81 Wainberg et al., 'Assessment of food disposal options in multi-unit dwellings in Sydney' (Sydney: Cooperative Research Centre for Waste Management & Pollution Control Limited, 2000), p. 8.
82 Strutz, 'Life cycle comparison of five engineered systems', p. 7.
83 Ibid.
84 Mithraratne et al., *Sustainable Living*, p. 218.
85 Ibid.
86 Strutz, 'Life cycle comparison of five engineered systems', p. 7.
87 A. Ravetz and R. Turkington, *The Place of Home: English Domestic Environments 1914–2000* (London: Spon, 1995), p. 54.
88 http://www.insinkerator.com:8765/iseb2c2/query.html?qt=evolution+excel+specification&col=iseb2c2&x=9&y=30 (viewed 15 November 2007).
89 http://www.gladore.com/faq1.asp (viewed 15 November 2007).
90 Mithraratne et al., *Sustainable Living*, p. 218.
91 Strutz, 'Life cycle comparison of five engineered systems', p. 7.
92 http://www.composters.com/camarillo/camarillo.html (viewed 15 November 2007).
93 Mithraratne et al., *Sustainable Living*, p. 218.
94 Mithraratne et al., *Sustainable Living*, p. 219.
95 Mithraratne et al., *Sustainable Living*, p. 218.

96 http://whatcom.wsu.edu/ag/compost/wormbins.htm (viewed 15 November 2007).

97 Mithraratne et al., *Sustainable Living*, p. 219.

98 Wainberg et al., 'Assessment of food disposal options', p. 8.

CHAPTER 2: TRANSPORT

1 Kenneth Grahame, *The Wind in the Willows* (London: Methuen, 1908).

2 http://www.whatwouldjesusdrive.org (viewed 2 October 2007).

3 http://www.msnbc.msn.com/id/12040753/ (viewed 4 September 2007).

4 *National Greenhouse Gas Inventory: Analysis of Recent Trends and Greenhouse Indicators 1990 to 2002*, and *Australian Methodology for the Estimation of Greenhouse Gas Emissions and Sinks 2002* (both Canberra: Australian Greenhouse Office, 2002).

5 http://www.volkswagen.com.au/pdf/Brochures/Golf_Brochure_310807.pdf (viewed 28 September 2007).

6 http://www.morris-minor.co.uk/p13.htm (viewed May 2008).

7 http://www.smartaustralia.com.au/fortwo/Tech-specs-.html (viewed 28 September 2007).

8 http://www.volkswagen.com.au/pdf/Brochures/Golf_Brochure_310807.pdf (viewed 28 September 2007).

9 Data for Holden Commodore Omega from http://www.holden.com.au/pdf/chooseavehicle/techdata/VE_Weights.pdf; http://www.holden.com.au/pdf/chooseavehicle/techdata/VE_Commodore_Specifications.pdf; http://www.holden.com.au/pdf/chooseavehicle/techdata/GM_Holden_fuel_economy_VE.pdf (all viewed 8 October 2007).

10 http://www.toyota.com.au/toyota/vehicle/Specification/0,4668,2141_704_363,00.html (viewed 28 September 2007).

11 From http://www.greenhouse.gov.au/fuelguide (viewed 31 July 2007).

12 Produced from data in *2001–2002 Fuel Consumption Guide* (Canberra: Australian Greenhouse Office, 2002).

13 http://www.nottinghamshire.gov.uk/home/environment/greenissues/greentransport/greendriving.htm (viewed 28 September 2007).

14 http://www.edmunds.com/advice/fueleconomy/articles/106842/article.html (viewed 28 September 2007).

15 Data derived from Tables 6.2 and 6.3 at http://72.14.253.104/search?q=cache:EdOApyCDCm0J: www.dft.gov.uk/pgr/statistics/datatablespublications/personal/mainresults/nts2004/sectionsixotherfactorsaffect 5253+average+occupancy+of+cars&hl=en&ct=clnk&cd=2& gl=nz (viewed 8 October 2007).

16 A. Perkins and S. Hamnett, 'The significance of urban form in creating more greenhouse-friendly cities', paper presented at the 8th International Conference of the Asian Planning Schools Association, Penang, 12–13 September 2005, p. 7.

17 B. N. Fildes, S. J. Lee and J. C. Lane, *Vehicle Mass, Size and Safety*, Report CR133 (Canberra: Federal Office of Road Safety, Department of Transport and Communications, 1993), p. 47.

18 http://www.roadandtravel.com/autonewsandviews/2005/whypeoplebuycars.htm (viewed 9 October 2007).

19 Ibid.

20 http://www.euroncap.com/carsearch.aspx (viewed 8 October 2007).

21 Combined fuel consumption from http://www.vcacarfueldata.org.uk/search/fuelConSearch.asp (viewed 16 April 2008).

22 http://www.tfl.gov.uk/roadusers/congestioncharging/6733.aspx, and http://www.energysavingtrust.org.uk/uploads/documents/fleet/-%20PowerShift%20Register%2029%202% 2020081. pdf (viewed 16 April 2008).

23 Based on an Advertising Standards Authority report into misleading advertising for the Toyota Prius, available at http://www.asa.org.uk/asa/focus/background_briefings/Environmental+Claims.htm (viewed 18 April 2008).

24 Audi A2 1.2 TDI: http://en.wikipedia.org/wiki/Audi_A2; Volkswagen Lupo 1.2 TDI: http://en.wikipedia.org/wiki/Volkswagen_Lupo (both viewed 16 April 2008).

25 http://www.lupo80days.com/tage/tag80_ticker_de.html (viewed 16 April 2008).

26 Honda Insight 1.0: http://en.wikipedia.org/wiki/Honda_Insight (viewed 16 April 2008).

27 http://www.volkswagen.de/vwcms_publish/vwcms/master_public/virtualmaster/de3/unternehmen/mobilitaet _und_nachhaltigkeit/technik___innovation/Forschung/1_Liter_Auto.html (viewed 16 April 2008).

28 http://www.fhwa.dot.gov/policy/ohim/hs05/motor_vehicles.htm (viewed 27 April 2008).

29 US Department of Transportation data, quoted at http://www.infoplease.com/ipa/A0004727.html (viewed 28 April 2008).

30 http://tatanano.inservices.tatamotors.com/tatamotors (viewed 28 April 2008).

31 http://www.automotiveworld.com/WVMA/content.asp?contentid=65687 (viewed 28 April 2008).

32 Data from http://www.juliaross.net/horsefax.html (viewed 29 April 2008).

33 http://www.juliaross.net/horsefax.html (viewed 29 April 2008).

34 http://www.bridlerides.co.uk/hints.html (viewed 29 April 2008).

35 http://www.newrider.com/Library/Misc_Tips/land_horse.html (viewed 29 April 2008).

36 Data from http://www.thewayofhorses.com/calories_0406.html (viewed 29 April 2008).

37 www.efrc.com/manage/authincludes/article_uploads/horses.doc (viewed 29 April 2008).

38 http://www.worldwatch.org/node/1537 (viewed 23 October 2007).

39 http://www.emigratenz.org/ReallyAndTruly.html (viewed 23 October 2007).

40 http://www.med.govt.nz/upload/48437/003-200707-a.pdf (viewed 23 October 2007).

41 Data from http://journeytoforever.org/biodiesel_yield.html (viewed 3 January 2008).

42 M. Duke, D. Andrews, T. Anderson and A. Fow, *The Feasibility of Battery Electric Cars in New Zealand*, PowerPoint presentation, University of Waikato, 2007.

43 Hale & Twomey, *Enabling Biofuels: Biofuel Supply Options* (Wellington, NZ: Ministry of Transport, 2006), p. 12.

44 Based on Table 2.2 in L. R. Brown, *Plan B 2.0: Rescuing a Planet Under Stress and a Civilization in Trouble* (New York: W. W. Norton and Co., 2006), p. 32.

45 Data from Table 6 in H. Shapouri, J. A. Duffield and M. Wang, *The Energy Balance of Corn Ethanol: An Update*, Agricultural Economic Report No. 813 (Washington, D.C.: US Department of Agriculture, Office of the Chief Economist, Office of Energy Policy and New Uses, 2002), p. 9.

46 F. Talbot, *All About Inventions and Discoveries: The Romance of Modern Scientific and Mechanical Achievements* (London: Cassell and Co., 1916).

47 *New Zealand Energy Strategy to 2050: Towards a Sustainable Low Emissions Energy System* (Wellington, NZ: Ministry of Economic Development, 2007), p. 31.

48 http://www.transport07.co.nz/uploads/File/ppt/m%20Duke.ppt#358,27 Energy Supply from Wind (viewed 30 October 2007).

49 All data from New Zealand Wind Energy Association, at http://www.windenergy.org.nz/FAQ/proj_dom.htm# potential (viewed 5 November 2007).

50 http://www.windenergy.org.nz/FAQ/ proj_dom.htm#current (viewed 5 November 2007).

51 From Fig. 4 in *Wellington Regional Land Transport Strategy 2007–2016* (Wellington, NZ: Greater Wellington Council, adopted July 2007), p. 9.

52 *Project West Wind* (Wellington, NZ: Meridian Energy, n.d.), p. 2.

53 http://www2.stats.govt.nz/domino/external/web/commprofiles.nsf/htmldocs/Wellington+Region+Community+Profile#households (viewed 6 November 2007).

54 http://www.toyota.co.uk/vs2/pdf/PS2_63_spec.pdf (viewed 9 July 2007).

55 B. Vale and R. Vale, 'Zero energy housing retrofit', *Proceedings PLEA 2006 – The 23rd Conference of Passive and Low Energy Architecture*, Geneva, 6–8 September 2006.

56 Data from 'Wind Power Project Site Identification & Land Requirements: A Part of the NYSERDA Wind Power Toolkit' (2005), prepared for New York State Energy Research and Development Authority, pp. 5–6.

57 http://usgovinfo.about.com/library/weekly/aa012202a.htm (viewed 5 November 2007).

58 U. Bossel, 'Does a hydrogen economy make sense?', *Proceedings of the Institute of Electrical and Electronic Engineers*, 94:10 (October 2006), pp. 1826–37.

59 Calculated from NZ electricity production, 41.59 billion kWh in 2005: https://www.cia.gov/library/publications/the-world-factbook/print/nz.html (viewed 3 December 2007).

60 Bossel, 'Does a hydrogen economy make sense?', Fig. 9, p. 1835.

61 Figures from http://www.nutristrategy.com/activitylist3.htm (viewed 4 July 2007).

62 Conversions all from http://www.convertworld.com/en/energy/kcal.html (viewed 4 July 2007).

63 http://www.greenhouse.gov.au/fuelguide/ (viewed 31 July 2007).

64 Australian Greenhouse Office, *National Greenhouse Gas Inventory: Analysis of Recent Trends and Greenhouse Indicators 1990 to 2002* (2007); and Department of Climate Change, *Australian Methodology for the Estimation of Greenhouse Gas Emissions and Sinks 2002: Energy (Transport)* (2007), both quoted at http://www.ptua.org.au/myths/energy.shtml (viewed 11 September 2007).

65 http://digilander.libero.it/felixpetrelli/vinicio.htm (viewed 11 September 2007).

66 A. Alcorn, *Embodied Energy and CO$_2$ Coefficients for New Zealand Building Materials* (Wellington, NZ: Victoria University of Wellington, Centre for Building Performance Research, 2001), p. 19.

67 Ibid.

68 http://www.grantadesign.com/resources/materials/casestudies/helmet.htm (viewed 11 September 2007).

69 http://walking.about.com/od/beginners/a/cheap.htm (viewed September 2007).

70 http://www.aaireland.ie/toptips/costofmotoring2004.asp (viewed September 2007).

71 http://www.deakin.edu.au/news/upload/170707energycalculator.pdf (viewed 30 July 2007).

72 G. Baird, personal communication with the authors, 30 July 2007.

73 Derived from data at http://www.wvda.org/calcs/mcals.htm (viewed 30 July 2007).

74 P. Chapman, *Fuel's Paradise* (Harmondsworth: Penguin, 1975).

75 http://www.mcdonalds.com/app_controller.nutrition.index1.html (viewed 4 September 2007).

76 A. Carlsson-Kanyama and M. Faist, *Energy Use in the Food Sector: A Data Survey*, AFR Report 291 (Stockholm: AFN, Naturvårdsverket, 2000), at http://www.infra.kth.se/fms/pdf/energyuse.pdf (viewed 4 September 2007), p. 12.

77 Alcorn, *Embodied Energy and CO$_2$ Coefficients*, p. 7.

78 Insight data from Canada's 2005 EnerGuide, at http://www.rncan.gc.ca/media/newsreleases/2005/200507a_e.htm (viewed 4 September 2007).

79 http://www.organicgardening.org.uk/hsl/index.php (viewed 4 September 2007).

80 http://www.seedsavers.org (viewed 4 September 2007).

81 Derived from http://hgic.clemson.edu/factsheets/hgic4254.htm (viewed 7 August 2007).

82 http://fastcooking.ca/pressure_cookers/energy_savings_pressure_cooker.php (viewed 7 August 2007).

83 Alcorn, *Embodied Energy and CO$_2$ Coefficients*, p. 7.

84 http://www.gbcaus.org/docs/greenstar/tools/GreenStar_OfficeDesign.xls (viewed 7 August 2007).

85 http://www.greenhouse.gov.au/yourhome/technical/fs21.htm#showers (viewed 6 August 2007).

86 E. Ghisi and D. F. Ferreira, 'Potential for potable water savings by using rainwater and greywater in a multi-storey residential building in southern Brazil', *Building and Environment*, 42:7 (July 2007), pp. 2512–22.

87 http://hyperphysics.phy-astr.gsu.edu/hbase/thermo/spht.html (viewed 24 September 2008).

88 Based on data from Bradley MJ & Associates, *Comparison of Energy Use & CO$_2$ Emissions From Different Transportation Modes*, May 2007, prepared for the American Bus Association, Washington, D.C., p. 5.

89 http://www.mfe.govt.nz/publications/ser/enz07-dec07/html/chapter5-energy/figure-5-11.html (viewed 26 April 2008).

90 B. Vale and R. Vale, 'Sustainable transport in the twenty-first century', a lecture delivered to the Engineers for Social Responsibility (Auckland branch) on 26 November 1998, School of Engineering, University of Auckland.

91 E. Boyapati, A. Hartono and J. Rowbottom, 'Comparison of emissions from the public transport system and private cars', paper given at the 8th International Conference on Energy and Environment, Cairo, 5 January 2003.

92 M. Lenzen (1999), data published by Victoria Transport Policy Institute (Canada), at http://www.vtpi.org/tdm/tdm59.htm (viewed 26 April 2008).

93 Data from Table 1, 'Greenhouse gas efficiency (Kg CO$_2$ equiv./pass-km) of Australian urban passenger transport, 1994/5', in *The Australian Transport Task, Energy Consumed and Greenhouse Gas Emissions* (Canberra: Australian Government Consulting Group, 1997).

94 G. J. Treloar, P. E. D. Love and R. H. Crawford, 'Hybrid life-cycle inventory for road construction and use', *Journal of Construction Engineering and Management*, 130:43 (Jan./Feb. 2004), p. 47.

95 Adapted from data from the Royal Commission on Environment and Pollution (1994), given in M. Bell, R. Lowe and P. Roberts, *Energy Efficiency in Housing* (Aldershot: Avebury, 1996), p. 67. The percentages in brackets are typical vehicle occupancies, assumed by the Royal Commission in order to calculate the energy figures.

96 B. Wiesmüller, 'Scale drawings: Deutsche Bundesbahn ETA 176/ESA 176', *Continental Modeller* (January 2007), pp. 50–51.

97 http://www.railcar.co.uk/hisOthers/BMUdesc.htm (viewed 27 April 2008).

98 http://www.railcar.co.uk/hisOthers/BMUops.htm (viewed 27 April 2008).

99 Bossel, 'Does a hydrogen economy make sense?', p. 1835.

100 J. Carlton, *Perth's Electric Rail System: Past Successes and Future Prospects* (Perth: Government of Western Australia, Department of the Premier and Cabinet, Sustainability Policy Unit, 2002), Fig. 4, p. 4.

101 Ibid., p. 3.

102 http://www.tc.gc.ca/programs/Environment/utsp/otrainlightrailproject.htm (viewed 8 January 2008).

103 www.tbus.org.uk/whythetrolleybus.doc (viewed 8 January 2008).

104 http://www.blacksea-crimea.com/Places/trolleybuses.html, and http://www.answers.com/topic/crimean-trolleybus (viewed 9 January 2008).

105 http://www.worldmapper.org/display.php?selected=36# (viewed 9 January 2008).

106 http://en.wikipedia.org/wiki/Transport_Licensing_Act_1931 (viewed 15 January 2008).

107 C. J. Allen, *Eagle Book of Trains* (London: Hulton Press, 1953), p. 95.

108 http://bioenergy.ornl.gov/papers/misc/energy_conv.html (viewed 28 January 2008).

109 Details of train composition derived from Allen, *Eagle Book of Trains*, pp. 118–27.

110 B. Vale and R. Vale, *The Self-Sufficient House* (London: Macmillan, 1980), p. 12.

111 E. Newby, *The Last Grain Race* (London: Secker and Warburg, 1958), Appendix, p. 235.

112 W. Donald, personal communication with the authors, 1 January 2007.

113 Marine Environment Protection Committee, *Prevention of Air Pollution from Ships: Atmospheric CO_2 and Emissions from Ships*, 42nd session, September 1998.

114 Calculated from data in S. Becken and J. E. Hay, *Tourism and Climate Change: Risks and Opportunities* (Clevedon: Multilingual Matters, 2007), p. 195.

115 http://www.nzmaritime.co.nz/oriana.htm (viewed 11 January 2008).

116 G. Raine, 'A sea change in shipping; 50 years ago, container ships altered the world', *San Francisco Chronicle*, 5 February 2006.

117 http://www.freighterworld.com/places/austnz.html (viewed 11 January 2008).

118 *International Shipping: Carrier of World Trade* (London: International Maritime Organization, 2005), p. 3.

119 F. E. Dodman, *The Observer's Book of Ships* (London: Frederick Warne and Co. Ltd., 1959), p. 39.

120 http://www.ciderpresspottery.com/ZLA/greatzeps/german/Hindenburg.html (viewed 25 September 2007).

121 Calculated from data at http://www.boeing.com/commercial/747family/pf/pf_facts.html (9 January 2008).

122 http://www.airliners.net/info/stats.main?id=100 (viewed January 2008).

123 http://www.ocean.washington.edu/courses/envir215/energynumbers.pdf (viewed 25 September 2007).

124 http://en.wikipedia.org/wiki/Specific_fuel_consumption#Typical_values_of_SFC_for_thrust_engines (viewed 25 September 2007).

125 http://www.chevron.com/products/prodserv/fuels/bulletin/aviationfuel/4_at_fuel_comp.shtm (viewed 25 September 2007).

126 Calculated from figures at http://www.hq.nasa.gov/office/pao/History/SP-468/ch10-2.htm (viewed 25 September 2007).

127 http://www.searates.com/reference/portdistance/?fcity1=6923&fcity2=513&speed=14&ccode=3968 (viewed 27 April 2008).

128 http://www.airrouting.com/content/TimeDistanceForm.aspx (viewed 27 April 2008).

129 D. L. Daggett, R. C. Hendricks, R. Walther, E. Corporan, *Alternate Fuels for Use in Commercial Aircraft* (Seattle: Boeing Company, 2007), p. 5.

130 P. G. Cooksley, *Advanced Jetliners*, vol. 4 of B. Gunston (ed.), *The Illustrated International Aircraft Guide* (London: Phoebus/BPC, 1980), pp. 62–63.

131 http://www.tupolev.ru/English/Show.asp?SectionID=82 (viewed 16 January 2008).

132 http://www.esa.int/techresources/ESTEC-Article-fullArticle_item_selected-6_1_01_par-30_1129904712655.html (viewed 16 January 2008).

133 http://www.tkk.fi/Units/AES/projects/renew/fuelcell/posters/hydrogen.html (viewed 29 April 2008).

134 http://www.reactionengines.co.uk/lapcat.html (viewed 16 January 2008).

135 Data from http://www.justtheflight.co.uk/cheap-flights-from-LON/SYD-sydney.html (viewed 16 January 2008).

136 http://ec.europa.eu/research/growth/gcc/projects/in-action-cryoplane.html (viewed 17 January 2008).

137 E. Vale, personal communication with the authors, 31 January 2008.

CHAPTER 3: BUILDINGS

1 B. Vale and R. Vale, *The New Autonomous House* (London: Thames & Hudson, 2000).

2 http://www.nabers.com.au/page.aspx?code=RATEHOME&site=3 (viewed 22 April 2008).

3 *2nd Annual Demographia International Housing Affordability Survey: 2006*, p. 16, at http://www.demographia.com/dhi2006.pdf (viewed 6 February 2008).

4 http://greenisland.net.au/wp-content/uploads/pdf/2_1_2_CL_Edited.pdf (viewed 6 February 2008). This reference is no longer available, but there is a brochure for the Eco House at http://mams.rmit.edu.au/94nr028f7cvb1.pdf (viewed 29 Sep 2008).

5 *2nd Annual Demographia International Housing Affordability Survey: 2006*, p. 16, at http://www.demographia.com/dhi2006.pdf (viewed 6 February 2008).

6 http://www.gts-timber-frame.com/html/online.php?planid=3 (viewed 6 February 2008).

7 http://www.gts-timber-frame.com/html/online.php?planid=4 (viewed 6 February 2008).

8 http://www.channel4.com/4homes/ontv/grand-designs (viewed 6 February 2008).

9 http://www.housebuildersupdate.co.uk/2007/04/on-stamp-duty-tax-breaks-for-zero.html (viewed 6 February 2008).

10 BRANZ Study Report 155, *Energy Use in New Zealand Households – Executive Summary: Year 10* (2006), p. iv, at http://www.branz.co.nz/branzltd/pdfs/SR155(2006)_HEEP _Yr10_ExecSum.pdf?PHPSESSID=ef828f56b1ecf26ee192 9b2b13feca4d (viewed 6 February 2008).

11 Calculated as 55% of total based on 4-bed house plan at http://www.ozehouseplans.com.au/houseplans.php?plan= HPD-04-310%20-%20Turon%20Homestead (viewed 6 February 2008).

12 http://www.buildingcommission.com.au/resources/ documents/Appendix_2_AbsFinaL.pdf (viewed 6 February 2008).

13 Calculated at 45% of total based on 3-bed (space for 4 bed in upper floor) plan at http://www.homeplans.com/exec/action/ plans/browsemode/details/filter/Sle.True%3bSQFTMax.22 50%3bSQFTMin.2000/hspos/hsnet/page/1/planid/20189 /section/homeplans?pvs=tot.eNozNLIwAAAB%2fgDM (viewed 6 February 2008).

14 http://www.eia.doe.gov/emeu/recs/recs2001/ce_pdf/ spaceheat/ce2-52u_sqft_demo2001.pdf. The calculation was based on a 4-person house with 2,104 ft² heated and consumption of 22 × 1,000 Btu/ft². (viewed 6 February 2008).

15 http://www.eia.doe.gov/emeu/recs/recs2001/ce_pdf/ aircondition/ce3-52u_sqft_demo2001.pdf (viewed 6 February 2008). The calculation was based on a 4-person house with 2138 ft² cooled and consumption of 5,000 Btu/ft².

16 Based on 172 m² house of 3 bedrooms with integral garage added into the overall area of house, to give 213 m²: see http://www.blueprintplan.co.nz/design817.htm (viewed 6 February 2008).

17 BRANZ Study Report 155, *Energy Use in New Zealand Households – Executive Summary: Year 6*, p. 3, gives average household energy use in 2001 as 10,000–11,000 kWh/annum (37.8 GJ/annum): http://www.branz.co.nz/ branzltd/pdfs/HEEP6Exe.pdf?PHPSESSID=79023244fbf 8185b73f5ad0461aaf210. Roughly one third is for space heating (12.6 GJ/annum). Statistics New Zealand states in a 2001 census that 47.5% of privately occupied dwellings had 3 bedrooms: http://www.stats.govt.nz/NR/rdonlyres/ F04D7190-B1C9-4EAA-94E4-77A36B487879/0/ cssnap12.pdf. A 3-bedroom house in NZ is approx. 100–120 m², so value of 110 m² is assumed to use 12.6 GJ/annum and figure is adjusted for the larger house (all viewed 6 February 2008).

18 Taken as percentage, 6.8 heated rooms and 3 heated bedrooms from a Canadian 1997 survey of household energy use at http://oee.nrcan.gc.ca/publications/ infosource/pub/energy_use/sheu_e/sheu_1.cfm (viewed 6 February 2008).

19 1990 average value before R-2000 programme came in: http://oee.nrcan.gc.ca/corporate/statistics/neud/dpa/table shandbook2/res_00_12_e_2.cfm?attr=0 (viewed 6 May 2008).

20 To meet the R-2000 standard, a house needs to reduce energy to operate it by about 30% compared to conventional houses: see http://oee.nrcan.gc.ca/residential/personal/ new-homes/r-2000/standard/standard.cfm?attr=12 (viewed 6 February 2008).

21 2005 average at http://oee.nrcan.gc.ca/corporate/ statistics/neud/dpa/tableshandbook2/res_00_12_e_2.cfm? attr=0 (viewed 6 May 2008).

22 Taken from a plan with 2 bedrooms, 1 bathroom, 1 kitchen/dining room, 1 living room at http://www.meadowsmottram.com/plans.php (viewed 6 February 2008).

23 http://www.bioregional.com/programme_projects/ ecohous_prog/bedzed/BedZED%20Monitoring%20Summ ary%2003-04.pdf (viewed 6 February 2008).

24 Taken from plan with 3 bedrooms, kitchen/dining room, living room, bathroom, cloakroom, at http://www.meadowsmottram.com/plans.php (viewed 6 February 2008).

25 http://www.bioregional.com/programme_projects/ ecohous_prog/bedzed/BedZED%20Monitoring%20Summ ary%2003-04.pdf (viewed 6 February 2008).

26 http://www.canopy.org.au/index.php?page=embodied-energy (viewed 23 April 2008).

27 http://ublib.buffalo.edu/libraries/projects/cases/ footprint/calculations%20housing.html (viewed 27 April 2008).

28 http://www.recovery-insulation.co.uk/energy.html (viewed 23 April 2008).

29 N. Mithraratne, B. Vale and R. Vale, *Sustainable Living: The Role of Whole Life Costs and Values* (London: Butterworth-Heinemann, 2007), p. 160.

30 http://www.optimumpopulation.org/ opt.af.footprint2.carbon.PDF (viewed 13 August 2007).

31 http://earthtrends.wri.org/pdf_library/feature/ for_fea_roundwood_complete.pdf (viewed 13 August 2007).

32 M. Wackernagel and W. Rees, *Our Ecological Footprint: Reducing Human Impact on the Earth* (Gabriola Island, British Columbia: New Society Publishers, 1996).

33 http://www.fao.org/fileadmin/user_upload/foodclimate/ presentations/EM56/Flavell.pdf (viewed 6 May 2008).

34 J. R. Moriera, 'Global energy biomass potential', prepared for the Expert Workshop on Greenhouse Gas Emissions and Abrupt Climate Change: Positive Options and Robust Policy, Paris 30 September – 1 October 2004: http://cc.msnscache.com/cache.aspx?q=73255430669797 &mkt=en-NZ&lang=en-NZ&w=d152c012,ec05f7a7&FORM =CVRE2 (viewed 6 May 2008).

35 http://www.selfbuildland.co.uk/self-build-houses.asp (viewed 23 April 2008).

36 http://www.whatprice.co.uk/home.html (viewed 23 April 2008).

37 http://www.openecosource.org/renewable-energy/the-economics-installing-solar-panels-wwwazomcom (viewed 23 April 2008).

38 http://www.emigratenz.org/ NewZealandSunshine.html (viewed 23 April 2008).

39 Data from G. Hammond and C. Jones, 'Inventory of carbon and energy', Version 1.6a (2008), University of Bath, Department of Mechanical Engineering, Sustainable Energy Research Team; available at www.bath.ac.uk/mech-eng/sert/embodied (viewed 23 April 2008).

40 V. Fthenakis and E. Alsema, 'Photovoltaics energy payback times, greenhouse gas emissions and external costs: 2004–early 2005 status', *Progress in Photovoltaics: Research and Applications*, 14 (2006), pp. 275–80, at http://www.clca.columbia.edu/papers/Photovoltaic_Energy _Payback_Times.pdf (viewed 24 April 2008).

41 Mithraratne et al., *Sustainable Living*, pp. 215–18.

42 http://www.grisb.org/publications/pub33.htm (viewed 24 April 2008).

43 Mithraratne et al., *Sustainable Living*. p. 154.

44 http://eere.energy.gov/buildings/info/components/envelope/framing/strawbale.html (viewed 25 April 2008).

45 N. Stone, 'Thermal performance of straw bale wall systems' (n.d.), at http://www.ecobuildnetwork.org/pdfs/Thermal_properties.pdf (viewed 25 April 2008)

46 http://www.nelsoncitycouncil.co.nz/environment/environment_matters/Downloads/Energy%20Efficiency%20Actions.pdf (viewed 25 April 2008).

47 http://www.esc.mtu.edu/EarthWeek2006/Sustainable_Construction.pdf (viewed 25 April 2008).

48 http://www.earthbuilding.org.nz/forum/view.php?id=188 (viewed 25 April 2008). The R-value is a measure of how insulated a wall, roof or floor is. The 'R' stands for 'resistance', since it is a measure of resistance to the passage of heat through the element of a building. The higher the R-value, the greater the level of insulation, and the passage of heat from inside to outside in a heated building is therefore slower. In the UK the insulation value is usually given as a U-value, which is a measure of the transmittance of heat (W) through a specified area of a building (m²) for every degree of temperature difference between inside and outside (°C). This gives the unit for the U-value as W/m² °C, so that the lower the U-value, the greater the insulation. The R-value is the inverse of this, so its units are m² °C/W. R-values are commonly used in the US, Canada and Australasia.

49 http://www.fastonline.org/CD3WD_40/CD3WD/CONSTRUC/H2380E/EN/B987_4.HTM#B987_4_3_4 (viewed 25 April 2008).

50 http://www.earthbuilding.org.nz/forum/view.php?id=188 (viewed 25 April 2008).

51 M. R. Fay, *Comparative Life Cycle Energy Studies of Typical Australian Suburban Dwellings*, PhD thesis (Deakin University, Australia, 1999), p. 423.

52 Ibid., p. 429.

53 Ibid., p. 422.

54 Ibid., p. 429.

55 Mithraratne et al., *Sustainable Living*, p. 166.

56 http://www.abs.gov.au/ausstats/abs@.nsf/b06660592430724fca2568b5007b8619/0aac8bfae9dd3241ca2568a90013942a!OpenDocument (viewed 27 April 2008).

57 E. Hodgins, *Mr. Blandings Builds his Dream House* (London: Michael Joseph, 1947), pp. 75–78.

58 http://rangioraecovillage.co.nz/images/uploads/rangiora_example_plan.pdf (viewed 27 April 2008).

59 Weight for most items is taken from Mithraratne et al., *Sustainable Living*, p. 156, and embodied energy coefficients from the same source, pp. 241–49.

60 Ibid., p. 159.

61 BRANZ Study Report 155, *Energy Use in New Zealand Households – Executive Summary: Year 6*, p. 3, gives average household energy use in 2001 as 10,000–11,000 kWh/annum: http://www.branz.co.nz/branzltd/pdfs/HEEP6Exe.pdf?PHPSESSID=79023244fbf8185b73f5ad0461aaf210 (viewed 27 April 2008).

62 Mithraratne et al., *Sustainable Living*, p. 134.

63 http://www.yourhome.gov.au/technical/fs21.htm (viewed 27 April 2008).

64 http://www.ci.wixom.mi.us/LocalGov/Water_Sewer/Water%20Usage/How%20Much%20Water.pdf (viewed 28 April 2008).

65 http://www.worldwar2exraf.co.uk/Online%20Museum/Govnt%20Publications/Picture%20Pages/Use%20Less%20Water.htm (viewed 28 April 2008); http://www.wartimememories.co.uk/women.html (viewed 29 September 2008).

66 N. Chambers, C. Simmons and M. Wackernagel, *Sharing Nature's Interest* (London: Earthscan, 2000), p. 98.

67 E. Ghisi and D. F. Ferreira, 'Potential for potable water savings by using rainwater and greywater in a multi-storey residential building in southern Brazil', *Building and Environment*, 42:7 (2007), pp. 2512–22.

68 http://www.sustainability.govt.nz/water/adjusting-toilet (viewed 28 April 2008).

69 Ibid.

70 http://blog.behavioralecology.net/2007/07/how-often-do-you-flush-the-toilet (viewed 28 April 2008).

71 http://www.sustainability.govt.nz/goal/reduce-water-usage (viewed 28 April 2008).

72 N. Mitraratne and R. Vale, 'Rain tanks or reticulated water supply?' (2007) at http://www.landcareresearch.co.nz/publications/researchpubs/Mithraratne_Vale_Sydney_2007.pdf (viewed 28 April 2008).

73 Ibid.

74 Ibid.

75 http://www.epa.gov/iaq/voc.html#Steps%20to%20Reduce%20Exposure (viewed 28 April 2008).

76 http://www.fashionproducts.com/personal-care-overview.html (viewed 28 April 2008).

77 J. Gabe, personal communication with the authors, 1 May 2008.

78 http://www.lung.ca/_resources/DevelopingaScentfreePolicyforaWorkplace.pdf (viewed 28 April 2008).

79 http://www.lung.ca/protect-protegez/pollution-pollution/indoor-interieur/scents-parfums_e.php (viewed 28 April 2008).

80 http://www.lesstoxicguide.ca/index.asp?fetch=household (viewed 28 April 2008).

81 http://www.ab.lung.ca/environment/scents.php (viewed 28April 2008).

82 http://www.cleaning101.com/cleaning/history (viewed 28 April 2008).

83 http://inventors.about.com/library/inventors/blsoap.htm (viewed 28 April 2008).

84 http://www.bbc.co.uk/science/humanbody/body/factfiles/smell/smell_animation.shtml (viewed 28 April 2008).

85 http://www.environmentalsummit.org/news.cfm?nd=1669 (viewed 28 April 2008).

86 http://www.aela.org.au/standards/GECA%2022-2004%20-%20Shampoos%20and%20Soaps.pdf (viewed 28 April 2008).

87 http://www.shellchemicals.com/aboutus/1,1098,52,00.html (viewed 29 April 2008).

88 http://teepol.co.uk (viewed 29 April 2008).

89 http://www.laundry-and-dishwasher-info.com/Environmental-Issues.html (viewed 29 April 2008).

90 http://www.ecojoes.com/dishwasher-versus-hand-washing (viewed 29 April 2008).

91 Mithraratne et al., *Sustainable Living*, p. 218.

92 Ibid., p. 135.

93 http://www.fisherpaykel.com/dishwashing/index.cfm?productUid=41299IF3-B15D-ADB9-B76C1101F499A7E3&section=benefits (viewed 29 April 2008).

94 http://www.homeimprovementspot.com/energy-efficiency.html (viewed 29 April 2008).
95 http://images.lowes.com/product/822843/822843884728.pdf (viewed 29 April 2008).
96 http://www.nsc.org/ehc/indoor/home.htm (viewed 29 April 2008).
97 Le Corbusier, trans. F. Etchells, *Towards a New Architecture* (London: Architectural Press, 1946).
98 A. Forty, *Objects of Desire: Design and Society, 1750–1980* (London: Thames & Hudson, 1986).
99 http://www.burrows.com/hist.html (viewed 11 November 2007).
100 Mithraratne et al., *Sustainable Living*, p. 219.
101 Ibid.
102 http://www.coatings.org.uk/default.asp?edit_id=295&nav=293&branch=5 (viewed 11 November 2007).
103 Mithraratne et al., *Sustainable Living*, p. 217.
104 http://www.johnlewis.com/47_Care+of+flooring/Content.aspx (viewed 11 November 2007).
105 http://www.tradepriced.co.uk/tredaire_carpet_underlay.html (viewed 11 November 2007).
106 Mithraratne et al., *Sustainable Living*, p. 218.
107 http://www.tradepriced.co.uk/enviro_felt_underlay.html (viewed 11 November 2007).
108 http://www.cavbrem.co.nz/cbconsumer/home-owners/buying/frequently-asked-questions/frequently-asked-questions_home.cfm (viewed 11 November 2007).
109 http://www.tretfordcarpets.com/technical-specification.asp (viewed 11 November 2007).
110 http://www.mrscleannw.com/tips/cleaning-carpet.html (viewed 11 November 2007).
111 http://www.sciencedirect.com/science?_ob=ArticleURL&_udi=B6VDX-4MH2C0W-1&_user=1495406&_coverDate=07%2F31%2F2007&_rdoc=1&_fmt=&_orig=search&_sort=d&view=c&_acct=C00005 3190&_version=1&_urlVersion=0&_userid=1495406&md5 =4b071f9a8078ba593783484ed0d2b1be (viewed 11 November 2007).
112 http://www.aela.org.au/Tarkett.htm (viewed 11 November 2007).
113 M. Gorree, J. B. Guinee, G. Huppes and L. van Oers, *Environmental Life Cycle Assessment of Linoleum: Final Report* (Leiden: Leiden University Centre of Environmental Science, 2000), p. 17: http://www.leidenuniv.nl/cml/ssp/publications/lcalinoleum.pdf (viewed 12 November 2007).
114 Mithraratne et al., *Sustainable Living*, p. 217.
115 http://strategis.ic.gc.ca/epic/site/dsib-tour.nsf/en/qq00062e.html (viewed 12 November 2007).
116 Personal communication with the authors, November 2007.
117 http://www.buildingdesign.co.uk/arch-technical/tarkett-marley-t/industrial-floor-selection-guide-heavy-duty-linoleum-lino.pdf (viewed 15 November 2007).
118 http://www.ribaproductselector.com/Docs/1/03121/external/20080686.pdf?ac= (viewed 15 November 2007).
119 http://irc.nrc-cnrc.gc.ca/ccmc/registry/09/preface/0965l_e.pdf (viewed 15 November 2007).
120 http://www.armstrong.si/commflreu/en-si/life_cycle_costs.html (viewed 15 November 2007).
121 http://strategis.ic.gc.ca/epic/site/dsib-tour.nsf/en/qq00062e.html (viewed 15 November 2007).
122 http://www.forbo-flooring.com/Default.aspx?MenuId=2088 (viewed 15 November 2007).
123 Mithraratne et al., *Sustainable Living*, p. 219.
124 http://www.jameshardieeu.com/downloads/hbacker_specif_en.pdf (viewed 20 April 2008).
125 Mithraratne et al., *Sustainable Living*, p. 215.
126 Ibid., p. 216.
127 http://www.concretefloorsolutions.com/product_2.htm (viewed 20 April 2008).
128 http://www.concretenetwork.com/concrete/interiorfloors/Caring.htm (viewed 20 April 2008).
129 E. Hasselaar, *Health Performance of Housing* (Amsterdam: IOS Press/Delft University Press, 2006), p. 140.
130 http://news.bbc.co.uk/1/hi/health/828622.stm (viewed 21 April 2008).
131 http://www.canadiancarpet.org/carpet_and_health/air_quality/scientific_studies.php (viewed 21 April 2008).
132 http://ec.europa.eu/environment/ecolabel/pdf/vacuum_cleaners/technicalstudy_may01.pdf (viewed 16 November 2007).
133 http://www.carpet-rug.org/about-cri/what-is-cri/frequently-asked-questions.cfm (viewed 16 November 2007).
134 http://www.goodhousekeeping.com/home/products/vacuum-cleaner-faqs-1101 (viewed 16 November 2007).
135 http://www.greenfloors.com/HP_Linoleum_Index.htm#Linoleum%20is%20made%20from%20all%20natural%2 0materials (viewed 16 November 2007).
136 http://friendswoodbrooms.com/guarantee.html (viewed 16 November 2007).
137 Mithraratne et al., *Sustainable Living*, p. 219.
138 http://www.asthma.org.uk/all_about_asthma/asthma_triggers_az/housedust_mites.html (viewed 29 April 2008).
139 http://www.buildinggreen.com/auth/productDetail.cfm?ProductID=1174 (viewed 29 April 2008).
140 Hasselaar, *Health Performance of Housing*, p. 203.
141 http://www.hc-sc.gc.ca/ewh-semt/air/out-ext/faq_e.html (viewed 29 April 2008).
142 http://www.market-lofts.com/Ralphs_layout.pdf (viewed 29 April 2008).
143 P. Jurasovich, *The Environmental Impact of New Ways of Working in the Office*, PhD thesis (University of Auckland, 2003), p. 496.
144 U.-M. Mroueh et al., *Life Cycle Assessment of Road Construction*, Finnish National Road Association (1999), pp. 27–28, at http://alk.tiehallinto.fi/tppt/pdf/lca_17-00.pdf (viewed 30 April 2008).
145 http://www2.dupont.com/Typar/en_US/assets/downloads/installation_guidelines/hr/Typar_HR_generic_car_park.pdf (viewed 30 April 2008).
146 Embodied energy coefficients from Mithraratne et al., *Sustainable Living*, pp. 214–18.
147 http://www.heatpumpcentre.org/Projects/Annex_31.asp (viewed 30 April 2008).
148 http://www.energystar.gov/ia/business/challenge/learn_more/Supermarket.pdf (viewed 30 April 2008).
149 http://www.epa.gov/cleanrgy/documents/sector-meeting/4biii_supermarket.pdf (viewed 30 April 2008).
150 http://www.aseanenergy.org/download/projects/promeec/2005-2006/building/vn/Heritage%20Halomg%20Hotel.pdf (viewed 30 April 2008).
151 http://www.energystar.gov/ia/business/challenge/learn_more/Supermarket.pdf (viewed 30 April 2008).
152 http://www.epa.gov/cleanrgy/documents/sector-meeting/4biii_supermarket.pdf (viewed 30 April 2008).
153 http://www.bwea.com/business/lec.html (viewed 30 April 2008).

154 http://www.gaff.org.uk/?lid=1919 (viewed 30 April 2008).

155 Stan Swan, personal communication with the authors, April 2008.

156 http://www.sheffieldplastics.com/web_docs/PDS061.pdf (viewed 30 April 2008).

157 Mithraratne et al., *Sustainable Living*, pp. 214–19.

158 Ibid., p. 159.

159 I. M. Johnstone, 'Energy and mass flows of housing: estimating mortality', *Building and Environment*, 36:1 (2001), pp. 43–51.

160 Z. Zhang, X. Wu, X. Yang and Y. Zhu, 'BEPAS – A life cycle building environmental performance assessment model', *Building and Environment*, 41:5 (2006), pp. 669–75.

161 K. K. Chen, *The Sustainable Apartment Building*, MArch thesis (University of Auckland, 2005).

162 *New Tricks with Old Bricks* (London: The Empty Homes Agency, 2008), at http://www.emptyhomes.com/documents/publications/reports/New%20Tricks%20With%20Old%20Bricks%20-%20final%2012-03-081.pdf (viewed 1 May 2008).

163 http://www.rcep.org.uk/urban/report/eci-appe_embodied_energy.pdf (viewed 1 May 2008).

164 Data from G. Hammond and C. Jones, 'Inventory of carbon and energy'; and Mithraratne et al., *Sustainable Living*, p. 215, as value for new-technology brick-making.

165 Mithraratne et al., *Sustainable Living*, p. 159.

166 http://www.baggeridge.co.uk/brick_calc_popup.htm (viewed 1 May 2008).

167 http://www.midlandbrick.com.au/docs/techspecs/bricksblocks/bricks_standard_face.asp?site=Midland&AUD=&toggleItem=5&menuItem=bricksblocks (viewed 1 May 2008).

168 http://www.bioregional.com/programme_projects/ecohous_prog/bedzed/bedzed_hpg.htm (viewed 1 May 2008).

169 R. Fay, R. Vale and B. Vale, 'Assessing the importance of design decisions on life cycle energy and environmental impact', *Proceedings of the Passive and Low Energy Architecture Conference*, Cambridge, UK, 2000.

170 G. Treloar, 'Extracting embodied energy paths from input–output tables: towards an input–output-based hybrid energy analysis method', *Economic Systems Research*, 9:4 (1997), pp. 375–92.

171 http://www.britishgas.co.uk/pdf/EnergyEfficiencyReport.pdf (viewed 2 May 2008).

172 http://money.cnn.com/2007/09/06/real_estate/valueadded_september.moneymag/index.htm (viewed 2 May 2008).

173 G. S. Sirmans, L. MacDonald, D. A. Macpherson and E. N. Zietz, *The Value of Housing Characteristics: A Meta Analysis* (2005), at http://realtytimes.com/rtpages/20040209_valueadded.htm (viewed 2 May 2008).

174 http://www.msnbc.msn.com/id/20895851 (viewed 2 May 2008).

175 http://www.home-remodeling4u.com/kitchen/kitchen-renovation.htm (viewed 2 May 2008).

176 http://www.sustainability.govt.nz/news/2008/get-rid-your-old-inefficient-fridge-porirua (viewed 2 May 2008).

177 http://www.arcainc.com (viewed 2 May 2008).

178 http://www.metrokc.gov/dnrp/swd/wdidw/category.asp?catid=20 (viewed 2 May 2008).

179 Mithraratne et al., *Sustainable Living*, p. 218.

CHAPTER 4: STUFF WE HAVE AT HOME

1 J. Soth, C. Grasser and R. Salerno, *The Impact of Cotton on Fresh Water Resources and Ecosystems: A Preliminary Synthesis* (1999), WWF Background Paper, p. 16, at http://assets.panda.org/downloads/impact_long.pdf (viewed 11 July 2007).

2 http://www.fundinguniverse.com/company-histories/Dyersburg-Corporation-Company-History.html (viewed 11 July 2007).

3 http://www.whitehouse.gov/history/grounds/06.html (viewed 7 May 2008).

4 http://www.ext.vt.edu/pubs/sheep/410-366/410-366.html#L1 (viewed 11 July 2007).

5 http://rovianconspiracy.blogspot.com/2007/04/yet-another-reason-no-impact-wont-catch.html (viewed 8 August 2007).

6 http://texmin.nic.in/msy_20010427.htm (viewed 11 July 2007).

7 http://r0.unctad.org/infocomm/anglais/cotton/market.htm (viewed 11 July 2007).

8 http://www.biotech-info.net/WWF_inter_update.pdf (viewed 12 September 2007).

9 http://www.regional.org.au/au/asa/1996/contributed/156court.htm (viewed 8 August 2007).

10 http://www.ienica.net/fibresseminar/vandam.pdf (viewed 8 August 2007).

11 http://mojo.calyx.net/~olsen/HEMP/IHA/jiha6107.html (viewed 8 August 2007).

12 http://www.binhaitimes.com/hemp.html (viewed 8 August 2007).

13 http://www.eartheasy.com/wear_tencel.htm (viewed 9 August 2007).

14 http://iis-db.stanford.edu/pubs/20711/forest-plantations-vision.pdf (viewed 9 August 2007).

15 http://www.fpl.fs.fed.us/documnts/fplgtr/fplgtr77.pdf (viewed 9 August 2007).

16 http://www.rightsandtrade.org/events/2006.9.20.Beijing/_docs/C%20Barr%20-%20S%20China%20Plantations%20(Eng).ppt#276,1, 'How cost competitive is wood pulp production in South China?' (viewed 9 August 2007).

17 http://www.ifm.eng.cam.ac.uk/sustainability/projects/mass/UK_textiles.pdf (viewed 9 August 2007).

18 http://ard.unl.edu/rn/0304/8_9.pdf (viewed 9 August 2007).

19 http://my.execpc.com/~drer/cornfuel.htm (viewed 9 August 2007).

20 http://www.bambrotex.com/second/aboutus.htm (viewed 9 August 2007).

21 http://www.bioversityinternational.org/publications/Web_version/572/ch24.htm (viewed 13 August 2007).

22 http://indiansilk.kar.nic.in/sericulture.html (viewed 13 August 2007).

23 http://indiansilk.kar.nic.in/statistics.html (viewed 13 August 2007).

24 http://www.sciencemuseum.org.uk/objects/plastics_and_modern_materials/1965-480.aspx (viewed 14 August 2007).

25 http://www.costumes.org/ADVICE/TEXTILES/NYLONArticle.htm (viewed 14 August 2007).

26 http://www.ifm.eng.cam.ac.uk/sustainability/projects/mass/UK textiles.pdf (viewed 14 August 2007).

27 http://www.fibersource.com/f-tutor/LCA-Chapter%202.htm#RESULTS%20AND%20DISCUSSION (viewed 14 August 2007).

28 http://www.patagonia.com/pdf/en_US/common_thread_exec_summary.pdf (viewed 14 August 2007).

29 http://www.fibersource.com/f-tutor/LCA-Chapter%202-1.htm (viewed 7 May 2008).

30 Shakespeare, *A Midsummer Night's Dream*, III.iii.76.

31 http://www.npr.org/templates/story/story.php?storyId=10874230 (viewed 7 May 2008).

32 Jaime Rios Calleja, personal communication with the authors, August 2007.

33 K. Slater, *Environmental Impact of Textiles* (Cambridge: Woodhead Publishing Ltd, 2003), p. 91.

34 J. Allwood, S. E. Laursen, C. M. de Rodriguez and N. M. P. Bocken, *Well Dressed?* (Cambridge: University of Cambridge Institute for Manufacturing, 2006), p. 16.

35 Ibid., p. 29.

36 http://www.defra.gov.uk/environment/statistics/land/kf/ldkf05.htm (viewed 14 August 2007).

37 http://www.defra.gov.uk/environment/statistics/land/kf/ldkf05.htm (viewed 14 August 2007).

38 Allwood et al., *Well Dressed?*, p. 38.

39 http://www.fibersource.com/f-tutor/LCA-Page.htm# EXECUTIVE%20SUMMARY (viewed 7 May 2008).

40 Ibid., p. 27.

41 http://www.defra.gov.uk/environment/consumerprod/energylabels/energylabel.pdf (viewed 4 September 2007).

42 http://www.energyrating.gov.au/appsearch/cwashers_srch.asp?sort=%5BNew+SRI%5D+DESC&list=basic&Elec=&HElec=&HUses=&Years=&type=All&capacity=all&brand=All&runout=on&B1=SEARCH (viewed 4 September 2007).

43 http://search.waterrating.com.au/cwashers_srch.asp?sort=%5Bwater_rating%5D+DESC&list=basic&Elec=&HElec=&HUses=&Years=&type=All&capacity=all&brand=All&B1=SEARCH (viewed 4 September 2007).

44 K. E. Fletcher and J. Dixon, *Laundry Work* (London: Pitman and Sons, 1963), p. 15.

45 Anon., *Laundry Washing and Bleaching* (n.p.: ICI Chemical Industries Ltd, n.d. [c. 1930]), p. 32.

46 The Woman's Institute, *Care of Clothing* (London: International Educational Publishing Company, 1925), p. 32.

47 Fletcher and Dixon, *Laundry Work*, p. 11.

48 http://www.ukcpi.org/educ/index.html (viewed 7 September 2007).

49 http://www.environmental-expert.com/articles/article1150/article1150.htm (viewed 7 September 2007).

50 http://cahe.nmsu.edu/pubs/_c/c-503.html (viewed 17 October 2007).

51 http://www.scienceinthebox.com/en_UK/sustainability/laundrydetergent_en.html (viewed 7 September 2007).

52 A. Steinemann, 2004, 'Human exposure, health hazards, and environmental regulation', *Environmental Impact Assessment Review*, 24 (Oct./Nov. 2004), pp. 695–710.

53 B. Philip, M. M. Mumtaz, J. R. Latendresse and H. M. Mahendale, 'Impact of repeated exposure on toxicity of perchloroethylene in Swiss Webster mice', *Toxicology*, 232:1/2 (2007), pp. 1–14.

54 http://www.hsrc-ssw.org/update3.pdf (viewed 7 September 2007).

55 http://www.mntap.umn.edu/drycl/54-ReductAlt.htm (viewed 12 September 2007).

56 http://www.mntap.umn.edu/drycl/22-AltDryCl.htm (viewed 12 September 2007).

57 J. Craik, *Uniforms Exposed: From Conformity to Transgression* (Oxford: Berg Publishers, 2005), p. 58.

58 http://www.nomarmiteintunisia.co.uk/educationintunisia.htm (viewed 12 September 2007).

59 D. R. Lockyer and R. A. Champion, *Agriculture, Ecosystems & Environment*, 86:3 (2001), pp. 237–46.

60 http://www.sciencedirect.com/science?_ob=ArticleURL&_udi=B7581-4KC47H6-D&_user=1495406&_coverDate=07%2F31%2F2006&_rdoc=1&_fmt=&_orig=search&_sort=d&view=c&_acct=C000053190&_version=1&_urlVersion=0&_userid=1495406&md5=a1ef47c03ace266a6d0fa48294fcde7d (viewed 12 September 2007).

61 http://www.maf.govt.nz/mafnet/rural-nz/sustainable-resource-use/climate/greenhouse-gas-policies/greengas-14.htm (viewed 14 September 2007).

62 http://www.maf.govt.nz/mafnet/rural-nz/sustainable-resource-use/climate/abatement-of-agricultural-greenhouse-gas-emissions/abatement-of-agricultural-greenhouse-gas-emissions-12.htm (viewed 14 September 2007).

63 http://www.maf.govt.nz/forestry/pfsi/carbon-sequestration-rates.htm (viewed 14 September 2007).

64 N. C. Ruck, *Building Design and Human Performance* (New York: Van Nostrand Reinhold, 1989), pp. 7–8.

65 T. Markus and E. N. Morris, *Buildings, Climate and Energy* (London: Pitman, 1980), p. 44.

66 http://www.sd48.bc.ca/pdf/MoE%20-%20Class%20Size%20-%20SD48.pdf (viewed 19 September 2007).

67 http://www.cdnportable.com/Classrooms.7.xpc (viewed 19 September 2007).

68 T. Arimes, *HVAC and Chemical Resistance Handbook for the Engineer and Architect* (n.p.: BCT Inc., 1994), pp. 11–34.

69 N. Mithraratne, B. Vale and R. Vale, *Sustainable Living: The Role of Whole Life Costs and Values* (London: Butterworth-Heinemann, 2007), p. 16.

70 http://www.timesonline.co.uk/tol/news/world/article525496.ece (viewed 5 October 2007).

71 http://www.aquilar.co.uk/refrigerant.php (viewed 5 October 2007).

72 http://business.fullerton.edu/finance/journal/papers/pdf/past/vol11no2/v11p183.pdf (viewed 5 October 2007).

73 BRECSU/ETSU, 'Energy use in offices', *Energy Consumption Guide 19* (2000), UK Government Energy Efficiency Best Practice Programme, p. 21, at http://www.cibse.org/pdfs/ECG019.pdf (viewed 5 October 2007).

74 *The Ampere Strikes Back: How Consumer Electronics are Taking Over the World* (London: Energy Saving Trust, 2007), p. 3.

75 Data derived from J. I. Utley and L. D. Shorrock, *Domestic Energy Fact File* (Watford: Building Research Establishment, 2006), Fig. 86, p. 67, and Table 56, p. 122.

76 Calculated from data given at http://www.statistics.gov.uk/CCI/nugget.asp?ID=7&Pos=1&ColRank=1&Rank=224 (viewed 29 April 2008).

77 http://reviews.cnet.com/4520-6475_7-6400401-3.html?tag=arw (viewed 4 January 2007).

78 Calculated from http://www.ukenergy.co.uk/pages/calculation.html (viewed 29 April 2008).

79 http://www.eeca.govt.nz/labelling-and-standards/standby-power/index.html (viewed 1 May 2008).

80 http://standby.lbl.gov/faq.html (viewed 7 May 2008).

81 http://berkeley.edu/news/media/releases/2001/02/09_energ.html (viewed 1 May 2008).

82 http://www.rsa.org.uk/projects/weee_man.asp (viewed 1 May 2008).

83 http://www.iowadnr.com/waste/recycling/
hazards.html (viewed 1 May 2008).
84 http://ublib.buffalo.edu/libraries/projects/
cases/footprint/calculations%20housing.html
(viewed 7 May 2008).
85 Interpreted from values for television, dvd and
computer from Mithraratne et al., *Sustainable Living*, p. 136.
86 Panasonic 42" High Definition Plasma TVTH-
42PV700AZ weighs 30.0 kg: http://panasonic.co.nz/
product-detail$product$894$.html (viewed 8 May 2008).
87 Sky+ set-top box assumed as 160 GB hard disk recorder:
Sony RDRHX750B Hard Disk Drive/DVD recorder, 160 GB
(4.4 kg): see http://www.sony.co.nz/products/product/blu-
ray-and-dvd/dvd-recorder/rdrhx750b.jsp
(viewed 8 May 2008).
88 Sony HTDDW7000 in-a-box home theatre, weight
adjusted to allow for assumed packaging etc.:
http://www.sony.co.nz/products/product/home-theatre/
theatre-systems/htddw7000.jsp (viewed 15 January 2009).
89 HP Pavilion Media Center a1310n Desktop PC (AMD
Athlon 64 3700+ Processor, 1 GB RAM, 200 GB Hard
Drive, Dbl Layer DVD+/-R/RW Drive), 24 lb (10.9 kg): see
http://www.amazon.com/Pavilion-Center-a1310n-Desktop-
Processor/dp/B000E1VZ7M (viewed 8 May 2008).
90 Canon Pixma ip4200 printer, 14.8 lb (6.7 kg): see
http://www.usa.canon.com/consumer/controller?act=Model
InfoAct&fcategoryid=184&modelid=11641#ModelTechSpecs
Act (viewed 8 May 2008).
91 CanoScan LiDE90 Color Image Scanner, 3.5 lb (1.6 kg):
see http://www.usa.canon.com/consumer/controller?act=
ModelInfoAct&tabact=ModelTechSpecsTabAct&fcategoryid
=119&modelid=15562 (viewed 8 May 2008).
92 Xbox 360, 7.7 lb (3.5 kg): see http://www.xbox.com/en-
AU/support/xbox360/manuals/xbox360specs.htm
(viewed 8 May 2008).
93 Mithraratne et al., *Sustainable Living*, p. 219.
94 http://www.ita.doc.gov/td/ocg/petfood_overview04.pdf
(viewed 6 May 2008).
95 http://www.ita.doc.gov/td/ocg/exp311111.htm
(viewed 6 May 2008).
96 http://www.ita.doc.gov/td/ocg/imp311111.htm
(viewed 6 May 2008)
97 http://www.stats.govt.nz/store/2006/05/subnational-
population-estimates-jun00-mr.htm (viewed 12 January 2008).
98 http://www.petfoodnz.co.nz/market.htm
(viewed 12 January 2008).
99 http://www.mapsofworld.com/world-top-ten/
countries-with-most-pet-cat-population.html
(viewed 12 January 2008).
100 http://uk.encarta.msn.com/encyclopedia_761573010/
United_States_of_America.html (viewed 12 January 2008).
101 http://www.petfoodnz.co.nz/market.htm
(viewed 12 January 2008).
102 F. C. Baldock, L. Alexander and S. J. More, 'Estimated
and predicted changes in the cat population of Australian
households from 1979 to 2005', *Australian Vet Journal*, 81:5
(2003), p. 289.
103 http://www.petfoodnz.co.nz/market.htm
(viewed 13 January 2008).
104 http://uk.encarta.msn.com/text_761553483__1/
United_Kingdom.html (viewed 13 January 2008).
105 http://www.rds-online.org.uk/pages/
page.asp?i_ToolbarID=2&i_PageID=2456
(viewed 2 March 2008).
106 http://uk.encarta.msn.com/text_761573055__1/
China.html (viewed 19 January 2008).
107 http://www.capital.net/com/phuston/cateating.html
(viewed 19 January 2008).
108 http://www.stats.govt.nz/store/2006/05/subnational-
population-estimates-jun00-mr.htm
(viewed 19 January 2008).
109 http://catchow.com/catcarecenter_3_adult_1.aspx?
storyID=60&category=5 (viewed 2 March 2008).
110 http://www.associatedcontent.com/article/468122/
eating_dry_food_does_not_cause_a_cat.html
(viewed 5 March 2008).
111 http://www.bluebuff.com/products/cats/wilderness-
cat.shtml (viewed 5 March 2008).
112 http://www.purinaone.com/Products/
ProductDetails.aspx?ProductId=B8F05F79-DB9E-4E28-
9BE2-B78DE28E37F0 (viewed 5 March 2008).
113 http://www.fsis.usda.gov/Fact_Sheets/Water_in_Meats/
index.asp (viewed 5 March 2008).
114 http://www.patentstorm.us/patents/6818241-
claims.html (viewed 7 March 2008).
115 http://www.fatcatinc.com/html_site/yourcat_archive.
shtml?15 (viewed 7 March 2008).
116 http://products.peapod.com/491.html
(viewed 7 March 2008).
117 http://www.mapsofworld.com/world-top-ten/countries-
with-most-pet-cat-population.html (viewed 7 March 2008).
118 http://www.felinecrf.org/tinned_food.htm
(viewed 7 March 2008).
119 http://www.fsis.usda.gov/Fact_Sheets/Water_in_Meats/
index.asp (viewed 7 March 2008).
120 K. A. Houpt, *Domestic Animal Behaviour* (Oxford:
Blackwell Publishing, 2005), p. 330:
http://books.google.co.nz/books?id=ZFQAs8Ag1z0C&pg=
PA330&lpg=PA330&dq=do+cats+prefer+fish&source=web
&ots=zRRiXfwV4T&sig=JfwlpuUQq_QpENKiqkYdbrjAeX
A&hl=en (viewed 9 March 2008).
121 http://www.onlynaturalpet.com/products/Natures-
Variety-Freeze-Dried-Diets/131056.aspx
(viewed 9 March 2008).
122 http://mstecker.com/pages/nz_fp.htm
(viewed 9 March 2008).
123 http://www.catinfo.org/commercialcannedfoods.htm
(viewed 9 March 2008).
124 http://www.bret.org.uk/soc1.htm (viewed 9 March 2008).
125 http://pethealth101.com/Senior_pets/
senior_life_expectancy.shtml (viewed 9 March 2008).
126 http://www.rds-online.org.uk/pages/
page.asp?i_ToolbarID=2&i_PageID=2456
(viewed 9 March 2008).
127 http://www.braintree.gov.uk/Braintree/environment/
streetscene/Promotions/RatCampaign.htm
(viewed 9 March 2008).
128 http://www.ratbehavior.org/WildRats.htm
(viewed 9 March 2008).
129 Ibid.
130 http://www.dawsonfurs.co.nz/pooyum.html
(viewed 6 May 2008).
131 http://www.compostthis.co.uk/item/cat-waste-and-
litter (viewed 12 March 2008).
132 http://www.sfgate.com/cgi-bin/article.cgi?f=/g/a/
2007/11/13/petscol.DTL (viewed 12 March 2008).
133 http://environment.about.com/od/renewableenergy/a/
animalwaste.htm (viewed 12 March 2008).

134 http://www.uswitch.com/news/energy/AprJun2005/
uk-homes-to-get-methane-gas.cmsx?ref=live_com
(viewed 12 March 2008).
135 B. Vale and R. Vale, *The Self-Sufficient House* (London:
Macmillan, 1980), p. 27.
136 http://library.thinkquest.org/C001472/en/
development/beaufort.html (viewed 14 March 2008).
137 *CIBSE Guide Volume A* (London: The Chartered
Institution of Building Services Engineers, 1970),
Table A7.3, p. A7-4.
138 B. Vale and R. Vale, *The New Autonomous House*
(London: Thames & Hudson, 2000), p. 95.
139 Ibid., p. 199.
140 http://www.doc.govt.nz/templates/Multipage
DocumentPage.aspx?id=39664 (viewed 14 March 2008).
141 For example, http://www.cvni.org/biodiversity/advice/
gardens/wildlife_garden (viewed 14 March 2008).
142 http://www.ehsni.gov.uk/other-index/education/edu-
resources/factsheets/fs-wildlifegardening.htm
(viewed 16 March 2008).
143 https://www.abcbirds.org/abcprograms/policy/cats/
materials/predation.pdf (viewed 16 March 2008).
144 D. Vackar, *Ecological Footprint and Biodiversity* (n.d.),
at http://www.brass.cf.ac.uk/uploads/Vackar_M74.pdf
(viewed 16 March 2008).
145 http://www.petsandpeople.org/cat-ther.htm
(viewed 16 March 2008).
146 http://www.wcu.edu/pubinfo/news/
Herzogdog04.htm (viewed 16 March 2008).
147 http://mapsofworld.com/world-top-ten/countries-with-
most-pet-dog-population.html (viewed 16 March 2008).
148 S. Chansomsak and S. Hengrasmee, personal
communication with the authors, 27 March 2008.
149 http://www.cat-pregnancy-report.com/cat-food.html
(viewed 19 March 2008).
150 http://www.animed.org/dogs_and_cats_table_food. htm
(viewed 19 March 2008).
151 http://www.dogfacts.org/dog-diet-dog-facts.htm
(viewed 19 March 2008).
152 http://puppydogweb.com/caninebreeds/
cockerspaniel.htm (viewed 19 March 2008).
153 http://www.nextdaypets.com/directory/breeds/
1100045 (viewed 19 March 2008).
154 http://formulak.co.uk/about-fourmula-k.html
(viewed 19 March 2008).
155 http://formulak.co.uk/amount.htm
(viewed 19 March 2008).
156 http://www.unece.org/trans/main/ter/Countries/
italy.htm (viewed 19 March 2008).
157 http://www.nationmaster.com/time.php?stat=agr_agr_
lan_sq_km-agriculture-agricultural-land-sq-km&country=
it-italy (viewed 19 March 2008).
158 http://www.demographia.com/db-japancultura.htm
(viewed 19 March 2008).
159 Personal communication with the authors, March 2008.
160 http://www.kittenkaboodle.com/Merchant2/
merchant.mv?Session_ID=47D9F09C0004C45E000047
DE00000000&Screen=PROD&Product_Code=01615&
Category_Code=Dog-Houses (viewed 21 March 2008).
161 Mithraratne et al., *Sustainable Living*, p. 219.
162 http://www.petwebsite.com/hamsters/hamster_care.
htm (viewed 21 March 2008).
163 http://www.petwebsite.com/hamsters/hamster_mix.
htm (viewed 21 March 2008).

164 http://groups.msn.com/HamsterHouse-/
soyouthink.msnw (viewed 21 March 2008).
165 http://www.petplanet.co.uk/petplanet/kids/
kidshamster.htm (viewed 21 March 2008).
166 http://www.hamsterific.com/Nutrition.cfm
(viewed 21 March 2008).
167 http://www.seapets.co.uk/view-products/category/1193.
html (viewed 21 March 2008).
168 http://www.petwebsite.com/hamsters/
home_made_hamster_cages.htm (viewed 21 March 2008).
169 G. Burgess and J. G. Fernandez-Velasco, 'Materials,
operational energy inputs, and net energy ratio for
photobiological hydrogen production', *International Journal
of Hydrogen Energy*, 32:9 (2007), at
http://www.sciencedirect.com/science?_ob=ArticleURL&_
udi=B6V3F-4MHPHFM-2&_user=1495406&_rdoc=1&_
fmt=&_orig=search&_sort=d&view=c&_acct=C000053190
&_version=1&_urlVersion=0&_userid=1495406&md5=0a
4b932a1ef82f28913dc9139a7239bb#secx6
(viewed 21 March 2008).
170 http://www.8020.net/HT-Series-36.asp
(viewed 21 March 2008).
171 Mithraratne et al., *Sustainable Living*, p. 218.
172 http://www.petplanet.co.uk/product.asp?dept_id=63&
pf_id=6551 (viewed 21 March 2008).
173 http://www.p2pays.org/ref/24/23694.pdf
(viewed 21 March 2008).
174 Mithraratne et al., *Sustainable Living*, p. 217.
175 http://exoticpets.about.com/od/birds/f/birdlifespan.htm
(viewed 23 March 2008).
176 http://exoticpets.about.com/cs/birds/a/canaries.htm
(viewed 23 March 2008).
177 http://www.upatsix.com/faq/canary.htm
(viewed 23 March 2008).
178 http://www.msha.gov/CENTURY/CANARY/PAGE2.asp
(viewed 23 March 2008).
179 http://news.bbc.co.uk/onthisday/hi/dates/stories/
december/30/newsid_2547000/2547587.stm
(viewed 23 March 2008).
180 http://www.canaryadvisor.com/canary-seed.html
(viewed 23 March 2008).
181 http://www.upatsix.com/faq/canary.htm
(viewed 23 March 2008).
182 http://members.aol.com/PacificASC/artpelle.htm
(viewed 23 March 2008).
183 Ibid.
184 http://www.goldeneggs.com.au/nutrition/
what_is_an_egg.html (viewed 23 March 2008).
185 http://www.suite101.com/article.cfm/
small_hookbills/59414/2 (viewed 23 March 2008).
186 http://www4.shopping.com/xPC-Prevue_Hendryx_
Prevue_Hendryx_Cockatiel_Small_Parrot_Cage_22_W_
X_15_D_X_23_H_Black (viewed 23 March 2008).
187 http://news.bbc.co.uk/1/hi/world/asia-pacific/
7283299.stm (viewed 26 March 2008).
188 http://www.bristol-aquarists.org.uk/goldfish/
common/common.htm (viewed 26 March 2008).
189 http://www.goldfishpages.com/History%20Page.htm
(viewed 26 March 2008).
190 http://www.goldfishpages.com/
new_page_55311111111121112111121112113.htm
(viewed 26 March 2008).
191 http://www.wetpetz.com/goldfish.htm
(viewed 26 March 2008).

192 http://www.ehow.com/how_2990_feed-goldfish.html (viewed 26 March 2008).
193 http://www.goldfishinfo.com/general.htm#fed (viewed 26 March 2008).
194 http://www.vendian.org/envelope/diro/grain_feel.html (viewed 26 March 2008).
195 http://www.simetric.co.uk/si_kitchen.htm (viewed 26 March 2008).
196 http://www.brooklands.co.nz/wardley/wgold.htm (viewed 26 March 2008).
197 http://www.wetpetz.com/goldfish.htm (viewed 26 March 2008).
198 http://www.goldfishinfo.com/goldlife.htm (viewed 26 March 2008).
199 http://news.bbc.co.uk/2/hi/uk_news/england/devon/4341254.stm (viewed 26 March 2008).
200 http://www.thekrib.com/Fish/goldfish.html (viewed 26 March 2008).
201 http://www.petlibrary.com/goldfish/fishcare.htm (viewed 26 March 2008).
202 N. Chambers, C. Simmons and M. Wackernagel, *Sharing Nature's Interest* (London: Earthscan, 2000), p. 98.
203 http://www.uniquaria.com/articles/goldfish.html (viewed 26 March 2008).
204 http://saltaquarium.about.com/cs/aquariumdiy/l/blcustomtank.htm (viewed 26 March 2008).
205 Mithraratne et al., *Sustainable Living*, p. 217.
206 http://exoticpets.about.com/cs/rabbits/a/rabbitcare.htm (viewed 26 March 2008).
207 J. C. Sandford, *The Domestic Rabbit* (London: Granada Publishing Ltd, 3rd edn 1979), p. 223.
208 Ibid., p. 29.
209 Ibid., p. 201.
210 http://www.ardengrabbit.com/facts.html (viewed 26 March 2008).
211 Sandford, *The Domestic Rabbit*, p. 125.
212 http://www.age.psu.edu/extension/ip/IP729-31.pdf (viewed 2 April 2008).
213 Mithraratne et al., *Sustainable Living*, p. 219.
214 B. Martin, *Rabbits as a New Pet* (Neptune City, N.J.: T.F.H. Publications, 1990), p. 12.
215 http://www.meshdirect.co.uk/Chicken-Wire-Netting-13mm-hole-size-1200-mm-wide-x-10-metre-roll-pr-177.html (viewed 2 April 2008).
216 Sandford, *The Domestic Rabbit*, p. 105.
217 http://www.nationmaster.com/graph/agr_yie_cor-agriculture-yield-corn (viewed 2 April 2008).
218 http://www.nationmaster.com/graph/agr_yie_oat-agriculture-yield-oats (viewed 2 April 2008).
219 http://www.staff.ncl.ac.uk/r.s.shiel/Palace_Leas/weather.htm (viewed 2 April 2008).
220 http://eng.lenobl.ru/economics/agriculture/crops (viewed 2 April 2008).
221 Sandford, *The Domestic Rabbit*, p. 106.
222 Jaqui Macintosh, personal communication with the authors, 9 April 2008.
223 J. Worthington, *Natural Poultry Keeping* (London: Crosby, Lockwood and Son, 1970), p. 2.
224 http://www.downthelane.net/Page_7.html (viewed 2 April 2008).
225 http://www.downthelane.net/feedingchickens.html (viewed 2 April 2008).
226 http://www.marriagefeeds.co.uk/layers_pellets.htm (viewed 2 April 2008).
227 http://www.goldeneggs.com.au/nutrition/what_is_an_egg.html (viewed 2 April 2008).
228 http://www.greens.org.nz/searchdocs/other5330.html (viewed 2 April 2008).

CHAPTER 5: TIME TO SPARE

1 http://www.golf-research-group.com/start.html (viewed 5 November 2007).
2 http://www.golftoday.co.uk/news/yeartodate/news03/china.html (viewed 5 November 2007).
3 http://www.uneptie.org/pc/tourism/sust-tourism/env-3main.htm (viewed 5 November 2007).
4 S. Hengrasmee, *Indigenous Knowledge and Sustainable Community*, research report (University of Auckland, 2004).
5 http://www.scottishgolfhistory.net/eighteen_hole_round.htm (viewed 5 November 2007).
6 http://www.saa.gov.uk/practice_notes/e_to_i/mpc07.html (viewed 7 November 2007).
7 http://www.organicconsumers.org/corp/golf042604.cfm (viewed 7 November 2007).
8 N. Mithraratne and R. Vale, 'Water supply infrastructure and settlement patterns', *International Journal of Environmental, Cultural, Economic and Social Sustainability* 3:3 (2007), pp. 141–52.
9 N. Chambers, C. Simmons and M. Wackernagel, *Sharing Nature's Interest* (London: Earthscan, 2000), p. 98.
10 Anon., *The Hundred Best Houses: The Book of the House and Cottage Exhibition 1911* (London: The Exhibition Committee, 1911).
11 http://encarta.msn.com/encyclopedia_761572379/Soccer.html (viewed 7 November 2007).
12 http://www.fifa.com/flash/lotg/football/en/Laws1_01.htm (viewed 7 November 2007).
13 http://www.fifa.com/aboutfifa/media/newsid=529882.html (viewed 7 November 2007).
14 http://www.fifa.com/mm/document/fifafacts/bcoffsurv/bigcount.summaryreport_7022.pdf (viewed 7 November 2007).
15 Ibid.
16 http://www.aucklandcity.govt.nz/stadium/docs/PortStadiumBledisloeReport.pdf (viewed 7 November 2007).
17 http://www.westpactruststadium.co.nz/information/facts.cfm (viewed 7 November 2007).
18 http://zoomin.co.nz/nz/wellington/thorndon/-westpac+stadium (viewed 7 November 2007).
19 http://en.wikipedia.org/wiki/Sheffield_Wednesday_F.C.#Current_first-team_squad (viewed 7 November 2007).
20 http://www.itftennis.com/abouttheitf/rulesregs/rules.asp (viewed 12 November 2007).
21 http://www.newenglandsealcoating.com/tennis.htm (viewed 12 November 2007).
22 http://www.lowerhutttennisclub.com/AnReport06.pdf (viewed 12 November 2007).
23 http://www.karoritennis.co.nz (viewed 6 January 2008).
24 http://www.tennis.com/yourgame/asktheeditors/asktheeditors.aspx?id=1430 (viewed 12 November 2007).
25 http://www.norcal.usta.com/NEWS/fullstory.sps?iNewsid=367601&itype=1941 (viewed 12 November 2007).
26 http://www.census.gov/Press-Release/www/releases/archives/population/003161.html (viewed 12 November 2007).
27 http://www.norcal.usta.com/NEWS/fullstory.sps?iNewsid=367601&itype=1941 (viewed 12 November 2007).

28 http://www.jpricebath.co.uk/page4.html (viewed 14 January 2008).
29 http://www.speedski.com/HistoryofSkiing.htm (viewed 3 December 2007).
30 Ibid.
31 http://seattletimes.nwsource.com/html/outdoors/2003431890_nwwwhistler16.html (viewed 3 December 2007).
32 http://72.14.253.104/search?q=cache:Gv92T_K5CZYJ: whistlerrealestate.ca/%3Fwhistlerresort%26PHPSESSID%3D8bcf084d1fe65043f21f7703a23b85de+number+of+visitors+ski+resort&hl=en&ct=clnk&cd=2&gl=nz (viewed 3 December 2007).
33 http://www.whistlerblackcomb.com/index.htm (viewed 3 December 2007).
34 Data from M. Beyrouti, 'More skiers and snowboarders are visiting Canadian ski areas', Winter Statistics Canada, Travel-Log, 19:1 (2000), p. 3; available at http://www.statcan.gc.ca/pub/87-003-x/87-003-x2000001-eng.pdf (viewed 15 January 2009).
35 http://www.fips.cam.org/Member%20Countries.html (viewed 3 December 2007).
36 http://www.guardian.co.uk/travel/2006/dec/23/green.skiing.saturday?page=2 (viewed 3 December 2007).
37 http://www.ski-europe.com/about/environment.html (viewed 3 December 2007).
38 http://www.cipra.org/en/alpmedia/news/1036 (viewed 3 December 2007).
39 http://www.everydayswim.org/news_item.asp?section=0001000100010008&itemid=139&itemTitle=Everyday+Swim+shares+lessons+with+Industry (viewed 3 December 2007).
40 http://www.norfolkesinet.org.uk/FileSystem/upfile/j00007/Swimming_charter.pdf (viewed 5 December 2007).
41 http://www.cambridge.gov.uk/ccm/content/parks-and-recreation/pools/jesus-green.en (viewed 5 December 2007).
42 http://www.cambridge.gov.uk/ccm/content/policy-and-projects/population-statistics.en (viewed 5 December 2007).
43 http://www.theleys.net/extracurricular/sport/swimming.html (viewed 5 December 2007).
44 Anon., Everday Swim Half-time Report (2007), p. 1, available at http://www.everydayswim.org (accessed 15 January 2009).
45 http://www.statistics.gov.uk/CCI/nugget.asp?ID=6 (viewed 5 December 2007).
46 http://www.ema.org.nz/publications/papers/jamieson_tromop1996.pdf (viewed 14 March 2008).
47 Swimming Pool Issues (Kuranda, Qld.: International Non-toxic Water-treatment Association, 2005), p. 3.
48 E. Hood, 'Tap water and trihalomethanes: flow of concern continues', Environmental Health Perspectives, 113:7 (2005).
49 Swimming Pool Issues.
50 http://www.burlesontx.com/Acrobat/Swimming%20Pool%20Discharge%20Info.pdf (viewed 10 December 2007).
51 http://www.uneptie.org/pc/tourism/sust-tourism/env-3main.htm (viewed 10 December 2007).
52 http://www.mainlandragons.co.nz/introduction.html (viewed 10 December 2007).
53 http://www.idbf.org/documents/DB_History_Culture.pdf (viewed 10 December 2007).
54 http://us.tom.com/english/1853.htm (viewed 10 December 2007).
55 http://www.bbc.co.uk/history/ancient/greeks/greek_olympics_gallery_06.shtml (viewed 10 December 2007).
56 http://www.dickssportinggoods.com/sm-golf-club-set-buyers-guide—bg-222851.html (viewed 12 December 2007).
57 http://answers.yahoo.com/question/index?qid=20060926151559AARDTF0 (viewed 12 December 2007).
58 http://www.med.govt.nz/templates/ContentTopicSummary___21417.aspx (viewed 12 December 2007).
59 http://library.thinkquest.org/10556/english/high/history/histo5.htm (viewed 12 December 2007).
60 http://irpec.lgm.gov.my/prd_golf.html (viewed 12 December 2007).
61 S. Smith in Golf Digest, November 1999 issue.
62 http://www.consumerreports.org/cro/home-garden/sports-exercise-equipment/golf-balls-506/overview/index.htm (viewed 12 December 2007).
63 Mithraratne et al., Sustainable Living, p. 218.
64 Based on 1 PJ to run a city of 30,000, or the city of Nelson in New Zealand: Nigel Isaccs, personal communication with the authors, December 2007.
65 http://www.statistics.gov.uk/census2001/pyramids/pages/00ec.asp (viewed 12 December 2007).
66 http://hamilton.co.nz/page/pageid/2145833419 (viewed 12 December 2007).
67 http://stores.channeladvisor.com/lost-golf-balls-retail (viewed 14 March 2008).
68 http://www.edwinwattsgolf.com/category2_golf-balls_10001_10001_1134_-1_Y.htm (viewed 14 March 2008).
69 http://www.golf-research-group.com/start.html (viewed 17 December 2007).
70 http://www.ncaonline.org/products/golf-cars/index.shtml (viewed 17 December 2007).
71 http://www.ezgo.com/golf/fleet/txt.html (viewed 17 December 2007).
72 http://thesandtrap.com/columns/the_numbers_game/exercise (viewed 17 December 2007).
73 National Greenhouse Gas Inventory: Analysis of Recent Trends and Greenhouse Indicators 1990 to 2002; and Australian Methodology for the Estimation of Greenhouse Gas Emissions and Sinks 2002 (both Canberra: Australian Greenhouse Office, 2002).
74 http://www.affordable-solar.com/battery.discharge.life.htm (viewed 8 January 2008).
75 http://www.ezgo.com/golf/fleet/txt.html (viewed 8 January 2008).
76 http://www.trojan-battery.com/Products/GolfCart.aspx (viewed 8 January 2008).
77 http://www.motorculture.co.uk/servicing.html (viewed 8 January 2008).
78 http://www.thefreedictionary.com/round+of+golf (viewed 8 January 2008).
79 http://thesandtrap.com/forum/showthread.php?s=b393daaa274ae3b7634d5fe8dcddoa3a&p=70034#post70034 (viewed 8 January 2008).
80 http://wings.avkids.com/Tennis/Book/racquet-01.html (viewed 8 January 2008).
81 http://www.academy.com/index.php?page=content&target=sports_tips/tennis/raquets_made_of (viewed 11 January 2008).
82 http://www.tennis-warehouse.com/LC/Naturalgut.html (viewed 11 January 2008).
83 http://www.tennis-warehouse.com/LC/SelectingRacquet/SelectingRacquet.html (viewed 11 January 2008).
84 http://www.victoria.ac.nz/cbpr/documents/pdfs/ee-co2_report_2003.pdf (viewed 11 January 2008).

85 http://www.level.org.nz/fileadmin/downloads/ Materials/LevelMCarpet.pdf (viewed 11 January 2008).
86 http://query.nytimes.com/gst/abstract.html?res= 940CE2DA1739E233A25756C2A9619C946496D6CF (viewed 11 January 2008).
87 http://www.cliffrichardtennis.org/planet_tennis/ history.htm (viewed 14 January 2008).
88 http://www.itftennis.com/technical/equipment/balls/ history.asp (viewed 14 January 2008).
89 http://www.hollandandsherry.com/pages/apparel/ textile_guide/fabric_types.htm#14 (viewed 14 January 2008).
90 http://www.love-tennis.net/Tennis-Balls/Selecting-the-correct-tennis-balls.html (viewed 14 January 2008).
91 http://www.athleticscholarships.net/sports-equipment-tennis.htm (viewed 14 January 2008).
92 http://www.inive.org/members_area/medias/pdf/ Inive%5Cpalenc%5C2005%5CAlmeida.pdf (viewed 14 January 2008).
93 http://www.my-youth-soccer-guide.com/soccer-law-2. html (viewed 14 January 2008).
94 http://soccerballworld.com/Oldestball.htm (viewed 14 January 2008).
95 http://soccerballworld.com/Construction.htm#Ball%20 Construction (viewed 14 January 2008).
96 http://www.ipenz.org.nz/ipenz/publications/indexes/ transaction/transactions97/civil/7baird.pdf (viewed 14 January 2008).
97 http://www.fifa.com/mm/document/fifafacts/ bcoffsurv/bigcount.summaryreport_7022.pdf (viewed 7 November 2007).
98 http://www.madehow.com/Volume-2/Ski.html (viewed 14 January 2008).
99 Ibid.
100 http://www.telemarktips.com/TeleNews83.html (viewed 14 January 2008).
101 Mithraratne et al., *Sustainable Living*, p. 219.
102 Ibid., p. 218.
103 http://www.infinityskipoles.com/basket_overviewe.html (viewed 16 January 2008).
104 Mithraratne et al., *Sustainable Living*, p. 218.
105 http://www.recovery-insulation.co.uk/ insulation_comparison.html (viewed 16 January 2008).
106 http://www.corkdirect.com/plank.html (viewed 16 January 2008).
107 http://www.vintageskiworld.com/ Museum_of_vintage_antique_ski_poles_s/49.htm (viewed 16 January 2008).
108 http://www.goode.com/skipoles.html (viewed 16 January 2008).
109 http://www.infinityskipoles.com/shaft_overviewe.html (viewed 16 January 2008).
110 http://www.outdoormania.co.uk/ Product.aspx?Product=Transcender_Walking_Poles_(Pair) &ProductID=336 (viewed 16 January 2008).
111 http://www.ifyouski.com/Gear/Doc/FAQ (viewed 16 January 2008).
112 http://entertainment.howstuffworks.com/how-to-maintain-skis.htm (viewed 16 January 2008).
113 http://www.skilifts.org/glossary.htm (viewed 18 January 2008).
114 http://skilift.nashacanada.com (viewed 18 January 2008).
115 http://www.directboats.com/brigstrat5hp.html (viewed 18 January 2008).
116 Mithraratne et al., *Sustainable Living*, p. 218.
117 Ibid.
118 http://www4.briggsandstratton.com/display/ router.asp?DocID=80682 (viewed 18 January 2008).
119 from http://www.greenhouse.gov.au/fuelguide (viewed 31 July 2007).
120 http://www.city-data.com/forum/colorado/116216-so-how-often-do-you-really.html (viewed 18 January 2008).
121 http://www.skilifts.org/glossary.htm (viewed 21 January 2008).
122 http://www.dragonboat.org.hk/en/dbr/ boatspecification.html (viewed 21 January 2008).
123 http://www.spiritabreast.com/page.php?id=29 (viewed 21 January 2008).
124 http://www.miamidragon.com/about.html (viewed 21 January 2008).
125 Mithraratne et al., *Sustainable Living*, p. 218.
126 http://www.hkdbf-ny.org/ home.php?choice=history&PHPSESSID=4d4fe868242e95 847dc2bedd57663298 (viewed 21 January 2008).
127 Mithraratne et al., *Sustainable Living*, p. 219.
128 http://www.catalinatrading.com/sustainability.htm (viewed 21 January 2008).
129 http://www.eurodamnews.com/2007/11/19/ sustainable-teak-for-decking-comes-from-thailand (viewed 21 January 2008).
130 Calculated using the Friends of Conservation carbon off-set calculator at http://www.friendsofconservation.org.uk/min/ calculatenew1a.asp (viewed 14 March 2008).
131 M. Lenzen, 'Total requirements of energy and greenhouse gases for Australian transport', *Transportation Research D*, 4:4 (July 1999), pp. 265–90.
132 http://www.mstrain.org/products/firstclass/ westcoastexpress/index.htm (viewed 17 March 2008).
133 http://www.eurostar.com/UK/uk/leisure/ about_eurostar/environment/off_setting.jsp (viewed 17 March 2008).
134 http://www.seat61.com/Switzerland.htm (viewed 17 March 2008).
135 http://www.alleuroperail.com/eurorail-high-speed-train.htm (viewed 17 March 2008).
136 http://www.eurostar.com/UK/uk/leisure/ about_eurostar/environment/greener_than_flying.jsp (viewed 17 March 2008).
137 http://www.zurich.co.uk/zurichcares/home/news/ latestnews/Tour+de+Zurich+cycle+ride.htm (viewed 17 March 2008).
138 http://www.forcestravel.com/ferry.php (viewed 17 March 2008).
139 http://www.nutristrategy.com/activitylist3.htm (viewed 19 March 2008).
140 http://www.nutristrategy.com/activitylist.htm (viewed 19 March 2008).
141 http://www.hotlyrics.net/lyrics/E/Ella_Fitzgerald/ _T_Ain_t_What_You_Do_It_s_The_Way_That_You_Do _It.html (viewed 19 March 2008).
142 http://www.nutristrategy.com/activitylist3.htm (viewed 19 March 2008).
143 http://www.livingroot.org/modules.php?name= News&file=article&sid=92 (viewed 19 March 2008).
144 http://www.clevelandclinic.org/heartcenter/pub/ guide/prevention/exercise/howmuchisenough.htm (viewed 20 March 2008).

145 http://www.historyofsports.net (viewed 20 March 2008).

146 http://www.youtube.com/watch?v=FoU81dukvMc& feature=related (viewed 20 March 2008).

147 http://www.statsci.org/data/oz/swimming.html (viewed 20 March 2008). The figure of 19.72 seconds for a 25 m lap used here was averaged from 24 values for swimming the same distance.

148 http://www.nutristrategy.com/activitylist4.htm (viewed 20 March 2008).

149 The assumption is 15 seconds to climb a normal flight of stairs.

150 http://www.7is7.com/otto/countries.html (viewed 20 March 2008).

151 http://www.nationalpsychologist.com/articles/ art_v16n2_2.htm (viewed 20 March 2008).

152 http://findarticles.com/p/articles/mi_m0EIN/ is_1999_Sept_9/ai_55701525 (viewed 21 March 2008).

153 http://www.penguinclassics.co.uk/nf/shared/ WebDisplay/0,,47594_1_5,00.html (viewed 21 March 2008).

154 http://www.conservatree.org/learn/EnviroIssues/ TreeStats.shtml (viewed 21 March 2008).

155 H. Greenwood and S. Maynard, *Digest of Statistics 2006* (Loughborough: LISU, 2006).

156 http://www.pbs.org/wgbh/amex/goebbels/filmmore/ ps_bookspeech.html (viewed 8 May 2008).

157 http://www2.edf.org/papercalculator/select.cfm (viewed 21 March 2008).

158 http://www.geoffswoodwork.co.uk/ book%20weights.htm (viewed 21 March 2008).

159 Mithraratne et al., *Sustainable Living*, p. 16.

160 Chambers et al., *Sharing Nature's Interest*.

161 http://www.carbontrust.co.uk/resource/measuring_co2/ Measuring_CO2_Methodologies.htm (viewed 24 March 2008).

162 http://www.mfe.govt.nz/publications/climate/ emissions-trading/10-emissions-trading-waste-sep07/10-emissions-trading-waste-sep07.pdf (viewed 24 March 2008).

163 http://www.oup.com/ca/about/publishing/cost (viewed 24 March 2008).

164 Boardman et al., *Reducing the Environmental Impact of Housing* (2003), ECI Report 31, Appendix E (2007) at http://www.rcep.org.uk/urban/report/eci-appe_embodied_energy.pdf (viewed 24 March 2008).

165 Using 2,793 MJ/m² from Mithraratne et al., *Sustainable Living*, p. 168.

166 Mithraratne et al., *Sustainable Living*, p. 219.

167 http://www.ukerc.ac.uk/Downloads/PDF/07/ 0706ESMMARKALpresKR2.pdf (viewed 1 April 2008.)

168 http://www.level.org.nz/energy/space-heating-and-cooling (viewed 1 April 2008).

169 Mithraratne et al., *Sustainable Living*, p. 51.

170 J. Yang, P. S. Brandon and A. C. Sidwell (eds), *Smart and Sustainable Built Environments* (Oxford: Blackwell Publishing, 2005), p. 113.

171 Using 2,793 MJ/m² from Mithraratne et al., *Sustainable Living*, p. 168.

172 http://www.teapotisland.com/TeaPot%20Island.htm (viewed 25 March 2008).

173 http://shopping.msn.com/results/teapots/bcatid7830/ amazon.com/12-12/forsale?text=category:teapots+Seller: Amazon.com&page=3 (viewed 25 March 2008).

174 http://shopping.msn.com/results/teapots/ bcatid7830/portmeirion/2-4201649/forsale?text=category: teapots+Brand:Portmeirion (viewed 25 March 2008).

175 Mithraratne et al., *Sustainable Living*, p. 215.

176 http://www.worldcollectorsnet.com/teapots (viewed 25 March 2008).

177 http://www.teapotisland.com/Guinness%20Book%20 Of%20Records.htm (viewed 25 March 2008).

178 J. Palmer and B. Boardman, *DELight: Domestic Efficient Lighting* (1998), p. 18, at http://www.iaeel.org/IAEEL/ Archive/Right_Light_Proceedings/DELight/Delight2.pdf (viewed 25 March 2008).

179 M. Stokes, T. Crosbie and S. Guy, 'Shedding light on domestic energy use: a cross-discipline study of lighting homes', *Proceedings of the Annual Research Conference of the Royal Institution of Chartered Surveyors 2006*, London: University College London, 2006, at http://www.rics.org/ NR/rdonlyres/2AF76451-3121-4C76-BE24-F590D4C41F62/0/COB06Stokes_etal.pdf (viewed 25 March 2008).

180 http://www.teapotisland.com/TeaPot%20Island.htm (viewed 26 March 2008).

181 http://www.cardewclub.com/diary/archives/5 (viewed 26 March 2008).

182 http://www.teapotisland.com/TeaPot%20Island.htm (viewed 1 April 2008).

183 http://www.wellingtonnz.com/school_trips/ southward_car_museum (viewed 1 April 2008).

184 http://www.southward.org.nz/viewsection.php?id=53 (viewed 2 April 2008).

185 http://www.southward.org.nz/viewsection.php?id=60 (viewed 2 April 2008).

186 http://www.southward.org.nz/viewsection.php?id=53 (viewed 2 April 2008).

187 http://www.southward.org.nz/viewsection.php?id=59 (viewed 2 April 2008).

188 R. Thomas and M. Fordham (eds), *Sustainable Urban Design: An Environmental Approach* (London: Taylor and Francis, 2003), p. 91.

189 http://www.tourismresearch.govt.nz/RegionalData/ North+Island/Wellington+Region/Tourism+to+Wellington +Region/Graph-International-Visitor-Activities-Popular-Wellington.htm (viewed 3 April 2008).

190 http://www.tourismresearch.govt.nz/RegionalData/ North+Island/Wellington+Region/Tourism+to+Wellington +Region/Graph-International-Visitor-Activities-Popular-Wellington.htm (viewed 3 April 2008).

191 Statistics New Zealand, *A Measure of Cultural Experience* (2003), p. 35, at http://www.stats.govt.nz/NR/rdonlyres/ 16A5F989-7947-44D3-A81D-FCA30C3A0D21/0/ MeasureOfCulture.pdf (viewed 3 April 2008).

192 Ibid., p. 36.

193 http://www.tepapa.govt.nz/TePapa/English/ AboutTePapa/Media/MediaReleases/2007/visitors.htm (viewed 3 April 2008).

194 http://www.aquariumnz.org.nz/Appendicies/ App%208-Traffic%20Assessment/ McDermott%20Miller%20Marine%20Education%20Cent re%20Parking%20Review.pdf (viewed 3 April 2008).

195 http://www.liftshare.org/download/case-for-car-sharing.pdf (viewed 3 April 2008).

196 http://www.scoop.co.nz/stories/PO0711/S00433.htm (viewed 3 April 2008).

197 http://uk.cars.yahoo.com/car-reviews/car-and-driving/ ariel-atom-2-1004698.html (viewed 3 April 2008).

198 http://www.twoatlarge.com/ralph/rmisc/spy.html (viewed 8 May 2008).

199 Rae Lewis, personal communication with the authors, 8 April 2008.
200 http://www.guardian.co.uk/uk/2006/sep/03/politics.schools (viewed 9 April 2008).
201 E. Frazao (ed.), *America's Eating Habits: Changes and Consequences*, Agriculture Information Bulletin No. (AIB750) (1999), United States Department of Agriculture, pp. 213–14, at http://www.ers.usda.gov/publications/aib750/aib750l.pdf (viewed 9 April 2008).
202 J. Hughes, 'How much are we spending and what are we consuming when we eat out?', *Nutrition & Food Science*, 96:2 (1996), pp. 12–15, at http://www.emeraldinsight.com/Insight/ViewContentServlet;jsessionid=711956DB08DA489344CBD5D3DF0F24E5?Filename=Published/EmeraldFullTextArticle/Articles/0170960203.html#0170960203001.png (viewed 9 April 2008).
203 Ibid.
204 Frazao, *America's Eating Habits*, pp. 223–25.
205 http://www.pizzafusion.com (viewed 9 April 2008).
206 Anon., *Edmonds Cookery Book: Sure to Rise* (Auckland: Bluebird Foods Ltd., 1996), p. 134.
207 http://www.mathleague.com/help/data/data.htm (viewed 10 April 2008).
208 P. Fava, L. Piergiovanni and E. Pagliarini, 'Design of a functional box for take-away pizza', *Packaging Technology and Science*, 12 (1999), p. 58, at http://www3.interscience.wiley.com/cgi-bin/fulltext/61006765/PDFSTART (viewed 10 April 2008).
209 http://www.ciao.co.uk/Goodfella_s_Deep_Pan_Pizza_Cheese_Supreme__5303435 (viewed 10 April 2008).
210 Fava et al., 'Design of a functional box', p. 58.
211 http://www.teakcroft.co.uk/board-grades.php (viewed 10 April 2008).
212 http://www2.edf.org/papercalculator/process.cfm?calcType=1 (viewed 10 April 2008).
213 http://www.usatoday.com/money/industries/food/2004-01-16-pizzabowl_x.htm (viewed 10 April 2008).
214 http://findarticles.com/p/articles/mi_m3190/is_v20/ai_4220450 (viewed 10 April 2008).
215 http://www.food.gov.uk/science/surveillance/fsis2004branch/fsis5804 (viewed 10 April 2008).
216 L. Robertson, C. Flinders and B. Godfrey, *Laurel's Kitchen* (Tomales, Calif.: Nilgiri Press, 1976), p. 51.
217 http://www.birminghamuk.com/georgecadbury.htm (viewed 11 April 2008).
218 http://www.cadbury.co.uk/EN/CTB2003/about_chocolate/history_cadbury/social_pioneers/bournville_village.htm (viewed 11 April 2008).
219 D. Pritchard, *Vegetable Growing in the Home Garden*, Bulletin No. 229 (Wellington, NZ: Department of Agriculture, n.d.), p. 2.
220 *Number Crunching* (Auckland: The National Heart Foundation of New Zealand, 1993).
221 Pritchard, *Vegetable Growing*, pp. 32–33.
222 http://www.nutristrategy.com/activitylist.htm (viewed 11 April 2008).
223 Yvonne Shaw, personal communication with the authors, March 2008.
224 M. Norwak, *Self-Sufficiency for Children* (London, Pelham Books, 1980), pp. 15–16.
225 http://www.permaculture.org.uk/mm.asp?mmfile=whatispermaculture (viewed 11 April 2008).
226 See, for example, A. J. Macself, *French Intensive Gardening* (London: W. H. and L. Collingridge, n.d.).

227 Pritchard, *Vegetable Growing*, p. 5.
228 http://www.littlejumper.com (viewed 12 April 2008).
229 http://www.thistleandbroom.com/shopping/apparel/wool/glenfinnan_moreinfo.htm (viewed 12 April 2008).
230 http://www.sisterhood.co.nz/products/cw4hatcardie.html (viewed 12 April 2008).
231 http://www.alzheimers.org.uk/site/scripts/documents_info.php?categoryID=200171&documentID=120 (viewed 12 April 2008).
232 Mithraratne et al., *Sustainable Living*, p. 218.
233 Ibid., p. 219.
234 Ibid., p. 217.
235 Ibid., p. 219.
236 Ibid., p. 217.
237 Ibid., p. 218.
238 http://www.budgetkitchendoors.co.uk/default.asp?dp=48 (viewed 14 April 2008).
239 http://www.building.co.uk/story.asp?storyCode=9248 (viewed 7 May 2008).
240 http://www.adore-kitchen-doors.co.uk/kitchen-doors-urban-chic.htm (viewed 14 April 2008).
241 http://www.aa.co.nz/motoring/tips/ask-jack/Pages/Reasonable-kilometres-for-a-used-car.aspx (viewed 14 April 2008).

CHAPTER 6: WORK

1 http://www.neri.org.nz/articles/5-stimulating-energy-research-through-scholarships-and-collaboration (viewed 15 April 2008).
2 http://www.shawfloors.com/Shaw-Environmental/Sustainability (viewed 15 April 2008).
3 http://www.nzine.co.nz/views/newzealand_immigration.html (viewed 17 December 2007).
4 http://www.timeday.org (viewed 15 April 2008).
5 E. McGrattan and R. Rogerson, *Changes in the Distribution of Family Hours Worked Since 1950* (2008), p. 5, at http://www.minneapolisfed.org/research/SR/SR397.pdf (viewed 15 April 2008).
6 Ibid., p. 7.
7 http://www.personneltoday.com/articles/2007/11/28/43464/long-hours-working-is-on-the-increase-in-the-uk.html (viewed 15 April 2008).
8 http://rmc.library.cornell.edu/EAD/htmldocs/RMM03442.html (viewed 15 April 2008).
9 http://www.hants.gov.uk/schooltravelplans/cartravel.html (viewed 17 April 2008).
10 http://www.scotland.gov.uk/Publications/2002/09/15290/10427 (viewed 17 April 2008).
11 http://www.lho.org.uk/viewResource.aspx?id=8641 (viewed 17 April 2008).
12 http://www.nber.org/papers/w8928 (viewed 17 April 2008).
13 http://www.bartleby.com/65/wh/whitecol.html (viewed 17 April 2008).
14 http://www.eia.doe.gov/emeu/efficiency/ee_ch4.htm (viewed 17 April 2008).
15 N. Howard and P. Robert, 'Environmental Comparisons', *Architects' Journal*, 202:11 (1995), pp. 46–47.
16 P. Jurasovich, *The Environmental Impact of New Ways of Working in the Office*, PhD thesis (University of Auckland, 2003).
17 Based on ibid., Table 192.
18 Ibid., p. 605.

19 http://www.microsoft.com/uk/press/content/
presscentre/releases/2006/11/pr03755.mspx
(viewed 21 April 2008).
20 http://www.personneltoday.com/articles/
2008/03/20/45020/homeworking-eases-stress-levels-but-
leads-to-fear-of-being.html (viewed 21 April 2008).
21 M. Csikszentmihalyi, *Flow: The Psychology of Happiness*
(London: Rider, 1992).
22 R. Vale and B. Vale, 'The impact of PLEA – are we
making a difference; have we done enough?', in S. Wittkopf
and B. K. Tan (eds), *Sun, Wind and Architecture: The
Proceedings of the 24th International Conference of Passive
and Low Energy Architecture*, National University of
Singapore, 2007, pp. 281–84.
23 K. I. Takahashi, H. Tatemichi, T. Tanaka and S. Nishi,
*Environmental Impact of Information and Communication
Technologies Including Rebound Effects* (2004), at
http://ieeexplore.ieee.org/iel5/9100/28876/01299680.pdf
(viewed 21 April 2008).
24 A. J. Sellen and R. H. R. Harper, *The Myth of the
Paperless Office* (Cambridge, Mass.: MIT Press, 2001).
25 P. Muter and P. Maurutto, 'Reading and skimming from
computer screens and books: the paperless office
revisited?', *Behaviour and Information Technology*, 10:4
(1991), pp. 257–66, at http://www.psych.utoronto.ca/users/
muter/pmuter2.htm (viewed 1 May 2008).
26 http://www.vuw.ac.nz/annualreports/previous-
reports/2004/about/about.html (viewed 1 May 2008).
27 http://www2.edf.org/papercalculator
(viewed 1 May 2008).
28 http://www.onlineconversion.com/forum/
forum_1118773419.htm (viewed 1 May 2008).
29 http://www.agric.wa.gov.au/content/LWE/VEGT/
TREES/TREENOTE3.htm (viewed 1May 2008).
30 S. A. Segrest, D. L. Rockwood, J. A. Stricker and
A. E. S. Green, *Biomass Cofiring with Coal at Lakeland
Utilities* (1998), at http://cc.msnscache.com/
cache.aspx?q=7315622173 7694&mkt=en-NZ&lang=en-
NZ&w=616c3e16,515c8038&FORM=CVRE5
(viewed 1 May 2008).
31 http://www.srd.gov.ab.ca/lands/formspublications/
aboutpublicland/crowntimberresourcesonwhiteareapublic
land.aspx (viewed 1 May 2008).
32 http://recycling.stanford.edu/5r/recycledpaper.html
(viewed 1 May 2008).
33 http://www.wcl.govt.nz/wellington/currentindex.html
(viewed 1 May 2008).
34 G. Baird, A. Alcorn and P. Haslam, 'The energy
embodied in building materials – updated New Zealand
coefficients and their significance', *IPENZ Transactions*,
24:1 (1997), pp. 46–47, at http://www.ipenz.org.nz/ipenz/
publications/indexes/transaction/transactions97/civil/
7baird.pdf (viewed 1 May 2008).
35 Ibid.
36 http://www.ifias.ca/IFIASinfo/IFIASinfohist.html
(viewed 2 May 2008).
37 Robert Vale, personal discussion with Graham Treloar
over several years.
38 A. Francis and J. Wheeler, *One Planet Living in the Suburbs*
(2006), p. 98, at http://www.wwf.org.uk/filelibrary/pdf/
OPL_suburbs_fullrpt.pdf (viewed 2 May 2008).
39 Ibid., p. 20.
40 http://www.arup.com/environment/
project.cfm?pageid=10335 (viewed 2 May 2008).

41 http://www.equilibrium-economicum.net/
marketandenvironment.htm (viewed 2 May 2008).
42 http://www.correspondence.school.nz
(viewed 2 May 2008).
43 http://www.open.ac.uk/new/distance-learning.shtml
(viewed 2 May 2008).

CHAPTER 7: RITES OF PASSAGE
1 http://www.smartmoney.com/divorce/marriage/
index.cfm?story=wedding-cutcosts (viewed 11 March 2008).
2 D. McMillan, 'Report by the Director of Housing,
Regeneration and Environmental Services: Community
Safety and Environmental Services Committee, 2 August
2006; Subject: Clydebank Crematorium – Service Times'
(West Dunbartonshire Council, 2006), p. 2.
3 *Mercury Emissions from Crematoria. Consultation on an
Assessment by the Environment Agency's Local Authority Unit*
(London: DEFRA, 2003), p. 12.
4 http://www.smartmoney.com/10things/
index.cfm?story=march2005 (viewed 7 March 2008).
5 http://www.smartmoney.com/divorce/marriage/
index.cfm?story=wedding-cutcosts (viewed 7 March 2008).
6 http://www.weddingguideuk.com/articles/planning/
budget.asp (viewed 7 March 2008).
7 http://www.nativeenergy.com/pages/portovert/
168.php?afc=portovert (viewed 11 March 2008).
8 *Mercury Emissions from Crematoria*, Fig. 2, p. 20.
9 http://en.wikipedia.org/wiki/Eco-cemetery
(viewed 7 March 2008).
10 http://www.cremationassociation.org/docs/
WebConfirmed.pdf (viewed 11 March 2008).
11 Mithraratne et al., *Sustainable Living*, pp. 215–19.
12 D. J. Davies and L. H. Mates, *Encyclopedia of Cremation*
(Aldershot: Ashgate, 2005), p. 146.
13 L. Hickman, 'Should I ... be buried or cremated?',
Guardian, 18 October 2005, available at
http://www.guardian.co.uk/environment/2005/oct/18/
ethicalmoney.climatechange (viewed 5 March 2008).
14 http://www.teriin.org/tech_cardamom.php
(viewed 5 March 2008).
15 *Assessing the Groundwater Pollution Potential of Cemetery
Developments* (Bristol: Environment Agency, 2004), p. 5.
16 http://en.wikipedia.org/wiki/Coal
(viewed 5 March 2008).
17 H. Saddler, M. Diesendorf and R. Denniss, *A Clean
Energy Future for Australia* (Sydney: WWF Australia/
Clean Energy Future Group, 2004), p. 81.
18 'Report covering the year 2005 pursuant to Article 4(1)
of Directive 2003/30/EC, on the promotion of the use of
biofuels or other renewable fuels for transport', Annex 1,
p. 4, available at http://www.ebb-eu.org/legis/
Netherlands%203RDreport%20Dir%202003%2030%20
EN.pdf (viewed 5 March 2008).
19 Data from M. D. Murray, *Growth and Yield of a Managed
30-Year-Old Noble Fir Plantation* (1988), Research Note
PNW-RN-475, United States Department of Agriculture
Forest Service Pacific Northwest Research Station, at
http://www.simetric.co.uk/si_wood.htm
(viewed 7 March 2008).
20 J. J. Modi, *The Funeral Ceremonies of the Parsees: Their
Origin and Explanation* (Bombay: Fort Printing Press,
4th edn 1928).
21 R. M. Khanna, 'Experts differ on cause of vultures'
death', *Tribune*, 20 February 2004, available at

http://www.tribuneindia.com/2004/20040220/
edit.htm#7 (viewed 11 March 2008).

22 McMillan, 'Report by the Director of Housing'.

23 J. M. Clarke, *The Brookwood Necropolis Railway* (Oxford:
Oakwood Press, 1995). Pictures of what is left of this railway
can be seen at http://disused-rlys.fotopic.net/c1154765.html
(viewed 5 March 2008).

24 http://www.rookwoodcemetery.com.au/
history_of_rookwood_necropolis and
http://en.wikipedia.org/wiki/Cemetery_Station_No._1_
railway_station%2C_Sydney (viewed 5 March 2008).

25 Thanks are due to our colleague Nigel Isaacs for
suggesting that this aspect of marriage needed to be
considered.

26 A. Francis and J. Wheeler, *One Planet Living in the
Suburbs* (2006), p. 30, at
http://www.wwf.org.uk/filelibrary/pdf/OPL_suburbs_
fullrpt.pdf (viewed 2 May 2008).

27 F. M. Dieleman and R. J. Schouw, 'Divorce, mobility and
housing demand', *European Journal of Population/Revue
Européenne de Démographie*, 5:3 (1989), pp. 235–52.

CONCLUSION

1 M. Higgs (ed.), *Dan Dare: Pilot of the Future*, facsimile
reproduction (London: Hawk Books, 1997).

2 http://www.rte.ie/tv/scope/scope06/SCOPE3_show05_
survival_course.html (viewed 9 October 2007).

3 *Air Resources Board Research Note 94-11: Topic = How Much
Air Do We Breathe?* (Sacramento, Calif.: California
Environmental Protection Agency, 1994).

4 http://science.ksc.nasa.gov/facilities/vab.html
(viewed 24 September 2007).

5 http://www.lungusa.org/site/pp.asp?c=dvLUK9OoE&b=
35358 (viewed 2 December 2008).

6 http://www.npi.gov.au/database/substance-info/
profiles/77.html (viewed 9 October 2007).

7 http://hypertextbook.com/facts/1997/EricCheng.shtml
(viewed 28 March 2008).

8 http://www.ccmr.cornell.edu/education/ask/
index.html?quid=733 (viewed 28 March 2008).

9 P. von Sengbusch, 'The flow of energy in ecosystems –
productivity, food chain, and trophic level' (2003),
Botany Online – The Internet Hypertextbook, at
http://www.biologie.uni-hamburg.de/b-online/e54/54c.htm
(viewed 28 March 2008).

10 http://www.bbc.co.uk/schools/gcsebitesize/biology/
greenplantsasorganisms/0photosynthesisrev6.shtml
(viewed 28 March 2008).

11 http://www.alaskazoo.org/willowcrest/boris.htm
(viewed 28 March 2008).

12 http://ga.water.usgs.gov/edu/earthwherewater.html
(viewed 28 March 2008).

13 *Water: A Shared Responsibility. The United Nations World
Water Development Report 2* (Paris: UNESCO, Division of
Water Sciences, 2006), p. 25.

14 Data from FAO Aquastat, quoted in
http://news.bbc.co.uk/1/hi/sci/tech/3747724.stm
(viewed 10 April 2008).

15 *Water: A Shared Responsibility*, p. 12.

16 http://dnr.state.il.us/orep/ctap/atlas/Urban.pdf
(viewed 7 May 2008).

17 http://www.didjshop.com/shop1/AbCulturecart.html
(viewed 7 May 2008).

18 B. Gott, 'Fire as an Aboriginal management tool in
South-Eastern Australia', paper given at the Australian
Bushfire Conference, Albury, NSW, July 1999.

19 http://www.eia.doe.gov/emeu/aer/pdf/pages/sec1_13.
pdf (viewed 7 May 2008).

20 A. Richard and R. A. Easterlin, 'Diminishing marginal
utility of income? A caveat' (2004), *University of Southern
California Law and Economics Working Paper Series*, Paper 5,
at http://law.bepress.com/usclwps/lewps/art5
(viewed 10 December 2008).

21 http://www.princeton.edu/main/news/archive/S15/15/
09S18/index.xml?section=topstories (viewed 1 May 2008).

22 Said by chairman and CEO Charlie Wilson in 1955:
see http://www.carlist.com/autonews/2005/autonews_131.
html (viewed 1 May 2008).

23 http://209.85.173.104/search?q=cache:MToeC5b9OoMJ:
www.photovoltaics.org.nz/+cost+effectiveness+photovoltai
cs&hl=en&ct=clnk&cd=5&gl=nz (viewed 10 April 2008).

24 http://www.klaus.cz/klaus2/asp/
clanek.asp?id=XpAV39wT4A32 (viewed 10 April 2008).

25 http://www.hm-treasury.gov.uk/media/9/9/
CLOSED_SHORT_executive_summary.pdf
(viewed 10 April 2008).

26 http://www.reuters.com/article/newsOne/
idUSL1688484420080416?sp=true (viewed 1 May 2008).

27 This idea came from a letter to the *Mercury*, the daily
paper of Tasmania, from Alan Champion of Sandy Bay,
Hobart: 'Obvious smoke signals' in 'Your Tasmania, your
voice, quick views', *Mercury*, 21 April 2008, p. 15.

28 http://www.newadvent.org/cathen/07783a.htm
(viewed 7 May 2008).

29 *Switching Lifestyles: Global Growth without Disaster*,
report by the Centre for Economics and Business Research
Ltd (Amersham: Comino Foundation, 2007).

30 A. Collins, A. Flynn and A. Netherwood, *Reducing
Cardiff's Ecological Footprint: A Resource Accounting Tool for
Sustainable Consumption* (Cardiff: WWF Cymru, 2005),
Table 2, p. 13.

31 http://www.scotland.gov.uk/Publications/2008/04/
16110121/5 (viewed 10 May 2008).

32 J. Dargay and M. Hanly, *Volatility of car ownership,
commuting mode and time in the UK* (2004), at
http://eprints.ucl.ac.uk/1235/1/2004_13.pdf
(viewed 10 May 2008).

SOURCES AND RESOURCES

We have referred to hundreds of books and websites during the writing this book. Most have been very specific in scope, but the interested reader might like to explore some of the ideas behind sustainability for a wider appreciation of the subject. The following is a selective list of books and articles that we have found useful and/or inspirational over the years.

CLASSICS

Many of the matters being discussed now under the heading of 'sustainability' were raised over a hundred years ago, as demonstrated by the following works:

William Morris, *News from Nowhere, or, An Epoch of Rest* (1890)
First published in serial form in *Commonweal*, the journal of the Socialist League, it is now available as *News from Nowhere and Other Writings* (2005) by Penguin Classics. The full text can be accessed at http://www.marxists.org/archive/morris/works/1890/nowhere/nowhere.htm, and at http://www.gutenberg.org/etext/3261.
A novel by William Morris, the celebrated 19th-century designer and activist, describing a vision of a sustainable society in an imaginary future England.

E. M. Forster, 'The Machine Stops', *Oxford and Cambridge Review* (Nov. 1909); reissued 2008 by Dodo Press
Full text available at http://brighton.ncsa.uiuc.edu/prajlich/forster.html.
A chillingly prescient short story about a society completely dependent on technology.

P. Kropotkin, *Fields, Factories and Workshops: or Industry Combined with Agriculture and Brain Work with Manual Work* (London: Thomas Nelson & Sons, 1912)
Not currently in print, but the text is available at http://dwardmac.pitzer.edu/anarchist_archives/kropotkin/fields.html.
This work is as visionary as Morris's, but presented as a factual account rather than as a novel.

FROM THE 1970S

Most of the answers to problems we are facing now were available in the 1970s. If we had followed the advice of these authors, we would not now be in the situation we are in.

D. H. Meadows, D. L. Meadows, J. Randers and W. Behrens, *The Limits to Growth* (New York: Potomac Associates/Universe Books, 1972)
The first book to set out clearly the future impact of population growth and resource depletion.

E. Goldsmith and R. Allen, 'A Blueprint for Survival', *The Ecologist*, vol. 2, no. 1 (January 1972)
Goldsmith and Allen's article aroused so much interest that it was published as a book by Penguin in September 1972. It was one of the first complete presentations both of the problems of sustainability and of possible solutions.

E. F. Schumacher, *Small is Beautiful: A Study of Economics as if People Mattered* (New York: Harper & Row, 1973)
A classic, still entirely relevant, by the chief economic advisor to Britain's National Coal Board. This was one of the first mainstream books to question the wisdom of a global society based on conventional economics.

G. Boyle and P. Harper (eds), *Radical Technology* (London: Wildwood House, 1976)
Brings together in one place all the various strands that made up what was known as the 'alternative technology' movement.

MORE RECENT BOOKS AND RESOURCES

So many recent books on sustainability seem to take the view that if you change your lightbulbs and don't use plastic bags at the supermarket, the world will be saved. The works here have a more realistic viewpoint.

M. Wackernagel and W. Rees, *Our Ecological Footprint: Reducing Human Impact on the Earth* (Gabriola Island, British Columbia: New Society Publishers, 1996)
A very important text that offered a powerful and comprehensible new way of measuring the impact of human activities on the environment.

George Monbiot, *Heat: How to Stop the Planet Burning* (London: Allen Lane, 2006)
An excellent, and well-referenced, attempt to show what stopping global warming would mean in terms of daily life in Britain, by an author who really understands the nature of the problems we face.

T. Trainer, 'A Short Critique of the Stern Review', *Real-World Economics Review*, vol. 45 (15 March 2008), pp. 54–58
Available at http://www.paecon.net/PAEReview/issue45/Trainer45.pdf.

—— 'The Simpler Way', at http://ssis.arts.unsw.edu.au/tsw.
Another writer who knows that we cannot continue with 'business-as-usual'.

INDEX